Guidelines

A Cross-Cultural
Reading/Writing Text

Guidelines

A Cross-Cultural Reading/Writing Text

RUTH SPACK
Tufts University

ST. MARTIN'S PRESS
New York

Editor-in-Chief: Susan Anker
Editor: Kathleen Keller
Project Editor: Joyce Hinnefeld
Editorial Assistant: Robert Skiena
Production Supervisor: Alan Fischer
Text Design: Leon Bolognese & Assoc., Inc.
Graphics: Grafacon, Inc.
Cover Design: Darby Downey
Cover Art: Decoding the Invisible Leopard by Laurence M. Gartel. © Laurence M. Gartel "Decoding the Invisible Leopard," 1984, Polaroid SX-70 Mural, Polaroid Corporate Collection, Massachusetts.

Library of Congress Catalog Card Number: 88-63036

Manufactured in the United States of America.
43210
fedcba

For information, write:
St. Martin's Press, Inc.
175 Fifth Avenue
New York, NY 10010

ISBN: 0-312-25902-6

ACKNOWLEDGMENTS

page 3: Wu-tsu, Fa-yen. "Zen and the Art of Burglary" from Diasetz T. Suzuki, *Zen and Japanese Culture*, Bollingen Series 64. Copyright © 1959 by Princeton University Press.
page 9: Harris, Sydney J. "What True Education Should Do" © with permission of *The Chicago Sun-Times*, Inc., 1989.
page 20: Yezierska, Anzia. "College" from *Bread Givers*, a novel by Anzia Yezierska. 1925. (Persea Books, 1975) Copyright, Louise Levitas Henrickson.
page 27: Sarton, May. "The Rewards of Living a Solitary Life," April 8, 1974. Op-ed. Copyright 1974 by *The New York Times* Company. Reprinted by permission.
page 28: Sarton, May. Excerpt from "Moving In" from *Collected Poems* (1930–1973). © 1974. W. W. Norton.
page 32: Gelles, Judy. Photograph of "Best Friends" © 1979 by Judy Gelles.

Acknowledgments and copyrights are continued at the back of the book on page 331, which constitutes an extension of the copyright page.

To Norman, Rebecca, and Jonathan Spack
with love

PREFACE

Guidelines: A Cross-Cultural Reading/Writing Text acknowledges and provides cultural diversity in the college composition class through naturally sequenced, culturally relevant reading selections and writing assignments that challenge students to examine and reinterpret their experience and background knowledge. The text features integration of readings with essay assignments, emphasizing the connection between reading and writing.

Guidelines addresses the academic needs of students who can benefit from carefully structured support as they undertake tasks requiring increasingly complex analytic and critical thought. Building on language resources that students already have, guidelines within the text show students how to integrate new procedures and ideas with previously learned skills and information, thereby increasing their own knowledge base.

The Level

Guidelines is a textbook designed for composition courses with a cross-cultural emphasis and for advanced ESL programs.

The Readings

Guidelines contains fourteen professional essays and four complete student essays. The professional selections are drawn from publications for both general and academic audiences and include expressive essays, research studies, argumentative essays, and a news article. Reading selections include footnotes to explain culture-specific items, historical references, slang, and idiomatic expressions that students might not be able to guess from the context or find in a dictionary. The authors represent several fields, including anthropology, psychology, speech communications, and writing. The readings cover thought-provoking and culturally diverse topics that appeal to both native-speaking and ESL students: college life, friendship, cross-cultural communication, teaching and learning, and issues in the news.

Purposeful pre-reading and post-reading activities, which involve reading, writing, and small group discussions, are designed to foster critical thinking and to lead students toward developing ideas for their own essays.

The Essay Assignments

Guidelines contains four increasingly challenging essay assignments presented in a theoretically sound progression that allows students to build on what they learn from one assignment to the next. All assignments are supported by reading and writing tasks that allow students to write from their own perspectives as they examine the perspectives of others. Students begin with writing from experience and move to writing from course readings, using their experience and background knowledge to evaluate and analyze what they read. They then write from outside sources, using the academic skills practiced in previous assignments and synthesizing new material as they examine a controversial issue.

The Guidelines

Clear, innovative, and flexible guidelines accompany each essay assignment to help students analyze the directions and define corresponding academic audiences. The guidelines demonstrate many of the stages that four student writers underwent to fulfill the assignments. By observing these composing processes, students can learn how to develop their own essays from inception to completion, through strategies such as invention, journal writing, note taking, focusing, drafting, organizing, peer reviewing, and revising. Furthermore, to complete essays based on reading, students can follow guidelines for annotating, summarizing, paraphrasing, quoting, and citing and documenting sources.

The Structure

Guidelines is divided into an introduction and six parts.

1. The *Introduction* explains and demonstrates the process of keeping a reading/writing journal on the course work. Students are guided toward practicing several exploratory reading and writing strategies, including annotating and making double-entry notes, that will be useful for all subsequent assignments.
2. *Part One* contains the first essay assignment, which asks students to express a belief or share an insight based on their own experience. To fulfill this assignment, students practice strategies learned in the introductory chapter, adding summarizing and invention strategies and the processes of focusing, drafting, organizing, peer reviewing, revising, and completing an essay.
3. *Part Two* contains the second essay assignment, which asks students to evaluate the course reading by relating what they have read to what they know from experience. To fulfill this assignment, students practice previously learned strategies, adding the skills of note taking, paraphrasing, quoting, and citing course material.

4. *Part Three* contains the third essay assignment, which asks students to analyze an argumentative essay and to present and support opinions in reaction to ideas discussed in the reading. To fulfill this assignment, students practice previously learned strategies, adding the strategies of critical reading and argumentative writing.

5. *Part Four* contains the fourth essay assignment, which asks students to research a recent controversy and to establish and support a position on the controversial issue. To fulfill this assignment, students practice previously learned strategies, adding the processes of learning how to use the college library, conducting an interview, examining various sides of an issue, synthesizing material from several sources, making an oral presentation, and documenting outside sources.

6. *Part Five* provides expanded coverage of the skills of summarizing, paraphrasing, quoting, paragraphing, and citing and documenting sources. This part serves as a handy reference for students as they are writing and revising their own essays.

7. *Part Six* provides guidelines for proofreading and editing as well as a handbook for correcting errors, with brief exercises. A unique chapter on "Causes of Error" asks students to examine and categorize the logic of their errors.

Acknowledgments

For several years, my own students have been critically appraising earlier drafts of this text. I will always be grateful for their patience, curiosity, insight, and willingness to take risks.

Catherine Sadow has been a generous collaborator, critic, and cheerleader throughout the project. Roberta Steinberg has tested out materials in her classes and enthusiastically shared her students' writing with me. Vivian Zamel has positively influenced my thinking on every aspect of composing, from journal writing to grammar and the causes of error. I thank them all.

The following reviewers offered valued suggestions that helped to shape *Guidelines*: Frances Boyd, Columbia University; Ulla Connor, Purdue University; Franklin Horowitz, Columbia University; Stan Jones, Carleton University, Canada; Donna Jurich, San Francisco State; Robert N. Kantor, Ohio State University; Alexandra Kraples, University of South Carolina; Joanne Liebman, University of Arkansas, Little Rock; Denise Murray, San Jose State University; Elizabeth Rorschach, City College, CUNY; Sandra R. Schecter, University of California, Berkeley; Elaine Wilson, Massachusetts Bay Community College. I am pleased to have this opportunity to acknowledge their contribution.

Kathleen Keller and Joyce Hinnefeld, editor and project editor at St. Martin's Press, have made the final stages of writing this book a pleasure.

I appreciate their concern for the tone and design of the text and their attention to detail.

Susan Anker, my acquiring editor and now editor-in-chief at St. Martin's Press, has guided me through the process of composing with grace and tact. In doing so, she has allowed me to grow as a writer and enabled me to grow as a teacher of writing. I am indebted to her for that.

Ruth Spack

BRIEF CONTENTS

CONTENTS

Chapter Four Guidelines for Fulfilling Essay Assignment 2   102

PART THREE
Writing from Course Readings: Analyzing an Argumentative Essay   118

Chapter Five Responding to Reading   120

INTRODUCTION

Reading, Writing, and Keeping a Journal

Guidelines: A Cross-Cultural Reading/Writing Text offers a composition course that allows you to become actively engaged in the processes of reading and of writing about what you read. Throughout the course, you will be exploring ideas in discussion groups and through a variety of writing activities as you work toward completion of several essay assignments.

One way in which you will be asked to explore your responses to the course reading and writing is by keeping a reading/writing journal. The guidelines that follow will help you to understand why and how you should keep a journal.

What Is a Reading/Writing Journal?

A journal is a record of your impressions and thoughts related to the course reading and writing. Making regular entries in your journal can help you to improve your reading and writing skills.

In writing about what you read, you can discuss an author's ideas and your reaction to those ideas. You may develop a deeper understanding of a reading selection or identify why you do not understand it. You can discuss why a selection seems valuable or confusing or even boring. In the process of writing a journal entry, you may discover why you agree or disagree or identify with an author's point of view or experience. Your journal comments may lead you to develop a point of view for your own essay on a similar topic. By sharing these entries on the readings with your classmates and instructor, you can help to stimulate reflection on and discussion of the ideas in each reading selection.

In writing about your own writing, you can discuss issues and develop ideas that are tied to your essay assignments. Since the course readings cover such topics as language learning, adjustment to college life, solitude, friendship, communication, teaching and learning, and issues of importance in the news, these are appropriate topics for your journals. You can also write about class discussions, writing activities and exercises, or the process of writing itself. And you can keep a record of your progress. For example, you may write regularly about the research project that you will start near the beginning of the semester and finish by the end of the semester. By

1

sharing these journal entries with your instructor, you will be able to inform the instructor of any successes or difficulties you are having. Your instructor can then work with you to strengthen your skills and to help you develop effective writing strategies.

How and How Often Do I Keep a Journal?

The number of journal entries you write will be determined by your instructor. Since your instructor will be collecting and responding to some or all of the entries, write or type each entry on a separate piece of paper. An entry can then be handed in to the instructor on an assigned date and later kept in a loose-leaf notebook.

How Will My Journal Be Evaluated?

Journals will not be corrected or graded. They are read for ideas only. This approach allows you to write without fear of red marks and to experiment with words and ideas without the pressure of grades. The purpose of the journal assignment is to give you the opportunity to use written language informally to explore, develop, and communicate your thoughts.

How Do I Start?

It may be hard for you to get started on a journal entry, especially the first one. Instead of staring for a long time at a blank page, start writing and keep your pen moving, even if you just begin by saying "I have nothing to say today" or "This reading was really difficult." The act of writing itself will probably generate ideas.

The process of writing a journal entry may be slow at the beginning of the semester. But as you gain confidence and fluency, you will probably find that you can quickly produce even a lengthy entry.

What Do I Say?

It's hard to write anything in a journal unless you first develop some appropriate reading and writing strategies. As the semester progresses, you will develop your own strategies for writing journal entries. For now, you may be able to profit from the following guidelines.

Reading and Writing about What You Read

The reading selections in this textbook present varying degrees of difficulty. Some may be easy for you to read; others may be hard. Some will immediately provoke a reaction; others will take more thought. Some selections may require only one reading before you feel ready to write a journal entry. Others may at first appear easy but in fact involve complex ideas and require careful rereading.

The reading suggestions that follow are directed toward your journal writing. However, they can be useful for other reading and writing tasks as well.

A First Reading

In preparation for writing a journal entry on a reading, follow these guidelines for reading "Zen and the Art of Burglary" (below).

GUIDELINES	**Guidelines for a First Reading**

1. To help predict its content and purpose, preview the reading:
   a. Read the title.
   b. Read the brief background information about the author.
   c. Read the vocabulary explanation.
2. Then read the essay through once, without stopping to use a dictionary.

Zen[1] and the Art of Burglary[2]
by Wu-tsu Fa-yen

Wu-tsu Fa-yen was a Chinese Zen Buddhist priest who lived from 1025 to 1104.

If people ask me what Zen is like, I will say that it is like learning the art of burglary. The son of a burglar saw his father growing older and thought, "If he is unable to carry on his profession, who will be the bread-winner of the family, except myself? I must learn the trade." He intimated the idea to his father, who approved of it.   1

One night the father took the son to a big house, broke through the fence, entered the house, and, opening one of the large chests, told the son to go in and pick out the clothing. As soon as the son got into it, the father dropped the lid and securely applied the lock. The father now came out to the courtyard and loudly knocked at the door, waking up the whole family; then he quietly slipped away by the hole in the fence. The residents got excited and lighted candles, but they found that the burglar had already gone.   2

The son, who remained all the time securely confined in the chest, thought of his cruel father. He was greatly mortified, then a fine idea flashed upon him. He made a noise like the gnawing of a rat. The family told the maid to take a candle and examine the chest. When the lid was unlocked, out came the prisoner, who blew out the light, pushed away the maid, and   3

---

[1] **Zen:** a form of Buddhism
[2] **burglary:** the act of breaking into a building to commit a crime (theft)

fled. The people ran after him. Noticing a well by the road, he picked up a large stone and threw it into the water. The pursuers all gathered around the well trying to find the burglar drowning himself in the dark hole.

In the meantime he went safely back to his father's house. He blamed   4
his father deeply for his narrow escape. Said the father, "Be not offended, my son. Just tell me how you got out of it." When the son told him all about his adventures, the father remarked, "There you are, you have learned the art."   ●

Subsequent Readings: Annotating and Double-Entry Notes

A second or third reading can consist simply of reading the selection again. But you can achieve a closer reading by making notes as you read and reread. Making these notes, either in the margins of the text, within the text itself, or on a separate sheet of paper, is known as *annotating*. Annotating can be practiced in many ways. Two useful ways to annotate are (1) identifying unfamiliar vocabulary words and (2) making double-entry notes.

ANNOTATING: IDENTIFYING UNFAMILIAR VOCABULARY WORDS

As you read, underline or in some other way make note of some key vocabulary words: words whose meaning you do not know but that you need to know in order to understand the reading selection fully.

You will probably be tempted to look up the words in a dictionary. It is true that dictionaries can be helpful in developing vocabulary. But a dictionary cannot define all expressions, and the definitions you do find may not apply to your reading passage. Furthermore, you may not always have access to a dictionary, and using one can be tedious and time-consuming.

Another way to build your vocabulary is to guess at the general meanings of words, using contextual clues. Look at what precedes and follows the word or expression to determine its meaning. Consider how the word fits into the whole essay. Context will not always give you the precise meaning, but it will often give you enough clues about the meaning to understand a passage.

Use the dictionary only for words whose meaning you cannot guess from the context.

ACTIVITY: Guessing meaning from context

Working in a group of three or four students, define the words *intimated* (first paragraph) and *mortified* (third paragraph) in "Zen and the Art of Burglary" (p. 3) without using the dictionary. Read what precedes and what follows each word, and consider how the words fit into the whole essay. Compare your definitions with those of another group of students.   ●

ANNOTATING: MAKING DOUBLE-ENTRY NOTES

Annotating by making brief comments as you are reading is a way to summarize and record your reactions to a reading selection. This process not only helps you to focus on the reading task, but it also enables you to become involved in your reading, almost as if you were engaging in conversation with the author.

The following guidelines suggest that you annotate by writing brief double-entry notes to reveal a double perspective on the reading: (1) summary and (2) reaction. In other words, you separate what the author is saying (summary) from what you think (reaction).

GUIDELINES

Guidelines for a Second Reading: Double-Entry Notes

To write double-entry notes, you can write in the left and right margins of the reading selection, on the left and right sides of a sheet of paper folded in two lengthwise, or on two separate sheets of paper.

1. On the left side or sheet, write notes that *summarize* the essay you are reading, to help you understand and focus on what the author is saying. This can be done paragraph by paragraph or in larger chunks.
2. On the right side or sheet, write notes that *record your reactions* to what you have just read. This can be done paragraph by paragraph or in larger chunks. In this section, you should feel free to say whatever you want to say. For example, you can express pleasure, surprise, disagreement, or anger at what you've just read; recall personal associations; make connections with something else you've read or seen; or ask questions.

A STUDENT WRITER AT WORK

Reprinted on the next page is an example of how one student, Chrystalla Papaioannou, annotated "Zen and the Art of Burglary." Using the double-entry format, she summarized each paragraph in the left margin and recorded her reactions in the right margin.

Read this annotated version of the essay, paying attention to the marginal comments. Compare Chrystalla's impression of the story with your own, and discuss your responses with the class. Did Chrystalla capture the essence of the story in her summaries? Are her reactions similar to yours? If not, what is different? Have her reactions helped you to understand the story better? Why or why not?

Note: Chrystalla's language errors have not been corrected.

Chrystalla's Annotations

Zen and the Art of Burglary
by Wu-tsu Fa-yen

If people ask me what Zen is like, I will say that it is like learning the art of burglary. The son of a burglar saw his father growing older and thought, "If he is unable to carry on his profession, who will be the breadwinner of the family, except myself? I must learn the trade." He intimated the idea to his father, who approved of it.

One night the father took the son to a big house, broke through the fence, entered the house, and, opening one of the large chests, told the son to go in and pick out the clothing. As soon as the son got into it, the father dropped the lid and securely applied the lock. The father now came out to the courtyard and loudly knocked at the door, waking up the whole family; then he quietly slipped away by the hole in the fence. The residents got excited and lighted candles, but they found that the burglar had already gone.

The son, who remained all the time securely confined in the chest, thought of his cruel father. He was greatly mortified, then a fine idea flashed upon him. He made a noise like the gnawing of a rat. The family told the maid to take a candle and examine the chest. When the lid was unlocked, out came the prisoner, who blew out the light, pushed away the maid, and fled. The people ran after him. Noticing a well by the road, he picked up a large stone and threw it into the water. The pursuers all gathered around the well trying to find the burglar drowning himself in the dark hole.

In the meantime he went safely back to his father's house. He blamed his father deeply for his narrow escape. Said the father, "Be not offended, my son. Just tell me how you got out of it." When the son told him all about his adventures, the father remarked, "There you are, you have learned the art."

Annotations in the form of paragraph summaries are useful primarily if they provide a shorter version of the paragraph than the author has originally written. Their chief purpose is to help you glance down the margin or side and be quickly reminded of what the author has said and of the organization of the material. If the summaries are as long as the original or even longer, you might as well ignore the summaries and reread the original. Therefore, you should attempt to make paragraph summaries as short as possible.

EXERCISE: *Shortening paragraph summaries*

Reread Chrystalla's paragraph summaries of "Zen and the Art of Burglary" (in the left margin of the text). Working alone or with a partner, rewrite the summaries so that they are as short as possible while still capturing the essence of the story. The summaries do not have to be complete sentences. ●

Turning Annotations into a Journal Entry

There are no set rules for what a journal should look like. Your journal entries will be unique because they depend on your individual reactions to what you are reading.

Once you have annotated a reading, you can refer to your notes before you begin to write an entry. The annotations will give you a brief overview of the reading and remind you of how you responded to it. These notes can be the springboard for your journal writing. However, you should be aware that you may have new reactions as you reread or start to write. In other words, your annotations can be added to or changed.

A STUDENT WRITER AT WORK

Reprinted on page 8 is Chrystalla's journal entry on "Zen and the Art of Burglary." Read what Chrystalla has written, and discuss how she has turned her annotations into a journal entry.

Note: Chrystalla's journal entry has been reprinted just as it was written, so that you can see that students do make errors in their writing and that it is acceptable in a journal entry to cross things out or write over what you have written. The journal does not need to be a neat, polished work.

ACTIVITY: *Reading, annotating, and writing a journal entry on the essay, "What True Education Should Do," by Sydney J. Harris (p. 9)*

1. Preview the essay by reading the title and biographical information.
2. Read the essay through, without using a dictionary.
3. Annotate the passage, using double-entry notes.

Chrystalla's Journal Entry on "Zen and the Art of Burglary"

I liked this piece of writing very much cause it has something to give. A son watching his father growing old realises his responsibilities and wants to carry on the work.

~~His~~ father realizing that the best way to learn something is by living it, decides to try this on his son. So when they go to break in ~~the~~ a house he locks his son in a chest, ~~runs aw~~ and runs away after waking the residents. His bitter son although is clever enough to manage to get out of the chest and get away. When finally he accuses his father of what he~~x~~'s done he answers with the most wise and truthfull answear— 'Now you've learned the trade.' This teaches us that the only way to learn something is by experiencing it.

4. Write a journal entry in which you explore your reactions to the reading. (For example, you might want to answer these questions: What is the author's main point? Do I agree? Why or why not?) If you are confused by the reading, explain why.
5. Working in a small group of two or three students, share your journal responses. Work together to ensure that everyone in the group understands key vocabulary words and the overall message of the essay.   ●

What True Education Should Do
by Sydney J. Harris

Sydney J. Harris (1917–1986) was a writer for major newspapers in Chicago, Illinois. His syndicated column, "Strictly Personal," was published weekly throughout the United States and in several other countries.

When most people think of the word "education," they think of a pupil as a sort of animate sausage casing. Into this empty casing, the teachers are supposed to stuff "education." 1

But genuine education, as Socrates knew more than two thousand years ago, is not inserting the stuffings of information *into* a person, but rather eliciting knowledge *from* him; it is the drawing out of what is in the mind. 2

"The most important part of education," once wrote William Ernest Hocking, the distinguished Harvard philosopher, "is this instruction of a man in what he has inside of him." 3

And, as Edith Hamilton has reminded us, Socrates never said, "I know, learn from me." He said, rather, "Look into your own selves and find the spark of truth that God has put into every heart, and that only you can kindle to a flame." 4

In the dialogue called the "Meno," Socrates takes an ignorant slave boy, without a day of schooling, and proves to the amazed observers that the boy really "knows" geometry—because the principles and axioms of geometry are already in his mind, waiting to be called out. 5

So many of the discussions and controversies about the content of education are futile and inconclusive because they are concerned with what should "go into" the student rather than with what should be taken out, and how this can best be done. 6

The college student who once said to me, after a lecture, "I spend so much time studying that I don't have a chance to learn anything," was succinctly expressing his dissatisfaction with the sausage-casing view of education. 7

He was being so stuffed with miscellaneous facts, with such an indigestible mass of material, that he had no time (and was given no encouragement) to draw on his own resources, to use his own mind for analyzing and synthesizing and evaluating this material. 8

Education, to have any meaning beyond the purpose of creating well-   9
informed dunces, must elicit from the pupil what is latent in every human
being—the rules of reason, the inner knowledge of what is proper for men
to be and do, the ability to sift evidence and come to conclusions that can
generally be assented to by all open minds and warm hearts.

Pupils are more like oysters than sausages. The job of teaching is not   10
to stuff them and then seal them up, but to help them open and reveal the
riches within. There are pearls in each of us, if only we knew how to
cultivate them with ardor and persistence.   ●

SAMPLE STUDENT WRITING: READING/WRITING JOURNALS

Reprinted here are several student journal entries about issues related
to course writing and reading. You may be surprised when you read the
entries to discover that they contain no mechanical errors. That is not
because these students did not make errors when they wrote but because
their writing has been carefully edited for publication in this book. Errors
are expected in student writing as a natural part of the language-learning
process. However, since errors can shift a reader's attention away from the
writer's meaning, they have been removed from the student writing published in this book.

Student Journal Entry: Problems with Vocabulary in Writing

Sometimes I have trouble writing an English composition. For
example, when I write, I have a lot of good ideas, but I don't
know which English word to use because I think in my native
language. I used to take out a Vietnamese-English dictionary.
But after I found out the word, I couldn't continue the idea
which I had been thinking about. I then tried to control my
ideas by thinking about only those ideas which I could express
in English without seeing the dictionary. This action wasn't
helpful because it didn't satisfy what I wanted to write. I really
don't know how I can improve my English in writing. The best
way, I think, is to study a lot of English words first. Is that
right or not?

LY

Student Journal Entry: Problems Associated with Cultural Background in Reading and Writing

My essay was about bowing in the Japanese culture. After discussing my first draft with my classmates, Ramy and Luis, I felt
I could get about half of the message across. But I found it interesting that both of them were stuck at the part where I mentioned Buddhism. I was interested because I saw a similarity
with my own experience: I am always stuck when any essay
mentions Christianity. I am not Buddhist or Shintoist, but Japa-

nese culture is so much influenced by those religions that it is almost impossible to talk about Japan without them. The problem is that many concepts associated with these religions are nonexistent in Christian-influenced society (Western society). I do not know how to explain something that does not exist in the English-speaking world in the English language. And I do not know how to understand something that never existed in my frame of reference. To me it is almost as hard as solving complicated math problems.

DAISUKE

Student Journal Entry: Fulfilling a Writing Assignment

I'm glad that I finally finished the research essay. I think the experience of doing research is unique. Whenever I have a research paper to write, I feel tons of pressure pressing on me. When I get started on the paper, I am afraid that I will have nothing to say about the subject. Then when I collect the materials I need, I have to control myself so that I don't write a fifty-page paper. The last part and also the best part is finishing the paper. When the paper is done, I have a feeling of success and of completing a task, and I feel that I am an expert on that particular subject. Moreover, I feel I have the power to acquire any knowledge. Research writing is unique (but I'm not saying that I enjoy writing a research paper!).

GORDON

Student Journal Entry: Reflections on College Learning

I have always preferred to be exact rather than dealing with uncertainties. I think that's why I chose to be an engineer. I want everybody to have the same answer when a question is asked. The way the natural science problems are answered is exactly what I want.

On the other hand, when a politics question is raised in an International Relations class, the answers the professor gets vary a lot. A person from India answers it in a different way than an American does, and certainly for another person having a different point of view the answer is different. So which is the right answer? Everybody thinks their answer is right.

I believed until today that the natural sciences are exact courses. What I have learned today, which surprised me a lot, is that they are not actually as exact as I thought. In my Physics Recitation today, while I was discussing a question with my professor, he explained that in some cases there may be different answers to a question that are all perfectly correct.

This made me come to the conclusion that we actually are not exact in any subject.

HUSEYIN

PART ONE

Writing from Experience: Expressing a Personal Viewpoint

The first essay you will complete is a personal viewpoint essay: an essay in which you express a belief or share an insight that has been drawn from your own experience (see Essay Assignment 1 on p. 37).

One of the challenges of writing a personal viewpoint essay is to make your experiences and thoughts meaningful to others. To guide you toward that end, several reading selections have been included to reveal various ways in which writers can successfully describe experiences and transmit ideas. In addition, several composing strategies that can help you in your own exploration and reflection are demonstrated. As you develop this essay assignment, you may work concurrently with Part Five to practice the skills of summarizing and paragraphing.

CHAPTER ONE

Responding to Reading

Reading Strategies

The readings in Part One are autobiographical and personal essays. Each author reveals a unique world, yet each is able to transform the individual experiences into ideas and insights that others can understand or learn from. By reading and examining your reactions to these works, you can develop a sense of how a writer can succeed in capturing and holding a reader's interest.

Before Reading

You can understand what you read better if you have some idea about the subject from your previous experience and knowledge. The following guidelines will help you anticipate or predict the content and purpose of each reading selection:

1. Follow the instructions for the Write before You Read activity that precedes each reading selection. This activity will help you start thinking and writing about the subject before you begin reading. (This can be written in your journal notebook.)
2. Read the biographical information before each reading. This section includes the title of the reading and the name of the author. In addition, you will learn where the selection was originally published and, in some cases, why it was written.

Reading

The first time you read each selection, enter the world of the writer. Try to feel what the writer felt and to learn from the writer's experience. It is not necessary during this first reading to understand every word or detail.

Rereading

When you reread, make note of your responses. Annotate the reading selection (see the guidelines for annotating in the Introduction).

Making a Journal Entry

Write in your journal to explore your reactions. Try to understand why a reading affects or interests you (or does not). For example, you can do one or more of the following:

- Examine how the author uses examples to illustrate a point. Note examples that are memorable. Note examples that help to clarify a complex point.
- Note which details stand out: what can you "see," "hear," "smell," "taste," or "feel"?
- Identify the passages where the author reveals the significance of an experience.
- Identify favorite passages. Identify confusing ones.
- Explore and reflect on similar experiences or insights you have had.
- Formulate questions about the reading that you want to ask in class.

Summarizing

Summarizing a reading can help you to understand a writer's purpose better, because summarizing requires that you separate the writer's general statement or idea from the specific details of the experience.

Sometimes writers of personal essays directly state a message or an insight. You can usually find this message in the opening paragraph(s) or in the last paragraph(s). But writers of personal essays often do not directly state a main idea. When they do not, it is necessary for you to infer the message from the details of the experiences described.

In writing a one-sentence summary of a personal essay, include what you believe to be the author's message or insight. Ask yourself these questions: Why did the author describe this experience? What did the author learn from it? What does the author want the reader to gain from it? If you write more than one sentence, your summary can include a brief general description of the experience(s) the author has described; eliminate minor details. Your summary can be written in your journal notebook. (For further work on summarizing, see Part Five.)

Discussing and Taking Notes

Share your journal responses and summaries in class discussions on the reading. During class discussions, keep notes on any ideas that may help you find or develop a topic for your own essay. You might also want to write about the reading in your journal again, if the class discussions have given you new insight.

READINGS

Write before You Read

In the following reading selection, the writer shares his experiences learning to master a new language. Before you read this essay, write for 10 or 15 minutes, either in or out of class, on the following subject:

Describe one or more experiences you have had learning to master a new language.

Since this piece of writing will not be graded or corrected, you do not need to focus on the accuracy of your language use. Write instead with the purpose of recording your experience so that you can remember it well enough to share it with your classmates.   ●

Barriers
by Rolando Niella

Rolando Niella is from Paraguay. He wrote "Barriers" to fulfill a writing assignment for a composition course. What you will read is a finished composition, which has been carefully edited for publication in this book. Later in this chapter, you will see how Rolando got started on this assignment and trace the various stages of thinking and writing and rewriting he went through to produce his essay.

Rolando says that he spent many hours on the essay. He felt very motivated; he "really wanted to write well to make it in college." There is one thing he learned from his writing experience that he would like to share with other students: "Most students," he says, "have the idea that they are supposed to sit down and write perfectly out of their heads onto the paper. There are people like that; it's true. But most of us should remember that it is normal to have to spend a lot of time to produce writing that is well organized and makes sense."

A few months ago, I decided that I wanted to learn how to play tennis. Today, after much practice and a few classes, I know how to hold the racket and basically how to hit the ball; however, I still can't say that I actually play tennis. It is taking me so long to learn, and it is so difficult! It didn't look that hard when I saw my friends playing it so gracefully. Even so, I am still giving it a try. But to play a sport that I cannot master is becoming a pain. I feel so frustrated sometimes that I consider forgetting all about tennis. It is hurting my pride.

Today, tennis is not the main source of my frustrations. I have another problem that generates feelings and puts me in moods very similar to those that I experience when I play it. This is daily conversation with people. It may sound bizarre, but it is not. I am a foreign student, and in playing tennis as in speaking English, I am still in the learning process. That is why the best way I can explain these complex feelings created by my communication problem is by associating them with tennis.

One of the most common situations I find myself in, when I play tennis, is that people, either conscious or unconscious of my level, will start the game with a strong service or will answer my weak service with a fast ball that I cannot possibly hit back. Comparable examples are the ladies at the cafeteria telling me about the menu, while speaking at an incredible speed. This is often worsened by their personal style, the Somerville accent. I also encounter the same problem when my roommate speaks with his heavy Massachusetts accent. He is from Peabody, or "PEEB'dy."   3

Experiences like these are likely to happen when I speak to someone for the first time. Usually, however, once they realize my level, most of them will not "serve for the ace." But with those who still do, it is a different story. If, after asking them to repeat their serves many times and after repeatedly failing to return their balls, I don't give up, they will find an excuse to leave the court immediately, or they will simply tell me to "forget it." In daily conversation, even my friends will use this phrase when they give up trying to make their point or to understand my point. I do not blame them sometimes, but this little phrase is one of the most frustrating ones I have heard. It can take away my desire to talk and discourage me in my efforts to get my ideas across—making me leave the court frustrated and angry. I then isolate myself or look for a friend with whom I can speak a language I don't have to concentrate on and at which I am very good: Spanish. In like manner, when I am tired of tennis and still want to do some sport, I jog alone or play soccer.   4

Once a person is aware of my level and tries to go at my pace, I still confront some problems. First, in tennis, if you are a fairly experienced player, you should be familiar with some basic game plans. The way your opponent is sending the balls may lead you to realize which plan he is using to score upon you. In the same way, if in a language you have experience with the cultural patterns of expressing feelings and moods, and you distinguish the different connotations of words, you may understand the point he is trying to make to you. In tennis, I am not very good at predicting what play my opponent is trying to use; and when I do, it is usually too late. Likewise, in conversation, I usually don't react to a joke until it is too late. I also have a hard time realizing how annoyed my roommate gets, because he selects words to make his point; but the connotations of some of them sometimes don't reach me because of my inexperience. I don't know exactly which is worse to him, "mad," "angry," "disturbed," or "pissed off."   5

Second, in tennis, by observing your opponent's movements, you improve your chances to return the ball and prolong the volley. The swing of his racket, the way he hits the balls, and his position in relation with   6 the net, are good hints for predicting the direction and the power of the ball. I still can't tell precisely how fast the ball is coming or if I have to return it with a forehand or a backhand shot just by watching my opponent. It is not only that I am unfamiliar with these movements, but I am also too busy analyzing the movements I have done, and the ones I am about to do. At the same time, my opponent can tell very little about my next shot by observing me, because my style is very awkward. When talking to people, I also feel the necessity to be familiar with the nonverbal language of Americans. Yesterday, for example, the guy across the hall asked me to turn down my stereo. By the time I understood what he had said, he was gone. I wasn't sure what his talking from the doorway and the tone of his voice meant. Everything happened so fast, just like a cross-court backhand. I didn't feel happy with my vague answer, and I am sure he didn't either.

Playing tennis, for me, in general is an uncomfortable situation. I waste   7
too much energy and attention on every single movement of my hand, my racket, my feet, etc., and besides I also have to watch the player at the other side of the net; then I don't enjoy the game. In everyday conversation, it is also very annoying to pay so much attention to things that should be automatic and to give as much thought to almost every word the other person and I are using.

Exposed to so many unfamiliar rules and ways, I easily lose the train   8
of thought in my conversation. I feel that I am not being natural and start questioning the way I communicate and relate with people. I worry so much about the "how to" that conversation is not always as relaxing as it should be. This is a problem from which the only way to escape is by fully experiencing it. As in any sport, if you want to enjoy it, you have to practice until you master it.

So if you happen to be talking to a foreigner, be aware of this problem.   9
If you are a foreign student yourself, do not feel depressed. I believe that in the long run there will be a reward, a better understanding of ourselves and the vital phenomenon of communication.   ●

Write after You Read

1. Make a journal entry on "Barriers," following the suggestions on p. 15.
2. Write a one- to three-sentence summary of "Barriers," following the guidelines for summarizing the message of a personal essay on p. 15.   ●

Activities for Class Discussion

Working in a group of three or four students, share in the following activities.

1. Share your written summary of "Barriers." If you do not agree on the intended message of this essay, discuss the reasons for the different interpretations. If your group cannot determine an overall message, consult with another group or with your instructor.
2. Are there any unfamiliar words, for example, the tennis terms (*service, serve for the ace, prolong the volley, forehand or backhand shot, crosscourt backhand*)? If so, make sure that everyone in the group understands these terms. Try to guess the meaning of other unfamiliar words or expressions from the context. If your group cannot determine the meaning, consult with your instructor.
3. Rolando has provided a number of examples to support or illustrate points he is making. For example, in the seventh paragraph, he makes a point about playing tennis: "Playing tennis, for me, in general is an uncomfortable situation." He then gives examples to illustrate that discomfort: "I waste too much energy and attention on every single movement of my hand, my racket, my feet, etc., and besides I also have to watch the player at the other side of the net. . . ." These examples help his readers fully understand his point. Search for other combinations of points and examples in his essay (or share any you may have written about in your journal). Discuss the effectiveness of the examples you find. Which are most memorable? Which help clarify Rolando's points?
4. Rolando has provided many details that enable readers to "see" and "hear" what he has experienced. For example, in talking about his roommate's accent, he lets us hear the sound: "He is from Peabody, or 'PEEB'dy.' " Without looking at his essay, try to recall some of these details (or share any you may have written about in your journal.) Why do these details stand out in your mind?
5. Discuss your overall reaction to this essay. Did you like it? Why or why not? If you could advise Rolando to make changes in his essay, what would you recommend?
6. Before reading this essay, you were asked to write a Write before You Read entry (p. 16) about your own experience in learning to master a new language. Share your experience. How is your experience similar to or different from Rolando's? How might you write about it if you decided to make it the subject of your own personal essay? (What details and examples might you include? What points might you make?)   ●

ACTIVITY: *Observing and practicing strategies for composing a personal essay*

In Chapter 2, you can see the process Rolando went through to produce his essay "Barriers." By practicing some or all of the composing strategies presented, you can work toward the production of your own personal essay.

Study and practice these strategies, as you continue to read and discuss the reading selections.   ●

Write before You Read

In the following reading selection, the writer shares her first experiences at college. Before you read her essay, write for 10 to 15 minutes, either in or out of class, on the following subject:

Describe your first impressions of college life.

Since this piece of writing will not be graded or corrected, you do not need to focus on the accuracy of your language use. Write instead with the purpose of recording your impressions so that you can remember them well enough to compare them with your classmates'.   ●

College
by Anzia Yezierska

Anzia Yezierska (1883?–1970), a Russian immigrant, came to America as a young girl. Like many immigrants of that time, her large family lived in a poor, overcrowded section (ghetto) of New York City. When Anzia left home at the age of 17, she was determined to overcome the indignity of poverty through education. She later received a college diploma and became a writer. The following selection is taken from her autobiographical novel Bread Givers, *published in 1925.*

That burning day when I got ready to leave New York and start out   1
on my journey to college! I felt like Columbus starting out for the other
end of the earth. I felt like the pilgrim fathers who had left their homeland
and all their kin behind them and trailed out in search of the New World.

I had stayed up night after night, washing and ironing, patching and   2
darning my things. At last, I put them all together in a bundle, wrapped
them up with newspapers, and tied them securely with the thick clothes
line that I had in my room on which to hang out my wash. I made another
bundle of my books. In another newspaper I wrapped up my food for the
journey: a loaf of bread, a herring, and a pickle. In my purse was the
money I had been saving from my food, from my clothes, a penny to a
penny, a dollar to a dollar, for so many years. It was not much but I
counted out that it would be enough for my train ticket and a few weeks'
start till I got work out there.

It was only when I got to the train that I realized I had hardly eaten   3
all day. Starving hungry, I tore the paper open. *Ach!* Crazy-head! In my
haste I had forgotten even to cut up the bread. I bent over on the side of
my seat, and half covering myself with a newspaper, I pinched pieces out

of the loaf and ripped ravenously at the herring. With each bite, I cast side glances like a guilty thing; nobody should see the way I ate.

After a while, as the lights were turned low, the other passengers began   4
to nod their heads, each outsnoring the other in their thick sleep. I was the only one on the train too excited to close my eyes.

Like a dream was the whole night's journey. And like a dream mounting   5
on a dream was this college town, this New America of culture and education.

Before this, New York was all of America to me. But now I came to   6
a town of quiet streets, shaded with green trees. No crowds, no tenements. No hurrying noise to beat the race of the hours. Only a leisured quietness whispered in the air: Peace. Be still. Eternal time is all before you.

Each house had its own green grass in front, its own free space all   7
around, and it faced the street with the calm security of being owned for generations, and not rented by the month from a landlord. In the early twilight, it was like a picture out of fairyland to see people sitting on their porches, lazily swinging in their hammocks, or watering their own growing flowers.

So these are the real Americans, I thought, thrilled by the lean, straight   8
bearing of the passers-by. They had none of that terrible fight for bread and rent that I always saw in New York people's eyes. Their faces were not worn with the hunger for things they never could have in their lives. There was in them that sure, settled look of those who belong to the world in which they were born.

The college buildings were like beautiful palaces. The campus stretched   9
out like fields of a big park. Air—air. Free space and sunshine. The river at dusk. Glimmering lights on passing boats, the floating voices of young people. And when night came, there were the sky and the stars.

This was the beauty for which I had always longed. For the first few   10
days I could only walk about and drink it in thirstily, more and more. Beauty of houses, beauty of streets, beauty shining out of the calm faces and cool eyes of the people! Oh—too cool. . . .

How could I most quickly become friends with them? How could I   11
come into their homes, exchange with them my thoughts, break with them bread at their tables? If I could only lose myself body and soul in the serenity of this new world, the hunger and the turmoil of my ghetto years would drop away from me, and I, too, would know the beauty of stillness and peace.

What light-hearted laughing youth met my eyes! All the young people   12
I had ever seen were shut up in factories. But here were young girls and young men enjoying life, free from the worry for a living. College to them was being out for a good time, like to us in the shop a Sunday picnic. But in our gayest Sunday picnics there was always the under-feeling that Monday meant back to the shop again. To these born lucky ones joy seemed to stretch out for ever.

What a sight I was in my gray pushcart clothes against the beautiful   13 gay colours and the fine things those young girls wore. I had seen cheap, fancy style, Five- and Ten-Cent Store finery. But never had I seen such plain beautifulness. The simple skirts and sweaters, the stockings and shoes to match. The neat finished quietness of their tailored suits. There was no show-off in their clothes, and yet how much more pulling to the eyes and all the senses than the Grand Street richness I knew.

And the spick-and-span cleanliness of these people! It smelled from   14 them, the soap and the bathing. Their fingernails so white and pink. Their hands and necks white like milk. I wondered how did those girls get their hair so soft, so shiny, and so smooth about their heads. Even their black shoes had a clean look.

Never had I seen men so all shaved up with pink, clean skins. The   15 richest store-keepers in Grand Street shined themselves up with diamonds like walking jewellery stores, but they weren't so hollering clean as these men. And they all had their hair clipped so short; they all had a shape to their heads. So ironed out smooth and even they looked in their spotless, creaseless clothes, as if the dirty battle of life had never yet been on them.

I looked at these children of joy with a million eyes. I looked at them   16 with my hands, my feet, with the thinnest nerves of my hair. By all their differences from me, their youth, their shiny freshness, their carefreeness, they pulled me out of my senses to them. And they didn't even know I was there.

I thought once I got into the classes with them, they'd see me and we'd   17 get to know one another. What a sharp awakening came with my first hour!

As I entered the classroom, I saw young men and girls laughing and   18 talking to one another without introductions. I looked for my seat. Then I noticed, up in front, a very earnest-faced young man with thick glasses over his sad eyes. He made me think of Morris Lipkin, so I chose my seat next to him.

"What's the name of the professor?" I asked.   19

"Smith," came from his tight lips. He did not even look at me. He   20 pulled himself together and began busily writing, to show me he didn't want to be interrupted.

I turned to the girl on my other side. What a fresh clean beauty! A   21 creature of sunshine. And clothes that matched her radiant youth.

"Is this the freshman class in geometry?" I asked her.   22

She nodded politely and smiled. But how quickly her eyes sized me   23 up! It was not an unkind glance. And yet, it said more plainly than words, "From where do you come? How did you get in here?"

Sitting side by side with them through the whole hour, I felt stranger   24 to them than if I had passed them in Hester Street. Wasn't there some secret something that would open us toward one another?

In one class after another, I kept asking myself, "What's the matter   25 with me? Why do they look at me so when I talk with them?"

Maybe I'd have to change myself inside and out to be one of them.   26 But how?

The lectures were over at four o'clock. With a sigh, I turned from the   27 college building, away from the pleasant streets, down to the shabby back alley near the post office, and entered the George Martin Hand Laundry.

Mr. Martin was a fat, easy-going, good-natured man. I no sooner told 28
him of my experience in New York than he took me on at once as an ironer at fifty cents an hour, and he told me he had work for as many hours a day as I could put in.

I felt if I could only look a little bit like other girls on the outside, 29
maybe I could get in with them. And that meant money! And money meant work, work, work!

Till eleven o'clock that night, I ironed fancy white shirtwaists. 30

"You're some busy little worker, even if I do say so," said Mr. Martin, 31
good-naturedly. "But I must lock up. You can't live here."

I went home, aching in every bone. And in the quiet and good air, I 32
so overslept that I was late for my first class. To make matters worse, I found a note in my mailbox that puzzled and frightened me. It said, "Please report at once to the dean's office to explain your absence from Physical Education I, at four o'clock."

A line of other students was waiting there. When my turn came I asked 33
the secretary, "What's this physical education business?"

"This is a compulsory course," he said. "You cannot get credit in any 34
other course unless you satisfy this requirement."

At the hour when I had intended to go back to Martin's Laundry, I 35
entered the big gymnasium. There was a crowd of girls dressed in funny short black bloomers and rubber-soled shoes.

The teacher blew the whistle and called harshly, "Students are expected 36
to report in their uniforms."

"I have none." 37

"They're to be obtained at the bookstore," she said, with a stern look 38
at me. "Please do not report again without it."

I stood there dumb. 39

"Well, stay for to-day, and exercise as you are," said the teacher, taking 40
pity on me.

She pointed out my place in the line, where I had to stand with the 41
rest like a lot of wooden soldiers. She made us twist ourselves around here and there, "Right face!" "Left face!" "Right about face!" I tried to do as the others did, but I felt like a jumping-jack being pulled this way and that way. I picked up dumbbells and pushed them up and down and sideways until my arms were lame. Then she made us hop around like a lot of monkeys.

At the end of the hour, I was so out of breath that I sank down, my 42
heart pounding against my ribs. I was dripping with sweat worse than Saturday night in the steam laundry. What's all this physical education nonsense? I came to college to learn something, to get an education with my head, and not monkeyshines with my arms and legs.

I went over to the instructor. "How much an hour do we get for this 43
work?" I asked her, bitterly.

She looked at me with a stupid stare. "This is a two-point course." 44

Now I got real mad. "I've got to sweat my life away enough only   45
to earn a living," I cried. "God knows I exercised enough, since I was a
kid—"

"You properly exercised?" She looked at me from head to foot. "Your   46
posture is bad. Your shoulders sag. You need additional corrective exercises
outside the class."

More tired than ever, I came to the class next day. After the dumbbells,   47
she made me jump over the hurdles. For the life of me, I couldn't do it.
I bumped myself and scratched my knees on the top bar of the hurdle,
knocking it over with a great clatter. They all laughed except the teacher.

"Repeat the exercise, please," she said, with a frozen face.   48

I was all bruises, trying to do it. And they were holding their sides   49
with laughter. I was their clown, and this was their circus. And suddenly,
I got so wild with rage that I seized the hurdle and right before their eyes
I smashed it to pieces.

The whole gymnasium went still as death.   50

The teacher's face was white. "Report at once to the dean."   51

The scared look on the faces of the girls made me feel that I was to   52
be locked up or fired.

For a minute when I entered the dean's grand office, I was so confused   53
I couldn't even see.

He rose and pointed to a chair beside his desk. "What can I do for   54
you?" he asked, in a voice that quieted me as he spoke.

I told him how mad I was, to have piled on me jumping hurdles when   55
I was so tired anyway. He regarded me with that cooling steadiness of his.
When I was through, he walked to the window and I waited, miserable.
Finally he turned to me again, and with a smile! "I'm quite certain that
physical education is not essential in your case. I will excuse you from
attending the course."

After this things went better with me. In spite of the hard work in the   56
laundry, I managed to get along in my classes. More and more interesting
became the life of the college as I watched it from the outside.

What a feast of happenings each day of college was to those other   57
students. Societies, dances, letters from home, packages of food, midnight
spreads and even birthday parties. I never knew that there were people
glad enough of life to celebrate the day they were born. I watched the gay
goings-on around me like one coming to a feast, but always standing back
and only looking on.

One day, the ache for people broke down my feelings of difference   58
from them. I felt I must tear myself out of my aloneness. Nothing had
ever come to me without my going out after it. I had to fight for my living,
fight for every bit of my education. Why should I expect friendship and
love to come to me out of the air while I sat there, dreaming of it?

The freshman class gave a dance that very evening. Something in the   59
back of my head told me that an evening dress and slippers were part of
going to a dance. I had no such things. But should that stop me? If I had

waited till I could afford the right clothes for college, I should never have been able to go at all.

I put a fresh collar over my old serge dress. And with a dollar stolen   60 from my eating money, I bought a ticket to the dance. As I peeped into the glittering gymnasium, blaring with jazz, my timid fears stopped the breath in me. How the whole big place sang with their light-hearted happiness! Young eyes drinking joy from young eyes. Girls, like gay-coloured butterflies, whirling in the arms of young men.

Floating ribbons and sashes shimmered against men's black coats. I took   61 the nearest chair, blinded by the dazzle of the happy couples. Why did I come here? A terrible sense of age weighed upon me; yet I watched and waited for someone to come and ask me to dance. But not one man came near me. Some of my classmates nodded distantly in passing, but most of them were too filled with their own happiness even to see me.

The whirling of joy went on and on, and still I sat there watching,   62 cold, lifeless, like a lost ghost. I was nothing and nobody. It was worse than being ignored. Worse than being an outcast. I simply didn't belong. I had no existence in their young eyes. I wanted to run and hide myself, but fear and pride nailed me against the wall.

A chaperon must have noticed my face, and she brought over one of   63 those clumsy, backward youths who was lost in a corner by himself. How unwilling were his feet as she dragged him over! In a dull voice, he asked, "May I have the next dance?" his eyes fixed in the distance as he spoke.

"Thank you. I don't want to dance." And I fled from the place.   64

I found myself walking in the darkness of the campus. In the thick   65 shadows of the trees I hid myself and poured out my shamed and injured soul to the night. So, it wasn't character or brains that counted. Only youth and beauty and clothes—things I never had and never could have. Joy and love were not for such as me. Why not? Why not? . . .

I flung myself on the ground, beating with my fists against the endless   66 sorrows of my life. Even in college I had not escaped from the ghetto. Here loneliness hounded me even worse than in Hester Street. Was there no escape? Will I never lift myself to be a person among people?

I pressed my face against the earth. All that was left of me reached   67 out in prayer. God! I've gone so far, help me to go on. God! I don't know how, but I must go on. Help me not to want their little happiness. I have wanted their love more than my life. Help me be bigger than this hunger in me. Give me the love that can live without love. . . .

Darkness and stillness washed over me. Slowly I stumbled to my feet   68 and looked up at the sky. The stars in their infinite peace seemed to pour their healing light into me. I thought of the captives in prison, the sick and the suffering from the beginning of time who had looked to these stars for strength. What was my little sorrow to the centuries of pain which those stars had watched? So near they seemed, so compassionate. My bitter hurt seemed to grow small and drop away. If I must go on alone, I should still have silence and the high stars to walk with me.   ●

Write after You Read

1. Make a journal entry on "College," following the suggestions on p 15.
2. Write a two- or three-sentence summary of "College," following the guidelines for summarizing the message of a personal essay on p. 15.   ●

Activities for Class Discussion

Working in a group of three or four students, share in the following activities. Your group can decide the order in which to cover the material and the amount of time to spend on each question.

1. Share your written summary of "College." If you do not agree on the intended message of this essay, discuss the reasons for the different interpretations. If your group cannot determine an overall message, consult with another group or with your instructor.
2. Are there unfamiliar words or expressions? Does everyone in the group know what "the pilgrim fathers" refers to (in paragraph 1)? Do you all understand the meaning of *ravenously* (paragraph 3), *tenements* (6), *turmoil* (11), and *compulsory* (34)? If not, try to guess the meaning of these or other unfamiliar words from the context. If your group cannot determine the meaning, consult with your instructor.
3. Without looking at the text, try to remember and then describe one or two scenes that stand out in you mind (or share a scene you may have written about in your journal). Then, looking at the text, analyze why these scenes are particularly memorable. Ask yourself questions like these:
   a. Are these scenes memorable because of the special way the author has described them? If so, what is notable about the description?
   b. Are these scenes memorable because you do not like the way the author has described them? If so, what is distasteful to you about the description?
   c. Are these scenes memorable because you can identify with them? If so, what similar experiences have you had?
   d. Are these scenes memorable because they are so different from your own experience? If so, how has the author succeeded in capturing your attention?
4. One way to read about personal experiences is to imagine that you are part of them. To enter the world of this author, discuss the answers to these questions:
   a. If you were one of her classmates, how would you treat her?
   b. If you were one of her instructors, how would you behave toward her?
5. Before you were assigned to read this essay, you were asked to write about your own first impressions of college. Share those impressions

with your group. How are your impressions similar to or different from Yezierska's?

6. The way a writer organizes a personal essay is dependent on the writer's particular purpose and experience. Yezierska writes about an experience which began with high expectations and resulted in deep disappointment from which she gained some insight.

   a. Examine how the author has structured her essay:

     • *Expectation:* Where are details provided that reveal how she thought things would be?

     • *Disappointment:* At what point do you become aware that she is in for a disappointment? At what point does she begin to describe the incident or series of events that opened her eyes?

     • *Discovery:* At what point does she discover some meaning in her experience?

   b. Share experiences you have had involving expectation and disappointment, such as taking a trip, making a new friend, celebrating a holiday, attending your graduation, looking for a job, living in a different country, applying to college, coming to college, meeting your roommate, or taking a particular course. How might you write about one of these experiences if you were to make it the subject of you own personal essay? What details would you use to reveal the expectation? How much of the disappointing experience would you relate? What lesson did you learn, and how could you share that with your readers?   ●

Write before You Read

On the following page is a photograph of the writer May Sarton, along with an excerpt from one of her poems. Look at the picture, read the poetry, and then write for five or ten minues, in or out of class, in answer to the following question:

Do you like to be alone?

Since this piece of writing will not be graded or corrected, you do not need to focus on the accuracy of your language use. Write instead with the purpose of focusing on what you think before you are influenced by what you read. You can discuss what you have written with your classmates.   ●

The Rewards of Living a Solitary Life
by May Sarton

May Sarton (b. 1912), a poet and author, was born in Belgium but came to the United States as a child and now lives alone in Maine. Her many books include A Reckoning *(1978) and* Journal of Solitude

I moved into my house one day
In a downpour of leaves and rain,
"I took possession," as they say,
With solitude for my domain. . . .

I moved into my life one day
In a downpour of leaves in flood,
I took possession as they say,
And knew I was alone for good.

Excerpt from "Moving In," from *Collected Poems* (1930–1973), p. 210.
(Photograph of May Sarton reprinted by permission of Seacoast Life Magazine.)

(1973). The following essay was originally published in the New York Times *in 1974.*

The other day an acquaintance of mine, a gregarious and charming 1 man, told me he had found himself unexpectedly alone in New York for an hour or two between appointments. He went to the Whitney[1] and spent the "empty" time looking at things in solitary bliss. For him it proved to be a shock nearly as great as falling in love to discover that he could enjoy himself so much alone.

What had he been afraid of, I asked myself? That, suddenly alone, he 2 would discover that he bored himself, or that there was, quite simply, no self there to meet? But having taken the plunge, he is now on the brink of adventure; he is about to be launched into his own inner space, space as immense, unexplored and sometimes frightening as outer space to the as-tronaut. His every perception will come to him with a new freshness and, for a time, seem startlingly original. For anyone who can see things for himself with a naked eye becomes, for a moment or two, something of a genius. With another human being present vision becomes double vision, inevitably. We are busy wondering, what does my companion see or think of this, and what do I think of it? The original impact gets lost, or diffused.

"Music I heard with you was more than music." Exactly. And therefore 3 music *itself* can only be heard alone. Solitude is the salt of personhood. It brings out the authentic flavor of every experience.

"Alone one is never lonely: the spirit adventures, walking/In a quiet 4 garden, in a cool house, abiding single there."

Loneliness is most acutely felt with other people, for with others, even 5 with a lover sometimes, we suffer from our differences of taste, tempera-ment, mood. Human intercourse often demands that we soften the edge of perception, or withdraw at the very instant of personal truth for fear of hurting, or of being inappropriately present, which is to say naked, in a social situation. Alone we can afford to be wholly whatever we are, and to feel whatever we feel absolutely. That is a great luxury!

For me the most interesting thing about a solitary life, and mine has 6 been that for the last twenty years, is that it becomes increasingly rewarding. When I can wake up and watch the sun rise over the ocean, as I do most days, and know that I have an entire day ahead, uninterrupted, in which to write a few pages, take a walk with my dog, lie down in the afternoon for a long think (why does one think better in a horizontal position?), read and listen to music, I am flooded with happiness.

I am lonely when I am overtired, when I have worked too long without 7 a break, when for the time being I feel empty and need filling up. And I am lonely sometimes when I come back home after a lecture trip, when I have seen a lot of people and talked a lot, and am full to the brim with experience that needs to be sorted out.   •

[1] **the Whitney:** an art museum in New York City

Then for a little while the house feels huge and empty, and I wonder   8
where my self is hiding. It has to be recaptured slowly by watering the
plants, perhaps, and looking again at each one as though it were a person,
by feeding the two cats, by cooking a meal.

It takes a while, as I watch the surf blowing up in fountains at the end   9
of the field, but the moment comes when the world falls away, and the
self emerges again from the deep unconscious, bringing back all I have
recently experienced to be explored and slowly understood, when I can
converse again with my hidden powers, and so grow, and so be renewed,
till death do us part.[2]   ●

Write after You Read

1. Make a journal entry on "The Rewards of Living a Solitary Life,"
   following the suggestions on p. 15.
2. Write a one- or two-sentence summary of "The Rewards of Living
   a Solitary Life," following the guidelines for summarizing the message of a personal essay on p. 15.   ●

Activities for Class Discussion

Working in a group of three or four students, share in the following
activities. Your group can decide the order in which to cover the material
and how much time to spend on each question.

1. Share your written summary of "The Rewards of Living a Solitary
   Life." If you do not agree on the intended message of this essay,
   discuss the reasons for the different interpretations. If your group
   cannot determine an overall message, consult with another group or
   with your instructor.
2. If any words or expressions are unfamiliar, try to guess their meaning
   from the context. Make sure that everyone in the group understands
   the meaning of these words:

gregarious (paragraph 1)	abiding (4)
inevitably (2)	acutely (5)
diffused (2)	converse (9)

   In addition, determine the meaning and note the usage of these
   idiomatic expressions:

in solitary bliss (1)	on the brink of (2)
having taken the plunge (2)	full to the brim with (7)

3. Looking at the text (or at what you have written in your journal),

---

[2] **till death do us part:** part of the marriage vows spoken by a couple at their wedding
ceremony

select one or two significant quotations. The quotation may be one you like, one you don't like, one you think best illustrates the major message of the selection, or one you found difficult to understand. After you have selected the quotations, follow these guidelines:

   a. Take turns reading your quotations aloud.
   b. Discuss the meaning and significance of each quotation. Remember that each reader may have a different response. Be ready to accept different interpretations of the same passage.

4. Sarton's response to solitude is not the characteristic attitude. Can you determine from her essay the more typical response to being alone? If so, discuss answers to this question: How do these two responses compare with your own attitude toward solitude? (To answer this question, you may want to refer to your answer to the Write before You Read question, "Do you like to be alone?")

5. If Anzia Yezierska, the author of "College" (pp. 20–25), had been able to read Sarton's essay, do you think it would have helped her to deal with her own loneliness? Why or why not?

6. Examine the organization of the essay. One way to do this is to read or annotate paragraph by paragraph to see what is included in each paragraph. Then discuss the purpose or function of each paragraph. (For example, does the paragraph introduce the main idea of the essay? Does the paragraph make a new point? Does the paragraph exist primarily to provide an example to illustrate or clarify a point made in the previous paragraph?)

   a. What does Sarton accomplish in paragraph 1? paragraph 2? and so on.
   b. Which sentence or paragraph first makes you aware of the essay's focus, of what the essay is really about?   ●

Write before You Read

In the following essay, the writer discusses his friends. Before you read his essay, write for 10 to 15 minutes, in or out of class, on one of the following subjects:

1. To stimulate your memory about childhood friendships, look at the picture on the following page, titled "Best Friends." Then describe your relationship with one of your childhood friends. Try to remember a specific incident.
2. Explain the difference between your male and female friendships.

Since this piece of writing will not be graded or corrected, you do not need to focus on the accuracy of your language use. Write instead with the purpose of focusing on your friendships so that you can visualize them and share what you have written with your classmates.   ●

Best Friends. © 1979 Judy Gelles.

Focusing on Friends
by Steve Tesich

Steve Tesich was born in Yugoslavia in 1942. He came to America when he was 14 years old and achieved two degrees in Russian literature by 1967. The author of a novel and several plays, Tesich is best known for his screenplay of the movie Breaking Away, *for which he received an Academy Award in 1979. His essay "Focusing on Friends" reflects his interest in the cinema. The essay was originally published in 1983 in the* New York Times Magazine, *in a section called "About Men."*

When I think of people who were my good friends, I see them all, as   1
I do everything else from my life, in cinematic terms. The camera work is entirely different for men and women.

I remember all the women in almost extreme close-ups. The settings   2
are different—apartments, restaurants—but they're all interiors, as if I had never spent a single minute with a single woman outside. They're looking right at me, these women in these extreme close-ups; the lighting is exquisite, worthy of a Fellini or Fosse film,[1] and their lips are moving. They're telling me something important or reacting to something even more important that I've told them. It's the kind of movie where you tell people to keep quiet when they chew their popcorn too loudly.

The boys and men who were my friends are in an entirely different   3
movie. No close-ups here. No exquisite lighting. The camera work is rather shaky but the background is moving. We're going somewhere, on foot, on bicycles, in cars. The ritual of motion, or action, makes up for the inconsequential nature of the dialogue. It's a much sloppier film, this film that is not really a film but a memory of real friends: Slobo, Louie, Sam. Male friends. I've loved all three of them. I assumed they knew this, but I never told them.

Quite the contrary is true in my female films. In close-up after close-   4
up, I am telling every woman who I ever loved that I love her, and then lingering on yet another close-up of her face for a reaction. There is a perfectly appropriate musical score playing while I wait. And if I wait long enough, I get an answer. I am loved. I am not loved. Language clears up the suspense. The emotion is nailed down.

Therein lies the difference, I think, between my friendships with men   5
and with women. I can tell women I love them. Not only can I tell them, I am compulsive about it. I can hardly wait to tell them. But I can't tell the men. I just can't. And they can't tell me. Emotions are never nailed down. They run wild, and I and my male friends chase after them, on

[1] **Fellini, Fosse:** Federico Fellini and Bob Fosse, movie directors whose films are noted for visual extravagance

foot, on bicycles, in cars, keeping the quarry in sight but never catching up.

My first friend was Slobo. I was still living in Yugoslavia at the time, 6 and not far from my house there was an old German truck left abandoned after the war. It had no wheels. No windshield. No doors. But the steering wheel was intact. Slobo and I flew to America in that truck. It was our airplane. Even now, I remember the background moving as we took off down the street, across Europe, across the Atlantic. We were inseparable: The best of friends. Naturally, not one word concerning the nature of our feelings for one another was ever exchanged. It was all done in actions.

The inevitable would happen at least once a day. As we were flying 7 over the Atlantic, there came, out of nowhere, that wonderful moment: engine failure! "We'll have to bail out," I shouted. "A-a-a-a-a!" Slobo made the sound of a failing engine. Then he would turn and look me in the eye: "I can't swim," he'd say. "Fear not." I put my hand on his shoulder. "I'll drag you to shore." And, with that, both of us would tumble out of the truck onto the dusty street. I swam through the dust. Slobo drowned in the dust, coughing, gagging. "Sharks!" he cried. But I always saved him. The next day the ritual would be repeated, only then it would be my turn to say "I can't swim," and Slobo would save me. We saved each other from certain death over a hundred times, until finally a day came when I really left for America with my mother and sister. Slobo and I stood at the train station. We were there to say goodbye, but, since we weren't that good at saying things and since he couldn't save me, he just cried until the train started to move.

The best friend I had in high school was Louie. It now seems to me 8 that I was totally monogamous when it came to male friends. I would have several girl friends but only one real male friend. Louis was it at that time. We were both athletes, and one day we decided to "run till we drop." We just wanted to know what it was like. Skinny Louie set the pace as we ran around our high-school track. Lap after lap. Four laps to a mile. Mile after mile we ran. I had the reputation as being a big-time jock.[2] Louie didn't. But this was Louie's day. There was a bounce in his step and, when he turned back to look at me, his eyes were gleaming with the thrill of it all. I finally dropped. Louie still looked fresh; he seemed capable, on that day, of running forever. But we were the best of friends, and so he stopped. "That's it," he lied. "I couldn't go another step farther." It was an act of love. Naturally, I said nothing.

Louie got killed in Vietnam. Several weeks after his funeral, I went to 9 his mother's house, and, because she was a woman, I tried to tell her how much I had loved her son. It was not a good scene. Although I was telling the truth, my words sounded like lies. It was all very painful and embarrassing. I kept thinking how sorry I was that I had never told Louie himself.

[2] **jock:** (*slang*) a male athlete

Sam is my best friend now, and has been for many years. A few years 10
ago, we were swimming at a beach in East Hampton. The Atlantic! The
very Atlantic I had flown over in my German truck with Slobo. We had
swum out pretty far from the shore when both of us simultaneously thought
we spotted a shark. Water is not only a good conductor of electricity but
of panic as well. We began splashing like madmen toward shore. Suddenly,
at the height of my panic, I realized how much I loved my friend, what
an irreplaceable friend he was, and, although I was the faster swimmer, I
fell back to protect him. Naturally, the shark in the end proved to be
imaginary. But not my feelings for my friend. For several days after that
I wanted to share my discovery with him, to tell him how much I loved
him. Fortunately, I didn't.

I say fortunately because on reflection, there seems to be sufficient 11
evidence to indicate that, if anybody was cheated and shortchanged by me,
it was the women, the girls, the very recipients of my uncensored emotions.
Yes, I could hardly wait to tell them I loved them. I did love them. But
once I told them, something stopped. The emotion was nailed down, but,
with it, the enthusiasm and the energy to prove it was nailed down, too.
I can remember my voice saying to almost all of them, at one time or
another: "I told you I love you. What else do you want?" I can now recoil
at the impatient hostility of that voice but I can't deny it was mine.

The tyranny of self-censorship forced me, in my relations with male 12
friends, to seek alternatives to language. And just because I could never be
sure they understood exactly how I felt about them, I was forced to look
for ways to prove it. That is, I now think, how it should be. It is time to
make adjustments. It is time to pull back the camera, free the women I
know, and myself, from those merciless close-ups and have the background
move. ●

Write after You Read

1. Make a journal entry on "Focusing on Friends," following the suggestions on p. 15.
2. Write a two- or three-sentence summary of "Focusing on Friends," following the guidelines for summarizing a personal essay on p. 15. ●

Activities for Class Discussion

Working in a group of three or four students, share in the following
activities. Your group can decide the order in which to cover the material
and how much time to spend on each question.

1. Share your written summary of "Focusing on Friends." If you do
   not agree on the intended meaning of the essay, discuss the reasons

for the different interpretations. If your group cannot determine the author's point, consult with another group or with your instructor.

2. Make sure that everyone in the group understands the meaning or use of the cinematic terms in paragraphs 1, 2, and 4 and other words such as these:

inconsequential (3)   recipients (11)
compulsive (5)   uncensored (11)
quarry (5)   recoil (11)
monogamous (8)

If you cannot guess the meaning and use of these or other words from the context, consult with your instructor.

3. Looking at the text (or at what you have written in your journal), select one or two favorite passages. The passage may be one you like, one you think identifies the major message of the selection, or one you believe best captures or illustrates the meaning of friendship. After you have selected the passages, follow these guidelines:
   a. Take turns reading your passages aloud.
   b. Discuss the meaning and significance of each passage. Remember that each reader may have a different response. Be ready to accept different interpretations of the same passage.

4. Discuss the following questions:
   a. Are your friendships with members of the same sex similar to or different from Tesich's friendships with men? Explain.
   b. Are your friendships with members of the opposite sex similar to or different from Tesich's friendships with women? Explain.
   c. Do you agree with Tesich's conclusion?
   d. Has reading this essay caused you to reevaluate your approach to any of your friendships? Explain.

5. Examine the organization of the essay. One way to do this is to read (or annotate) paragraph by paragraph to see what is included in each paragraph. Then discuss the purpose of each paragraph or group of paragraphs. Ask yourself questions such as these:
   a. What does Tesich accomplish in paragraphs 1 through 4?
   b. Which sentence or paragraph first makes you aware of the essay's focus, of what the essay is really about?
   c. Does each paragraph add new ideas, or do some paragraphs exist primarily to emphasize or illustrate ideas already provided?
   Would another organization of this material have been possible? If so, how else could this essay have been organized?   ●

CHAPTER TWO

Guidelines for Fulfilling Essay Assignment 1

Essay Assignment 1

Write an essay in which you draw from your own experience to express a personal viewpoint. Describe in detail an event or experience (or series of events or experiences) that has led you to learn, believe, or understand something. Your purpose in writing this essay will be to reveal to your classmates and your instructor the significance of what you have experienced. ●

Understanding the Assignment

Before you begin writing an essay, you need to understand exactly what you are being assigned to write. You need to analyze the directions of the writing assignment so that you know both the essay's possibilities and its limitations. The following activity can help you fulfill that goal.

ACTIVITY: *Rereading and analyzing the writing assignment*

Working in a group of three or four students, have one student read the essay assignment aloud. Examine what the assignment asks you to do. What purpose will the essay serve? What material should it contain? If you are unclear as to the demands of the assignment, consult with your instructor. ●

Practicing Invention Strategies

To express a personal viewpoint, you need a topic to write about and something to say about that topic. If you have not already thought of a topic or if you have thought of one but don't know what to say about it, you need some strategies for getting started. The strategies suggested here, known as *invention strategies*, can help stimulate your thinking.

To observe how these strategies work, you can follow the writing process of one student, Rolando Niella, whose essay "Barriers" is reprinted on pp. 16–18. You will see how using these strategies led him to develop the essay.

Since all writers differ, the techniques that worked well for Rolando may not work as well for you. But practicing these strategies may lead you to discover a rich resource of ideas and experiences.

Invention strategies represent a way of thinking on paper. Whenever you use them, you write primarily for yourself. Therefore, you should not be overly concerned with language accuracy at this stage. Rolando made many language errors as he wrote; they have been edited for this book so that you can focus on the development of his ideas.

Making a List

Making a list can be a valuable first step in writing. If it works for you, it can help you to find a topic to write about. As you prepare to make a list of experiences and ideas, consider what prompts writers to write personal essays. For example, authors often recall and reflect on the following situations and experiences:

- Confronting a problem
- Facing a challenge
- Adapting to new circumstances
- Experiencing disappointment
- Making a choice or decision
- Discovering an identity
- Experiencing a turning point
- Suffering an illness or injury
- Rebelling against authority
- Being influenced by a special individual

To begin, you can list several experiences and concepts that might be good topics for a personal essay. Here are some examples:

EXPERIENCES
- Applying to college
- Leaving home
- Arriving in the United States
- Starting college

CONCEPTS
- Solitude
- Self-respect
- Fear
- Jealousy

ACTIVITY: Making a list

Working in a small group, add five topics to the lists of experiences and concepts. Share your lists with the other groups in the class. Discuss how some of the topics might be expanded into essays. What details and examples could be included that would help readers to "see," "hear," and "feel" the experience?   ●

A STUDENT WRITER AT WORK

Rolando was attracted to the idea of writing about confronting a problem. In preparation for his essay, he made a list of several problems he had experienced or was experiencing. He put a star next to the topics he thought he might want to write about.

Rolando's List

PROBLEMS

☆ • Culture shock
☆ • Making friends
   • Problems in my family
   • Problem between by brother and my father
   • Problems in adolescence
☆ • Defining my friends
   • Taking tests
   • Christian problem
   • good problems

ACTIVITY: *Making a list*

Make a list of topics you might want to write about in your own personal essay. Star the topics that seem most promising.   ●

Freewriting

Freewriting is a writing activity in which you write about a topic for several minutes without stopping. You write whatever comes into your mind about your topic, without trying to write a perfect essay. In other words, you talk to yourself on paper. This technique is one way to get started on your writing. If it works for you, it can help you to find out what is really on your mind.

A STUDENT WRITER AT WORK

Even after he had made his list of topics, Rolando was still not sure what to write about in his essay. He began to freewrite to try to discover which problem was most important to him. As you will see, although he has trouble thinking of a topic, the problem of culture shock emerges as the most important thing on his mind.

Rolando's Freewriting

I have to start writing. I just thought . . . I don't have other problems. There must be some other problems that I'm not aware of, but I can't think. I think it's because there is one problem that takes so much time and space in my head. THE

CULTURE SHOCK. Well that's a problem, to have a problem that goes around your head night and day and wears your brain away. What to do. I don't know. Well, there are some problems in my family, but they are so complicated. I have to look for some other problem not so complicated—what could it be? I don't really know. What else is a problem in the past, problem in the past . . . define my friends . . . problem in the past was to . . . I don't know. Well, I guess I'm running out of ideas about problems. Come on problems, come to my mind. I don't know. What a problem not to know.

ACTIVITY: *Freewriting*

Freewrite for five minutes to find a topic for your essay. If you have already decided on a topic, freewrite on that topic. Remember that you are not trying to write a perfect composition; you don't even have to write in complete sentences. Just talk to yourself on paper to find out what you are thinking.   ●

Looping

Looping[†] is a writing activity in which you loop (join together) two or more freewriting exercises and reflect on what you have written. If this technique works for you, it can help you to explore a topic in some depth.

GUIDELINES	## *Guidelines for Looping*

1. Freewrite on a topic for several minutes.
2. Stop.
3. Read what you have just written.
4. Find an idea in your freewriting that you want to pursue.
5. Write that idea in a new sentence.
6. Freewrite on that idea.
7. Repeat steps 2–7.

---

† Based on the work of Peter Elbow.

A STUDENT WRITER AT WORK

After his freewriting (pp. 39–40), Rolando realized that the number one problem on his mind was the culture shock he was experiencing living in the United States. He began to explore this subject by looping.

Rolando's Looping

1. Rolando wrote freely for several minutes, using the word *problem* as his topic:

   > I have of course many problems in my life like everybody has, but right now I am feeling new problems like the cultural shock. I got out of my country and came to study in the U.S.A. One of the biggest problems is to make friends, to make or have the good old friends I have back home. It's so hard here—you don't know how to act, whether you should ask them their telephone number or wait for them to do it, whether you should call them very often or not. Are they bothered by my language problem? Can they not carry on a conversation with me because they always talk about local or national subjects about which I am not informed? This is really hard and sometimes makes me feel like a stranger in a group where everybody is laughing and talking and they supposedly were my friends.

2. Rolando then stopped writing.
3. He read what he had just written.
4. He found an idea he wanted to pursue.
5. He wrote that idea in a new sentence:

   > Sometimes I feel like a stranger.

6. He began to freewrite on the idea in that sentence:

   > Yes, this is true, so I start wondering if my feelings are part of my imagination or not. I try to put myself into the same posi-tion—my having a foreign kid as a friend in Paraguay—and I realize that sometimes you just can't explain everything even though you still care for the person. I really care about my friends. I mean, whenever they know I like to be their friend, I care a lot about them. But I wonder, are these new friends like that? Is that the way they act but not what they mean? I know what the solution is: get together with the Latin people; but I don't want that. I don't want to be part of a minority and limit my circle of friends. I want to meet a lot of people.

7. Rolando then repeated steps 2–4 and came up with a new idea he wanted to pursue, this time creating two sentences:

   > I don't want to limit my circle of friends. I want to meet a lot of people.

8. He then began to freewrite on the idea:

> This is a hard experience. I don't know the solution for this problem. Otherwise I would have solved it already. But it seems to me that the only thing I can do is keep trying—try to get close to people very carefully—try to learn, not only the way they act, but their language and their culture. But there is so much to learn. I have to wait—I think waiting is the best thing—and be very observant and careful. But I have to watch out and not become paranoid and overanalyze every single aspect of what happens between me and my friends. I don't know if I am going to write about this problem. It seems so confusing that I don't even know if a good paper will come out of it. The least it could show is the total confusion I have in my head.

9. Rolando read over everything that he had written and decided that the problem that most affected him was communicating in a second language, because it interfered with his ability to make new friends.

ACTIVITY: *Looping*

Follow the guidelines below for looping to explore a topic for your essay. Working in small groups, share the experiences and ideas that have emerged. Discuss how your topics can be developed into essays. What details and examples could be included?

1. Freewrite on your topic for five to ten minutes.
2. Stop.
3. Read what you have just written.
4. Find an idea in your freewriting that you want to pursue.
5. Write that idea in a new sentence.
6. Freewrite on that idea.
7. Repeat steps 2–5. (Optional: Repeat steps 6 and 7.)

Cubing

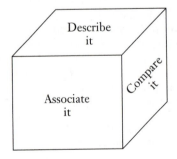
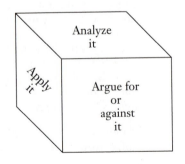

Cubing[†] is a writing activity that allows you to explore a specific topic

[†] Based on the work of Elizabeth Cowan.

from six different perspectives. Imagine that your topic is inside a cube and that you are looking at it through each of the six sides. Move quickly from one viewpoint to another, writing down whatever each perspective suggests to you about your subject. If this technique works for you, it can help you to find a way to approach your topic. In some cases, it may help you to find an organizational pattern for your essay.

GUIDELINES **Guidelines for Cubing**

Explore a topic through these six perspectives:

1. *Description:* Describe it. Look closely and tell what you see.
2. *Comparison:* Compare it. What is it similar to? What is it different from?
3. *Association:* Associate it. What does it remind you of? And what other associations come to mind?
4. *Analysis:* Analyze it. Tell how it's made.
5. *Application:* Apply it. Tell what you can do with it. How can it be used?
6. *Argument:* Argue for *and* against it.

A STUDENT WRITER AT WORK

To explore his topic, which he now called "The Language Barrier," Rolando used cubing. Rolando underlined certain sentences *after* he finished this writing activity. These were the ideas he decided to focus on in his essay.

Rolando's Cubing

TOPIC: THE LANGUAGE BARRIER

1. Rolando first described his topic:

   The language barrier is the idealistic or imaginary barrier that you feel in a country or group of people that speaks a different language than you do. You feel that barrier because even though you can speak the language and you can make yourself understand, you can't get your ideas across. You are speaking but you feel your words disintegrate before reaching their effect. You feel continuously that you have to think about every word you are saying when the natural thing is just to let your spirit express without thinking. You doubt youself; you feel insincere; you feel insecure; you feel false because you are choosing your words so much. But when you use them just like that you are misunderstood.

2. Then he compared it with other things:

It is hard to compare, but it is like you reach a point where you feel you are in a theater rehearsing where everybody is talking in a way that deep inside is not natural, that all talking doesn't belong to reality. It's like seeing a poem but you don't know its meaning. It's like when you have to write a letter and you don't have the paper to write on, or even you write but you don't know the zip code so you don't send your letter. It's like talking to yourself.

3. Then he made associations:

It reminds me of reading a very hard book and not understanding the meaning but yes the words. It's like being in a band and not singing with the group. Every time I feel the barrier of language, I feel how far I am from home and how necessary are cultures. Feeling the language barrier is like when I play tennis. I can't get a serve in and sometimes I can't even answer the ball. You don't know how to say what you want to say. Pain. Frustration.

4. Then he analyzed it:

Well . . . there are two sides, and you are trying to go over it, to make your ball go over the net. . . . There are two parts: (a) Make yourself understood and (b) understand the others.

a. You are always choosing the words.
   You don't know the words.
   You just shut up.
b. They talk and you can't understand them because of so many reasons. So they give up or they tell you "forget it," "it doesn't matter." This is the terrible part because these are the things that really enable you to participate, share, that make you feel part of the team, of a system of that "functioning" or "belongness" you were used to.

5. Then he tried to apply it:

What do you mean by "apply it"? It [the language barrier] is applied to me by force, because of you.

- When they tell jokes
- When they talk slowly
- When they say something good to you and you have to ask again
- When they complain to you
- When they give "trivial comments" that will help you
- When you want to express your inner feelings, being mean but nice, etc.

6. Finally he argued for and against it:

- For: because it makes you aware of everything, of every word;

develops your senses; gives you an idea of how important language is
- Against: frustrated, bad complex, unhappiness, paranoia, anxiety, wastes your time

7. After Rolando had covered all of the perspectives, he read what he had written. He decided that he would try to write an essay comparing learning to play tennis with learning a new language.

ACTIVITY: *Cubing*

Follow the guidelines for cubing to explore a topic from several perspectives. Spend only a few minutes on each perspective. Working in a small group, stop after one or two perspectives to share what you have written. After you have covered all six perspectives, read over your writing. Mark any sections that you think might lead you to writing an essay. Discuss perspectives you might take in an essay. How might an essay on one or more of the perspectives be organized?

1. Describe your topic.
2. Compare it.
3. Associate it.
4. Analyze it.
5. Apply it.
6. Argue for *and* against it.

Focusing Your Thoughts

When you practice invention, you generate ideas to develop your own understanding of your subject. When you write an essay, you share your understanding with others, bringing your thoughts into focus for your readers.

Developing a Focal Point

You can now observe the process Rolando went through to begin to focus his thoughts. Your own process will probably be different from his, but you should begin to plan how you will transmit an idea to your readers.

A STUDENT WRITER AT WORK

Rolando Focuses His Thoughts for Himself

After Rolando finished cubing, he went back over all his invention notes and underlined some phrases and sentences. He then made a list of key ideas discovered in invention, as well as some new ideas that he wanted to include in his essay about the language barrier.

ROLANDO'S LIST

PARTICIPATION
- Sharing
- Belongingness
- Become an operational and useful part of the team (sport/tennis) by understanding the way and the rules

YOU WANT TO
- GO BACK TO SOMETHING THAT YOU ALREADY KNOW
  - No risk
  - No pain or frustration
  - (Become paranoid)
- BE ABLE TO MANAGE THE WHOLE THING AND HAVE FUN PLAYING THE GAME
  - Without caring too much about the "how to" and worrying about style

"WHAT AM I DOING HERE?"

Rolando Focuses His Thoughts for His Readers

Rolando knew that he wanted to write his essay on the topic of the language barrier. He had a general list of items he wanted to cover in the paper. He now needed to turn the topic into an idea that he could share with his reading audience. To create a sentence that would tell his readers what the essay would be about, he asked himself, "What do I want to show my readers?" In searching for the answer to this question, Rolando started several different sentences:

> Problems . . .
>
> Language play . . .
>
> Learning to use . . .
>
> Learning how to use a foreign language is like a tennis . . .

He finally settled on this one:

> Learning a foreign language as a means of integration into a new culture is like learning how to play tennis.

As you can see by looking back at his essay (pp. 16–18), Rolando did not repeat the exact wording of this sentence in his essay. But this sentence did act as a focal point, to guide him as he drafted his essay.

The Focal Point and the Message or Insight of an Essay

Note that in Rolando's completed composition, the *focal point*, which tells readers what his essay will be about, is not the same as the *message* or *insight*, which reveals the significance of what he has experienced.

Focal point (second paragraph):
> . . . the best way I can explain these complex feelings created by my communication problem is by associating them with tennis.

Message (last paragraph):
> . . . in the long run, [as a result of the efforts to communicate successfully in a second language], there will be a reward, a better understanding of ourselves and the vital phenomenon of communication.

The difference between focal point and message or insight can be observed in other essays as well. See, for example, "Focusing on Friends" by Steve Tesich (pp. 33–35):

Focal point (first paragraph):
> When I think of people who were my good friends, I see them all, as I do everything else from my life, in cinematic terms.

(This sentence tells readers that in his essay, Tesich will focus on his friends and will discuss them in cinematic terms.)

Insight (last paragraph):
> It is time to pull back the camera, free the women I know, and myself, from those merciless close-ups and have the background move.

(This sentence reveals to readers what Tesich has learned from his experience: that he should change the nature of his relationships with his women friends.)

In both examples, the message or insight is placed in the last paragraph because each writer has chosen to organize his essay in this way. Each could have chosen to place the message at the beginning. The focal point could then have been the message. The important thing to remember is that readers of personal essays expect to read an essay (1) whose focus is clear and (2) whose point or significance is revealed.

ACTIVITY: *Focusing your thoughts*

Reread whatever you have written for this course up to this point: the Write before You Read entries, journal entries, lists, freewriting, looping, cubing, and class notes. If you haven't already done so, decide what the subject of your personal essay will be. Then ask yourself, "What do I want to show in my essay?" Try to answer this question by writing a sentence that can act as a focal point, to indicate what your essay will be about. To help you shape your ideas further, explain your focus to a small group of classmates to see if they understand what your essay will cover.

If you are not yet ready to establish a focal point, turn to the next section, on writing a trial draft, and use the drafting process to discover what you want to show in your essay.   ●

Writing a Trial Draft

Since each writer approaches writing differently, it is not possible to tell you exactly how to proceed once you are ready to begin the actual writing of your essay. Instead, as with the invention and focusing strategies, you will see how one student, Rolando, approached the writing of his essay. He went through a drafting process that produced several versions of his essay. He began by writing a *trial draft.*

A *trial draft* is a preliminary essay in which you test out the experiences and ideas discovered in invention to see how they will work together. It is not the final paper that your instructor will evaluate.

A STUDENT WRITER AT WORK

Rolando wrote a trial draft to determine whether or not the comparison of tennis and language learning, discovered during invention, would work. This draft, reprinted here, is much shorter than his finished composition, "Barriers" (pp. 16–18). As you will see, his essay became longer and longer as he wrote successive drafts. Since this may be the case with your own writing, you should not be overly concerned with length at this time. For example, a two- or three-paragraph trial draft may eventually be turned into a six- or eight-paragraph essay. Just begin by writing to see how your ideas and examples can work together.

Rolando's Trial Draft†

Have you ever tried to learn how to play tennis? Have you gone through the whole process of learning, from how to grab the racket and get the ball across the net to the complicated set of steps and rules? Well, if you have, you may understand the problem a foreign person has with language when he is in the process of integrating into the new culture.

The racket is the new language with which you have to carry on the game of life. Once you have that skill, you have already made a step into the new game. You may be accepted into your tennis class or club, but only by using the right way will you be able to participate in the game and become a useful part of the team.

The balls are the words. The combination of strength and direction, the way you hit the balls, will be the way you build your sentences and choose your words. The net is the barrier that will always be there but that you have to overcome with skill. It will stop your balls; it will change direction; it will frighten you, become an obsession to the point of stopping you from new attempts in the same day, making you play a sure hit. That is not interesting for the other one. The player on the

---

† Mechanical errors have been corrected.

other half of the court is the other one, who in our case is a good player; and he is the one you are trying to get along with. If he is a friend of yours, he might have patience and wait for your balls to come over the net or to catch your bad shots so that the game can continue. And of course he will try to be gentle. Other times you will find someone who won't try to catch your bad balls and who, once he answers your good ones, will return them so hard that you can't handle it. He may get tired very soon and tell you "forget it" and leave the court.

The rules are also very important. They tell you when to stop, when to count points, and what are the good manners. . . .

Rolando stopped in the middle of writing. When he came to the last words, he said to himself: "Stop! Great! I have the rules, the balls, the manners. I actually developed the comparison that I discovered in the cubing. This sounds good. I have enough material." And he put down the pen. He knew that he did not yet have a well-developed paper, but he had time to turn this trial draft into a more substantial and better-organized piece of writing.

GUIDELINES ## Guidelines for Writing a Trial Draft

1. Sit down and write.
2. Remember that a trial draft is a first try.
   a. Don't try to write the perfect paper now.
   b. Focus on the development of ideas rather than on grammar, spelling, or punctuation.
   c. If you can't think of a beginning, start in the middle.
   d. If you can't think of an ending, just stop.

A trial draft may be written for yourself only, or your instructor may provide class time for you to share this draft in a small group. If so, members of your group can share their reactions to your writing and give you ideas for proceeding.

If you are a writer who needs a more structured approach to writing a draft, refer to the next section for guidelines on organizing a personal essay.

Organizing the Essay

When to Organize

Your personal essay should be a well-organized piece, because structure enables you to communicate your ideas accurately and effectively to your readers. At some stage in the writing process, then, you need to focus your attention on the organization of your essay. When that stage occurs is dependent on several factors, for example, your own approach to writing and the subject you are writing about. You may need to plan the organization of your essay before you write a draft. Or you may find that you cannot determine the appropriate organization for your essay until you have written a draft. Follow these guidelines when you are ready to structure your writing.

How to Organize: Beginning, Middle, and Ending

There is no rigid formula that you must follow to organize a personal essay. As you could probably see from your reading and from class discussions of the readings, the organization of a personal essay is dependent on the experiences, ideas, and intentions of the writer.

Nevertheless, you can establish an overall organizational goal: to move your readers toward some sort of understanding or insight. And there is a basic organizational framework that you can keep in mind as you develop your essay: all personal essays have a *beginning*, a *middle*, and an *ending*. As a writer, you choose what to put into each of these sections of your paper. What guides your decision should be the logic of your material. Consider the relationship between ideas and examples as you plan a structure. If you begin with a certain idea, it is logical to continue with a related example. This logic should control the essay as a whole. Here are some examples.

1. BEGINNING
   - The beginning may simply be the retelling of the first stage of an experience.
   - The beginning may contain a focal point that guides your readers so that they know what the essay will be about.
   - The beginning may contain the overall message or insight that you want to share in your essay.

2. MIDDLE
   - If an essay has begun with the retelling of an experience, the middle of the essay may be the continuation of the experience.
   - If an essay has begun with a focal point, the middle may be the presentation of details and examples that illustrate the point.
   - If an essay has begun with the message or insight, the middle of the essay may be a complete description of the experience(s) that led to the message or insight.

3. ENDING
   - If an essay has begun with the retelling of an experience and has continued with the retelling of the experience, the ending may reveal the message or insight that is derived from the experience.

- If an essay has begun with a focal point and has continued with examples and details that support that point, the ending may reveal the overall message of the essay.
- If an essay has begun with the message or insight and has continued with a complete description of the experience(s) that led to the message or insight, the ending may discuss the importance of the message or insight.

Again, these are only some general possibilities that emerge as writers plan the structure of their essays. Review some of the readings in Chapter 1 to examine how the various writers have organized their work. (See also "Organizing Body Paragraphs," pp. 244–245). You can use the drafting process to experiment with organization; your early efforts can be revised later.

A STUDENT WRITER AT WORK

After writing his trial draft, Rolando made a preliminary plan for the organization of his essay. This plan was made in his head; he did not write it down.

Rolando's Preliminary Plan

1. *Beginning:* Discuss problem of communication and compare it with tennis.
2. *Middle:* Give examples: speaking problems and tennis problems.
3. *Ending:* I don't know yet.

ACTIVITY: *Organizing the essay*

If outlining is a useful practice for you, sketch out a preliminary organizational plan for your essay.[†]

1. Beginning
2. Middle
3. Ending

This plan can be as detailed as you want it to be; expand the list accordingly. Remember that you can vary the plan after you begin to write, to fit your experiences, ideas, and intentions.   ●

[†] Some writers prefer to write an outline only after they have written a draft, to check to seek if the organization is logical. Other writers create outlines only in their heads. Still other writers plan in their heads, write an outline before they write a draft, and write another outline after they have written a draft.

Writing a Draft to Present for Review

For Rolando, writing his essay meant going through a process of creating several different drafts. His first draft (pp. 48–49) was written primarily for himself. He then began to prepare another draft that would be brought to class for the purpose of being reviewed by his classmates and then handed in to his teacher for further evaluation.

A STUDENT WRITER AT WORK

Writing this next draft was a difficult and messy process, as Rolando tried to match his intentions with his concern for making his meaning understandable to his readers. He erased and crossed out many words, and he threw a lot of paper into the wastebasket. The draft you will read next is the one he presented for review.

As you read Rolando's draft, you will see that many details have been added since his previous draft. He was particularly careful to provide details that he knew would appeal to his reading audience: members of the same college community. Note, for example, his reference to his roommate's accent and to the ladies in the cafeteria.

The Draft Rolando Presented for Review[†]

I've been in the States for two months now, and even though my English is good enough to make myself understood, trying to communicate with people in a language that is not mine is a problem.

Whenever I talk to someone, I feel like I'm playing tennis. In tennis as in English, I am a novice. I know how to hold the racket and how to hit the ball, but that's not enough to carry on a complete game and enjoy it.

The origin of the problem is the dependence I still have on my opponent at the other side of the net. In a way—sometimes subtle, other times evident, voluntary or involuntary—he is the one who controls the game. This feeling of constant submission in daily communication becomes a very frustrating experience.

In fact, I'm depending too much on his consciousness of my level, on his style, his better knowledge of the rules, and I'm also depending on personality characteristics that wouldn't play any role had I known how to play well.

When I want to play tennis, I usually ask the people that I know will be willing to play with me—a beginner. Therefore, most of the time I can avoid unpleasant situations. But the need

---

[†] Mechanical errors have been corrected.

to talk to people is different. Playing tennis with every person you meet is not necessary, but you do need to talk to every person you encounter. Then I feel like having to play tennis with every person I meet.

The most unpleasant situation is when I find a person that will play hard on me and doesn't care or doesn't know my level. The worst ones either start with such a strong service that I just can't hit the ball back or will answer my serves with similar powerful balls. Typical examples are the phone operator and people that are on public service. Another problem is their style. Some opponents have such a wiser way of hitting the balls that I misinterpret their shots and run in the wrong direction or I just stand still watching the ball to see where it goes. In this group I may include the women in the cafeteria with their Medford accent or my roommate's accent from Peabody, read "PEEB'dy."

In these two cases, of unconsciousness and style, I sometimes get to play when my opponents realize my situation and are willing to cooperate by trying softer serves and slower balls. Otherwise, if I don't give up, they will be the ones to let me know they can't play anymore or they will just tell me "forget it" and leave the court. This is a painful experience because you feel rejected and impotent to communicate with people, whether to have information or to become friends. This is when personal characteristics such as patience, ignorance, or prejudice affect your deep or serious conversation as well as a simple act of asking for information.

ACTIVITY: *Reviewing Rolando's draft*

As a whole class or in a small group, review Rolando's draft by answering these questions orally:

1. Is the focus clear?
   a. If the answer is yes, what is the focal point of the essay?
   b. If the answer is no, can you suggest a way that the focus could be clarified?
2. Do the examples help you to understand the ideas?
   a. If the answer is yes, which examples help to clarify a point?
   b. If the answer is no, which examples are not helpful? Which examples need more development?

Raise and answer any other questions that you think would help Rolando to improve his paper.   ●

Follow these guidelines for preparing a draft to be read and reviewed by your classmates and instructor.

GUIDELINES

Guidelines for Writing a Draft to Present for Review

1. Reread your previous draft, if you have written one.
2. Reflect on the purpose of the assignment, its requirements, and the needs and expectations of your readers.
3. Devise an organizational plan for the essay.
4. Set aside some uninterrupted time and start to write. You may have to force yourself to begin. But once you get started, your writing will probably begin to flow.
5. Structure your writing so that it has a beginning, a middle, and an ending. Try to follow the organizational pattern you have planned, but be flexible in your approach. If the plan doesn't work, allow another organizational pattern to emerge from your material.
6. Develop details and examples to support all points you are making in your paper.
7. Understand that writing a draft may be a messy process, with cross-outs, additions, and so on. You may pause to re-read, rethink, and rewrite certain sections before you reach the end.
8. Prepare a legible copy of the essay to show to your class-mates and instructor.

Before you bring your paper to class, use the following checklist for content.

Checklist for Content: Self-Evaluation

1. Does my essay provide details and examples, to enable my readers to "see," "hear," and "feel" what I am describing?

   If the answer is no, add details and examples, or make a list of details and examples that you might add in your next draft. Show this list to your reviewers and instructor. If you are not sure whether you have enough details and examples, ask your reviewers for advice.
2. Does my essay have a section that reveals the significance of my experience: a message or insight that I have shared with my readers?

   If the answer is no, include such a section in your paper, or plan such a section on a separate sheet of paper. If you do not know what to write, ask your reviewers for help.

Peer Reviewing

In this course, you and your classmates have the opportunity to work in small groups to give and receive helpful criticism about each other's writing. This collaborative process is called *peer review*. By discussing work in progress, you can become aware of how readers react to writing and how writers react to their readers' responses. Peer reviewing can therefore be extremely valuable in training you to internalize criteria for evaluating written work. By asking other writers questions about their drafts and by having readers ask you questions about your draft, you can learn to ask yourself questions of yourself about your own writing. For example, you may ask yourself questions like these:

- What am I trying to say?
- What have I already said?
- How else could I have said this?
- How will my readers react when they read this? What questions might they ask?
- How does it sound? How does it look?
- What should I do next?

This process will lead you to become a critical reader of your own writing. And you must learn to become a critic of your own writing because your English instructor will not always be there. Eventually you will be on your own when you write.

Peer review groups provide a place for exploration and discovery of ideas. The criticism that is offered should point out strengths as well as weaknesses. The writer should learn what is successful and where problems exist. The writer's response to the criticism should not be defensive but should acknowledge that the reviewer has accepted the responsibility of helping to develop the writer's writing ability.

To prepare for peer review, read the recommendations on page 56 for giving and accepting criticism. The recommendations are reprinted from a book on problem solving by Don Koberg and Jim Bagnall titled *The Revised All New Universal Traveler*. To get their points across, Koberg and Bagnall humorously refer to problem solving as a journey, and they give advice in the form of tips for travelers.

ACTIVITY: *Discussing guidelines for giving and accepting criticism*

Read and discuss the recommendations on page 56. Use this opportunity to express your concerns and to ask questions about peer review.   ●

The peer review form on page 57 is based on the recommendations for giving and accepting criticism. You can use this format for criticizing each of the essay assignments in this book.

HOW TO CRITICIZE PAINLESSLY

The need for assertive criticism often emerges
in the realm of conscious problem-solving.

Here is a fool-proof method for telling yourself
or someone else that something is wrong without
fear of losing a friendship or of starting a
battle.

The trick is to place the criticism within a
context of positive reinforcements . . . just
simple diplomacy.

1. BEGIN WITH TWO POSITIVE
   REINFORCEMENTS
   "You really are a well-seasoned traveler."
   "You have all of the best gear for hiking."
2. INSERT YOUR CRITICISM
   "I wish we could stay in step when we hike
   together."
3. ADD ONE MORE POSITIVE REINFORCEMENT
   "I notice that you can adapt easily to most
   things."
4. FINISH WITH A RAY OF HOPE
   "If we work on this together, I'm sure we'll be
   able to get harmony into our stride."

Now you try it!

HOW TO ACCEPT CRITICISM

It is easier to feel a discontent than it is to accept the challenge of construc-
tively improving the situation. And it is also easier, as the old saying goes,
"to give criticism than it is to receive it." Being "defensive" of our position,
which we imagine to be under attack from outside, is wasted motion. But it
is also far more normal than an outlook of receptive self-improvement.

Be *abnormal*. Instead of wasting time with defenses and soothing
self-inflicted, imaginary hurts, get procedural. *Accept* the comments for further
ANALYSIS and DEFINITION. If the criticism then seems appropriate, "try it
on for size." If not, discard it as irrelevant and the matter is finished.

Reprinted, with permission, from *The Universal Traveler* by Don Koberg and Jim
Bagnall. Copyright © 1981 by William Kaufmann, Inc. Los Altos, CA 94022. All
rights reserved.

Peer Review Form

Writer's name: _____   Reviewer's Name: _____

Directions: Your goal in reviewing a paper is to help the writer. Unless errors interfere with your ability to understand what the writer is saying, read for meaning only.

1. *Begin with positive reinforcement.* Tell the writer what you like about the paper and what you think should not be changed.

2. *Insert your criticism.* Tell the writer what confused you, misled you, bothered you, or left you wanting more. Be specific.

3. *Finish with a ray of hope.* Remind the writer of what you like, and then tell the writer how this draft can be improved. Be specific. If you were the writer of this paper, what would you do to make it clearer or more interesting?

GUIDELINES

Guidelines for Peer Reviewing

1. Form groups of two or three students.
2. Decide whether the writer will read aloud or all will exchange drafts and read silently.
3. Use the peer review form (p. 57) as a guideline for giving critical commentary. Your teacher will tell you whether to provide written or oral feedback.
4. Discuss the responses to the draft, helping the writer to understand what is good about the paper and what can be done to make it better.
5. When your paper is being discussed, take notes.

ACTIVITY: Peer Reviewing

Bring your draft to class, and exchange papers with one or two students. Review each other's papers by examining (1) what you like about the paper and (2) what you think can be done to improve it. Determine whether the writer has described in detail an event or experience (or series of events or experiences) in such a way as to lead you to learn, believe, or understand something. Unless errors interfere with your ability to understand what the writer is saying, read for meaning only. Use the peer review form (p. 57), the questions used to review Rolando's draft (p. 53), and the checklist for content (p. 54) as guidelines for your responses.

After the discussions, write a note to your instructor, explaining what you may do to improve your paper.

Hand in your paper and the note to the instructor for review. Your instructor will read and return the paper in a few days, with responses to what your peer reviewer wrote (if the comments were written down) and with suggestions for revision. Take time to discuss these comments in and out of class so that you know how to proceed.   ●

Responding to Reviewers' Comments

A STUDENT WRITER AT WORK

After he received comments and suggestions from his classmates and his instructor, Rolando began to rewrite his draft. Some of those comments and the changes Rolando made are reprinted here. The opening paragraphs of the draft Rolando wrote for review are included, along with a reviewer's comments, and then Rolando's revised paragraphs. The reviewer's comments about the need for specific examples and Rolando's revision are also included.

Opening Paragraphs of Rolando's Draft

I've been in the States for two months now, and even though my English is good enough to make myself understood, trying to communicate with people in a language that is not mine is a problem.

Whenever I talk to someone, I feel like I'm playing tennis. In tennis as in English, I am a novice. I know how to hold the racket and how to hit the ball, but that's not enough to carry on a complete game and enjoy it.

Reviewer's Comments on the Opening Paragraphs

I think your comparison with tennis is unique. But I think you need more background information about your experience with tennis before you talk about language. Now, the first sentence of the second paragraph is too confusing, too abrupt.

Rolando's Revision of the Opening Paragraphs

A few months ago, I decided that I wanted to learn how to play tennis. Today, after much practice and a few classes, I know how to hold the racket and basically how to hit the ball; however, I still can't say that I actually play tennis. It is taking me so long to learn, and it is so difficult! It didn't look that hard when I saw my friends playing it so gracefully. Even so, I am still giving it a try. But to play a sport that I cannot master is becoming a pain. I feel so frustrated sometimes that I consider forgetting all about tennis. It is hurting my pride.

Today, tennis is not the main source of my frustrations. I have another problem that generates feelings and puts me into moods very similar to those that I experience when I play it. This is daily conversation with people. It may sound bizarre, but it is not. I am a foreign student, and in playing tennis as in speaking English, I am still in the learning process. That is why the best way I can explain these complex feelings created by my communication problem is by associating them with tennis.

Reviewer's Comments on the Need for Specific Examples

I like the examples about the women in the cafeteria and your roommate's accent. I think you should put in more examples to show your experience.

Rolando's Revision (Material Added)

I also have a hard time realizing how annoyed my roommate gets, because he selects words to make his point; but the connotations of some of them sometimes don't reach me because of my inexperience. I don't know exactly which is worse to him, "mad," "angry," "disturbed," or "pissed off."

Revising

By now, one or more students and your instructor have commented on your paper. If you have followed the recommendations for accepting criticism (Figure 2-1), you have accepted the comments for further analysis. Now is the time to analyze. You need to determine which comments are most helpful and how to revise the paper to meet your readers' needs and expectations.

Revising entails more than just rewriting a paper. It means making decisions about what to keep, what to add, what to delete, what to change, what to rearrange, and what to rethink. Like drafting, revising allows you to think about your thinking, to take a new look, to reshape and refine your thoughts.

There can be no hard and fast rules for revision, of course, because each of you has a different paper and different reviewer responses. But the following questions should help you sift through the criticism you have received.

What Should I Keep?

Reread your reviewers' comments and your own notes to remember what your readers liked about your paper. Though it may not be possible to save everything that appealed to them, you should keep their positive impressions in your mind as you rewrite.

What Should I Add?

Reread the comments and notes to discover whether any of your readers needed more background information to understand your subject. If so, determine from your reviewers' comments where you need more information. This might mean adding only as little as a brief phrase or as much as a few explanatory sentences.

Reread the comments and notes to discover whether more details and examples or other evidence are needed to illustrate or support points you have made. If so, make note of the spots where your readers want to know more. It might be helpful at this point to look at some passages of the reading selections in this book to see how the published authors achieved detailed writing. Invention strategies can also be useful in helping you generate new ideas or examples.

What Should I Delete?

It is possible that one of your readers suggested that you used too much detail or included too much information. This is especially difficult criticism to hear because this reviewer may be recommending deletion of some of your favorite parts. Before you take anything out, remember that this is one reader's reaction. As with all criticism, you might determine that the suggestion is not appropriate and decide to include the material in your revision. However, if another reader made the same comment, this is probably advice worth taking.

What Should I Change?

If any of your readers expressed confusion, make note of the section or sections of your draft that caused the problem. Since you have already discussed the draft with your readers, you probably know why the confusion exists. In fact, you may have already solved the problem just by explaining to your reviewers what you meant to say. Now you need to rewrite the confusing section. You may want to experiment with two versions. Then read them aloud to yourself or show them to a classmate or your instructor. They can help you determine which version is clearer.

What Should I Rearrange?

If you have been told that your paper is not well organized, it might be a good idea to outline your draft briefly, paragraph by paragraph, summarizing each paragraph. Then look at your outline to see where the logic of the organization breaks down. Revise the outline to reflect a better organization. Then rearrange the material in your draft.

Once you have attended to the overall organization of your paper, you can examine the connections within and between paragraphs and sentences (see Chapter 13). Does the first sentence of each new paragraph relate what you have just said to what you are about to say? Have you shown the relationship between ideas and examples through transitions or other connective devices? Have you used too many transitions, making your writing sound artificial and mechanical? If relationships are not clear, make connections. If there are too many connective devices, delete some.

What Should I Rethink?

It is possible that despite all of your efforts, you may not have revealed your point of view (your insight, message, or position) to your readers. It is also possible that you have not done so because you yourself do not really know what you want to say. Since that might be true, you will have to reconsider what you have written. Try an invention strategy such as looping on your topic, or discuss your topic with a classmate or friend or the instructor to find what is important to you about this topic.

Once you have come to an understanding of the idea you want to share, you need to find a way to transmit that thought in the paper. In some cases, that will involve rewriting the beginning. In some cases, that will mean rewriting the ending. In any case, insert commentary, reveal emotions, or provide contrasts with earlier sections of the paper to allow readers to understand or accept your point of view.

Completing the Essay

Once you have revised your draft, there are at least three more steps you can take to complete the final essay.

Guidelines for Completing the Essay

1. *Evaluate the essay as a whole.* Concentrate on pulling everything together into a whole essay where every part fits other parts. The beginning, middle, and ending should merge with each other smoothly. Make sure that if a point is made in the beginning, it is discussed in the middle of the paper and that the ending relates to the material presented in the beginning and middle.

2. *Proofread and edit the essay.* Turn your attention to grammar, punctuation, spelling, and mechanics. Give your essay a final check to catch any errors you might have made. (See Part Six, "The Editing Process.")

3. *Follow the guidelines for preparing a final manuscript* (see pp. 329–330).

PART TWO

Writing from Course Readings: Relating Reading to Experience

To fulfill the first essay assignment, the personal viewpoint essay, you were asked to write from your own experience. To fulfill the next essay assignment, you will be asked to draw from your experience *and* from the readings as well (see Essay Assignment 2 on p. 102). The writing assignment instructs you to examine the relationship between what you read and what you know from experience. The challenge in such an assignment is to compare or contrast your experiences and attitudes with the generalizations, theories, or experiences of another writer. In doing so, you will be testing the truth or value of what you have read.

To fulfill this assignment, you will use many of the invention, summarizing, and paragraphing strategies you used to develop your personal essay. In addition, you will practice various ways to incorporate key ideas and relevant facts from your course reading into your own writing. As you develop this essay assignment, you will work concurrently with Part Five to practice the skills of paraphrasing, quoting, and citing and documenting sources.

CHAPTER THREE

Responding to Reading

Reading Strategies

In the essays in Part One, the authors share insights drawn from their personal experiences so that readers can identify with and learn from these experiences. The reading selections in Part Two are essays and reports, both informal and formal, based on the authors' research into their subjects. The authors go beyond personal experience, drawing ideas and information from conversations, observations, interviews, and other field research. They present their findings on the assumption that they will be of value to readers.

One or more of these readings will become the source material for your own essay.

Before Reading

Prereading activities help you to anticipate or predict the content, purpose, and organization of a reading selection. This can in turn lead you to a more efficient understanding of what you read.

1. Follow the instructions for the Write before You Read activity that precedes each reading selection. This activity will enable you to get your own ideas about the topic on paper before you are influenced by what you read.
2. Read the biographical information before each reading. This information will provide the name of the author, the title, the original publication, and perhaps the original audience of the selection.
3. Preview the reading:
   a. Look at its length and the length of its paragraphs. This will help you plan the amount of time it will take you to read.
   b. Look at headings or subheadings, if they are provided. This will help you determine the organization and content of the reading.
   c. Look for words or phrases that are in boldface (darker print) or in *italics*. This may help you pick up key concepts.
   d. Look at graphs or illustrations, if there are any. These will give you clues as to the content.

Reading

The first time you read each selection, read for overall meaning. It is not necessary at this stage to understand every word. Aim to understand the most important general ideas in a paragraph or section. Note how supporting examples serve to clarify or illustrate ideas. As you read, relate the information to what you already know about the topic and to what you have just read. Allow yourself to identify with the reading, to question it, to judge it, to be changed by it.

Rereading

As you reread, keep track of your responses. Annotate or take notes on the reading selection. You can, for example, make a list of key points of information. And you can underline or copy down sections of the essay or article that seem to present the overall findings of the research.

Making a Journal Entry

Write in your journal to discuss your response to the reading. For example, you can do one or more of the following:

- Write about specific experiences—your own or those of others—that relate to the topic. You may include experiences that support or experiences that contradict what the author has said.
- Examine how the author uses examples to illustrate a point. Note examples that are memorable, either because you like them or because you don't. Note examples that help to clarify a point.
- Formulate questions about the reading that you want to ask in class.

Summarizing

Summarizing these readings is important not only to help you understand the author's purpose better but also because Essay Assignment 2 requires that you include a summary of the reading in your essay.

Because the reading selections are based on the authors' research into their subjects, your goal in summarizing the readings is to discover the findings of the research.

You will find that the selections follow different formats because the authors have published their work in different publications and have therefore written for different audiences. Two of the selections (Viorst, Mead and Metraux) were published in a popular magazine geared toward a general audience. One of the selections (Barna) was published in an academic journal read by an audience of professionals in the field. The fourth selection (Levine and Wolff) was published in a magazine that makes research findings understandable to a nonprofessional audience.

Since the formats are different, you will not always discover the findings in the same place. Sometimes the findings may be reported in the introduction, and some of the findings may be reported in the body of the paper; research findings are usually summarized in the conclusion. You need to read through the whole essay to determine what the author has found.

In a one-sentence summary, you should simply report the results of the research. Ask yourself, What conclusion did the researcher come to as a result of the research? If you write more than one sentence, you can briefly describe the research project that the author undertook; eliminate minor details.

Discussing and Taking Notes

Share your journal responses and summaries in class discussions on the reading. During class discussions, keep notes to help you understand the reading selection better. Write about the reading again in your journal, if the class discussions have given you more ideas.

READINGS

Write before You Read

The following two reading selections deal with the subject of friendship. Before reading the essays, write for 10 to 15 minutes to finish this statement:

A friend is . . .

Write with the purpose of getting your views on paper to find out what you really think before you are influenced by your reading. Share what you have written with your classmates, either by reading aloud or by telling them what you have written.   ●

Friends, Good Friends—and Such Good Friends
by Judith Viorst

A professional writer, Judith Viorst was born in Newark, New Jersey, in 1936. She is a poet, a journalist, and the author of several books of fiction and nonfiction for children and adults. The following essay, written in a very informal style, first appeared in 1977 in Redbook, *a magazine at that time directed primarily toward an audience of nonworking women. Her awareness of that audience is revealed in many of the examples she uses to illustrate her points. Nevertheless, her essay can relate to the experiences of men and working women as well. Through personal recollections and conversations with other women, Viorst reveals a characteristic American approach toward friendship.*

Women are friends, I once would have said, when they totally love   1
and support and trust each other, and bare to each other the secrets of their
souls, and run—no questions asked—to help each other, and tell harsh
truths to each other (no, you can't wear that dress unless you lose ten
pounds first) when harsh truths must be told.

Women are friends, I once would have said, when they share the same   2
affection for Ingmar Bergman, plus train rides, cats, warm rain, charades,
Camus, and hate with equal ardor Newark and Brussel sprouts and Law-
rence Welk and camping.

In other words, I once would have said that a friend is a friend all the   3
way, but now I believe that's a narrow point of view. For the friendships
I have and the friendships I see are conducted at many levels of intensity,
serve many different functions, meet different needs and range from those
as all-the-way as the friendship of the soul sisters mentioned above to that
of the most nonchalant and casual playmates.

Consider these varieties of friendship: 4

1. Convenience friends. These are women with whom, if our paths   5
weren't crossing all the time, we'd have no particular reason to be friends:
a next-door neighbor, a woman in our car pool, the mother of one of our
children's closest friends or maybe some mommy with whom we serve juice
and cookies each week at the Glenwood Co-op Nursery.

Convenience friends are convenient indeed. They'll lend us their cups   6
and silverware for a party. They'll drive our kids to soccer when we're
sick. They'll take us to pick up our car when we need a lift to the garage.
They'll even take our cats when we go on vacation. As we will for them.

But we don't, with convenience friends, ever come too close or tell too   7
much; we maintain our public face and emotional distance. "Which means,"
says Elaine, "that I'll talk about being overweight but not about being
depressed. Which means I'll admit being mad but not blind with rage.
Which means that I might say that we're pinched this month but never
that I'm worried sick over money."

But which doesn't mean that there isn't sufficient value to be found in   8
these friendships of mutual aid, in convenience friends.

2. Special-interest friends. These friendships aren't intimate, and they   9
needn't involve kids or silverware or cats. Their value lies in some interest
jointly shared. And so we may have an office friend or a yoga friend or a
tennis friend or a friend from the Women's Democratic Club.

"I've got one woman friend," says Joyce, "who likes, as I do, to take   10
psychology courses. Which makes it nice for me—and nice for her. It's
fun to go with someone you know and it's fun to discuss what you've
learned, driving back from the classes." And for the most part, she says,
that's all they discuss.

"I'd say that what we're doing is *doing* together, not being together,"   11
Suzanne says of her Tuesday-doubles friends. "It's mainly a tennis relationship, but we play together well. And I guess we all need to have a
couple of playmates."

I agree.   12

My playmate is a shopping friend, a woman of marvelous taste, a woman   13
who knows exactly *where* to buy *what*, and furthermore is a woman who
always knows beyond a doubt what one ought to be buying. I don't have
the time to keep up with what's new in eyeshadow, hemlines and shoes
and whether the smock look is in or finished already. But since (oh shame!)
I care a lot about eyeshadows, hemlines and shoes, and since I don't *want*
to wear smocks if the smock look is finished, I'm very glad to have a shopping
friend.

3. Historical friends. We all have a friend who knew us when . . .   14
maybe way back in Miss Meltzer's second grade, when our family lived in
that three-room flat in Brooklyn, when our dad was out of work for seven
months, when our brother Allie got in that fight where they had to call
the police, when our sister married the endodontist from Yonkers and when,
the morning after we lost our virginity, she was the first, the only, friend
we told.

The years have gone by and we've gone separate ways and we've little   15
in common now, but we're still an intimate part of each other's past. And
so whenever we go to Detroit we always go to visit this friend of our
girlhood. Who knows how we looked before our teeth were straightened.
Who knows how we talked before our voice got un-Brooklyned.[1] Who knows
what we ate before we learned about artichokes. And who, by her presence,
puts us in touch with an earlier part of ourself, a part of ourself it's important
never to lose.

"What this friend means to me and what I mean to her," says Grace,   16
"is having a sister without sibling rivalry. We know the texture of each
other's lives. She remembers my grandmother's cabbage soup. I remember
the way her uncle played the piano. There's simply no other friend who
remembers those things."

4. Crossroads friends. Like historical friends, our crossroads friends are   17
important for *what was*—for the friendship we shared at a crucial, now
past, time of life. A time, perhaps, when we roomed in college together;
or worked as eager young singles in the Big City together; or went together,
as my friend Elizabeth and I did, through pregnancy, birth and that scary
first year of new motherhood.

Crossroads friends forge powerful links, links strong enough to endure   18
with not much more contact than once-a-year letters at Christmas. And out
of respect for those crossroads years, for those dramas and dreams we once
shared, we will always be friends.

5. Cross-generational friends. Historical friends and crossroads friends   19
seem to maintain a special kind of intimacy—dormant but always ready to
be revived—and though we may rarely meet, whenever we do connect,
it's personal and intense. Another kind of intimacy exists in the friendships
that form across generations in what one woman calls her daughter-mother
and her mother-daughter relationships.

[1] **Brooklyn:** part of New York City known for its residents' accents

Evelyn's friend is her mother's age—"but I share so much more than   20
I ever could with my mother"—a woman she talks to of music, of books
and of life. "What I get from her is the benefit of her experience. What
she gets—and enjoys—from me is youthful perspective. It's a pleasure for
both of us."

I have in my own life a precious friend, a woman of 65 who has lived   21
very hard, who is wise, who listens well; who has been where I am and
can help me understand it; and who represents not only an ultimate ideal
mother to me but also the person I'd like to be when I grow up.

In our daughter role we tend to do more than our share of self-revelation;   22
in our mother role we tend to receive what's revealed. It's another kind of
pleasure—playing wise mother to a questioning younger person. It's another
very lovely kind of friendship.

6. Part-of-a-couple friends. Some of the women we call our friends we   23
never see alone—we see them as part of a couple at couples' parties. And
though we share interests in many things and respect each other's views,
we aren't moved to deepen the relationship. Whatever the reason, a lack of
time or—and this is more likely—a lack of chemistry, our friendship remains in the context of a group. But the fact that our feeling on seeing
each other is always, "I'm *so* glad she's here" and the fact that we spend
half the evening talking together says that this too, in its own way, counts
as a friendship.

(Other part-of-a-couple friends are the friends that came with the mar-   24
riage, and some of these are friends we could live without. But sometimes,
alas, she married our husband's best friend; and sometimes, alas, she *is* our
husband's best friend. And so we find ourselves dealing with her, somewhat
against our will, in a spirit of what I'll call *reluctant* friendship.)

7. Men who are friends. I wanted to write just of women friends, but   25
the women I've talked to won't let me—they say I must mention man-
woman friendships too. For these friendships can be just as close and as
dear as those that we form with women. Listen to Lucy's description of
one such friendship:

"We've found we have things to talk about that are different from what   26
he talks about with my husband and different from what I talk about with
his wife. So sometimes we call on the phone or meet for lunch. There are
similar intellectual interests—we always pass on to each other the book
that we love—but there's also something tender and caring too."

In a couple of crises, Lucy says, "he offered himself for talking and   27
for helping. And when someone died in his family he wanted me there.
The sexual, flirty part of our friendship is very small—but *some*—just
enough to make it fun and different." She thinks—and I agree—that the
sexual part, though small, is always *some*, is always there when a man and
a woman are friends.

It's only in the past few years that I've made friends with men, in the   28
sense of a friendship that's *mine*, not just part of two couples. And achieving
with them the ease and the trust I've found with women friends has value

indeed. Under the dryer at home last week, putting on mascara and rouge, I comfortably sat and talked with a fellow named Peter. Peter, I finally decided, could handle the shock of me minus mascara under the dryer. Because we care for each other. Because we're friends.

8. There are medium friends, and pretty good friends, and very good 29 friends indeed, and these friendships are defined by their level of intimacy. And what we'll reveal at each of these levels of intimacy is calibrated with care. We might tell a medium friend, for example, that yesterday we had a fight with our husband. And we might tell a pretty good friend that this fight with our husband made us so mad that we slept on the couch. And we might tell a very good friend that the reason we got so mad in that fight that we slept on the couch had something to do with that girl who works in his office. But it's only to our very best friends that we're willing to tell all, to tell what's going on with that girl in his office.

The best of friends, I still believe, totally love and support and trust 30 each other, and bare to each other the secrets of their souls, and run—no questions asked—to help each other, and tell harsh truths to each other when they must be told.

But we needn't agree about everything (only 12-year-old girl friends 31 agree about *everything*) to tolerate each other's point of view. To accept without judgment. To give and to take without ever keeping score. And to *be* there, as I am for them and as they are for me, to comfort our sorrows, to celebrate our joys.

Write after You Read

1. Make a journal entry on "Friends, Good Friends—and Such Good Friends," following the suggestions on p. 67.
2. Write a one- to three-sentence summary of "Friends, Good Friends— and Such Good Friends," following the guidelines for summarizing the findings of a research study on pp. 67–68. ●

Activities for Class Discussion

Working in a group of three or four students, share in the following activities. Your group can decide the order in which to cover the material and the amount of time to spend on each question.

1. Share your written summary of "Friends, Good Friends—and Such Good Friends." If you do not agree on the conclusion Viorst has reached as a result of her personal experience and her conversations with other women, discuss the reasons for the different interpretations. If your group cannot determine an overall message, consult with another group or with your instructor.
2. Are there unfamiliar words or expressions? Make sure that everyone in the group understands the meaning of these terms:

ardor (2)   dormant (19)
soul sisters (3)   revived (19)
nonchalant (3)   lack of chemistry (23)
sibling rivalry (16)   calibrated (29)
forge (18)

Try to guess the meaning of these or other unfamiliar words from the context. If your group cannot determine the meaning, consult with your instructor.

3. Examine the organization of Viorst's essay. Compare the first paragraph with the last two paragraphs. What is different? What purpose does the rest of the essay serve?
4. Can you place your friends in any of Viorst's categories? If so, describe some of those friends.
5. Do you have friends who don't fit into any of the categories? Describe those friends. What category could you create for them?
6. Do you have friends who fit into more than one category? Describe those friends.
7. Would you use the term *friend* in another language you speak or have studied to describe all of the categories Viorst discusses? Explain.
8. Do you agree with Viorst's definition of what it means to be the best of friends? If you do not agree with her definition, how would you define true friendship?   ●

Write before You Read

In the following reading selection, the authors discuss different styles of friendship in different lands. Before reading, write for 10 to 15 minutes, in or out of class, in response to this quotation from the reading selection:

> The difficulty when strangers from two countries meet is not a lack of appreciation of friendship, but different expectations of what constitutes friendship and how it comes into being.

Write with the purpose of understanding the quotation so that you can discuss it with your classmates.   ●

On Friendship
by Margaret Mead and Rhoda Metraux

Margaret Mead (1901–1978) was a noted cultural anthropologist, professor, and author whose work continues to be important and influential. She spent much of her life studying foreign societies, attempting to understand what people value in their culture. Among her many books are Coming of Age in Samoa *(1928) and* Childhood in Contemporary Cultures

(1955). Rhoda Metraux (b. 1914), also an anthropologist, collaborated with Mead on a collection of essays reprinted in the book A Way of Seeing *(1970), from which the following reading selection was taken. "On Friendship" originally appeared in* Redbook *magazine in 1966 under the title "Different Lands, Different Friendships."*

Few Americans stay put for a lifetime. We move from town to city to   1
suburb, from high school to college in a different state, from a job in one
region to a better job elsewhere, from the home where we raise our children
to the home where we plan to live in retirement. With each move we are
forever making new friends, who become part of our new life at that time.

For many of us the summer is a special time for forming new friend-   2
ships. Today millions of Americans vacation abroad, and they go not only
to see new sights but also—in those places where they do not feel too
strange—with the hope of meeting new people. No one really expects a
vacation trip to produce a close friend. But surely the beginning of a friendship is possible? Surely in every country people value friendship?

They do. The difficulty when strangers from two countries meet is not   3
a lack of appreciation of friendship, but different expectations about what
constitutes friendship and how it comes into being. In those European
countries that Americans are most likely to visit, friendship is quite sharply
distinguished from other, more casual relations, and is differently related
to family life. For a Frenchman, a German or an Englishman friendship is
usually more particularized and carries a heavier burden of commitment.

But as we use the word, "friend" can be applied to a wide range of   4
relationships—to someone one has known for a few weeks in a new place,
to a close business associate, to a childhood playmate, to a man or woman,
to a trusted confidant. There are real differences among these relations for
Americans—a friendship may be superficial, casual, situational or deep and
enduring. But to a European, who sees only our surface behavior, the
differences are not clear.

As they see it, people known and accepted temporarily, casually, flow   5
in and out of Americans' homes with little ceremony and often with little
personal commitment. They may be parents of the children's friends, house
guests of neighbors, members of a committee, business associates from
another town or even another country. Coming as a guest into an American
home, the European visitor finds no visible landmarks. The atmosphere is
relaxed. Most people, old and young, are called by first names.

Who, then, is a friend?   6

Even simple translation from one language to another is difficult. "You   7
see," a Frenchman explains, "if I were to say to you in France, 'This is
my good friend,' that person would not be as close to me as someone about
whom I said only, 'This is my friend.' Anyone about whom I have to say
more is really less."

In France, as in many European countries, friends generally are of the   8
same sex, and friendship is seen as basically a relationship between men.

Frenchwomen laugh at the idea that "women can't be friends," but they also admit sometimes that for women "it's a different thing." And many French people doubt the possibility of a friendship between a man and a woman. There is also the kind of relationship within a group—men and women who have worked together for a long time, who may be very close, sharing great loyalty and warmth of feeling. They may call one another *copains*—a word that in English becomes "friends" but has more the feeling of "pals" or "buddies." In French eyes this is not friendship, although two members of such a group may well be friends.

For the French, friendship is a one-to-one relationship that demands a   9
keen awareness of the other person's intellect, temperament and particular interests. A friend is someone who draws out your own best qualities, with whom you sparkle and become more of whatever the friendship draws upon. Your political philosophy assumes more depth, appreciation of a play becomes sharper, taste in food or wine is accentuated, enjoyment of a sport is intensified.

And French friendships are compartmentalized. A man may play chess   10
with a friend for thirty years without knowing his political opinions, or he may talk politics with him for as long a time without knowing about his personal life. Different friends fill different niches in each person's life. These friendships are not made part of family life. A friend is not expected to spend evenings being nice to children or courteous to a deaf grandmother. These duties, also serious and enjoined, are primarily for relatives. Men who are friends may meet in a café. Intellectual friends may meet in larger groups for evenings of conversation. Working people may meet at the little *bistro*[1] where they drink and talk, far from the family. Marriage does not affect such friendships; wives do not have to be taken into account.

In the past in France, friendships of this kind seldom were open to any   11
but intellectual women. Since most women's lives centered on their homes, their warmest relations with other women often went back to their girlhood. The special relationship of friendship is based on what the French value most—on the mind, on compatibility of outlook, on vivid awareness of some chosen area of life.

Friendship heightens the sense of each person's individuality. Other   12
relationships commanding as great loyalty and devotion have a different meaning. In World War II the first resistance groups[2] formed in Paris were built on the foundation of *les copains*. But significantly, as time went on these little groups, whose lives rested in one another's hands, called themselves "families." Where each had a total responsibility for all, it was kinship ties that provided the model. And even today such ties, crossing every line of class and personal interest, remain binding on the survivors of these small, secret bands.

In Germany, in contrast with France, friendship is much more artic-   13

[1] *bistro:* (*French*) small café
[2] **resistance groups:** secret groups of citizens formed to fight against German occupation

ulately a matter of feeling. Adolescents, boys and girls, form deeply sentimental attachments, walk and talk together—not so much to polish their wits as to share their hopes and fears and dreams, to form a common front against the world of school and family and to join in a kind of mutual discovery of each other's and their own inner life. Within the family, the closest relationship over a lifetime is between brothers and sisters. Outside the family, men and women find in their closest friends of the same sex the devotion of a sister, the loyalty of a brother. Appropriately, in Germany friends usually are brought into the family. Children call their father's and their mother's friends "uncle" and "aunt." Between French friends, who have chosen each other for the congeniality of their point of view, lively disagreement and sharpness of argument are the breath of life. But for Germans, whose friendships are based on mutuality of feeling, deep disagreement on any subject that matters to both is regarded as a tragedy. Like ties of kinship, ties of friendship are meant to be irrevocably binding. Young Germans who come to the United States have great difficulty in establishing such friendships with Americans. We view friendship more tentatively, subject to changes in intensity as people move, change their jobs, marry, or discover new interests.

English friendships follow still a different pattern. Their basis is shared 14 activity. Activities at different stages of life may be of very different kinds—discovering a common interest in school, serving together in the armed forces, taking part in a foreign mission, staying in the same country house during a crisis. In the midst of the activity, whatever it may be, people fall into step—sometimes two men or two women, sometimes two couples, sometimes three people—and find that they walk or play a game or tell stories or serve on a tiresome and exacting committee with the same easy anticipation of what each will do day by day or in some critical situation. Americans who have made English friends comment that, even years later, "you can take up just where you left off." Meeting after a long interval, friends are like a couple who begin to dance again when the orchestra strikes up after a pause. English friendships are formed outside the family circle, but they are not, as in Germany, contrapuntal to the family nor are they, as in France, separated from the family. And a break in an English friendship comes not necessarily as a result of some irreconcilable difference of viewpoint or feeling but instead as a result of misjudgment, where one friend seriously misjudges how the other will think or feel or act, so that suddenly they are out of step.

What, then, is friendship? Looking at these different styles, including 15 our own, each of which is related to a whole way of life, are there common elements? There is the recognition that friendship, in contrast with kinship, invokes freedom of choice. A friend is someone who chooses and is chosen. Related to this is the sense each friend gives the other of being a special individual, on whatever grounds this recognition is based. And between friends there is inevitably a kind of equality of give-and-take. These similarities make the bridge between societies possible, and the American's characteristic openness to different styles of relationship makes it possible for him to find new friends abroad with whom he feels at home.   ●

Write after You Read

1. Make a journal entry on "On Friendship," following the suggestions on p. 67.
2. Write a one- to three-sentence summary of "On Friendship," following the guidelines for summarizing a research study on pp. 67–68.   ●

Activities for Class Discussion

Working in a group of three or four students, share in the following activities. Your group can decide the order in which to cover the material and how much time to spend on each question.

1. Share your written summary of "On Friendship." If you do not agree on the conclusion the authors have reached as a result of their research, discuss the reasons for the different interpretations. If your group cannot determine an overall conclusion, consult with another group or with your instructor.
2. Are there any unfamiliar words? Make sure everyone in the group understands the meaning of these terms:

particularized (3)	compatibility (11)
confidant (4)	congeniality (13)
landmarks (5)	mutuality (13)
accentuated (9)	irrevocably (13)
compartmentalized (10)	contrapuntal (14)
niches (10)	irreconcilable (14)
enjoined (10)	

   Try to guess the meaning of the words from the context. If your group cannot determine the meaning, consult with another group or with your instructor, or consult a dictionary.
3. What is the word for *friend* in another language that you speak or have studied? Does it have more than one meaning? Is there more than one word for *friend*? If so, what is the difference in meaning between the words?
4. How would you contrast the concept of friendship in your culture or group with the American concept, as presented by Mead and Metraux?
5. How would you compare or contrast the concept of friendship in your culture or group with the French concept, the German concept, and the English concept, as presented by Mead and Metraux?

6. Examine the relationship between the authors' ideas and their examples. Which examples, in your opinion, do the best job of illustrating or clarifying ideas? Discuss what effect the essay might have on you as a reader if there were no, or almost no, examples.

7. Examine the organization of the essay.
   a. Which sentence or paragraph first makes you aware of the essay's focus, of what the essay is really about?
   b. What do you think is the purpose of the first paragraph? The second?
   c. Distinguish among the beginning (introduction), middle (body), and ending (conclusion). If there is disagreement within the group, consult with another group or with your instructor.
   d. Make a brief outline of the essay, and compare your outline with that of another group. Discuss the similarities and differences.

8. Based on your reading of this essay, explain what Mead and Metraux mean by this quotation:

> The difficulty when strangers from two countries meet is not a lack of appreciation of friendship, but different expectations about what constitutes friendship and how it comes into being.

Compare your explanation with what you wrote in the Write before You Read activity that precedes "On Friendship."   ●

Write before You Read

The following two readings are reports of research on cross-cultural communication. Before reading these articles, write for 10 to 15 minutes on the following topic:

> Describe some difficulty you have had in making yourself understood in another culture or place or in understanding someone or something from another culture or place.

Share what you have written with your classmates.   ●

Intercultural Communication Stumbling Blocks
by LaRay M. Barna

LaRay M. Barna, a professor in the Department of Speech Communication at Portland State University in Oregon, wrote "Intercultural Communication Stumbling Blocks" (1976) to report on her classroom research with American and international students. In it, she discusses the barriers ("stumbling blocks") that prevent successful cross-cultural interaction. The article was originally published in Kentucky Speech Arts Journal, *a journal for professionals in the field of communication. Because Barna is reporting research to an academic reading audience, she is careful to document her sources, providing detailed endnotes for each quotation or reference. These endnotes ("References") correspond to bracketed numbers within the text.*

Note: *Because this article was written for professional readers, it will be more difficult for you to read than previous essays. But since the research is based on students' comments, you may already have firsthand knowledge of its content.*

Introduction

There are many viewpoints regarding the practice of intercultural communication but a familiar one is that "people are people," basically pretty much alike; therefore increased interaction through travel, student exchange programs, and other such ventures should result in more understanding and friendship between nations. Others take a quite different view, particularly those who have done research in the field of speech communication and are fully aware of the complexities of interpersonal interaction, even *within* cultural groups. They do not equate contact with communication, do not believe that the simple experience of talking with someone insures a successful transfer of meanings and feelings. Even the basic commonalities of birth, hunger, family, death, are perceived and treated in vastly different ways by persons with different backgrounds [1]. If there *is* a universal, it might be that each has been so subconsciously influenced by his own cultural upbringing that he assumes that the needs, desires, and basic assumptions of others are identical to his own [2].

It takes a long time of noninsulated living[1] in a new culture before a foreigner can relax into new perceptions and nonevaluative thinking so that he can adjust his reactions and interpretations to fit what's happening around him. The few who achieve complete insight and acceptance are outstanding by their rarity. After nine years of monitoring dyads[2] and small group discussions between U.S. and international students, this author, for one, is inclined to agree with Charles Frankel, who says: "Tensions exist within nations and between nations that never would have existed were these nations not in such intense cultural communication with one another" [3]. The following typical reactions of three foreign students to one nonverbal behavior that most Americans expect to bridge gaps—the smile—may serve as an illustration:

[1] **noninsulated living:** participating socially
[2] **monitoring dyads:** observing groups of two people

Japanese student: On my way to and from school I have received a smile by nonacquaintance American girls several times. I have learned they have no interest for me; it means only a kind of greeting to a foreigner. But if someone smiles at a stranger in Japan, especially a girl, she can assume he is either a sexual maniac or an impolite person.

Korean student: An American visited me in my country for one week. His inference was that people in Korea are not very friendly because they didn't smile or want to talk with foreign people. That's true because most Korean people take time to get to be friendly with people. We never talk or smile at strangers.

Vietnamese student: The reason why certain foreigners may think that Americans are superficial—and they are, some Americans even recognize this—is that they talk and smile too much. For people who come from placid cultures where nonverbal language is more used, and where a silence, a smile, a glance have their own meaning, it is true that Americans speak a lot. The superficiality of Americans can also be detected in their relations with others. Their friendships are, most of the time, so ephemeral compared to the friendships we have at home. Americans make friends very easily and leave their friends almost as quickly, while in my country it takes a long time to find out a possible friend and then she becomes your friend—with a very strong sense of the term. Most Americans are materialistic and once they are provided with necessities, they don't feel the need to have a friend. Purposes of their friendships are too clear, and you can hardly find a friendship for friendship's sake.

An American girl in the same class gives her view:

In general it seems to me that foreign people are not necessarily snobs but are very unfriendly. Some class members have told me that you shouldn't smile at others while passing them by on the street. To me I can't stop smiling. It's just natural to be smiling and friendly. I can see now why so many foreign people stick together. They are impossible to get to know. It's like the Americans are big bad wolves. How do Americans break this barrier? I want friends from all over the world but how do you start to be friends without offending them or scaring them off—like sheep? [4]

One reason for the long delay in tackling the widespread failure to   3
achieve understanding across cultures might be that it is not readily apparent when there has been miscommunication at the interpersonal level. Unless there is overt reporting of assumptions³ such as in the examples above, which seldom happens in normal settings, there is no chance for comparing impressions. The foreign visitor to the United States nods, smiles, and gives affirmative comments, which the straightforward, friendly American confidently translates as meaning that he has informed, helped, and pleased

³ **overt reporting of assumptions:** open explanations of basic beliefs and practices

the newcomer. It is likely, however, that the foreigner actually understood very little of the verbal and nonverbal content and was merely indicating polite interest or trying not to embarrass himself or his host with verbalized questions. The conversation may even have confirmed his stereotype that Americans are insensitive and ethnocentric.[4]

In a university classroom U.S. students often complain that the inter-   4
national members of a discussion or project seem uncooperative or unin-
terested. The following is a typical statement from the international's point
of view:

> I had difficulty with the opinion in the class where peoples in group
> discuss about subject. I was surrounded by Americans with whom I
> couldn't follow their tempo of discussion half of the time. I have dif-
> ficulty to listen and speak, but also with the way they handle the group.
> I felt uncomfortable because sometimes they believe their opinion
> strongly. I had been very serious about the whole subject but I was
> afraid I would say something wrong. I had the idea but not the
> words. [4]

Typically, the method used to improve chances for successful inter-   5
cultural communication is to gather information about the customs of the
other country and a smattering of the language. The behaviors and attitudes
are sometimes researched, but almost always from a secondhand source.
The information is seldom sufficient and may or may not be helpful. Knowing "what to expect" too often blinds the observer to all but what is confirmatory to his image or preconception. Any contradictory evidence that
does filter through is likely to be treated as an exception [5].

A better approach is to study the history, political structure, art, lit-   6
erature, and language of the country if time permits. But more important,
one should develop an investigative nonjudgmental attitude[5] and a high
tolerance for ambiguity[6]—which means lowered defenses. Margaret Mead
suggests sensitizing persons to the kinds of things that need to be taken
into account instead of developing behavior and attitude stereotypes, mainly
because of the individual differences in each encounter and the rapid changes
that occur in a culture pattern [6]. Edward Stewart concurs with this
view [7].

The Stumbling Blocks

Language

One way to reach an improved state of awareness and sensitivity to   7
what might go wrong is to examine five variables in the communication
process that seem to be major stumbling blocks when the dyad or small

[4] **ethnocentric:** tending to believe that one's own culture is superior
[5] **investigative nonjudgmental attitude:** the objective position a researcher takes toward the
    research subject
[6] **high tolerance for ambiguity:** willingness to accept uncertainty and complexity

group is cross-cultural. The first is so obvious it hardly needs mentioning—
language. Vocabulary, syntax, idioms, slang, dialects, and so on, all cause
difficulty, but the person struggling with a different language is at least
aware when he's in this kind of trouble. A worse language problem is the
tenacity with which someone will cling to "*the*" meaning of a word or phrase
in the new language once he has grasped one, regardless of connotation or
context. The infinite variations, especially of English, are so impossible to
cope with that they are waved aside. The reason the problem is "worse"
is because each thinks he understands. The nationwide misinterpretation
of Khruschev's sentence "We'll bury you" is a classic example.[7] Even "yes"
and "no" cause trouble. When a Japanese hears, "Won't you have some
tea?" he listens to the literal meaning of the sentence and answers, "No,"
meaning that he wants some. "Yes, I won't" would be a better reply because
this tips off the hostess that there may be a misunderstanding. In some
cultures, also, it is polite to refuse the first or second offer of refreshment.
Many foreign guests have gone hungry because their U.S. hostess never
presented the third offer.

Nonverbal Signs and Symbols

Learning the language, which most foreign visitors consider their *only*   8
barrier to understanding, is actually only the beginning. As Frankel says,
"To enter into a culture is to be able to hear, in Lionel Trilling's phrase,
its special 'hum and buzz of implication' " [8]. This brings in *nonverbal areas*
and the second stumbling block. People from different cultures inhabit
different nonverbal sensory worlds. Each sees, hears, feels, and smells only
that which has some meaning or importance for him. He abstracts whatever
fits into his personal world of recognitions and then interprets it through
the frame of reference[8] of his own culture.

An Oregon girl in an intercultural communication class asked a young   9
man from Saudi Arabia how he would signal nonverbally that he liked her.
His response was to smooth back his hair which, to her, was just a common
nervous gesture signifying nothing. She repeated her question three times.
He smoothed his hair three times and, finally realizing that she was not
recognizing this movement as his reply to her question, automatically ducked
his head and stuck out his tongue slightly in embarrassment. This behavior
was noticed by the girl, and she interpreted it as the way he would express
his liking for her.

The lack of comprehension of obvious nonverbal signs and symbols   10
such as gestures, postures, and vocalizations[9] is a definite communication
barrier, but it is possible to learn the meaning of these messages (once they

---

[7] **"We'll bury you":** Nikita Khrushchev, leader of the Soviet Union from 1953 to 1964, was
referring to *economic* competition with the West, but Americans misunderstood it as a
military boast.

[8] **frame of reference:** a set or system of beliefs against which other ideas are tested

[9] **vocalizations:** sounds made with the voice

are perceived) in much the same way as a verbal language is learned. It is more difficult to correctly note the unspoken codes of the other culture that are further from awareness, such as the handling of time and spatial relationships, subtle signs of respect or formality, and many others.

Preconceptions and Stereotypes

The third stumbling block is the presence of *preconceptions* and *stereotypes*.   11 If the label "inscrutable" has preceded the Japanese guest, it is thus we explain his constant and inappropriate smile. The stereotype that Arabs are "inflammable" causes U.S. students to keep their distance when an animated and noisy group from Libya is enjoying lunch in the cafeteria. A professor who "knows" of the bargaining habits of natives of certain countries may unfairly interpret a hesitation by one of his foreign students as a move to "squirm out" of a commitment. Stereotypes help do what Ernest Becker [9] says the anxiety-prone human race *must* do, and that is to reduce the threat of the unknown by making the world predictable. Indeed, this is one of the basic functions of culture: to lay out a predictable world in which the individual is firmly oriented. Stereotypes are overgeneralized beliefs that provide conceptual bases from which to "make sense" out of what goes on around us. In a foreign land they increase our feeling of security and are psychologically necessary to the degree that we cannot tolerate ambiguity or the sense of helplessness resulting from inability to understand and deal with people and situations beyond our comprehension.

Stereotypes are stumbling blocks for communicators because they in-   12 terfere with objective viewing of stimuli.[10] Unfortunately, they are not easy to overcome in others or in ourselves by demonstrations of the "truth," hoping to teach a lesson of tolerance or cultural relativity.[11] They persist because they sometimes rationalize prejudices or are firmly established as myths or truisms by one's own national culture. They are also sustained and fed by the tendency to perceive selectively only those pieces of new information that correspond to the image. The Asian or African visitor who is accustomed to privation and the values of denial and self-help cannot fail to experience American culture as materialistic and wasteful. The stereotype for him turns into a concrete reality.

The Tendency to Evaluate

Another deterrent to an understanding between persons of differing   13 cultures or ethnic groups is the *tendency to evaluate*, to approve or disapprove, the statements and actions of the other person or group rather than to try to completely comprehend the thoughts and feelings expressed. Each person's culture, his own way of life, always seems right, proper, and natural.

---

[10] **objective viewing of stimuli:** the ability to look at things without making judgments about them

[11] **cultural relativity:** the evaluation of a custom in relation to other customs of a particular group

This bias prevents the open-minded attention needed to look at the attitudes and behavior patterns from the other's point of view. A midday siesta[12] changes from a "lazy habit" to a "pretty good idea" when someone listens long enough to realize the midday temperature in that country is 115° Fahrenheit. . . .

The communication cut-off caused by immediate evaluation is height-   14
ened when feelings and emotions are deeply involved; yet this is just the time when listening with understanding is most needed. It takes both aware-ness of the tendency to close our minds and courage to risk change in our own values and perceptions to dare to comprehend why someone thinks and acts differently from us. As stated by Sherif, Sherif, and Nebergall, "A person's commitment to his religion, politics, values of his family, and his stand on the virtue of his way of life are ingredients in his self-picture— intimately felt and cherished" [10]. It is very easy to dismiss strange or different behaviors as "wrong," listen through a thick screen of value judg-ments, and therefore fail miserably to receive a fair understanding. The impatience of the American public over the choice of the shape of the conference table at the Paris Peace talks[13] and their judgment of a "poor reception" for the President of the United States because there were no bands or flag-waving throngs waiting for Nixon as he was driven through towns in New China on his historic visit[14] are two examples.

The following paragraph written by an international student from Korea   15
illustrates how a clash in values can lead to poor communication and result in misunderstanding and hurt feelings:

> When I call on my American friend, he had been studying his lesson. Then I said, "May I come in?" He said through window, "I am sorry. I have no time because of my study." Then he shut the window. I thought it over and over. I couldn't understand through my cultural background. In our country, if someone visits other's house, house owner should have welcome visitor whether he likes or not and whether he is busy or not. Then next, if the owner is busy, he asks to visitor, "Would you wait for me?" Also the owner never speaks without opening his door. [11]

This example also illustrates how difficult it is to bring one's own cultural norm into awareness. It is unlikely the "American friend" ever knew that he insulted the young Korean.

High Anxiety

The fifth stumbling block is *high anxiety*, separately mentioned for the   16
purpose of emphasis. Unlike the other four (language, illusive nonverbal

---

[12] **siesta:** (*Spanish*) a brief nap or rest after the noon meal
[13] **Paris Peace talks:** talks between Vietnamese and United States representatives in the early 1970s whose purpose was to end the Vietnam War
[14] **Nixon's historic visit:** In 1972, Richard Nixon became the first U.S. President to visit the People's Republic of China.

cues, preconceptions and stereotypes, and the practice of immediate evaluation), the stumbling block of anxiety is not distinct but underlies and
compounds the others. The presence of high anxiety/tension is very common in cross-cultural experiences because of the uncertainties present. An
international student says it well:

> During those several months after my arrival in the U.S.A., every day
> I came back from school exhausted so that I had to take a rest for a
> while, stretching myself on the bed. For all the time, I strained every
> nerve in order to understand what the people were saying and make
> myself understood in my broken English. When I don't understand
> what American people are talking about and why they are laughing, I
> sometimes have to pretend to understand by smiling, even though I
> feel alienated, uneasy and tense.
>
> In addition to this, the difference in culture or customs, the way
> of thinking between two countries, produces more tension because we
> don't know how we should react to totally foreign customs or attitudes,
> and sometimes we can't guess how the people from another country
> react to my saying or behavior. We always have a fear somewhere in
> the bottom of our hearts that there are much more chances of breakdown
> in intercultural communication than in communication with our own
> fellow countrymen.[12]

The native of the country is uncomfortable when talking with a foreigner   17
because he cannot maintain the normal flow of verbal and nonverbal interaction to sustain the conversation. He is also threatened by the unknown
other's knowledge, experience, and evaluation—the visitor's potential for
scrutiny and rejection of himself and his country. The inevitable question,
"How do you like it here?" which the foreigner abhors, is the host's quest
for reassurance, or at least the "feeler" that reduces the unknown and gives
him ground for defense if that seems necessary.

The foreign member of the dyad is under the same threat, with the   18
added tension of having to cope with the differing pace, climate, and culture.
The first few months he feels helpless in coping with messages that swamp
him and to which his reactions may be inappropriate. His self-esteem is
often intolerably undermined unless he employs such defenses as withdrawal
into his own reference group[15] or into himself, screening out or misper-
ceiving stimuli, rationalizing, overcompensating,[16] even hostility—none of
which leads to effective communication.

Conclusion

Since all of the communication barriers mentioned are hard to remove,   19
the only simple solution seems to be to tell everybody to stay home. This

---

[15] **reference group:** the group of people with whom one has something in common, such as
     nationality or native language
[16] **overcompensating:** trying too hard

advice obviously is unacceptable, so it is fortunate that a few paths are being laid around the obstacles. Communication theorists are continuing to offer new insights and are focusing on problem areas of this complex process [13]. Educators and linguists are improving methods of learning a second language. The nonverbal area, made familiar by Edward T. Hall in his famous books *The Silent Language* and *The Hidden Dimension*, is getting a singular amount of attention [14]. The ray of hope offered by Hall and others is that nonverbal cues, culturally controlled and largely out-of-awareness, can be discovered and even understood when the communicator knows enough to look for them, is alert to the varying interpretations possible, and is free enough from tension and psychological defenses to notice them.

In addition, textbooks are appearing and communication specialists are   20 improving means for increasing sensitivity to the messages coming from others in an intercultural setting [15]. Professional associations are giving increased amounts of attention to intercultural communication, and new societies such as the Society for Intercultural Education, Training and Research are being developed. The International and Intercultural Communication Annual [16] has a complete listing of these.

What the interpersonal intercultural communicator must seek to achieve   21 can be summarized by two quotations. The first is by Roger Harrison, who says:

> The communicator cannot stop at knowing that the people he is working with have different customs, goals, and thought patterns from his own. He must be able to feel his way into intimate contact with these alien values, attitudes, and feelings. He must be able to work with them and within them, neither losing his own values in the confrontation nor protecting himself behind a wall of intellectual detachment. [17]

Robert T. Oliver phrases it thus: "If we would communicate across   22 cultural barriers, we must learn what to say and how to say it in terms of the expectations and predispositions of those we want to listen" [18].

References

1. Marshall R. Singer, "Culture: A Perceptual Approach," in *Readings in Intercultural Communication*. Vol. I (Regional Council for International Education, University of Pittsburgh), and Edward T. Hall, *The Hidden Dimension* (New York: Doubleday and Company, Inc., 1966), p. 2.
2. Edward T. Hall, *The Silent Language* (Greenwich, Conn.: Fawcett Publications, Inc., 1959).
3. Charles Frankel, *The Neglected Aspect of Foreign Affairs* (Washington, D.C.: Brookings Institution, 1965), p. 1.
4. Taken from student papers in a course in intercultural communication taught by the author.
5. For one discussion of this concept, see Daryl J. Bem, *Beliefs, Attitudes, and Human Affairs* (Belmont, Calif.: Brooks/Cole Publishing Co., 1970), p. 9.
6. Margaret Mead, "The Cultural Perspective," in *Communication or Conflict*, ed. Mary Capes (Association Press, 1960).

7. Edward C. Stewart, *American Cultural Patterns: A Cross-cultural Perspective* (Pittsburgh, Pa.: Regional Council for International Education, University of Pittsburgh, April 1971), p. 14.

8. Frankel, *The Neglected Aspect of Foreign Affairs*, p. 103.

9. Ernest Becker, *The Birth and Death of Meaning* (New York: Free Press, 1962), pp. 84–89.

10. Carolyn W. Sherif, Musafe Sherif, and Roger E. Nebergall, *Attitude and Attitude Change* (Philadelphia: W. B. Saunders Co., 1965) p. vi.

11.&12. Taken from a student's paper in a course in intercultural communication taught by the author.

13. An early book, now in its second edition, which adapted the language of information theory to communication and stressed the influence of culture, remains one of the best sources: *Communication: The Social Matrix of Psychiatry* by Jurgen Ruesch and Gregory Bateson (New York: W. W. Norton & Co., 1968).

14. See, for example, *Silent Messages* by Albert Mehrabian (Belmont, Calif.: Wadsworth Publishing Co., 1971).

15. Sources include: Edward D. Stewart, "The Simulation of Cultural Differences," *The Journal of Communication*, Vol. 16, December 1966; Alfred J. Kraemer, *The Development of Cultural Self-awareness Design of a Program of Instruction* (George Washington University, Human Resources Research Office, Professional Paper 27–69, August 1969); David Hoopes, ed., *Readings in Intercultural Communication*, Vols. I–IV. (Regional Council for International Education, University of Pittsburgh).

16. *International and Intercultural Communication Annual*, Vol. 1, December 1974, published by Speech Communication Association, Statler Hilton Hotel, New York.

17. Roger Harrison, "The Design of Cross-cultural Training: An Alternative to the University Model," in *Explorations in Human Relations Training and Research* (Bethesda, Md.: National Training Laboratories, 1966), NEA No. 2, p. 4.

18. Robert T. Oliver, *Culture and Communication: The Problem of Penetrating National and Cultural Boundaries* (Springfield, Ill.: Charles C. Thomas, 1962), p. 154.

●

Write after You Read

1. Make a journal entry on "Intercultural Communication Stumbling Blocks," following the suggestions on p. 67.

2. Write a one- to three-sentence summary of "Intercultural Communication Stumbling Blocks," following the guidelines for summarizing a research study on pp. 67–68.   ●

Activities for Class Discussion

Working in a group of three or four students, share in the following activities. Your group can decide the order in which to cover the material and how much time to spend on each question.

1. Share your written summary of "Intercultural Communication Stumbling Blocks." If you do not agree on the overall research findings, discuss the reasons for the different interpretations. If your

group cannot determine the research findings, consult with another group or with your instructor.

2. Discuss any words that interfere with your understanding of the article. Make sure that everyone in the group understands the meaning of these terms:

a universal (1)   persist (12)
tackling (3)   rationalize (12)
affirmative (3)   truisms (12)
smattering (5)   privation (12)
a secondhand source (5)   a concrete reality (12)
confirmatory (5)   deterrent (13)
preconception (5)   bias (13)
concurs (6)   cultural norm (15)
tenacity (7)   illusive (16)
implication (8)   scrutiny (17)
abstracts (8)   abhors (17)
anxiety-prone (11)   predispositions (22)
oriented (11)

Try to guess the meaning of these or other unfamiliar words from the context. If your group cannot determine the meaning, consult with your instructor or consult a dictionary.

3. Can you identify with any or all of the five major stumbling blocks (listed here) that interfere with successful communication across cultures? Have you had any humorous, difficult, or confusing experiences that you can share? Reread each section as you discuss each stumbling block:
   a. Language problems (paragraph 7)
   b. Nonverbal misunderstanding (paragraphs 8–10)
   c. The presence of preconceptions and stereotypes (11–12)
   d. The tendency to evaluate (13–15)
   e. High anxiety (16–18)

4. Do any of your experiences contradict what Barna is saying?

5. Has Barna overlooked other common cross-cultural communication barriers? If so, what are they?

6. Are Barna's solutions to this problem reasonable? Are they potentially successful? Can you provide other solutions, based on your own experience?

7. Following the guidelines for paraphrasing (p. 226), put the first sentence of this reading selection into your own words:

There are many viewpoints regarding the practice of intercultural communication but a familiar one is that "people are people," basically pretty much alike; therefore increased interaction through travel, student exchange programs, and other such ventures should result in more understanding and friendship between nations.

Your goal is to preserve and yet clarify the meaning of the passage. Share your paraphrase with another group. Discuss the similarities and the differences.   ●

Write before You Read

In the following reading selection, the author examines the sense of time and pace of life in different places. Before reading, write for 10 to 15 minutes, in or out of class, about the following quotation (taken from the reading selection):

Ideas of time and punctuality vary considerably from place to place.

Write with the purpose of providing an example of a different concept of time or punctuality (being on time) in different places you have been. Share what you have written with your classmates.   ●

Social Time: The Heartbeat of Culture
by Robert Levine with Ellen Wolff

Robert Levine, professor of psychology at California State University at Fresno, collaborated with Ellen Wolff, a freelance writer, to write "Social Time: The Heartbeat of Culture." The article combines a narrative of Levine's personal experience as a visiting professor in Brazil with a description of his research on time sense and pace of life in different cultures. The article was published in 1985 in Psychology Today, *a monthly magazine that makes research findings about human experience available to a nonprofessional audience.*

"If a man does not keep pace with his companions, perhaps it is because he hears 1
a different drummer." This thought by Thoreau strikes a chord in so many people that it has become part of our language. We use the phrase "the beat of a different drummer" to explain any pace of life unlike our own. Such colorful vagueness reveals how informal our rules of time really are. The world over, children simply "pick up" their society's time concepts as they mature. No dictionary clearly defines the meaning of "early" or "late" for them or for strangers who stumble over the maddening incongruities between the time sense they bring with them and the one they face in a new land.

I learned this firsthand, a few years ago, and the resulting culture shock 2
led me halfway around the world to find answers. It seemed clear that time "talks." But what is it telling us?

My journey started shortly after I accepted an appointment as visiting 3
professor of psychology at the federal university in Niteroi, Brazil, a mid-sized city across the bay from Rio de Janeiro. As I left home for my first

New York, New York: pounding the pavement at a pretty pace.

day of class, I asked someone the time. It was 9:05 a.m., which allowed me time to relax and look around the campus before my 10 o'clock lecture. After what I judged to be half an hour, I glanced at a clock I was passing. It said 10:20! In panic, I broke for the classroom, followed by gentle calls of "Hola, professor" and "Tudo bem, professor?" from unhurried students, many of whom, I later realized, were my own. I arrived breathless to find an empty room.

Frantically, I asked a passerby the time. "Nine forty-five" was the   4
answer. No, that couldn't be. I asked someone else. "Nine fifty-five." Another said: "Exactly 9:43." The clock in a nearby office read 3:15. I had learned my first lesson about Brazilians: Their timepieces are consistently inaccurate. And nobody minds.

My class was scheduled from 10 until noon. Many students came late,   5
some very late. Several arrived after 10:30. A few showed up closer to 11. Two came after that. All of the latecomers wore the relaxed smiles that I came, later, to enjoy. Each one said hello, and although a few apologized

briefly, none seemed terribly concerned about lateness. They assumed that I understood.

The idea of Brazilians arriving late was not a great shock. I had heard   6
about "mānha," the Portuguese equivalent of "mañana" in Spanish. This term, meaning "tomorrow" or "the morning," stereotypes the Brazilian who puts off the business of today until tomorrow. The real surprise came at noon that first day, when the end of class arrived.

Back home in California, I never need to look at a clock to know when   7
the class hour is ending. The shuffling of books is accompanied by strained expressions that say plaintively, "I'm starving. . . . I've got to go to the bathroom. . . . I'm going to suffocate if you keep us one more second." (The pain usually becomes unbearable at two minutes to the hour in undergraduate classes and five minutes before the close of graduate classes.)

When noon arrived in my first Brazilian class, only a few students left   8
immediately. Others slowly drifted out during the next 15 minutes, and some continued asking me questions long after that. When several remaining students kicked off their shoes at 12:30, I went into my own "starving/bathroom/suffocation" routine.

I could not, in all honesty, attribute their lingering to my superb   9
teaching style. I had just spent two hours lecturing on statistics in halting Portuguese. Apparently, for many of my students, staying late was simply of no more importance than arriving late in the first place. As I observed this casual approach in infinite variations during the year, I learned that the "mānha" stereotype oversimplified the real Anglo/Brazilian differences in conceptions of time. Research revealed a more complex picture.

With the assistance of colleagues Laurie West and Harry Reis, I com-   10
pared the time sense of 91 male and female students in Niteroi with that of 107 similar students at California State University in Fresno. The universities are similar in academic quality and size, and the cities are both secondary metropolitan centers with populations of about 350,000.

We asked students about their perceptions of time in several situations,   11
such as what they would consider late or early for a hypothetical lunch appointment with a friend. The average Brazilian student defined lateness for lunch as 33½ minutes after the scheduled time, compared to 19 minutes for the Fresno students. But Brazilians also allowed an average of about 54 minutes before they'd consider someone early, while the Fresno students drew the line at 24.

Are Brazilians simply more flexible in their concepts of time and punc-   12
tuality? And how does this relate to the stereotype of the apathetic, fatalistic and irresponsible Latin temperament? When we asked students to give typical reasons for lateness, the Brazilians were less likely to attribute it to a lack of caring than the North Americans were. Instead, they pointed to unforeseen circumstances that the person couldn't control. Because they seemed less inclined to feel personally responsible for being late, they also expressed less regret for their own lateness and blamed others less when they were late.

Tokyo, Japan: Lead, follow or get out of the way.

We found similar differences in how students from the two countries   13
characterized people who were late for appointments. Unlike their North
American counterparts, the Brazilian students believed that a person who
is consistently late is probably more successful than one who is consistently
on time. They seemed to accept the idea that someone of status is expected
to arrive late. Lack of punctuality is a badge of success.

Even within our own country, of course, ideas of time and punctuality   14
vary considerably from place to place. Different regions and even cities
have their own distinct rhythms and rules. Seemingly simple words like
"now," snapped out by an impatient New Yorker, and "later," said by a
relaxed Californian, suggest a world of difference. Despite our familiarity
with these homegrown differences in tempo, problems with time present a
major stumbling block to Americans abroad. Peace Corps volunteers told
researchers James Spradley of Macalester College and Mark Phillips of the
University of Washington that their greatest difficulties with other people,
after language problems, were the general pace of life and the punctuality
of others. Formal "clock time" may be a standard on which the world
agrees, but "social time," the heartbeat of society, is something else again.

How a country paces its social life is a mystery to most outsiders, one   15
that we're just beginning to unravel. Twenty-six years ago, anthropologist
Edward Hall noted in *The Silent Language* that informal patterns of time

Florence, Italy: living at a leisurely pace, particularly at the post office.

"are seldom, if ever, made explicit. They exist in the air around us. They are either familiar and comfortable, or unfamiliar and wrong." When we realize we are out of step, we often blame the people around us to make ourselves feel better.

Appreciating cultural differences in time sense becomes increasingly   16
important as modern communications put more and more people in daily contact. If we are to avoid misreading issues that involve time perceptions, we need to understand better our own cultural biases and those of others.

When people of different cultures interact, the potential for misunder-   17
standing exists on many levels. For example, members of Arab and Latin cultures usually stand much closer when they are speaking to people than we usually do in the United States, a fact we frequently misinterpret as aggression or disrespect. Similarly, we assign personality traits to groups with a pace of life that is markedly faster or slower than our own. We build ideas of national character, for example, around the traditional Swiss and German ability to "make the trains run on time." Westerners like ourselves define punctuality using precise measures of time: 5 minutes, 15 minutes, an hour. But according to Hall, in many Mediterranean Arab cultures there are only three sets of time: no time at all, now (which is of varying duration) and forever (too long). Because of this, Americans often find difficulty in getting Arabs to distinguish between waiting a long time and a very long time.

Solo, Indonesia: Volleyball, anyone? There's always time for a friendly game.

According to historian Will Durant, "No man in a hurry is quite   18
civilized." What do our time judgments say about our attitude toward life?
How can a North American, coming from a land of digital precision, relate
to a North African who may consider a clock "the devil's mill"?

Each language has a vocabulary of time that does not always survive   19
translation. When we translated our questionnaires into Portuguese for my
Brazilian students, we found that English distinctions of time were not
readily articulated in their language. Several of our questions concerned
how long the respondent would wait for someone to arrive, as compared
with when they hoped for arrival or actually expected the person would
come. In Portuguese, the verbs "to wait for," "to hope for" and "to expect"
are all translated as "esperar." We had to add further words of explanation
to make the distinction clear to the Brazilian students.

To avoid these language problems, my Fresno colleague Kathy Bartlett   20
and I decided to clock the pace of life in other countries by using as little
language as possible. We looked directly at three basic indicators of time:
the accuracy of a country's bank clocks, the speed at which pedestrians
walked and the average time it took a postal clerk to sell us a single stamp.
In six countries on three continents, we made observations in both the
nation's largest urban area and a medium-sized city: Japan (Tokyo and
Sendai), Taiwan (Taipei and Tainan), Indonesia (Jakarta and Solo), Italy

(Rome and Florence), England (London and Bristol) and the United States
(New York City and Rochester).

What we wanted to know was: Can we speak of a unitary concept   21
called "pace of life"? What we've learned suggests that we can. There appears
to be a very strong relationship (see chart) between the accuracy of clock
time, walking speed and postal efficiency across the countries we studied.

We checked 15 clocks in each city, selecting them at random in down-   22
town banks and comparing the time they showed with that reported
by the local telephone company. In Japan, which leads the way in accuracy,
the clocks averaged just over half a minute early or late. Indonesian clocks,
the least accurate, were more than three minutes off the mark.

I will be interested to see how the digital-information age will affect   23
our perceptions of time. In the United States today, we are reminded of
the exact hour of the day more than ever, through little symphonies of
beeps emanating from people's digital watches. As they become the norm,
I fear our sense of precision may take an absurd twist. The other day,
when I asked for the time, a student looked at his watch and replied, "Three
twelve and eighteen seconds."

" *'Will you walk a little faster?' said a whiting to a snail. 'There's a porpoise*   24
close behind us, and he's treading on my tail.' "

So goes the rhyme from *Alice in Wonderland*, which also gave us that   25
famous symbol of haste, the White Rabbit. He came to mind often as we
measured the walking speeds in our experimental cities. We clocked how
long it took pedestrians to walk 100 feet along a main downtown street
during business hours on clear days. To eliminate the effects of socializing,
we observed only people walking alone, timing at least 100 in each city.
We found, once again, that the Japanese led the way, averaging just 20.7
seconds to cover the distance. The English nosed out the Americans for
second place—21.6 to 22.5 seconds—and the Indonesians again trailed the
pack, sauntering along at 27.2 seconds. As you might guess, speed was
greater in the larger city of each nation than in its smaller one.

THE PACE OF LIFE IN SIX COUNTRIES			
	Accuracy of Bank Clocks	*Walking Speed*	*Post Office Speed*
Japan	1	1	1
United States	2	3	2
England	4	2	3
Italy	5	4	6
Taiwan	3	5	4
Indonesia	6	6	5

Numbers (1 is the top value) indicate the comparative rankings of each country
for each indicator of time sense.

Our final measurement, the average time it took postal clerks to sell   26
one stamp, turned out to be less straightforward than we expected. In each
city, including those in the United States, we presented clerks with a note
in the native language requesting a common-priced stamp. . . . They were
also handed paper money, the equivalent of a $5 bill. In Indonesia, this
procedure led to more than we bargained for.

At the large central post office in Jakarta, I asked for the line to buy   27
stamps and was directed to a group of private vendors sitting outside. Each
of them hustled for my business: "Hey, good stamps, mister!" "Best stamps
here!" In the smaller city of Solo, I found a volleyball game in progress
when I arrived at the main post office on Friday afternoon. Business hours,
I was told, were over. When I finally did get there during business hours,
the clerk was more interested in discussing relatives in America. Would I
like to meet his uncle in Cincinnati? Which did I like better: California or
the United States? Five people behind me in line waited patiently. Instead
of complaining, they began paying attention to our conversation.

When it came to efficiency of service, however, the Indonesians were   28
not the slowest, although they did place far behind the Japanese postal
clerks, who averaged 25 seconds. That distinction went to the Italians,
whose infamous postal service took 47 seconds on the average.

"A man who wastes one hour of time has not discovered the meaning of life. . . ."   29

That was Charles Darwin's belief, and many share it, perhaps at the   30
cost of their health. My colleagues and I have recently begun studying the
relationship between pace of life and well-being. Other researchers have
demonstrated that a chronic sense of urgency is a basic component of the
Type A, coronary-prone personality. We expect that future research will
demonstrate that pace of life is related to rate of heart disease, hypertension,
ulcers, suicide, alcoholism, divorce and other indicators of general psychological and physical well-being

As you envision tomorrow's international society, do you wonder who   31
will set the pace? Americans eye Japan carefully, because the Japanese are
obviously "ahead of us" in measurable ways. In both countries, speed is
frequently confused with progress. Perhaps looking carefully at the different
paces of life around the world will help us distinguish more accurately
between the two qualities. Clues are everywhere but sometimes hard to
distinguish. You have to listen carefully to hear the beat of even your own
drummer.   ●

Write after You Read

1. Make a journal entry on "Social Time: The Heartbeat of Culture,"
   following the suggestions on p. 67.
2. Write a one- to three-sentence summary of "Social Time: The Heartbeat of Culture," following the guidelines for summarizing research
   findings on pp. 67–68.   ●

Activities for Class Discussion

In a group of three or four students, share in the following activities. Your group can decide the order in which to cover the material and how much time to spend on each question.

1. Share your written summary of "Social Time: The Heartbeat of Culture." If you do not agree on the research findings, discuss the reasons for the different interpretations. If your group cannot determine the research findings, consult with another group or with your instructor.
2. Are there any unfamiliar words? Make sure everyone in the group understands the meaning of these terms:

strikes a chord (1)	hypothetical (11)
incongruities (1)	explicit (15)
shuffling (7)	aggression (17)
plaintively (7)	articulated (19)
attribute (9)	respondent (19)
lingering (9)	infamous (28)

   Try to guess the meaning of the words from the context. If your group cannot determine the meaning, consult with another group or with your instructor, or consult a dictionary.
3. Have you experienced a difference in time sense in adapting to a new culture or place? If so, can you share some humorous, difficult, or confusing experiences? How have these experiences changed your attitude or behavior?
4. Have you noticed a different pace of life in adapting to a new culture or place? If so, explain how the pace of life is different by comparing specific examples from the two cultures or places. How have these experiences affected your attitude or behavior?
5. Has reading this article influenced the way you perceive people in a different culture? Explain.
6. Has reading this article helped you to understand your own culture better? Explain.
7. Based on your reading of this article, explain what Levine and Wolff mean by the following quotations:
   a. "When people of different cultures interact, the potential for misunderstanding exists on many levels." (paragraph 17)
   b. "Each language has a vocabulary of time that does not always survive translation." (paragraph 19)
8. Following the guidelines for paraphrasing on p. 226, put the quotations in 7 into your own words. Share your written paraphrases with another group. Discuss the similarities and differences. ●

Facing a Different Culture
by Doxis Doxiadis

Doxis Doxiadis is from Greece. He wrote "Facing a Different Culture" to fulfill a writing assignment for a composition course. What you will read is a finished composition, carefully edited for publication in this book. Later in this chapter, you will see how Doxis got started on this assignment and the various stages of thinking, writing, and rewriting he went through to produce this essay.

In his essay, Doxis compares his own experiences and those of his friends with the findings of LaRay Barna's "Intercultural Communication Stumbling Blocks." Doxis says that initially he wanted to write about Viorst's "Friends, Good Friends—and Such Good Friends," but he felt he had said everything he wanted to say about it during class discussions. He chose to write about Barna's article instead so that he could explore the reading beyond what was discussed in class and therefore comprehend it more fully.

My first visit to the U.S. was quite a disappointment. I expected to find a lot of new friends in this country, but I soon realized that this would not be so easy. A number of problems, generated from the first minute I stepped into this country, did not allow me to fulfill my expectations and forced me to seek the company of other foreigners with similar cultural backgrounds to my own. These problems, discussed in LaRay Barna's article "Intercultural Communication Stumbling Blocks," are experienced, to different extents, by most foreign students and force them to form groups among themselves in order to find a shelter where their problems can be shared and understood. 1

The basic problem that an international student faces, as Barna very correctly says, is the language. It doesn't matter if a foreigner was a class A student in English back in his country. The difficulties still remain. When I studied English back in Greece, I didn't learn the idioms and expressions of the language and of course couldn't "get" expressions such as "beat it" or "hot dog." To make matters worse, every American seems to have his own pronunciation. I couldn't, and still can't, understand what someone from Texas, Tennessee, or South Carolina was saying. Initially my inability to understand what my classmates or friends were saying frustrated me, and I tried to avoid talking altogether. 2

However, as Barna points out, language is not the only problem a foreigner will face. When I first came to the U.S., I found out that my values, preferences, and habits were totally different from those of Americans. I thought that people here were ruder according to my standards. I could never ask someone the personal—and maybe too friendly—questions they asked me from the very first minute of our acquaintance. I remember 3 that I couldn't understand why all the students were smiling and greeting me. My roommates behaved as though I was a long-lost friend of theirs; and such friendliness embarrassed me since I could not, or thought I did not, respond accordingly. This behavior seemed to me quite shallow, and I don't think that this impression was mine alone. As a Vietnamese student says in the Barna article, "Foreigners . . . think that Americans are super-ficial" (paragraph 2). In the eyes of a foreigner, Americans look like happy fools, even though, as I found out, this is certainly not true. However, the first impression of Americans will make most foreigners avoid them and they won't therefore find their true self.

One of the most interesting and unfortunately true notions in the Barna   4 article is the fact that lack of communication and comprehension between Americans and foreigners often results in "hurt feelings" and serious mis-understandings (paragraph 15). A friend of mine from Saudi Arabia told me that he was often insulted by Americans because they showed the soles of their feet to him, which is an insult to his people. I, as well, was often offended at first by what Americans consider innocent jokes. I used to run red-hot whenever someone made a joke about Greeks even though he usually didn't intend to insult me. It took me a long time to learn what is considered an insult in the U.S. and what is a simple joke.

Another true notion that Barna discusses is that Americans often do   5 not realize that customs and habits are different between people from dif-ferent countries. While I was writing this essay, I had a conversation with an American friend of mine who couldn't even understand the topic of my essay. He didn't believe that there could be important differences in the behavior of people even if they came from a different country.

Barna's article, however, leaves some things underdeveloped. Americans   6 avoid foreigners just as foreigners avoid Americans. Even though most Americans want to consider themselves as good hosts and open-minded people, they are often embarrassed by foreigners and do not feel comfortable in front of them. They are afraid of giving them a bad impression, and they don't know what could possibly offend them. So sometimes they prefer to avoid them or at least to leave the first move to the foreigner, a move that doesn't come often.

Finally, another underdeveloped problem that foreigners face in the   7 U.S. is the pace of life. As is noted in Robert Levine and Ellen Wolff's essay "Social Time: The Heartbeat of Culture," the U.S. has a much faster pace of life than most countries, including, of course, Greece. When I encountered the quick way of living in the U.S. that is guided by the idea that "time is money," I was completely unprepared for it. Life in Greece is much more relaxed and is focused on the enjoyment of life. So I found out that I had to change my whole concept of living if I didn't want to be always late for class. This change, however, resulted in increased anxiety and stress, which added to all the other problems that I faced.

Now that I am finally acclimated, I can look back and laugh at the   8 problems and anxieties I faced initially. This is not, however, a laughing matter. A lot of other foreign students will face crushing pressure resulting from the aforementioned problems, which will make them, until they finally surpass these problems, curse their decision to attend an American college. Unfortunately, I cannot provide a solution to this problem, so I can only hope that someone else will find a way to lift the burden international students carry in a foreign country.   ●

Write after You Read

1. Make a journal entry on "Facing a Different Culture."
2. Write a one-sentence summary of the essay by answering this question: What is Doxis trying to show?   ●

Activities for Class Discussion

Working with the whole class, share in the following activities.

1. On the board, write a one-sentence summary of Doxis's essay. If you cannot agree on the focal point and message, discuss the reasons for the different interpretations.
2. Discuss your reaction to Doxis's essay.
3. Doxis makes several references to the reading, Barna's "Intercultural Communication Stumbling Blocks." Discuss whether these references are sufficient to reveal the purpose and content of the reading.
   a. Which references do you find most helpful? Why?
   b. If you think Doxis has not made enough references to the reading, where can more references be added? Can you suggest specific references that might be helpful?
4. Doxis provides several personal examples in his essay. Discuss whether these examples are sufficient to support points he makes about the reading.
   a. Which examples do the best job of clarifying a point? Why?
   b. If you think more examples are needed, where could they be added? Can you suggest the types of examples that might be helpful?
5. Examine the paragraph units of the essay.
   a. Which sentence or paragraph first makes you aware of the essay's focus, of what the essay is about?
   b. Go through the essay paragraph by paragraph, and determine the purpose or function of each paragraph. For example, does the paragraph introduce the main idea of the essay? Does the paragraph make a new point? Does the paragraph exist primarily to provide an example to illustrate or clarify a point made in the preceding paragraph?
   c. If a paragraph makes a new point, does the paragraph contain

enough details and examples to support or illustrate that point?
Are all the details and examples logically connected to that point?

d. The first sentence of each new paragraph should help the reader
to move smoothly from what the writer has just said to what the
writer is about to say. Does each first sentence make a link
between what Doxis has just said and what he is about to say?

e. Look for connections within and between paragraphs. Identify
words or expressions that connect ideas and examples, and show
how they are related to one another.

- If you find connective words, do they help you as a reader to
follow Doxis's way of thinking about his subject?
- If there are any missing connections, where would you add
connective words or expressions?
- If you find any connectives that are distracting (sometimes a
writer can include more connectives than a reader needs), explain where they are and why you would delete them.   ●

ACTIVITY: *Observe one student in the process of writing an essay*

On pp. 104–114, you can observe the process Doxis went through to
produce his essay. Use the guidelines to compose your own essay relating
reading to experience.   ●

CHAPTER FOUR

Guidelines for Fulfilling Essay Assignment 2

Essay Assignment 2

Write an essay in which you examine the relationship between ideas in the reading and your own experiences and attitudes. Refer to one or more of the readings in Part Two. Show how the generalizations or theories or experiences of another writer compare to what you have learned from experience, or show how they help you make sense of your own world. In writing this essay, your purpose will be to illuminate, evaluate, or test the validity of the ideas contained in the reading. Direct references to the reading—in the form of summary, paraphrase, and quotation—are necessary.   ●

Understanding the Assignment

Before you begin writing an essay, you need to understand exactly what you are being assigned to write. You need to analyze the directions of the writing assignment so that you know both the essay's possibilities and its limitations. The following activity can help you fulfill that goal.

ACTIVITY: *Rereading and analyzing the writing assignment*

Working in a group of three or four students, have one student read the essay assignment aloud. Examine what the assignment asks you to do. What purpose will the essay serve? What material should it contain? If you are unclear as to the demands of the assignment, consult with your instructor.   ●

Defining Your Audience

Being aware of your reading audience as you plan an essay can help you to shape your thoughts. Though in this course, your classmates are readers and reviewers of your work in progress, ultimately it is your instructor who does the final evaluation of your work. It is therefore important for you to understand this audience's needs and expectations.

ACTIVITY: *Defining your audience*

Although this activity can be done in small groups, it is a good idea to define your audience by communicating directly with that audience, your instructor. As a class, you can discuss some answers to these questions:

1. What does the instructor already know about the topic?
2. What does the instructor want to learn from you?
3. What material do you need to provide to ensure that the instructor learns what needs to be learned?
4. Why does the instructor need a summary of a reading that is familiar to the instructor?
5. Why does the instructor need paraphrases when the original material is available?
6. Why does the instructor want to see quotations of passages that are well known to the instructor?

Raise any other questions that will help you define the audience. ●

Finding and Developing a Topic

To develop an essay relating reading to experience, you need to use not only invention strategies that help you remember and explore your experiences but also different strategies that help you use the reading in productive ways.

The strategies listed here suggest approaches you can take to fulfill the assignment. You may not need to follow every one of the suggestions or to follow the suggestions in the order in which they are given. But you will find them helpful as guidelines. Excerpts from the writing of one student, Doxis Doxiadis, are included to show some of the strategies he used to write his essay, "Facing a Different Culture" (pp. 98–100). All of his mechanical errors have been corrected so that you can focus on his idea development.

By comparing Doxis's composing strategies with those of Rolando Niella, who wrote on a similar topic in his essay "Barriers" (pp. 16–18), you can see how the process of writing an essay relating reading to experience differs from the process of writing an essay drawn only from experience.

Reviewing Your Writing and Selecting a Reading

The first step in finding or developing a topic can be to reread all of the assigned readings to determine which one you want to discuss in your essay. A more efficient approach is to review all the writing you have done so far about the readings: the Write before You Read entries, your marginal annotations or reading notes, your journal entries, and any notes you might have taken during class discussions. After reading what you have written, you will see which subject has been of interest to you or which passages remind you of experiences you want to write about. You may then be able to select a reading quickly. If you still cannot decide, discuss the choices with a classmate or with your instructor.

A STUDENT WRITER AT WORK

After reviewing his writing, Doxis decided he would write about LaRay Barna's "Intercultural Communication Stumbling Blocks." In explaining how the journal helped him to choose to write about Barna's article, Doxis said: "My journal reminded me that I thought the article was interesting. But also, my journal didn't say enough. I wanted to think more about what Barna was saying. Is it true? Is it complete?"

Doxis's Reactions to Barna's Article, As Revealed in His Journal

> This essay about intercultural communication is very interesting to me, as I believe it would be to any international student. I liked especially what the international students were saying, and I must say that I agree with most of what they say. I don't mind the friendly look of Americans, but I find it a little bit strange. When someone you don't know smiles at you, you don't really know how to react since you are not used to it. It is true that Americans smile too much and are overfriendly but not true friends. You might get the impression that you are very close to someone but you might just be another acquaintance for him. It is often embarrassing to talk to people you have hardly met about problems they are having since this is not very common in my country. In Greece people will be friendly to a stranger but will not be friends, and the stranger knows that. Here, on the other hand, everyone behaves as though you are his best friend and this is quite confusing. However, I don't believe that Americans have friendships in order to gain something. In general, however, I agree with the essay.

Rereading and Taking Notes on the Source

Reread the reading you have selected. Knowing that you will be writing about this reading, read carefully: you will need to present the author's ideas fairly and accurately in your essay. One or more of these strategies may be helpful:

1. Make additional annotations. Connect the ideas you are reading about with experiences you remember. If any of your experiences contradict what the author is saying, make note of them.
2. Take notes, recording the author's key ideas or main facts.
3. Review the discussion questions following the reading, and write down answers to the most relevant questions.
4. Decide which passages from the reading you are most likely to refer

to in your own essay, and mark them by underlining or circling them or copying them over into your notebook.

A STUDENT WRITER AT WORK

In describing the process he went through, Doxis said:

> I usually do not make notes on the articles. I write down [on another sheet of paper] what parts or ideas I want to use or the ones I disagree about and then write down some quotes. But I never mark the article. I do not like writing on articles because I cannot use them again without emphasizing the same points and finding the same ideas.

Look at some of Doxis's notes. He listed key information and quotations from Barna's article that he thought he might want to use in his paper.

Doxis's Reading Notes

- Americans behave too friendly—smile a lot, superficial
- Problems with language—misunderstanding
- People offended (foreigners) by American actions
- Different customs, values
- Stereotypes
- Different ideas, behaviors, and likings
- Anxiety
- QUOTATIONS:
  - (paragraph 2) "The reason why certain foreigners may think that Americans are superficial—and they are, some Americans even recognize this—is that they talk and smile too much."
  - (paragraph 15) "A clash of values can lead to poor communication and result in misunderstanding and hurt feelings."
  - (paragraph 12) "Stereotypes are stumbling blocks for communicators because they interfere with objective viewing of stimuli."
  - (paragraph 13) "Another deterrent to an understanding between persons of differing cultures or ethnic groups is the tendency to evaluate . . . rather than to try to completely comprehend the thoughts and feelings expressed."
  - (paragraph 16) "The presence of high anxiety/tension is very common in cross-cultural experiences because of the uncertainties present."

Selecting and Developing Experiences That Relate to the Reading

In addition to selecting material from the reading, you also need to select experiences that support or contradict some of the statements made by the author. You may already know what you are going to write about, but the following suggestions may be helpful in developing specific details and examples:

1. Use one or more invention strategies (making a list, freewriting, looping, cubing) or any other strategy that you find productive to uncover and develop experiences that you can write about in your essay.

A STUDENT WRITER AT WORK
Doxis's List of His Own Problems

- Learning idioms
- Understanding pronouns
- Being on time
- Their personal questions
- Their jokes
- Making friends—Americans avoid foreign students (but they act friendly)
- Different habits

2. Speak to friends who may have had similar experiences. You can use one of their experiences or reactions to emphasize a point you want to make. You may also use an example or comment made by a classmate during a class discussion of the reading.

A STUDENT WRITER AT WORK

Curious as to what an American citizen would think of the Barna article, Doxis spoke to someone he knew on campus. He included the result of that discussion in his paper:

> While I was writing this essay, I had a conversation with an American friend of mine who couldn't even understand the topic of my essay. He didn't believe that there could be important differences in the behavior of people even if they came from a different country.

Doxis also spoke to a friend from Saudi Arabia, who told him about a specific miscommunication between Americans and Saudis. He decided to use that example in his paper.

3. Make a list showing the relationship between the parts of the reading you will refer to and the specific experiences you will describe.

A STUDENT WRITER AT WORK

In describing how he made a list showing how he related experiences to the article, Doxis said:

After I wrote the main themes, I thought about my experiences and I added some factors or took out some others that did not seem that important. Then I went back to the points from the article [his reading notes] and found some quotes that could fit in my paper. I do not remember how many I did find, but from those I chose only a few. I then took points from the article, and under each point listed personal experiences on these points; then I made a list of not mentioned points.

Doxis's List of Major Points and Examples

I. language problem
- idioms/expressions
   "beat it"
   "hot dog"
   pronunciation

II. language not the only problem
- values/habits
   personal questions
   Americans superficial
- hurt feelings and misunderstanding
   Saudi Arabia/soles of feet
   jokes/insults

III. things not developed enough by Barna
   Americans avoid foreigners
   pace of life/Levine's essay

This new combined list would act as a preliminary organizational plan for Doxis's essay.

Focusing Your Thoughts

After spending time taking notes on the reading and generating your own ideas, it is useful to stop and think about what you want to focus on in your essay.

A STUDENT WRITER AT WORK

Doxis knew the general focus of his essay almost from the time he received the assignment: he wanted to relate the ideas in Barna's essay to his own experience. By taking notes, talking with other students, and making lists, he began to see that he would focus specifically on two of the stumbling blocks Barna discusses: language and nonverbal signs. This was a decision he made mentally; he did not write out a focal point until he began drafting the essay.

ACTIVITY: *Focusing your thoughts*

Reread everything you have written in connection with the reading selection you will discuss: the Write before You Read entry, journal entries, lists, freewriting, class notes. If you haven't done so already, decide what the specific focus of your essay will be. As a start, decide which of the author's ideas you will write about. (You do not have to discuss every idea in an article.) Ask yourself, "What do I want to show?" Try to answer this question by formulating a sentence that can act as a focal point, to indicate what your essay will be about. To help you shape your ideas further, explain your focus to a small group of classmates to see if they understand what your essay will cover.   ●

If you are not yet ready to establish a focal point, you may want to write a trial draft of your essay, to use the drafting process to discover what you want to show in your essay. Remember that in writing a trial draft, you do not have to try to write a complete paper. You can begin in the middle if you don't have an introduction, and if you can't think of an ending, you can just stop. But look back at the middle and see what issues and examples are most important to you. Decide what ideas keep emerging. Then write a sentence that can act as a focal point for your essay. This sentence does not have to appear exactly as it will appear in your final paper. It can be revised as you continue to work on your essay.

If you are a writer who needs an even more structured approach to writing a draft, continue reading for guidelines on organizing an essay that relates reading to experience.

Organizing the Essay

At some point after developing your responses to the reading, you need to think about how you will organize your essay. Like Doxis, you may be a list maker, and an appropriate organization for your essay may emerge as you reread and take notes on a reading selection. If that is the case, you can outline your ideas and examples before you begin to write a draft. But list making may not be an approach you are comfortable with. Or perhaps your early efforts on this particular assignment will not result in the discovery of a logical organization. In that case, you may need to write one or more drafts to explore your subject further and to see what logical organization does emerge. When you are ready to structure your writing, you can follow the guidelines given here.

Like the personal essay, an essay relating reading to experience needs a carefully constructed arrangement: a beginning, a middle, and an ending. These sections of an academic essay are known, respectively, as the *introduction*, the *body*, and the *conclusion*.

1. Introduction

The purpose of the introduction is to focus on the topic: to tell the readers what the essay is about. The introduction serves to involve readers in your perspective on the topic and to supply the information they need to understand the purpose of the essay. This is usually accomplished in one or two paragraphs.

You can choose from a variety of approaches to involve your readers in the topic at the beginning of your essay. For example, you can provide background information on your topic (see Mead and Metraux, p. 74), quote a famous saying (see Levine and Wolff, p. 89), tell a brief story or anecdote (see Sarton, p. 29), make a shocking statement (see Neusner, p. 130), or ask a question that invites your readers to reconsider their position on the subject or identify with the material you are about to present.

The introduction is flexible. Its content and form are dependent on your subject matter and individual writing style. But there are certain features your readers will need and expect to see in an introduction to an essay relating reading to experience.

COMMON FEATURES OF THE INTRODUCTION

The introduction of your essay relating reading to experience should accomplish three things, though not necessarily in this order:

1. Identify the reading by title (within quotation marks) and author (full name).
2. Summarize the reading.
3. Indicate the focus of your paper: the relationship of the reading to your experience.

It can be difficult to write a fully developed introduction in a first draft. You can spend hours trying to write the "perfect" introduction before you even get started on the body of the essay. To save yourself valuable time, you might want to follow this advice: In the first draft of your introduction, simply identify and summarize the reading and then indicate how it relates to your experiences. You can later add the background material that will involve readers in your topic and supply the information they need to understand the purpose of the essay.

A STUDENT WRITER AT WORK

Doxis took the preceding advice to write the first draft of his introduction: he simply summarized the article and showed its relationship to real-life experiences.

First Draft of Doxis's Introduction

LaRay Barna states in her essay "Intercultural Communication Stumbling Blocks" a number of reasons that do not allow, or make more difficult, communication between Americans and foreigners. Most of the reasons that she explains are unfortunately true, and I, as a foreign student, have experienced almost every one during my visits in the U.S.

Reviewer's Comments

After reading Doxis's review draft, one reviewer made this comment: "The introduction would work better with more detailed background information—about you, about Barna's article, or more about other students, or something like that." Doxis then revised his paper.

Revision of Doxis's Introduction

My first visit in the U.S. was quite a disappointment. I expected to find a lot of new friends in this country, but I soon realized that this would not be so easy. A number of problems, generated from the first minute I stepped into this country, did not allow me to fulfill my expectations and forced me to seek the company of other foreigners with similar cultural backgrounds to my own. These problems, discussed in LaRay Barna's article "Intercultural Communication Stumbling Blocks," are experienced, to different extents, by most foreign students and force them to form groups among themselves in order to find shelter where their problems can be shared and understood.

ACTIVITY: *Evaluating introductions*

The following passages are introductions to student essays relating reading to experience. Some are first drafts, others are revisions; all have been edited for errors. Working in a small group, evaluate each introduction. Read the introductions in two ways:

1. Look for the common features of an introduction:
   a. *Identification of the reading:* Has the writer included the name of the author and the title of the article being discussed?
   b. *Summary of the reading:* Can you tell what the reading is about by reading this summary?
   c. *A focus:* Can you tell what the writer will discuss in the essay?
2. Examine your response. Discuss your overall impression of each introduction with your classmates. Does it involve you in the topic? (Does it make you want to read the rest of the essay?) Why or why not? Do you like the writing style? Why or why not? If you think the introduction should be revised, what suggestions would you have for the writer? Allow for differences of opinion in your group.

A

Friends. Whenever this word comes to my mind, images of my friends will pop up. The friendships I shared with these friends may vary enormously, ranging from those of bosom friends to those of casual acquaintances. As Judith Viorst depicts in her article "Friends, Good Friends—and Such Good Friends," friends can be grouped into different categories, according to the nature of interaction and level of intensity of the relationship. Among them are special-interest friends, crossroads friends, and historical friends. As Viorst does, I can also classify my friends into different categories; however, I find that the boundary between these categories is not a rigid one. For as our friendship grows and deepens, one of my friends, Mimi, can be best described as a special-interest, crossroads, and historical friend at the same time.

AGNES

B

We have learned many different authors' views in the matters of friendship and cross-cultural communication. I would like to discuss Margaret Mead and Rhoda Metraux's "On Friendship," where they write about what friendships are like in other countries and compare this to their personal view on how Americans consider friendship. Since I am a new foreign student in the U.S., I would like to compare their views with my own personal experiences.

HANS

C

One thing about myself that I can say without any hesitation is that I'm not a quiet type of person. But this saying is true only when I'm at home in Thailand. Back home, I'm very outgoing, and I love to be surrounded by people that I like and feel comfortable with: my friends. I have a lot of friends. I talk and laugh a lot with them. Back home, my life is great, and I'm content by that fact. The problem is that I don't understand why I became a different person the moment I set foot in America for the first time.

NUALPAN

D

When I first came to college in the United States, all I could think of was how I would get along with American students. But soon I found out that I was facing a new problem: time synchronization. I couldn't understand how it was possible for professors and students to be so exact about time when I had always lived in a country where five minutes more or less would not mean a thing. Reading Robert Levine's article, "Social Time: The Heartbeat of Culture," was very interesting to me, for I saw my own problem through the eyes of a man who had the exact experience as I had trying to adjust to the time sense of another country.

PATRICIA

●

2. Body

The body of the paper is its longest section. In several paragraphs, you develop the general idea stated in your introduction. The body therefore consists of an explanation of the reading through paraphrased and quoted references. (See Part Five on paraphrasing and quoting.) It also consists of descriptions of personal experiences. The focus of your discussion should be on the relationship between the ideas in the reading and your experiences. There are several ways to organize this group of paragraphs.

SUGGESTED ORGANIZATIONAL PATTERNS

None of the patterns listed below represents a rigid formula. You may try variations on these structures or devise another structure that is better suited to your topic. You can use the drafting process to experiment with organization; these first attempts can later be revised.

1. *Explore several ideas from the reading one by one, devoting at least one paragraph to each idea.* State the idea from the reading; your statement can appear at the beginning of a new paragraph. Explain the author's point. Then in the paragraph (you may need more than one paragraph), describe your experiences in detail to show how they relate to the idea. Repeat this procedure for each idea you want to discuss.

   Be sure that the ideas are presented in a logical order. Here are two possibilities:
   a. Begin with what you think is the less or least important idea and end with the most important, or vice versa.
   b. First discuss the ideas that your experiences support, and then discuss the ideas that your experiences contradict.
2. *Explore one major idea from the reading.* Explain one of the author's major ideas. Then describe one or more of your own experiences in detail to show how they support or contradict that idea. Most of the body will be devoted to a discussion of your experiences, but references to the reading are necessary to remind readers of points made in the article and to reveal the full meaning of the experiences.
3. *Explore several ideas from the reading, and then explore one or more ideas that the reading does not develop enough or neglects altogether.*
   • *First part:* State an idea from the reading that you will discuss; your statement can appear at the beginning of a paragraph. Explain the author's point. Then in the paragraph (you may need more than one paragraph), de-

scribe your experiences in detail to show how they relate to the reading. Repeat this procedure for each idea you want to discuss.

- *Second part:* State an idea that the reading ignores. Provide specific, detailed information that is not included in the reading to show how it relates to your idea. Repeat this procedure for each idea you want to discuss.

A STUDENT WRITER AT WORK

Doxis's reading notes showed him that he was interested in discussing two ideas from Barna's article (language and nonverbal communication) and two ideas that he felt Barna did not develop enough (American avoidance of foreigners and the pace of life). He therefore decided to organize his essay using the third organizational pattern in the list just presented. The fifth and sixth paragraphs of his eight-paragraph essay are reprinted here. The ideas that are discussed are underlined. Editorial comments in the left margin highlight the ideas and the examples that support those ideas.

Paragraphs from Doxis's Essay:

idea from the reading

Another true notion that Barna discusses is that Americans often do not realize that customs and habits are different between people from different countries. While I was writing this essay, I had a conversation with an American friend of mine who couldn't even understand the topic of my essay. He didn't believe that there could be important differences in the behavior of people even if they came from a different country.

specific experience related to the reading

reference to an idea not developed enough in the reading

Barna's article, however, leaves some things underdeveloped. Americans avoid foreigners just as foreigners avoid Americans. Even though most Americans want to consider themselves good hosts and open-minded people, they are often embarrassed by foreigners and do not feel comfortable in front of them. They are afraid of giving them a bad impression, and they don't know what could possibly offend them. So sometimes they prefer to avoid them or at least to leave the first move to the foreigner, a move that doesn't come often.

information not emphasized in the reading

3. Conclusion

The conclusion grows out of the rest of the essay. The important points have already been covered; now is the time to discuss their implications. If your essay is very long, you might want to review the main points of your paper. Even if your paper is short, it is a good idea to remind readers of the main focus of your paper. Once that is accomplished, there are several strategies you can use to bring your essay to its end.

SUGGESTIONS FOR A CONCLUDING DISCUSSION

In concluding your essay relating reading to experience, you can use one or more of these strategies:

1. Emphasize the importance of what has been said.
2. Invite readers to apply the knowledge or insight that you gained from your reading and writing to their own lives.
3. Predict future experiences or state hope for the future.
4. Discuss the effect that your reading and writing have had on your outlook on the topic or on your life.

Even though the conclusion is a natural outgrowth of the rest of the essay, it can be difficult to write. You may need several tries before you are satisfied. At first, you can just write one sentence to show that your paper has come to an end. Later you can revise your work.

A STUDENT WRITER AT WORK

First Draft of Doxis's Conclusion

> It is easy to understand why there are so many problems be-
> tween Americans and foreigners, but I can't see any solutions to
> this situation.

Doxis's Final Revision of His Conclusion

> Now that I am finally acclimated, I can turn back and laugh at
> the problems and anxieties I faced initially. This is not, how-
> ever, a laughing matter. A lot of other foreign students will face
> crushing pressure resulting from the aforementioned problems,
> which will make them, until they finally surpass these problems,
> curse their decision to attend an American college. Unfortu-
> nately, I cannot provide a solution to this problem, so I can only
> hope that someone else will find a way to lift the burden inter-
> national students carry in a foreign country.

ACTIVITY: Organizing the essay

Either in your head or on paper (or both), sketch out a preliminary organizational plan for your essay. Read over your reading notes to see which and how many ideas in the reading you want to discuss. If you plan to discuss several ideas, the first suggested organizational pattern for the body of your paper may work best. If only one major idea has captured your interest, the second pattern may fit your material. If you are interested in discussing ideas that the reading ignores, the third pattern may be most useful for you. Of course, other alternatives exist. If a pattern has not emerged from your material, ask your instructor for advice.   ●

Writing a Draft to Present for Review

Prepare a draft of your essay to be read and reviewed by your classmates and instructor. Before you bring your paper to class, use the checklist for content.

Checklist for Content: Self-Evaluation

Does my essay provide all of the following details?

1. The title and the name of the author of the reading I am writing about
2. A summary of the reading
3. A focal point that reveals the relationship between the ideas in the reading and my experience
4. Paraphrased and quoted references to the reading
5. Examples of experiences that support points made about the reading

If the answer to any of the questions is no, either add the missing material to your draft before bringing it in for review or prepare to explain to your reviewers and instructor what you will include in your revision of this essay. If you are not sure what to include, ask for advice.

Peer Reviewing

Bring your draft to class to exchange papers with your classmates. Review each other's papers by examining (1) what you like about the paper and (2) what you think can be done to improve it. Determine whether the writer has successfully related material from the reading to life experiences in order to illuminate, evaluate, or test the validity of the ideas contained in the reading. Use the peer review form (p. 57) and the following questions to shape your responses.

1. Is the focus clear?
   a. If the answer is yes, what is the focal point of the essay?
   b. If the answer is no, can you suggest a way in which the focus could be clarified?
2. Does the writer make enough references (through summary, para-

phrase, and quotation) to the reading to reveal its purpose and content?

    a. If the answer is yes, which references did you find most helpful? Why?

    b. If the answer is no, where can more references be added? Can you suggest specific references that might be helpful? If so, what are they?

3. Does the writer provide enough detailed summaries of personal experiences to support points made about the reading?

    a. If the answer is yes, which examples do the best job of clarifying a point?

    b. If the answer is no, where should more detailed examples be added? Should any examples be deleted?

Evaluate the organization of the essay, and raise and answer any other questions that you think will help the writer to improve the paper.

Revising

After you have received feedback on your draft from your classmates and instructor, revise your paper by asking these questions (see pp. 60–61 for fuller discussion):

- What should I keep?
- What should I add?
- What should I delete?
- What should I change?
- What should I rearrange?
- What should I rethink?

Completing the Essay

Once you have revised the essay, read it over to evaluate the essay as a whole. Make sure that there is a smooth flow from paragraph to paragraph and that every part fits logically. Check to see that the issues raised in the introduction are discussed throughout the body and that the conclusion grows out of the rest of the essay. Proofread and edit the essay, and prepare a neat final manuscript to hand in for evaluation.

Y our next essay assignment will be an analysis of an argumentative essay (see Essay Assignment 3, p. 154). An argumentative essay is one in which a writer presents a strong opinion on an issue and attempts to convince the reader to accept or support the writer's viewpoint or to understand the importance of the issue. To write your own essay, you will need to determine how effective an author's argument is by determining what the author says, analyzing how well the author's points are made, and deciding what points may have been ignored. You will also present and support your opinion in reaction to ideas discussed in the reading. The challenge in such an assignment is to represent another writer's ideas fairly and accurately whether you agree or disagree with the point of view presented.

To fulfill this assignment, you will use some invention strategies as well as many of the strategies you used to develop your essay relating reading to experience, including summarizing, paraphrasing, quoting, and citing and documenting sources (discussed in detail in Part Five). In addition, you will learn how to read and respond critically and to present your own views forcefully.

CHAPTER FIVE

Responding to Reading

Reading Strategies

The reading selections in this chapter are argumentative essays. In these essays, the authors are presenting their opinions, favoring one side of an issue. This means that the material has been carefully arranged so that you, the reader, will be convinced to believe what the author believes or will be led to recognize the importance of the issue discussed.

One of these readings will become the source material for your next essay.

Before Reading

1. Follow the instructions for the Write before You Read activity that precedes each reading selection.
2. Read the biographical information before each reading.
3. Preview the reading, to help you plan the amount of time it will take you to read:
   a. Look at its length.
   b. Look at the length of the paragraphs.

Reading

The first time you read each selection, read for overall meaning. It is not necessary at this stage to understand every word. Aim to understand the most important general ideas in a paragraph or section. Note how supporting examples serve to clarify or illustrate ideas. As you read, relate the information to what you already know about the topic and to what you have just read. You may find yourself questioning what you are reading and examining your own views.

Rereading

As you reread, keep track of your responses. Annotate or take notes on the reading selection. You might make a list of key points along with the examples that support those points. You could underline or copy down sections of the essay or article that seem to present the author's overall point or argument.

Making a Journal Entry

Write in your journal to discuss your responses to the reading. For example, you can do one or more of the following:

- Discuss ideas you agree with.
- Discuss ideas you disagree with.
- Write about specific experiences or ideas that relate to the topic. You may include experiences or ideas that support or ones that contradict what the author has said.
- Examine how the author uses examples to illustrate a point. Note examples that are memorable. Note examples that help to clarify a point.
- Identify passages to which you had a strong reaction, either negative or positive.
- Formulate questions that you want to ask in class about the reading.

Reading Critically

Analyzing an argumentative essay requires critical reading. Critical reading involves not just identifying what the author is saying but also determining whether the author has argued convincingly or effectively.

You can appreciate the quality of an argument without necessarily agreeing with the author's point of view. An essay may be effective if the author has persuaded you by the end or if the author has clarified the issue for you. In other words, an argument can be valid even if you disagree with the author.

GUIDELINES

Guidelines for Analyzing an Argumentative Essay

1. Summarize the author's purpose and major point. ("What is the author trying to prove?")
2. Evaluate the supporting material. ("Does the evidence support the author's point?")

Summarizing the Author's Purpose and Major Point

Summarizing enables you to examine an essay's content and structure to develop an understanding of the author's meaning. By including a summary of the reading selection in your own essay, you demonstrate your understanding and clarify meaning for your own readers.

Your aim in summarizing an argumentative essay is to identify the author's purpose and the author's major point. (The major point in an argumentative essay is sometimes referred to as a *thesis*, a *claim*, or a *proposition*.) Identifying purpose and major point will provide the gist, or essence, of the argument.

To identify the author's purpose and major point, you need to answer the question, What is the author trying to prove? For example, the author of an argumentative essay may be trying to prove that a condition exists or that something is true (e.g., "Adjustment to college life is difficult for many"), that one thing is more (or less) desirable than another (e.g., "Lecturing is a superior form of teaching"), or that some change should be instituted to solve a problem (e.g., "To allow students more freedom of choice, the number of distribution requirements should be reduced").

In some essays, the author's thesis may be clearly stated in the introduction. But when this is not the case, you need to read through the entire essay to uncover the major point. Your task is to examine each of the points the author makes in support of an argument and to try to understand how the points are connected. Then, in a one-sentence summary, create a statement that captures the gist of the argument. Ask yourself, What is the most important issue to this author? Which issue includes all of the points made?

SUMMARIZING AN ARGUMENTATIVE ESSAY

In the Introduction to this book, you were asked to read, annotate, and write a journal entry on Sydney J. Harris's essay "What True Education Should Do" (p. 9). Reread the essay now so that you can follow the analysis of the essay in this chapter.

Author's purpose and major point

What is Harris trying to prove? Harris acknowledges in the first paragraph that most people think education means stuffing knowledge into students. But he rejects that definition in the second paragraph, when he says that genuine education means drawing out what is already in the student. He is making a judgment in his essay and is trying to prove that one thing (teaching students to analyze) is more desirable than another (stuffing knowledge into students). A one-sentence summary of the essay could be:

> Sydney J. Harris believes that true education means helping students to think for themselves rather than simply filling them with information.

Harris's purpose is not to change his readers' opinion but primarily to stimulate them to think.

Evaluating the Supporting Material

All points made in an argument should be supported. To decide whether an argument is strong or weak, you need to examine the material the author has used to support the major point. Supporting material consists of (a) *evidence*—examples, facts (including statistics), and opinions—and (b) *appeals* to the needs and values of the audience.

It is not always possible to know when a point is valid, when evidence is sound, or when the appeals to the audience are appropriate. But there are many ways to verify and evaluate information and ideas presented in a reading selection. When you analyze an argumentative essay, you can first rely on your background knowledge and the knowledge you gain through class discussions of the reading. As you probably discovered while writing an essay relating reading to experience, many facts stated by another writer can be verified by your own experience or by the experiences of people you know. Other facts can be verified by consulting an authority such as your instructor, a book, an academic essay, or a news article.

Your evaluation of the emotional appeals a writer makes to an audience can also be based on your background knowledge. By analyzing the intended audience with your classmates and instructor, you can come to an understanding of the relationship between the writer and the readers.

ANALYZING AN ARGUMENT

To determine the soundness of the evidence and the appropriateness of the appeals, ask these questions. Again, use Harris's essay as an example.

What is the gist of the argument?
Harris claims that genuine education is not stuffing knowledge into students but rather involves teaching students to think for themselves.

What evidence is used to support the argument?
Harris provides evidence in the form of example (the example of an overworked college student), fact (the fact that many of the discussions about the content of education are concerned with what should go into the student), opinions of experts (Socrates, Hocking, Hamilton), and Harris's own opinions.

Is there enough evidence?
The amount of evidence that any writer provides is dependent on the length of the essay and the complexity of the subject. In a long essay or one that covers a complex topic, such as a research essay on the safety of nuclear power plants, readers will need and expect several examples to support each side of the issue. In a shorter essay, two or three examples may be adequate.

Since Harris was writing a column for a newspaper, he had to limit the amount of evidence he included. It was therefore necessary for him to select evidence carefully to support his point. What is more important in an analysis of his essay, then, is not the amount but the quality of evidence. That leads to the next question.

Are the examples representative?
In an essay, a writer must limit the number of examples used to support the truth of a generalization. Therefore, the examples that are included should be representative, that is, similar to or typical of many other examples that are not included.

To show that students who are stuffed with knowledge receive an inferior education, Harris provides the example of a college student who says that he spends so much time studying that he does not have the opportunity to learn anything. In analyzing the evidence, you should ask, "Is the experience of this student typical of the experience of most college students?" If your answer is yes, you may conclude that the evidence is representative and that it therefore strengthens the argument. If your answer is no, you may conclude that the argument is weak.

Are the opinions provided by qualified sources?

When writers use opinions to support generalizations, they can include both their own opinions and the testimony of others. You must decide whether the sources of the opinions are qualified to give an opinion on the subject.

In analyzing whether an author is qualified to give an opinion on the subject, you need to know something about the author. By reading the biographical information that precedes "What True Education Should Do," you can learn that Harris was a writer for major newspapers in one of America's largest cities. You can also learn that Harris had his own syndicated column, a place where he could regularly express his opinion, and that this column was published in newspapers in several countries. You can deduce that Harris was a respected writer with a large reading audience. However, there is no evidence that Harris was a professional educator. If you determine that he is qualified to comment on the subject of education because he is a respected writer, you may conclude that his opinion strengthens the argument. On the other hand, if you are not willing to accept his opinion because there is no evidence that he was a professional educator, you may conclude that his argument is weakened. (Actually, further investigation would reveal that Harris also taught at the University of Chicago.)

Harris includes opinions from several sources presented as experts: Socrates, William Ernest Hocking, and Edith Hamilton. You must decide whether these experts are qualified to comment on the subject of education. You can rely on your own background knowledge, on information given by the author, or on information provided by an authority. As an educated person, you probably know that Socrates is generally regarded as one of the wisest persons of all time. His opinions are therefore highly respected. You are less likely to know of William Ernest Hocking, but Harris refers to him as "the distinguished Harvard philosopher." You may therefore assume that Hocking's comments on education are based on years of experience. No information is given about Edith Hamilton, but Harris's words suggest that she is an expert on the subject of Socrates. If you need more background information about Hamilton, you may want to consult an authority such as your instructor or a biographical source in the library. As a result of this analysis, you will probably decide that the experts are qualified. You may therefore conclude that their opinions strengthen Harris's argument. Nevertheless, you may wish that Harris had included the comments of other sources.

Are the sources biased?

Sources may be qualified but still not be reliable. Sometimes sources are biased; that is, they have a special interest in the subject that makes it impossible for them to remain objective. For example, bias can exist if an expert is being paid to advertise a product, if the expert's religious beliefs or political loyalties are involved, or if the expert has had a bad experience connected to the subject that has influenced the opinion. You cannot always know when bias exists, but if you suspect the motive of a source, including the author, you may conclude that an argument is weak. In the essay by Harris, there is little evidence of bias, although it is possible that the author had a bad experience as a student that has colored his perception. (Harris never finished college. You can speculate on how that might have influenced what he wrote.)

Is the evidence relevant?

You may find that even though you accept the qualifications of the sources, you question the relevance of the opinions. In other words, the sources may be qualified, but what they say may not be closely related to the subject of the essay. Likewise, the examples provided by the writer may be interesting but irrelevant. If this is your judgment, you may conclude that the evidence weakens the argument.

Since all of the evidence Harris provides is connected to the subject of genuine education, it may be safe to conclude that the evidence is relevant. Nevertheless, you may feel that Harris should have included other evidence to support his points.

Are the facts accurate?

A fact is defined in the dictionary as "something that has actually happened or is true." Writers often supply facts (examples, statistics, testimony) to prove or to further a point. They know these facts primarily from their experience, their reading, their observation, or their research.

Facts are considered accurate if they can be verified. For example, someone may tell you that 5 percent of the students at your university are from foreign countries. If you want to, you can verify that statement by checking with an authoritative source such as an admission officer at the university or by reading a written report from the international center. But you may not feel the need to verify the statement. If the person who gives you this information is a trustworthy source, such as a professor who specializes in teaching international students, you may simply assume that the information is accurate.

When you analyze an argument, you need to decide if the facts are accurate. Since you do not have knowledge of all facts, you are largely dependent on your trust in the writer. If, based on the criteria for evaluating sources, you decide that the sources are qualified, reliable, and unbiased, you may assume that the facts are accurate. If the opposite is true, you may question some or all of the facts provided. You may need to verify the facts by checking with an authoritative source. If you know or find that any fact is untrue, you can conclude that the argument is weak. In fact, if a writer deliberately provides untrue evidence, the writer is guilty of dishonesty, and the entire argument can be dismissed. More often, however, a writer may present only some true evidence, ignoring other evidence that does not support a point. Of course, it is possible that certain evidence is ignored simply because the author is unaware of it.

How you decide what evidence is missing is dependent on your own background knowledge of the topic. Some topics require extensive research (see Essay Assignment 4 in Part Four: "Researching a Controversy"). But it is possible to base your analysis of the readings in Part Three, which deal with the subject of teaching and learning, on what you already know or can determine through discussion with your classmates and instructor.

To support his argument that most people have the wrong idea about what education is, Harris includes the fact that "many of the discussions and controversies about the content of education . . . are concerned with what should 'go into' the student rather than with what should be taken out." If you believe that Harris is a trustworthy source, you may conclude that this fact can be verified and that it is therefore accurate. But if you think that Harris may be biased, you may wonder why he includes so few facts in his essay. You may suspect, for example, that he has ignored some facts that might weaken his argument. If you know of facts that may disprove or challenge one or more of his points, you can conclude that his argument is weak.

Is the evidence up to date?

Whether evidence is up to date depends on the subject. With certain subjects, writers must be careful to supply evidence that is available close to the time they are writing. For example, a writer writing in 1990 about the problem of nuclear waste in 1990 should rely on information known up to 1990; an argument on nuclear waste in 1990 would be weak if the writer supplied evidence only from 1972 to 1984.

With other subjects, the issue of up-to-date evidence is less important. Harris's subject of the nature of genuine education falls into that category. Since he is discussing an issue that has been discussed at least since the time of Socrates, he could but is not obligated to provide recent research on educational systems. His example is drawn from a current time so that he can show that the issue is an important one at the time he is writing. Nevertheless, you may conclude that the lack of recent research weakens Harris's argument.

Are the emotional appeals appropriate for the audience?

When a writer publishes an essay, there is an intended audience: the readers of the publication. The writer must understand the needs and values of the audience if the argument is to be effective. For example, if readers are not already interested in the subject, the writer must try to make them care about the subject.

All writers have their own set of values, which may be similar to or different from those of the readers. The writer must therefore write in such a way as to enable readers to understand, accept, or identify with the writer's values. If the readers fail to appreciate them, the argument will not be effective.

To appeal to readers who may not care about the subject, may disagree with the writer, or may not share the writer's values, the writer should consider many sides to an issue. To present only one point of view without revealing that there may be opposing viewpoints, the writer can fail to reach an audience. The audience may reject the writer's view not because the view is wrong but simply because the argument has not taken another viewpoint into account.

The language a writer uses is also important in determining the effectiveness of an argument. Writers of arguments often use words that express and arouse emotion, reveal their attitude toward their subject, and influence their readers to see things as they do. Such use of language is considered acceptable in argumentative essays. However, when writers use language in a deliberately slanting way—for example, when they cruelly attack someone rather than providing evidence to support a point or to reveal the other side of an issue—they weaken their own arguments.

Harris wrote for a major Chicago newspaper; his column was reproduced in papers in several countries. Though this was a large audience, you may assume something about them: they probably read the newspaper to discover the important issues and events of the day. If they chose to read Harris's essay on the day it was published, it may be because they valued education. Harris could therefore appeal to an audience that shared his concern about what education should accomplish. He may have selected Socrates and Hocking as sources to appeal to his readers' higher values, assuming that they too respected the ancient Greeks and Harvard University. He may have carefully chosen the words "stuff" and "a sort of animate sausage casing" to create a powerful image in the minds of his readers. By talking about students as stuffed skins rather than as human beings, he could make his readers regret any time they wasted as passive students in a classroom. They may therefore have found his argument strong.

If your own experience has been different, you might not share Harris's values. For example, you may have been educated in a system in which students are filled with information and feel nevertheless that you are a well-educated person. Therefore, you might not reject the type of educational approach that Harris assumes is bad. Since Harris's essay does not take your point of view into account, you may conclude that his argument is weak.

Are the examples appropriate for the audience?

Readers use their own experience and background knowledge to judge the validity of an argument. If the examples a writer provides contradict or do not match the readers' experience, or if the examples are extremely negative, the readers may reject the writer's point.

Harris's audience is, of course, a large one, and it would be difficult to determine whether all of these readers would like or object to Harris's example of the overworked college student. If you believe that anyone who would read an essay titled "What True Education Should Do" has probably had college experience, you might conclude that Harris's example is appropriate for the audience. If you believe that Harris's audience would not be interested in the experience of a college student, you might conclude that this example is inappropriate.

Discussing and Taking Notes

Share your journal responses and summaries in class discussions on the reading. Use the questions just discussed for analyzing the reading. During class discussions, keep notes that help you to analyze the reading selection. Write about the reading again in your journal, perhaps revising your summary or summarizing the important ideas that you and your fellow students brought up about the reading or adding reasons why you agree or disagree with the author.

READINGS

Write before You Read

The next two readings deal with the subject of student academic life. Before reading these essays, write for 10 to 15 minutes on the following topic:

> Look at the picture on the accompanying page. Then speculate on what the student in the picture may be experiencing, thinking, and feeling.

Share your speculations with your classmates.   ●

The Commencement Speech[1] You'll Never Hear
by Jacob Neusner

Jacob Neusner (b. 1932) is a university professor and distinguished scholar at Brown University in Rhode Island. As the title suggests, the commencement speech was not delivered at the college graduation but was published as an essay. "The Commencement Speech You'll Never Hear" was pub-

---

[1] **commencement speech:** talk given by an invited speaker at a graduation ceremony

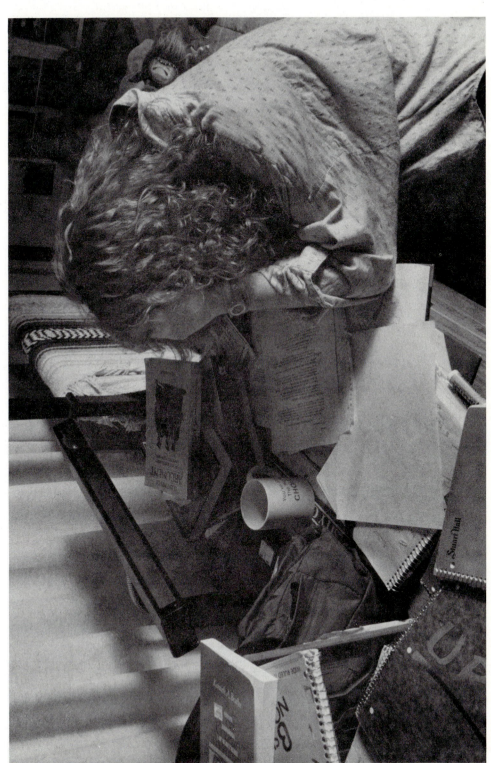

lished in the Brown University campus newspaper, the Daily Herald, *on June 12, 1981.*

We the faculty take no pride in our educational achievements with you.   1
We have prepared you for a world that does not exist, indeed, that cannot
exist. You have spent four years supposing that failure leaves no record.
You have learned at Brown that when your work goes poorly, the painless
solution is to drop out. But starting now, in the world to which you go,
failure marks you. Confronting difficulty by quitting leaves you changed.
Outside Brown, quitters are no heroes.

With us you could argue about why your errors were not errors, why   2
mediocre work really was excellent, why you could take pride in routine
and slipshod presentation. Most of you, after all, can look back on honor
grades for most of what you have done. So, here grades can have meant
little in distinguishing the excellent from the ordinary. But tomorrow, in
the world to which you go, you had best not defend errors but learn from
them. You will be ill-advised to demand praise for what does not deserve
it, and abuse those who do not give it.

For years we created an altogether forgiving world, in which whatever   3
slight effort you gave was all that was demanded. When you did not keep
appointments, we made new ones. When your work came in beyond the
deadline, we pretended not to care.

Worse still, when you were boring, we acted as if you were saying   4
something important. When you were garrulous and talked to hear your-
selves talk, we listened as if it mattered. When you tossed on our desks
writing upon which you had not labored, we read it and even responded,
as though you earned a response. When you were dull, we pretended you
were smart. When you were predictable, unimaginative and routine, we
listened as if to new and wonderful things. When you demanded free lunch,
we served it. And all this why?

Despite your fantasies, it was not even that we wanted to be liked by   5
you. It was that we did not want to be bothered, and the easy way out
was pretense: smiles and easy Bs.

It is conventional to quote in addresses such as these. Let me quote   6
someone you've never heard of: Prof. Carter A. Daniel, Rutgers University
(*Chronicle of Higher Education*, May 7, 1979):

> College has spoiled you by reading papers that don't deserve to be read,
> listening to comments that don't deserve a hearing, paying attention
> even to the lazy, ill-informed and rude. We had to do it, for the sake
> of education. But nobody will ever do it again. College has deprived
> you of adequate preparation for the last 50 years. It has failed you by
> being easy, free, forgiving, attentive, comfortable, interesting, unchal-
> lenging fun. Good luck tomorrow.

That is why, on this commencement day, we have nothing in which   7
to take much pride.

Oh, yes, there is one more thing. Try not to act toward your co-   8
workers and bosses as you have acted toward us. I mean, when they give
you what you want but have not earned, don't abuse them, insult them,
act out with them your parlous relationships with your parents. This too
we have tolerated. It was, as I said, not to be liked. Few professors actually
care whether or not they are liked by peer-paralyzed adolescents, fools so
shallow as to imagine professors care not about education but about pop-
ularity. It was, again, to be rid of you. So go, unlearn the lies we taught
you. To Life!   ●

Write after You Read

1. Make a journal entry on "The Commencement Speech You'll Never
   Hear," following the suggestions on p. 121.
2. Write a one-sentence summary of "The Commencement Speech
   You'll Never Hear," following the guidelines for summarizing an
   argumentative essay on pp. 121–122.   ●

Activities for Class Discussion

Working in groups of three or four students, share in the following
activities. (Activities 4 and 5 may be done by the class as a whole.)

1. Share your written summary of "The Commencement Speech You'll
   Never Hear." If you do not agree on the gist of the argument,
   discuss the reasons for the different interpretations. If your group
   cannot determine the gist of the argument, consult with another
   group or with your instructor.
2. Are there unfamiliar words or expressions? Make sure that everyone
   in the group understands the meaning of these terms:

   mediocre (2)   parlous (8)
   slipshod (2)   peer-paralyzed (8)
   garrulous (4)

   Try to guess the meaning of these and other unfamiliar words from
   the context. If your group cannot determine the meaning, consult
   with another group or with your instructor, or consult a dictionary.
3. Outline the organization of the essay. Compare your outline with
   that of another group. Discuss the similarities and differences.
4. Following the guidelines on pp. 122–128, evaluate the supporting
   material of Neusner's argument. Ask these questions:
   • What evidence is used to support the argument?
   • Is there enough evidence?
   • Are the examples representative?
   • Are the opinions provided by qualified sources?
   • Are the sources biased?

- Is the evidence relevant?
- Are the facts accurate?
- Is the evidence up to date?
- Are the emotional appeals appropriate for the audience?
- Are the examples appropriate for the audience?

While or after you analyze the argument, share what you have written in your journal. State your reasons for agreeing or disagreeing with Neusner. What evidence do you have to support or refute his points?

5. When Neusner's essay was published in the Brown University newspaper, the *Daily Herald*, it created quite a debate on the college campus. Hundreds of letters were sent to the "Letters to the Editor" section of the newspaper. Speculate on what the letters might have said.

6. Write letters in response to Neusner's essay. Decide whether each group or person should write two letters or if the task of writing the letters should be divided among the groups or individual class members.

   a. Write a letter to the editor of the *Daily Herald*, explaining your reaction to reading "The Commencement Speech You'll Never Hear." (First decide who the editor might be, consider why the editor decided to publish Neusner's essay, and determine who the readers would be if your letter was published in the newspaper.)

   b. Write a letter to Neusner, explaining your reaction to reading his essay.

After the letters have been written, share them with the whole class. Then discuss the differences between writing to the editor and writing to Neusner. Are there different examples? Are the emotional appeals to the readers different?   ●

Write before You Read

Before reading the following essay, write for 10 to 15 minutes, in or out of class, in response to this quotation, taken from the reading:

Defeat is as instructive as victory.

Write with the purpose of understanding the quotation so that you can discuss it with your classmates.   ●

College Pressures
by William Zinsser

William Zinsser (b. 1922) is an American writer, educator, and film critic. His many books include On Writing Well. *In the 1970s, Zinsser taught nonfiction writing at Yale University in Connecticut. "College Pressures," written in response to his experience at Yale, was originally published in the magazine* Blair and Ketchum's Country Journal *in 1979. This publication, which provides information on country living, has a national readership.*

Note: *The monetary figures mentioned in the reading reflect 1979 statistics and information. As you read, you can increase Zinsser's figures to match today's numbers. The basic economic problem that Zinsser discusses continues today.*

Dear Carlos: I desperately need a dean's excuse for my chem midterm which will begin in about 1 hour. All I can say is that I totally blew it this week. I've fallen incredibly, inconceivably behind.

Carlos: Help! I'm anxious to hear from you. I'll be in my room and won't leave it until I hear from you. Tomorrow is the last day for . . .

Carlos: I left town because I started bugging out again. I stayed up all night to finish a take-home make-up exam & am typing it to hand in on the 10th. It was due on the 5th. P.S. I'm going to the dentist. Pain is pretty bad.

Carlos: Probably by Friday I'll be able to get back to my studies. Right now I'm going to take a long walk. This whole thing has taken a lot out of me.

Carlos: I'm really up the proverbial creek. The problem is I really *bombed* the history final. Since I need that course for my major . . .

Carlos: Here follows a tale of woe. I went home this weekend, had to help my Mom, & caught a fever so didn't have much time to study. My professor . . .

Carlos: Aargh! Trouble. Nothing original but everything's piling up at once. To be brief, my job interview . . .

Hey Carlos, good news! I've got mononucleosis.

Who are these wretched supplicants,[1] scribbling notes so laden with   1
anxiety, seeking such miracles of postponement and balm?[2] They are men and women who belong to Branford College, one of the twelve residential colleges at Yale University, and the messages are just a few of hundreds that they left for their dean, Carlos Hortas—often slipped under his door at 4 A.M.—last year.

---

[1] **wretched supplicants:** miserable people making urgent requests for help
[2] **balm:** something that comforts

But students like the ones who wrote those notes can also be found on   2
campuses from coast to coast—especially in New England and at many
other private colleges across the country that have high academic standards
and highly motivated students. Nobody could doubt that the notes are real.
In their urgency and their gallows humor[3] they are authentic voices of a
generation that is panicky to succeed.

My own connection with the message writers is that I am master of   3
Branford College. I live in its Gothic quadrangle and know the students
well. (We have 485 of them.) I am privy to their hopes and fears—and
also to their stereo music and their piercing cries in the dead of night ("Does
anybody *ca-a-are?*"). If they went to Carlos to ask how to get through
tomorrow, they come to me to ask how to get through the rest of their
lives.

Mainly I try to remind them that the road ahead is a long one and that   4
it will have more unexpected turns than they think. There will be plenty
of time to change jobs, change careers, change whole attitudes and approaches. They don't want to hear such liberating news. They want a
map—right now—that they can follow unswervingly to career security,
financial security, Social Security and, presumably, a prepaid grave.

What I wish for all students is some release from the clammy grip of   5
the future. I wish them a chance to savor each segment of their education
as an experience in itself and not as a grim preparation for the next step.
I wish them the right to experiment, to trip and fall, to learn that defeat
is as instructive as victory and is not the end of the world.

My wish, of course, is naive. One of the few rights that America does   6
not proclaim is the right to fail. Achievement is the national god, venerated
in our media—the million-dollar athlete, the wealthy executive—and glorified in our praise of possessions. In the presence of such a potent state
religion, the young are growing up old.

I see four kinds of pressure working on college students today: economic   7
pressure, parental pressure, peer pressure, and self-induced pressure. It is
easy to look around for villains—to blame the colleges for charging too
much money, the professors for assigning too much work, the parents for
pushing their children too far, the students for driving themselves too hard.
But there are no villains; only victims.

"In the late 1960s," one dean told me, "the typical question that I got   8
from students was 'Why is there so much suffering in the world?' or 'How
can I make a contribution?' Today it's 'Do you think it would look better
for getting into law school if I did a double major in history and political
science, or just majored in one of them?' " Many other deans confirmed
this pattern. One said: "They're trying to find an edge—the intangible
something that will look better on paper if two students are about equal."

Note the emphasis on looking better. The transcript has become a sacred   9
document, the passport to security. How one appears on paper is more

---

[3] **gallows humor:** something funny but also grim

important than how one appears in person. *A* is for Admirable and *B* is for Borderline, even though, in Yale's official system of grading, *A* means "excellent" and *B* means "very good." Today, looking very good is no longer good enough, especially for students who hope to go on to law school or medical school. They know that entrance into the better schools will be an entrance into the better law firms and better medical practices where they will make a lot of money. They also know that the odds are harsh. Yale Law School, for instance, matriculates 170 students from an applicant pool of 3,700; Harvard enrolls 550 from a pool of 7,000.

It's all very well for those of us who write letters of recommendation   10 for our students to stress the qualities of humanity that will make them good lawyers or doctors. And it's nice to think that admission officers are really reading our letters and looking for the extra dimension of commitment or concern. Still, it would be hard for a student not to visualize these officers shuffling so many transcripts studded with *A*s that they regard a *B* as positively shameful.

The pressure is almost as heavy on students who just want to graduate   11 and get a job. Long gone are the days of the "gentleman's *C*," when students journeyed through college with a certain relaxation, sampling a wide variety of courses—music, art, philosophy, classics, anthropology, poetry, religion—that would send them out as liberally educated men and women. If I were an employer I would rather employ graduates who have this range and curiosity than those who narrowly pursued safe subjects and high grades. I know countless students whose inquiring minds exhilarate me. I like to hear the play of their ideas. I don't know if they are getting *A*s or *C*s, and I don't care. I also like them as people. The country needs them, and they will find satisfying jobs. I tell them to relax. They can't.

Nor can I blame them. They live in a brutal economy. Tuition, room,   12 and board at most private colleges now comes to at least $7,000, not counting books and fees. This might seem to suggest that the colleges are getting rich. But they are equally battered by inflation. Tuition covers only 60 percent of what it costs to educate a student, and ordinarily the remainder comes from what colleges receive in endowments, grants, and gifts. Now the remainder keeps being swallowed by the cruel costs—higher every year—of just opening the doors. Heating oil is up. Insurance is up. Postage is up. Health-premium costs are up. Everything is up. Deficits are up. We are witnessing in America the creation of a brotherhood of paupers—colleges, parents, and students, joined by the common bond of debt.

Today it is not unusual for a student, even if he works part time at   13 college and full time during the summer, to accrue $5,000 in loans after four years—loans that he must start to repay within one year after graduation. Exhorted at commencement to go forth into the world, he is already behind as he goes forth. How could he not feel under pressure throughout college to prepare for this day of reckoning?[4] I have used "he," incidentally, only for brevity. Women at Yale are under no less pressure to justify their

---

[4] **day of reckoning:** time when something must be paid back

expensive education to themselves, their parents, and society. In fact, they are probably under more pressure. For although they leave college superbly equipped to bring fresh leadership to traditionally male jobs, society hasn't yet caught up with this fact.

Along with economic pressure goes parental pressure. Inevitably, the   14
two are deeply intertwined.

I see many students taking pre-medical courses with joyless tenacity.   15
They go off to their labs as if they were going to the dentist. It saddens me because I know them in other corners of their life as cheerful people.

"Do you want to go to medical school?" I ask them.   16

"I guess so," they say, without conviction, or "Not really."   17

"Then why are you going?"   18

"Well, my parents want me to be a doctor. They're paying all this   19
money and . . ."

Poor students, poor parents. They are caught in one of the oldest webs   20
of love and duty and guilt. The parents mean well; they are trying to steer their sons and daughters toward a secure future. But the sons and daughters want to major in history or classics or philosophy—subjects with no "practical" value. Where's the payoff on the humanities? It's not easy to persuade such loving parents that the humanities do indeed pay off. The intellectual faculties developed by studying subjects like history and classics—an ability to synthesize and relate, to weigh cause and effect, to see events in perspective—are just the faculties that make creative leaders in business or almost any general field. Still, many fathers would rather put their money on courses that point toward a specific profession—courses that are pre-law, pre-medical, pre-business, or, as I sometimes heard it put, "pre-rich."

But the pressure on students is severe. They are truly torn. One part   21
of them feels obligated to fulfill their parents' expectations; after all, their parents are older and presumably wiser. Another part tells them that the expectations that are right for their parents are not right for them.

I know a student who wants to be an artist. She is very obviously an   22
artist and will be a good one—she has already had several modest local exhibits. Meanwhile she is growing as a well-rounded person and taking humanistic subjects that will enrich the inner resources out of which her art will grow. But her father is strongly opposed. He thinks that an artist is a "dumb" thing to be. The student vacillates and tries to please everybody. She keeps up with her art somewhat furtively and takes some of the "dumb" courses her father wants her to take—at least they are dumb courses for her. She is a free spirit on a campus of tense students—no small achievement in itself—and she deserves to follow her muse.[5]

Peer pressure and self-induced pressure are also intertwined, and they   23
begin almost at the beginning of freshman year.

"I had a freshman student I'll call Linda," one dean told me, "who   24

---

[5] **muse:** artistic inspiration

came in and said she was under terrible pressure because her roommate, Barbara, was much brighter and studied all the time. I couldn't tell her that Barbara had come in two hours earlier to say the same thing about Linda."

The story is almost funny—except that it's not. It's symptomatic of 25 all the pressures put together. When every student thinks every other student is working harder and doing better, the only solution is to study harder still. I see students going off to the library every night after dinner and coming back when it closes at midnight. I wish they would sometimes forget about their peers and go to a movie. I hear the clacking of typewriters in the hours before dawn. I see the tension in their eyes when exams are approaching and papers are due: *"Will I get everything done?"*

Probably they won't. They will get sick. They will get "blocked." They 26 will sleep. They will oversleep. They will bug out. *Hey Carlos, help!*

Part of the problem is that they do more than they are expected to do. 27 A professor will assign five-page papers. Several students will start writing ten-page papers to impress him. Then more students will write ten-page papers, and a few will raise the ante to fifteen. Pity the poor student who is still just doing the assignment.

"Once you have twenty or thirty percent of the student population 28 deliberately overexerting," one dean points out, "it's bad for everybody. When a teacher gets more and more effort from his class, the student who is doing normal work can be perceived as not doing well. The tactic works, psychologically."

Why can't the professor just cut back and not accept longer papers? 29 He can, and he probably will. But by then the term will be half over and the damage done. Grade fever is highly contagious and not easily reversed. Besides, the professor's main concern is with his course. He knows his students only in relation to the course and doesn't know that they are also overexerting in their other courses. Nor is it really his business. He didn't sign up for dealing with the student as a whole person and with all the emotional baggage the student brought along from home. That's what deans, masters, chaplains, and psychiatrists are for.

To some extent this is nothing new: a certain number of professors 30 have always been self-contained islands of scholarship and shyness, more comfortable with books than with people. But the new pauperism has widened the gap still further, for professors who actually like to spend time with students don't have as much time to spend. They also are overexerting. If they are young, they are busy trying to publish in order not to perish, hanging by their fingernails onto a shrinking profession. If they are old and tenured, they are buried under the duties of administering departments— as departmental chairmen or members of committees—that have been thinned out by the budgetary axe.

Ultimately it will be the students' own business to break the circles in 31 which they are trapped. They are too young to be prisoners of their parents' dreams and their classmates' fears. They must be jolted into believing in themselves as unique men and women who have the power to shape their own future.

"Violence is being done to the undergraduate experience," says Carlos   32
Hortas. "College should be open-ended: at the end it should open many, many roads. Instead, students are choosing their goal in advance, and their choices narrow as they go along. It's almost as if they think that the country has been codified in the type of jobs that exist—that they've got to fit into certain slots. Therefore, fit into the best-paying slot.

"They ought to take chances. Not taking chances will lead to a life of   33
colorless mediocrity. They'll be comfortable. But something in the spirit will be missing."

I have painted too drab a portrait of today's students, making them   34
seem a solemn lot. That is only half of their story; if they were so dreary I wouldn't so thoroughly enjoy their company. The other half is that they are easy to like. They are quick to laugh and to offer friendship. They are not introverts. They are usually kind and are more considerate of one another than any student generation I have known.

Nor are they so obsessed with their studies that they avoid sports and   35
extracurricular activities. On the contrary, they juggle their crowded hours to play on a variety of teams, perform with musical and dramatic groups, and write for campus publications. But this in turn is one more cause of anxiety. There are too many choices. Academically, they have 1,300 courses to select from; outside class they have to decide how much spare time they can spare and how to spend it.

This means that they engage in fewer extracurricular pursuits than their   36
predecessors did. If they want to row on the crew and play in the symphony they will eliminate one; in the '60s they would have done both. They also tend to choose activities that are self-limiting. Drama, for instance, is flourishing in all twelve of Yale's residential colleges as it never has before. Students hurl themselves into these productions—as actors, directors, carpenters, and technicians—with a dedication to create the best possible play, knowing that the day will come when the run will end and they can get back to their studies.

They also can't afford to be the willing slave of organizations like the   37
Yale Daily News. Last spring at the one-hundredth anniversary banquet of that paper—whose past chairmen include such once and future kings as Potter Stewart,[6] Kingman Brewster,[7] and William F. Buckley, Jr.[8]—much was made of the fact that the editorial staff used to be small and totally committed and that "newsies" routinely worked fifty hours a week. In effect they belonged to a club; Newsies is how they defined themselves at Yale. Today's student will write one or two articles a week, when he can, and

---

[6] **Potter Stewart:** a former Supreme Court Justice
[7] **Kingman Brewster:** a former president of Yale
[8] **William F. Buckley, Jr.:** an influential journalist

he defines himself as a student. I've never heard the word Newsie except at the banquet.

If I have described the modern undergraduate primarily as a driven   38
creature who is largely ignoring the blithe spirit inside who keeps trying to come out and play, it's because that's where the crunch is, not only at Yale but throughout American education. It's why I think we should all be worried about the values that are nurturing a generation so fearful of risk and so goal-obsessed at such an early age.

I tell students that there is no one "right" way to get ahead—that each   39
of them is a different person, starting from a different point and bound for a different destination. I tell them that change is a tonic and that all the slots are not codified nor the frontiers closed. One of my ways of telling them is to invite men and women who have achieved success outside the academic world to come and talk informally with my students during the year. They are heads of companies or ad agencies, editors of magazines, politicians, public officials, television magnates, labor leaders, business executives, Broadway producers, artists, writers, economists, photographers, scientists, historians—a mixed bag of achievers.

I ask them to say a few words about how they got started. The students   40
assume that they started in their present profession and knew all along that it was what they wanted to do. Luckily for me, most of them got into their field by a circuitous route, to their surprise, after many detours. The students are startled. They can hardly conceive of a career that was not pre-planned. They can hardly imagine allowing the hand of God or chance to nudge them down some unforeseen trail.   ●

Write after You Read

1. Make a journal entry on "College Pressures," following the suggestions on p. 121.
2. Write a one-sentence summary of "College Pressures," following the guidelines for summarizing an argumentative essay on pp. 121–122.   ●

Activities for Class Discussion

Working in a group of three or four students, share in the following activities. (Activities 4 and 5 may be done by the class as a whole.)

1. Share your written summary of "College Pressures." If you do not agree on the gist of the argument, discuss the reasons for the different interpretations. If your group cannot determine the gist of the argument, consult with another group or with your instructor.

2. Are there unfamiliar words or expressions? Make sure that everyone in the group understands the meaning of these terms:

laden with (1)	vacillates (22)
privy to (3)	ante (27)
unswervingly (4)	codified (32)
savor (5)	introverts (34)
venerated (6)	predecessors (36)
exhilarate (11)	blithe spirit (38)
a brotherhood of paupers (12)	tonic (39)
exhorted (13)	circuitous route (40)
tenacity (15)	

Try to guess the meaning of these and other unfamiliar words from the context. If your group cannot determine the meaning, consult with another group or with your instructor, or consult a dictionary.

3. Briefly outline the organization of the essay. Compare your outline with that of another group. Discuss the similarities and differences.

4. Following the guidelines on pp. 122–128, evaluate the supporting material of Zinsser's argument. Ask these questions:
   - What evidence is used to support the argument?
   - Is there enough evidence?
   - Are the examples representative?
   - Are the opinions provided by qualified sources?
   - Are the sources biased?
   - Is the evidence relevant?
   - Are the facts accurate?
   - Is the evidence up to date?
   - Are the emotional appeals appropriate for the audience?
   - Are the examples appropriate for the audience?

   While or after analyzing the argument, share what you have written in your journal. State your reasons for agreeing or disagreeing with Zinsser. What evidence do you have to support or refute his argument?

5. Discuss answers to these questions: Do you think Zinsser's argument could effect a change on college campuses? Why or why not?

6. Working in pairs, paraphrase the following passage, or select a passage from the essay that is not completely clear to you and rewrite it in your own words to clarify its meaning.

   One of the few rights that America does not proclaim is the right to fail. Achievement is the national god, venerated in our media—the million-dollar athlete, the wealthy executive—and glorified in our praise of possessions. In the presence of such a potent state religion, the young are growing up old.

7. Based on your reading of this essay, explain what Zinsser means by the statement

   Defeat is as instructive as victory.

Compare your explanation with what you wrote in the Write before You Read activity that precedes "College Pressures."

8. Write letters in response to your reading. Decide whether each group or person should write two letters or if the task of writing the letters should be divided among the groups or individual class members.

   a. Write a letter from William Zinsser to Jacob Neusner expressing what you believe would be Zinsser's response to "The Commencement Speech You'll Never Hear."

   b. Write a letter from Jacob Neusner to William Zinsser expressing what you believe would be Neusner's response to "College Pressures."

   Take turns reading the letters aloud, and discuss the differences in emotional appeals to the reader. ●

Write *before* You Read

Take the following quiz to test your knowledge.

Briefly identify the following:

1. Mussolini	10. the author of *The Canterbury Tales*
2. Dostoevski	11. Romeo and Juliet
3. Belgrade	12. Donkey Kong
4. Prague	13. Shakespeare
5. Kabul	14. Lyndon Johnson
6. Karachi	15. Ho Chi Minh
7. Hamlet	16. Hirohito
8. Buenos Aires	17. the Periodic Table
9. tacos	18. a river in Brazil

Compare your results with those of your classmates. What do the results reveal about the knowledge level of the class? To answer this question, you might try to classify the material according to categories such as geography, literature, and history. Then determine which categories the class knows best or least, and try to explain why this is so. ●

We Should Cherish Our Children's Freedom to Think
by Kie Ho

Kie Ho, who grew up in Indonesia, is now a southern California business executive. In the following essay, he compares the educational system in the United States with that of Indonesia and many other countries in the world. The essay originally appeared in 1983 in the Los Angeles Times *newspaper.*

Americans who remember "the good old days" are not alone in com-   1
plaining about the educational system in this country. Immigrants, too,
complain, and with more up-to-date comparisons. Lately I have heard a
Polish refugee express dismay that his daughter's high school has not taught
her the difference between Belgrade and Prague. A German friend was
furious when he learned that the mathematics test given to his son on his
first day as a freshman included multiplication and division. A Lebanese
boasts that the average high-school graduate in his homeland can speak
fluently in Arabic, French and English. Japanese businessmen in Los Angeles send their children to private schools staffed by teachers imported
from Japan to learn mathematics at Japanese levels, generally considered at
least a year more advanced than the level here.

But I wonder: If American education is so tragically inferior, why is   2
it that this is still the country of innovation?

I think I found the answer on an excursion to the Laguna Beach Museum   3
of Art, where the work of schoolchildren was on exhibit. Equipped only
with colorful yarns, foil paper, felt pens and crayons, they had transformed
simple paper lunch bags into, among other things, a waterfall with flying
fish, Broom Hilda the witch and a house with a woman in a skimpy bikini
hiding behind a swinging door. Their public school had provided these
children with opportunities and direction to fulfill their creativity, something
that people tend to dismiss or take for granted.

When I was 12 in Indonesia, where education followed the Dutch   4
system, I had to memorize the names of all the world's major cities, from
Kabul to Karachi. At the same age, my son, who was brought up a Californian, thought that Buenos Aires was Spanish for good food—a plate of
tacos and burritos, perhaps. However, unlike his counterparts in Asia and
Europe, my son had studied *creative* geography. When he was only 6, he
drew a map of the route that he traveled to get to school, including the
streets and their names, the buildings and traffic signs and the houses that
he passed.

Disgruntled American parents forget that in this country their children   5
are able to experiment freely with ideas; without this they will not really
be able to think or to believe in themselves.

In my high school years, we were models of dedication and obedience;   6
we sat to listen, to answer only when asked, and to give the only correct
answer. Even when studying word forms, there were no alternatives. In
similes, pretty lips were *always* as red as sliced pomegranates, and beautiful
eyebrows were *always* like a parade of black clouds. Like children in many
other countires in the world, I simply did not have a chance to choose, to
make decisions. My son, on the contrary, told me that he got a good laugh—
and an A—from his teacher for concocting "the man was as nervous as
Richard Pryor[1] at a Ku Klux Klan[2] convention."

---

[1] **Richard Pryor:** a comedian who is African-American
[2] **Ku Klux Klan:** a secret society hostile to African-Americans and other minority groups

There's no doubt that American education does not meet high standards   7
in such basic skills as mathematics and language. And we realize that our
youngsters are ignorant of Latin, put Mussolini in the same category as
Dostoevski, cannot recite the Periodic Table by heart. Would we, however,
prefer to stuff the developing little heads of our children with hundreds of
geometry problems, the names of rivers in Brazil and 50 lines from *The
Canterbury Tales*? Do we really want to retard their impulses, frustrate their
opportunities for self-expression?

When I was 18, I had to memorize Hamlet's "To be or not to be"   8
soliloquy flawlessly. In his English class, my son was assigned to write a
love letter to Juliet, either in Shakespearean jargon or in modern lingo. (He
picked the latter; his Romeo would take Juliet to an arcade for a game of
Donkey Kong.)

Where else but in America can a history student take the role of Lyndon   9
Johnson in an open debate against another student playing Ho Chi Minh?
It is unthinkable that a youngster in Japan would dare to do the same
regarding the role of Hirohito in World War II.

Critics of American education cannot grasp one thing, something that   10
they don't truly understand because they are never deprived of it: freedom.
This most important measurement has been omitted in the studies of the
quality of education in this century, the only one, I think, that extends
even to children the license to freely speak, write and be creative. Our
public education certainly is not perfect, but it is a great deal better than
any other.   ●

Write after You Read

1. Make a journal entry on "We Should Cherish Our Children's Freedom to Think," following the suggestions on p. 121.
2. Write a one-sentence summary of the essay, following the guidelines
   for summarizing an argumentative essay on pp. 121–122.   ●

Activities for Class Discussion

Working in a group of three or four students, share in the following
activities. (Activities 4, 5, and 6 may be done by the class as a whole.)

1. Share your written summary of "We Should Cherish Our Students
   Freedom to Think." If you do not agree on the gist of the argument,
   discuss the reasons for the different interpretations. If your group
   cannot determine the gist of the argument, consult with another
   group or with your instructor.
2. Are there unfamiliar words or expressions? Make sure that everyone
   in the group knows the meaning of these terms:

   innovation (2)   retard (7)
   excursion (3)   soliloquy (8)

disgruntled (5)   flawlessly (8)
similes (6)   jargon (8)
concocting (6)   lingo (8)
recite (7)   extends . . . the license to (10)

Try to guess the meaning of these or other unfamiliar words from the context. If your group cannot determine the meaning, consult with another group or with your instructor, or consult a dictionary.

3. Briefly outline the organization of the essay. Compare your outline with that of another group. Discuss the similarities and differences.

4. Following the guidelines on pp. 000–000, evaluate the supporting material of Ho's argument. Ask these questions:
   - What evidence is used to support the argument?
   - Is there enough evidence?
   - Are the examples representative?
   - Are the opinions provided by qualified sources?
   - Are the sources biased?
   - Is the evidence relevant?
   - Are the facts accurate?
   - Is the evidence up to date?
   - Are the emotional appeals appropriate for the audience?
   - Are the examples appropriate for the audience?

   While or after analyzing the argument, share what you have written in your journal. State your reasons for agreeing or disagreeing with the author. What evidence do you have that supports or refutes the author's points?

5. List the advantages and disadvantages of the two educational systems Ho discusses. If you have been educated under one of the systems, share your experiences. If you have had a different educational experience, explain it.

6. Based on your own experiences as a student, discuss what an ideal educational system might be. Then list the advantages and disadvantages of such a system. ●

Write before You Read

The following essay, written by a college professor, deals with the subject of evaluation of teachers. Before reading this essay, write for 10 to 15 minutes in answer to one or both of the following:

1. Do you want to have the opportunity to write written evaluations of your teachers? Why or why not?

2. Do you think students should sign their names to written evaluations of their teachers?

Write with the purpose of getting your views on paper to find out what you really think before you are influenced by your reading. Share what you have written with your classmates. ●

We Should Abolish Anonymous Evaluations of Teachers by Their Students
by Paul McBrearty

Paul McBrearty is an English professor at St. Louis Community College at Meramec, in Missouri. In the following essay, he discusses the evaluations that students write of their teachers at the end of a course. The essay originally appeared in 1982 in the Chronicle of Higher Education, *a weekly publication read by college and university faculty and administration.*

Note: *As a college student, you will probably be asked to evaluate your teachers, if you haven't done so already. Your evaluations will be anonymous; that is, you will not have to give your name. Therefore, the person reading the evaluation (usually the person in charge of hiring, firing, and promoting the teachers in the department) will not be able to identify you as the author of the evaluation.*

Anonymity in student evaluations of teachers—so we have often been told and many of us believe—encourages students to be frank.[1] To the uncritical, frankness implies honesty, and surely it follows that what is said frankly and honestly must be true.   1

Now frankness is, of course, a virtue in certain contexts. However, it must never be mistaken for acuteness of perception, objectivity, or even accuracy, all of which may well be—and often are—missing from the "frankest" student evaluation.   2

Far more valuable for purposes of evaluation and improvement of instruction are the accuracy and reliability of the information supplied. It goes without saying that absolute accuracy and reliability in evaluations are unattainable. But we must not let that fact mislead us into imagining that if we encourage frankness by guaranteeing anonymity to evaluators we will secure more accurate observations and more reliable judgments than would otherwise be the case. Indeed, a few moments of reflection should make us realize that in many cases guaranteeing anonymity will result in just the opposite.   3

Anonymity, after all, fosters not merely frankness; more ominously (for teachers) it fosters irresponsibility, a trait of character (or a kind of behavior, if we prefer) that we ought never to encourage in the young. Formal evaluation of teachers by their students, at one time unheard of, was seen as a privilege when it was first introduced, but quite soon it came to be looked upon as a right.   4

Like all rights, however, the right to evaluate carries with it a corre-   5

[1] **frank:** free in expressing one's thoughts; honest even to the point of insensitivity

sponding obligation: the obligation of the evaluators to take responsibility for what they say or write. When we assure students that we will not under any circumstances reveal their identities, we in effect tell the weak, the confused, the vindictive, the morally obtuse, and the less courageous among them that they may say what they please without having to stand behind their words.

That is a foolish and dangerous thing to do. To give power without   6
responsibility is to ask for abuse; to give it to students—many of whom are by definition immature, and some of whom may be enrolled in courses beyond their capacities—is unfair to us and a perversion of our duty to them.

We owe our students rather more than lectures on Keynesian theory,   7
computer language, and topic sentences. We owe them the opportunity to learn to behave as mature people with full responsibility for the actions they take. Guaranteeing them anonymity in their evaluations of faculty members guarantees them precisely the avoidance of that responsibility. That is bad pedagogy, bad institutional policy, and certainly bad morality.

Anonymous testimony is discounted or ignored nearly everywhere out-   8
side the peculiar world of higher education *because* it is anonymous and therefore of doubtful authenticity. Only in investigative police work is anonymous information officially acted upon, and even then never without verification. In law, it has no standing whatsoever. It is therefore intolerable that administrative and personnel decisions affecting the lives and careers of professionals are sometimes taken on the basis (to whatever extent) of unverified anonymous information. Teachers should be accorded at least the standing presently granted known lawbreakers and those accused of crimes.

Student anonymity is unfair to the faculty. As teachers, we are con-   9
tinually called upon to defend our grading methods and standards—not only to students but also occasionally to parents and administrators—by producing verifiable support for the grades we give. At my institution, among others, administrators are required to document their negative evaluations of faculty members with specific evidence. Only students are exempt from the necessity of supporting and defending the "grades" they give, and teachers are denied the privilege of confronting their graders.

Lacking the steadying influence that would be provided by the knowl-   10
edge that their evaluations, too, are subject to verification, students are under no obligation even to tell the simple truth about factual matters and cannot be called to account as teachers frequently are.

Anonymity in student evaluations virtually assures lowered academic   11
standards and inflated grades. The pressures on teachers to *give* good grades so as to *get* good grades are severe, pervasive, unremitting, and inescapable. Historically, the beginning of the use of student evaluations on a large scale coincides precisely with the beginning of nearly universal grade inflation.[2]

---

[2] **grade inflation:** a gradual rise in grades, resulting in higher average college grades than in the past

There is no doubt that other influences contributed to the upward spiral, but there is also no doubt that student evaluation of teachers has been the principal one.

There is a discouragingly widespread view—among students, admin-   12
istrators, and the general public—that high student grades are a mark of superior teaching, despite the fact, which should be obvious to anyone of ordinary intelligence, that nothing is easier to manipulate than grades. In the face of that widely held, if unsophisticated, view, some teachers have the best possible grounds for fearing retaliation from students whose grades are lower than the students had—for whatever reason—expected. More practical-minded teachers (more cynical or more "flexible," perhaps) adjust their grading so as to reflect the "success" of their teaching. Only a fool will refuse to see what can (and does) become of academic standards and professional integrity when teachers are placed in a double-bind of this sort.

Anonymity in student evaluations obviates any meaningful research   13
into possible relationships between student behavior and student ratings. How can we justify this extraordinary refusal to procure valuable and relevant data on a matter of such importance? Incredibly, and almost uniquely, in the context of student evaluations alone, we assert—contrary to all ordinary experience and common sense—that it does not matter who says what under what conditions; in student evaluations only *what is said* matters.

In our courses we teach our students, as an elementary principle of   14
discourse, that he who asserts must prove. We teach them that ignoring context is a form of falsification. Furthermore, we teach them—or we should—that when they offer the testimony of outside sources in support of a proposition, they must identify those sources fully so that their readers or hearers may judge or verify the knowledgeability of the source and the veracity of the testimony.

When students evaluate a teacher, however, the previous involvement   15
of the witnesses with the subject of their testimony, and the witnesses' experience, their qualifications, their knowledge, their intelligence, their maturity, their judgment, their veracity, their *character* are suddenly of no account whatever. What more egregious instance can we find of the perverse violation of our own high principles?—and all presumably in the cause of assuring "frankness."

With no information as to which student is saying what, we cannot   16
determine, for example, how the item "Informs students about how they will be graded on tests and assignments" was marked by a student who was absent on the days the tests and assignments were given or due; we cannot tell how the student who is never prepared or never able to respond in class marks the item "Explains material in response to questions." In fact, we cannot learn anything useful to help us form judgments as to the many student characteristics that may tend to correspond with particular responses.

Whenever student evaluations are used in any way by administrators   17
as a basis for the denial of promotion, retention, or salary increase, or for

assigning a less-than-satisfactory rating to a faculty member, the faculty member is denied the constitutional right of due process[3] if not permitted to confront what are in effect his or her accusers.

It would be easy to devise safeguards that would insure that faculty members would not be given access to identifying data except in a case of clear need, as in a grievance hearing.[4] Indeed, such a system was proposed to—and at first accepted by—the administration on my campus. In the end, however, administrators here felt that elaborate safeguards notwithstanding, even to hint to students that their identities might, under very restricted conditions, be revealed would invalidate the evaluations—since students would not, of course, give "honest" evaluations, but only favorable ones—the two evidently being mutually exclusive.[5] That there is an analogy between this situation and that of the instructor who gives high grades because he fears students will retaliate if he gives low ones either does not impress those administrators or does not occur to them.   18

The present method of administering student evaluations must be changed because: 19

Anonymity does not assure accuracy and reliability but more likely the opposite.

Anonymity encourages irresponsibility in students who should be learning to be responsible.

Anonymous and hence unchallengeable evaluations are inherently unfair to faculty members whose evaluations of students *are* subject to challenge.

Anonymity renders impossible most meaningful research on the reliability of student evaluations.

Anonymity in student evaluations may well result in denial of a faculty member's constitutional right to due process.

If, as administrators claim, the method itself cannot feasibly be changed, then student evaluations must no longer be a component in the process of faculty evaluation.   20   ●

Write after You Read

1. Make a journal entry on "We Should Abolish Anonymous Evaluations of Teachers by Their Students," following the suggestions on p. 121.

---

[3] **constitutional right of due process:** the right guaranteed to all Americans to fair judicial procedures (e.g., a fair trial)
[4] **grievance hearing:** a preliminary investigation of a complaint
[5] **mutually exclusive:** unable to coexist

2. Write a one-sentence summary of the essay, following the guidelines for summarizing an argumentative essay on pp. 121–122. ●

Activities for Class Discussion

Working in a group of three or four students, share in the following activities. (Activities 6, 7, and 8 may be done by the class as a whole.)

1. Share your written summary of "We Should Abolish Anonymous Evaluations of Teachers by Their Students." If you do not agree on the gist of the argument, discuss the reasons for the different interpretations. If your group cannot determine an overall message, consult with another group or with your instructor.

2. Are there unfamiliar words or expressions? Make sure that everyone in the group understands the meaning of these terms:

acuteness (2)	unremitting (11)
fosters (4)	retaliation (12)
ominously (4)	obviates (13)
vindictive (5)	procure (13)
morally obtuse (5)	asserts (14)
perversion (6)	veracity (14)
verification (8)	egregious (15)
intolerable (8)	retention (17)
standing (8)	feasibly (20)
pervasive (11)	

   Try to guess the meaning of these or other unfamiliar words from the context. If your group cannot determine the meaning, consult with another group or with your instructor, or consult a dictionary.

3. Briefly outline the organization of the essay. Compare your outline with that of another group. Discuss similarities and differences.

4. As a group, select a sentence or longer passage that is not completely clear to you, and rewrite it in your own words to clarify its meaning. Have one member of the group read aloud to the class the original passage and the group's paraphrase of the passage, and let the class decide whether the paraphrase both preserves and clarifies the author's meaning.

5. Select one quotation from the essay to which you have a strong response. Freewrite for five minutes to explain what the quotation means and why your reaction to it is so strong. Share your free-writing with members of your group.

6. Following the guidelines on pp. 122–128, evaluate the supporting material of McBrearty's argument. Ask these questions:
   - What evidence is used to support the argument?
   - Is there enough evidence?
   - Are the examples representative?

- Are the opinions provided by qualified sources?
- Are the sources biased?
- Is the evidence relevant?
- Are the facts accurate?
- Is the evidence up to date?
- Are the emotional appeals appropriate for the audience?
- Are the examples appropriate for the audience?

While or after analyzing the argument, share what you have written in your journal. State your reasons for agreeing or disagreeing with the author. What evidence do you have that supports or refutes the author's points?

7. Have you ever written an anonymous evaluation of a teacher? If so, describe what went through your mind as you began to write. Thinking back on the evaluation, do you now think you were fair in what you said? If you could, would you add to or change anything you said?

8. Create your own questions for an evaluation of teachers. Make a list of three or four questions that you think students should be asked in evaluating their teachers at the end of a semester. ●

College: An All-forgiving World?
by Ida Timothee

Ida Timothee wrote "College: An All-forgiving World?" to fulfill a writing assignment for a composition course. What you will read is a finished composition, carefully edited for publication in this book. Later in this chapter, you will see how Ida got started on this assignment and the various stages of thinking, writing, and rewriting she went through to produce this essay.

Ida's essay was chosen for publication as an example of one possible response to Neusner's "Commencement Speech You'll Never Hear": complete disagreement with two of his major points. There are many other possible responses to Neusner. For example, you may completely agree with him, or you may agree with some points but not with others, or you may completely disagree with him, as Ida does, but focus on different points or respond less emotionally. Therefore, you should try not to allow Ida's approach to have too strong an influence on your own writing.

In "The Commencement Speech You'll Never Hear," Jacob Neusner   1
argues that we have been made to believe, according to our college experience, that "failure leaves no record" (paragraph 1) and that things can be easily achieved. It seems to Neusner that college is not a good preparatory school for life because it is making us ready "for a world that does not exist" (paragraph 1).

There's no doubt that Neusner should have taken a closer look at what college life is really like before formulating such a strong opinion about it. He is completely ignoring all the pressures and hard times students go through to make it at college. It is not the way he describes it at all. 2

Is college not preparing us for real life, as Neusner puts it? Is what we are experiencing something not useful to learn for the real world? These are questions that pop into my mind when I think about what Neusner says. I think that he is very wrong. The college years, for many of us, are when we start to be independent, make crucial decisions on our own, and become responsible for them. At college, we must learn to budget our time (and money!) and to be tolerant (otherwise we wouldn't survive in a crowded triple room!). We meet people from different parts of the world that broaden our view of the world itself and help us understand each other better. If these things are not useful for the real world, then I don't know what could be. 3

Neusner believes that in college we are trained to think that "failure leaves no record" because we can supposedly get away with mistakes easily. I have news for him. If you fail a test, you can't take it again, or the teacher won't erase the grade even if he thinks you will hate him for the rest of your life. If you drop out of a class, next semester you will have to take more courses. If you get low grades, your chances of getting into a fine graduate school are almost none. If your grade point average is not reasonably high for a number of classes, you just don't get your degree. When midterms and finals come, no one can avoid taking them. When the going gets tough, the tough have to get down to work because, unlike what Neusner believes, college does not give "painless" solutions to mistakes (paragraph 1). It is not "an altogether forgiving world," and by no means have teachers "pretended not to care" (paragraph 3) when deadlines are not kept or when things aren't done at the time they are supposed to be. 4

To me, living in a crowded triple, having a one-day reading period before finals, tons of readings, papers, and midterms due the same week are not exactly my idea of " 'easy, free, forgiving, attentive, comfortable, interesting, unchallenging fun' " (paragraph 6). ● 5

Write after You Read

1. Make a journal entry on "College: An All-forgiving World?"
2. Write a one-sentence summary of the essay by answering this question: What is Ida trying to prove? ●

Activities for Class Discussion

Working with the whole class, share in the following activities.

1. On the board, write a one-sentence summary of Ida's essay. If you cannot agree on her purpose and main point, discuss the reasons for the different interpretations.

2. Discuss your reaction to Ida's essay.

3. Ida makes several references to Neusner's essay—through summary, paraphrase, and quotation. Are these references sufficient to remind you of and to clarify Neusner's ideas?

   a. If the answer is yes, which references are most helpful?

   b. If the answer is no, where should more references be added? Can you suggest any specific references that might be helpful?

4. Evaluate the supporting material of Ida's argument. Ask these questions:

   • What evidence is used to support the argument?
   • Is there enough evidence?
   • Are the examples representative?
   • Are the opinions provided by qualified sources?
   • Are the sources biased?
   • Is the evidence relevant?
   • Are the facts accurate?
   • Is the evidence up to date?
   • Are the emotional appeals appropriate for the audience?
   • Are the examples appropriate for the audience?

   While or after examining the essay, share what you have written in your journal. State your reasons for agreeing or disagreeing with Ida. Do you have additional evidence that could support or refute her argument?

5. Examine the paragraph units of Ida's essay.

   a. Which sentence or paragraph first makes you aware of the essay's focus, of what the essay is about?

   b. Go through the essay paragraph by paragraph and determine the purpose or function of each paragraph. For example, does the paragraph introduce the main idea of the essay? Does the paragraph make a new point? Does the paragraph exist primarily to provide an example to illustrate or clarify a point made in the preceding paragraph?

   c. If a paragraph makes a new point, does the paragraph contain enough details and examples to support or illustrate that point? Are all the details and examples logically connected to that point?

   d. The first sentence of each new paragraph should help the reader to move smoothly from what the writer has just said to what the writer is about to say. Does each first sentence make a link between what Ida has just said and what she is about to say?

   e. Look for connections within and between paragraphs. Identify words or expressions that connect ideas and examples and show how they are related to one another.

      • If you find connective words, do they help you as a reader to follow Ida's way of thinking about her subject?

      • If there are any missing connections, where should you add connective words or expressions?

- If you find any connectives that are distracting, explain where they are and why you should delete them. Sometimes a writer can include more connectives than a reader needs.   ●

ACTIVITY: *Observing one student in the process of composing an essay*

On pp. 156–166, you can observe the process Ida went through to produce her essay. Use the guidelines to compose your own essay analyzing an argument.   ●

CHAPTER SIX

Guidelines for Fulfilling Essay Assignment 3

Essay Assignment 3

Write an essay in which you analyze another author's argumentative essay. Analyze one of the readings in Part Three or Sydney J. Harris's essay in the Introduction (pp. 9–10). Determine what the author says, how well the author's points are made, and what points may have been overlooked. Establish and support your position by either agreeing or disagreeing with—or taking a mixed position toward—some key idea(s) or issue(s) raised in the reading. In writing this essay, your purpose will be to determine the effectiveness of the argument. ●

Understanding the Assignment

Before you begin writing an essay, you need to understand exactly what you are being assigned to write. You need to analyze the directions of the writing assignment so that you know both the essay's possibilities and its limitations. The following activity can help you fulfill that goal.

ACTIVITY: *Rereading and analyzing the writing assignment*

Working in a group of three or four students, have one student read the writing assignment above aloud. Examine what the assignment asks you to do. What purpose will the essay serve? What material should it contain? If you are unclear as to the demands of the assignment, consult with your instructor. ●

Defining Your Audience

Writers of argumentative essays need to consider how to connect with their readers and to move those readers toward some kind of insight, understanding, or change, depending on the writer's purpose. Likewise, when you write your essay, you need to connect with and move your audience. You must understand the needs and values of that audience if your argument is to be effective. The evidence you provide, the appeals you make, and the language you use will all work together to accomplish the goal of enabling your audience to understand, accept, or identify with your own values.

In writing this essay, you can share your knowledge, experiences, and beliefs. Your instructor is interested in learning your unique response to the course reading. Remember that this audience does not necessarily have to agree with you to appreciate the quality of your argument.

ACTIVITY: *Defining your audience*

This activity can be done in small groups. If possible, define your audience by communicating directly with that audience, your instructor. As a class, you can discuss some answers to the questions raised about audience in Part Two (p. 103). In addition, you can discuss the following questions:

1. What kind of evidence will be acceptable to support a student writer's agreement or disagreement with an author's points?
2. What kinds of appeals will be appropriate?

Raise any other questions that might help you to define your audience further. ●

Finding and Developing a Topic

To develop an essay analyzing an argumentative essay, you will need to use most of the strategies used in Part Two: selecting a reading, rereading and taking notes on the selection, summarizing, paraphrasing, and quoting. In addition, you need to analyze the author's arguments and to determine why you agree or disagree with certain points.

The strategies listed here suggest approaches you can take to fulfill the assignment. You do not have to follow the exact order of the suggestions. Use them as guidelines, rather than as rigid instructions. The writing of one student, Ida Timothee, is included to show some of the strategies she used to write her essay "College: An All-forgiving World?" (pp. 150–151). All of her mechanical errors have been corrected so that you can focus on her idea development.

Reviewing Your Writing and Selecting a Reading

The first step in analyzing an argumentative essay is deciding which essay to analyze. You should ask yourself, "Which reading caused the strongest reaction?" or "Which reading would I like to explore further?" To answer either or both of these questions, read whatever you have written in connection with the readings in Part Three: the Write before You Read exercises, your marginal annotations or reading notes, your journal entries, and your notes on class discussions.

If reviewing your writing does not help you find a topic, reread each of the assigned selections, or discuss the choices with a classmate or with your instructor.

A STUDENT WRITER AT WORK

Ida knew that she would write about Jacob Neusner's essay "The Commencement Speech You'll Never Hear" (pp. 130–131) because, as she said, "I was shocked when I read this article. *Really* shocked. It's so . . . cold, so rude, what's the word I want . . . pessimistic. This essay really made me mad."

Excerpt from Ida's Journal on Neusner

Ida had written a journal entry about Neusner's essay in which she discussed some parts she didn't agree with:

> When he said that we are forgiven for passing deadlines, [I thought,] it's not true; most of the time it will count negatively toward a lower grade and a lower job eventually. College is not fantasy and so much fun, not at all as he puts it.

But she said that it was her journal entry about Zinsser's "College Pressures" (pp. 133–139) that made her want to write about Neusner's essay.

> When I read my journal about pressures, I wanted to tell Neusner that he didn't understand what it means to be a college student. I really felt I wanted to write my essay because I had to prove that he was wrong.

Excerpt from Ida's Journal on "College Pressures"

> There's a lot of pressure in the simple fact of being away from home, living with someone you just met (especially if you don't get along with that person), getting adjusted to new schedules (some morning persons are forced to become night persons, or vice versa), adjusting to a different climate and/or culture perhaps, etc. And then you wonder how is it possible . . . to enjoy college life with all this pressure? And these are supposed to be our best years? I guess that with some organization it is possible to enjoy college life, even at the worst times. But before that, we probably will go through a trial-and-error learning process.

Rereading and Taking Notes on the Source

Before you can make any further judgments about the author's opinion, you must understand completely the argument the author is making and the reasons given for the position the author takes. That understanding calls for a close rereading of the source. One or both of these strategies may be helpful:

1. Make additional annotations. Underline or copy passages that raise significant issues.
2. Take notes on the reading. Aim to understand the author's main argument. Then look for supporting points and the evidence given to support each point. Make a list of key points. Or you may find it useful to outline the argument, step by step. Make a list of the main argument, its supporting points, and their supporting evidence, as follows:

I. Main argument
   A. Supporting point
      1. Evidence
      2. Evidence
   B. Supporting point
      1. Evidence
      2. Evidence

A STUDENT WRITER AT WORK

In preparation for her paper, Ida read Neusner's essay twice. The second time, she underlined some of Neusner's key points. Then she organized those points into a list. She did not list his supporting evidence because, as she said:

> I did not want to look at his examples. That's what made me really angry. I got too angry when he said things like we were "boring" and "dull." I was trying to concentrate on his major points so that I could argue logically with him, without too much angry emotion.

Ida's Reading Notes

1. College—forgiving world
2. Preparation for a world that is not real
3. Failure at college leaves no record
4. We think that teachers are concerned about being liked by us
5. College is "easy, free, . . . unchallenging," etc.
6. College offers "painless solutions" to problems

Analyzing the Author's Arguments

If you participated in the class discussions, you have already analyzed each reading selection. But now that you have chosen a particular reading to write about in your own essay, it can be useful to go through the reading, following the guidelines for analyzing an argumentative essay (pp. 122–128) again. You are likely to make more discoveries.

Identifying Points of Agreement and Disagreement

Reread the source again, this time to focus on your own reactions. Make note of particular points with which you agree and those with which you disagree. Again, your decisions are based on your own background knowledge. You might find it helpful to make separate lists of points of agreement and points of disagreement. Then review your lists to see if you can find a pattern in your reactions. For example, you may disagree with everything the author says, or you may agree on one main point but disagree on others, or you may agree and disagree on an equal number of points. It is also possible that you agree with the author's opinion completely but still have a problem with the way the author has presented it. Recognizing a pattern in your response will help you to organize your paper later.

A STUDENT WRITER AT WORK

In rereading the article, Ida recognized a pattern in her thinking. As she put it:

> I realized that I *completely* disagreed with Neusner. I couldn't see his side at all. So I knew that in my essay I would disagree. I looked back at my reading notes and chose three of Neusner's points that I wanted to write about in my paper. I didn't use certain points like the one about teachers wanting to be liked because I didn't have any personal evidence for that one (although someone in class did).

Ida's List of Points to Debate

1. Preparation for a world that is not real
2. Failure leaves no record
3. College is "easy, free, . . . unchallenging," etc.

Determining Why You Agree or Disagree

Just as the author has provided evidence to support each point, you need to provide evidence to support your argument. It's not enough in an academic paper simply to say, "I agree" or "I disagree." You need to explain your reasons fully, giving examples, relating experiences, and referring to other readings or information that you know. One of the following suggestions may be useful in helping you to recall the experiences, ideas, and information that led you to agree or disagree.

1. Use one or more of the invention strategies described in Chapter 1 (making a list, freewriting, looping, cubing) or any other strategy that you find productive to generate ideas.

A STUDENT WRITER AT WORK

Ida had a list of Neusner's points that she wanted to debate. Her next step was to

> think of examples to support my ideas. I did some freewriting for a few minutes to think about the best examples. After writing for a while, I got some good ideas. Then I just started thinking about what I would write in my draft. And then I got started. I mean, I started my draft. I tried to include a lot of examples so that I could prove I was right.

2. Discuss the reading with a classmate or group of friends. By engaging in conversation about the author's opinions, not only will you find reasons why you believe as you do, but you will also get some fresh ideas. You may use your friends' examples or experiences to support points you make in your paper.

Focusing Your Thoughts

It is important to stop and think after you have spent some time taking notes on the readings and generating your own ideas. By rereading what you have written and determining the focus of your thoughts, you can give shape to your writing so that later your readers will be able to understand what you want to say.

A STUDENT WRITER AT WORK

Ida explained:

> I knew why I thought Neusner was wrong, but I had to think about making my points clear. I tried to decide what idea tied everything together. I wanted to think about what is really wrong with Neusner's essay. So I wrote a sentence in my head that I thought would tell anyone who read my essay what I wanted to say.

Ida's Major Point

> College is not as easy and perfect for the student as Neusner presents it.

Ida continued:

> The funny thing is that I didn't use this sentence in my draft. I was thinking about it when I started my writing, but I got so excited that I forgot about my readers. So when they read my draft, they got really confused. It was a good thing I could revise.

ACTIVITY: *Focusing your thoughts*

Reread whatever you have written in connection with the reading selection you will analyze: the Write before You Read entry, journal entries, lists, freewriting, class notes. If you haven't done so already, decide what the focus of your essay will be. As a start, you can decide whether you will agree with, disagree with, or have a mixed position toward the author's ideas. Ask yourself, "What am I trying to prove?" Try to answer this question by composing a sentence that can act as a focal point, to indicate what your essay will be about. To help you shape your ideas further, explain your focus to a small group of classmates to see if they understand what your essay will cover.   ●

If you are not yet ready to establish a focal point, you may want to write a trial draft of your essay, to use the drafting process to discover what you want to prove in your essay. Remember that in writing a trial draft, you don't have to try to write a complete paper. You can begin in the middle if you don't have an introduction, and if you can't think of an ending, you can just stop. But look back at the middle and see what issues and examples are most important to you. Decide what overall idea ties everything together. Then write a sentence that captures that idea and can act as a focal point for your essay.

If you are a writer who needs an even more structured approach to writing a draft, continue reading for guidelines on organizing an essay that analyzes an argument.

Organizing the Essay

Once you have developed your ideas, you need to put them into an orderly sequence so that your readers can follow your line of reasoning. Your approach to writing in general and to this assignment in particular will determine the appropriate time for organizing. For example, you may need to write one or more drafts before a logical organizational pattern emerges, or you may need to conceive of or write a detailed plan before you can begin even a first draft of the paper. When you are ready to structure your writing, follow the guidelines given here.

1. Introduction

The purpose of the introduction is to focus on your topic, to let your readers know in one or two opening paragraphs what your essay is about. As with the introduction of an essay relating reading to experience (see p. 109), you can approach your topic in a variety of ways: providing background information, telling a story or an anecdote, quoting a passage, stating a shocking fact, or asking a question. As you write several drafts of the paper, you can experiment with different openings. But there are certain features that your readers will ultimately need and expect in the introduction to an essay that analyzes another writer's argument.

COMMON FEATURES OF THE INTRODUCTION

The introduction of your argumentative essay should accomplish these things, though not necessarily in this order.

1. Identify the reading by title (within quotation marks) and author (full name).
2. Summarize the gist of the argument.
3. Restate the idea or ideas in the reading that you are responding to in your essay. (If you are responding to the main argument which you have already summarized, this will not be necessary.)
4. Indicate the focus of your paper. Make clear whether you agree with, disagree with, or have a mixed position toward the author's idea(s). What are you trying to prove?

A STUDENT WRITER AT WORK

Like many writers, Ida had trouble writing her introduction. She forgot to include the gist of Neusner's argument.

First Draft of Ida's Introduction

There's no doubt that Jacob Neusner should have taken a closer look at what college life is really like before formulating such a strong opinion about it. To me, living in a crowded triple, having a one-day reading period before finals, tons of readings, papers, and midterms due the same week are not exactly my idea of " 'easy, free, forgiving, attentive, comfortable, interesting, and unchallenging fun.' "

Peer Reviewer's Comment on the Introduction

I was a bit frustrated in the first paragraph because I couldn't remember what Neusner wrote.

Instructor's Comment on the Introduction

I agree with Wendy that in the introduction you need to explain Neusner's strong opinion *before* you start criticizing it.

I also think the first paragraph is too specific. Save the details ("crowded triple," etc.) for a later point in the paper, and create a more general statement instead to show what your focus is.

Revision of Ida's Introduction

In "The Commencement Speech You'll Never Hear," Jacob Neusner argues that we have been made to believe, according to our college experience, that "failure leaves no record" (paragraph 1) and that things can be easily achieved. It seems to Neusner that college is not a good preparatory school for life because it is making us ready "for a world that does not exist" (paragraph 1).

There's no doubt that Neusner should have taken a closer look at what college life is really like before formulating such a strong opinion about it. He is completely ignoring all the pressures and hard times students go through to make it at college. It is not the way he describes it at all.

ACTIVITY: *Evaluating introductions*

The following passages are introductions to essays in which students analyze the arguments of the authors in Part Three. Some are first drafts, and others are revisions; all have been edited for errors. Read the introductions in two ways:

1. Look for the common features of an introduction:
   a. *Identification of the reading:* Has the writer included the name of the author and the title of the article being discussed?
   b. *Summary of the reading:* Has the writer explained the gist of the argument?
   c. *Restatement of the idea(s) the writer is responding to:* Has the writer made clear which of the author's ideas will be discussed in the essay?
   d. *Focus:* Is the writer's position clear?
2. Examine your response. Discuss your overall impression of each introduction with your classmates. Does it involve you in the topic? (Does it make you want to read the rest of the essay?) Why or why not? Do you like the writing style? Why or why not? If you think the introduction should be revised, what suggestions would you have for the writer? Allow for differences of opinion in your group.

A

When I first started reading William Zinsser's article "College Pressures," I thought it was written for me. I could read most of what I felt about college. My roommates used to tease me because I had a lot of things to do and it was hard for me to catch up with the pace of the classes.

It is true that college pressures are very high. The writer says that there are four main sources of pressure—economic pressure, parental pressure, peer pressure, and self-induced pressure—and I will agree with most of them.

CHRISTOS

B

Paul McBrearty wrote the article "We Should Abolish Anonymous Evaluations of Teachers by Their Students," which is about how unfair it is for professors to be evaluated by their students. I myself am a student, and as I was reading this article, I found it to be an insult. I know that many professors are well educated and can teach well. However, I also know that there are some professors who are well educated but do not know how to teach.

T<small>ANAPATI</small>

C

Jacob Neusner in his article "The Commencement Speech You'll Never Hear" states that all professors act and pretend in order to please the students and not be bothered by them. I cannot say this is wrong, but I cannot see why this should extend to the degree Professor Neusner takes it. Students always have enthusiasm; and this enthusiasm blinds them so they cannot see when they are becoming annoying, offensive, and disrespectful to their professors. I don't think, though, that professors should look at students' behavior as it appears but rather see through it and help them understand that what they are doing is incorrect. After all, this is the way everybody learns.

G<small>EORGE</small>

D

Kie Ho states that the public education in the States is "certainly not perfect, but it is a great deal better than any other" (paragraph 10). I cannot take a stand on this statement because there are aspects that I do not agree with and some I do. It is not necessarily true that the education is "a great deal better," but certainly it is, in a way, "better."

S<small>TEPHANIE</small>

●

2. Body

In several paragraphs, you develop the position that you stated in your introduction. The body therefore consists of paraphrased and quoted references to the reading as well as your reasons for agreeing or disagreeing with the author. Your reasons need to be supported by background knowledge in the form of examples, experiences, and references to other readings or information that you know. There are several ways to organize this group of paragraphs.

SUGGESTED ORGANIZATIONAL PATTERNS

None of the patterns suggested here represents a rigid formula. You may try variations on these structures or devise another structure that is better suited to your topic. You can use the drafting process to experiment with organization; your early efforts can later be revised.

1. *Explore several ideas from the reading one by one, devoting at least one paragraph to each idea.* State an idea from the reading that you agree or disagree with; your statement can appear at the beginning of a paragraph. Explain the author's point. Then in that same paragraph (you may need more than one paragraph), explain why you agree or disagree with that idea. Repeat this procedure for each point you want to discuss.

   Be sure that the ideas are presented in a logical order; here are three possibilities:
   a. Begin with what you think is the less or least important idea and end with the most important, so that your argument gets stronger.
   b. First discuss all the ideas from the reading that you agree with, and then discuss all the ideas that you disagree with.
   c. First discuss the author's main points as they are presented in the reading; then discuss ideas that present the opposing point of view.

2. *Explore one major idea from the reading.* State one major idea from the reading. Explain the author's point. Then describe one or more experiences or ideas in detail to reveal whether you agree or disagree with that major idea. Most of the body will be devoted to a discussion of your reasons, although references to the reading (through paraphrase or quotation) are necessary to remind readers of the points you are responding to.

3. *Explore several ideas from the reading, and then explore one or more ideas that the reading neglects.*
   - *First part:* State the idea from the reading that you will discuss; your statement can appear at the beginning of a paragraph. Explain the author's point. Then in that same paragraph (you may need more than one paragraph), explain why you agree or disagree. Repeat this procedure for each idea you want to discuss.
   - *Second part:* State the idea that the reading ignores. Then in that same paragraph or in one or more paragraphs, explain why that idea is important to consider. Repeat this procedure for each idea you want to discuss.

A STUDENT WRITER AT WORK

A workable organizational plan for her essay did not emerge until after Ida had written a draft and received feedback from her classmates and instructor. As she explained it:

> The first time I wrote the paper, I did not think about the order of ideas. I just wrote down all the examples I could think of to

show Neusner was wrong. After I presented my paper [for review], I knew my readers were confused. One of my classmates said, "I can't tell what's the most important thing to you," and that made me think about changing the order. So I decided I would put the idea about preparing us for life first, and then put the idea about "failure leaves no record," to emphasize it. Before I revised the paper, I made an outline of ideas and examples.

After her draft was reviewed, and upon learning that its disorganization made it difficult for her readers to understand her ideas, Ida made an outline to create a new and more logical order for her ideas and examples.

Ida's List of Neusner's Points and Her Counterexamples

1. Preparation for a world that is not real
   - We learn to be independent
   - learn to budget time and money
   - learn from diverse student body
   - we learn to be tolerant
2. Failure leaves no record
   - If you fail a test or a course, teacher won't change the grade
   - drop a class—you'll have to take more courses next semester
   - low GPA—no graduate school
3. College is "easy, free, . . . unchallenging," etc.
   - living in triple
   - one-day reading period
   - workload

This organization for the body of her paper is similar to the first organizational pattern suggested.

3. Conclusion

The conclusion grows out of the rest of the essay. You have restated what the author has said, analyzed how well the author's points are made, and explained why you agree or disagree with those points. Now is the time to make your final statement. It is important to remind your readers of the main focus of your paper: your position toward the author's ideas. You want to make your strongest statement at the end so that you can convince your readers of the validity of your point of view. You may also want to discuss the implications or consequences of accepting or supporting the author's view. There are several strategies you can use to bring your essay to its end.

SUGGESTIONS FOR A CONCLUDING DISCUSSION

In concluding your essay analyzing another writer's argument, you can use one or more of these strategies:

1. Emphasize the importance of your position.
2. Point out a basic flaw in the author's thinking.

3. Persuade readers to reject the author's arguments in favor of yours.
4. Propose a better way to view the topic.
5. Discuss the effect that your reading and writing have had on your view of the topic.

As with every other part of your paper, you may find that it takes several tries before you are satisfied with your conclusion. Again, remember that you will have the opportunity to rewrite your work after you have received suggestions from your reviewers.

A STUDENT WRITER AT WORK

Ida said:

> I didn't even have a conclusion in my first draft. I just wrote examples and then stopped. I had trouble deciding what my conclusion should be. Then I decided that I liked the details that I had in the introduction of my first draft and I wanted to use them. I couldn't use them in the introduction because the teacher thought the introduction shouldn't be so detailed. So I just moved that information and it became part of my conclusion, and I ended the paper with a strong statement.

Ida's Revised Conclusion

> To me, living in a crowded triple, having a one-day reading period before finals, tons of readings, papers, and midterms due the same week are not exactly my idea of " 'easy, free, forgiving, attentive, comfortable, interesting, unchallenging fun.' "

ACTIVITY: *Organizing the essay*

Either in your head or on paper (or both), sketch out a preliminary organizational plan for your essay. Read over your notes to determine your focus. If there are several ideas from the reading that you want to discuss, the first suggested organizational pattern for the body of your paper may work best. You will then need to decide the most logical order of the ideas. If there is only one major idea that you have a strong reaction to, the second pattern may fit your material. If you are interested in emphasizing ideas that the reading neglects, the third pattern may be most useful for you. Of course, other alternatives exist. If a pattern has not emerged from your material, ask your instructor for advice. ●

Writing a Draft to Present for Review

Prepare a draft of your essay to be read and reviewed by your classmates and instructor. Before you bring your paper to class, use the checklist for content.

> ## *Checklist for Content: Self-Evaluation*
>
> Does my essay provide all of the following details?
>
> 1. The title and the name of the author of the reading I am writing about
> 2. A summary of the gist of the argument in the reading
> 3. A statement of the idea or ideas in the reading that I am responding to (if this is different from the main argument)
> 4. A focal point that reveals my position toward the idea(s) from the reading that I am responding to
> 5. Paraphrased and quoted references to the reading
> 6. Well-supported reasons for agreeing or disagreeing with the author
>
> If the answer to any of the questions is no, either add the missing material to your draft before bringing it in for review, or prepare to explain to your reviewers and instructor what you will include in your revision of this essay. If you are not sure what to include, ask for advice.

Peer Reviewing

Bring your draft to class to exchange papers with your classmates. Review each other's papers by examining (1) what you like about the paper and (2) what you think can be done to improve it. Determine whether the writer has successfully analyzed the author's argument and established a position toward ideas discussed in the reading. Use the peer review form on p. 57 and the following questions to shape your responses.

1. Is the focus clear?
   a. If the answer is yes, what is the focal point of the essay?
   b. If the answer is no, can you suggest a way in which the focus could be clarified?
2. Does the writer make enough references (through summary, paraphrase, and quotation) to the reading to reveal its purpose and content?
   a. If the answer is yes, which references did you find most helpful? Why?
   b. If the answer is no, where can more references be added? Can you suggest specific references that might be helpful? If so, what are they?
3. Does the writer provide enough well-supported reasons for agreeing or disagreeing with the reading?
   a. If the answer is yes, which reason is most convincing?

b. If the answer is no, where should more reasons be added? Which reasons need fuller development? Which reasons are unconvincing?

Evaluate the organization of the essay, and raise and answer any other questions that you think will help the writer to improve the paper.

Revising

After receiving feedback from your classmates and instructor, revise your paper by asking and answering these questions (see pp. 60–61 for fuller discussion):

- What should I keep?
- What should I add?
- What should I delete?
- What should I change?
- What should I rearrange?
- What should I rethink?

Completing the Essay

Once you have revised the essay, read it over to evaluate the essay as a whole. Make sure that there is a smooth flow from paragraph to paragraph and that every part fits logically. Check to see that the issues raised in the introduction are discussed throughout the body and that the conclusion grows out of the rest of the essay. Proofread and edit the essay, and prepare a neat final manuscript to hand in for evaluation.

PART FOUR

Writing from Outside Sources: Researching a Controversy

READING

Angela Gan, "Asian-American Students: Why Is Their Success Becoming a Hindrance?" (student essay)

The essay you will complete at the end of Part Four is a *research essay*, that is, an essay in which you develop an opinion based on reading materials found through your own investigation (see Essay Assignment 4, p. 172). You will choose your topic from news stories and opinion pages published in recent issues of American newspapers and magazines. This assignment will therefore enable you to become better informed about issues that are covered in the American press. There are numerous challenges in such an assignment:

1. To find a topic that engages your interest
2. To formulate a question that your research will answer
3. To decide which research materials you will need
4. To evaluate the ideas and information in different sources
5. To synthesize (combine and integrate) ideas and information
6. To examine various sides to an issue
7. To establish a position in relation to the topic

To fulfill this assignment, you will use many of the strategies you have used in previous essays, including summarizing, paraphrasing, quoting, evaluating, and analyzing what you have read. You will also learn how to find information in the college library and through various organizations on and off campus. In addition, you will be asked to synthesize materials from several sources. Finally, you will learn formats for citing and documenting outside sources.

CHAPTER SEVEN

Preparing for Research

Since finding and synthesizing materials takes time, your research project should begin early in the semester. You will be working on your research essay as you are writing and revising other essays for this course.

Essay Assignment 4

Write an essay in which you establish and support a position on a controversial issue that has recently been covered in the news. (A *controversial* issue is one that is subject to a conflict of opinion.) Gather your sources of information about the issue from the library. You may also interview authorities on your subject. In writing this essay, you will need to evaluate and synthesize materials from several sources as you examine the various sides of the issue. To help you shape your ideas, you will be asked to make an oral presentation of your research to the class. Your purpose in fulfilling the assignment will be to explore and come to a fuller understanding of the importance of your chosen topic.
●

Understanding the Assignment

Before you begin writing an essay, you need to understand exactly what you are being assigned to write. You need to analyze the directions of the writing assignment so that you know both the essay's possibilities and its limitations. The following activity can help you fulfill that goal.

ACTIVITY: *Analyzing the assignment*

Working in a group of three or four students, examine what the writing assignment asks you to do. What purpose will the essay serve? What material should it contain? If you are unclear as to the demands of the assignment, consult with your instructor.
●

ACTIVITY: *Reading a sample student research essay*

Before you begin your own research, read the sample student research essay in this chapter. By reading and discussing this essay with your classmates, you can get an idea of what your own essay might look like.   ●

Asian-American Students: Why Is Their Success Becoming a Hindrance?
by Angela Gan

Angela Gan wrote the following research essay in 1987 to fulfill a writing assignment for a composition course. What you will read is a finished composition, carefully edited for publication in this book.

As you work through Chapters 8 and 9, you will see how Angela selected and developed her topic. By studying the process she went through, you can learn one approach to research writing.

> In the last ten years, Asian-Americans have scored higher than whites on the math portion of the Scholastic Aptitude Test, averaging 515 points out of a possible 800, as against 490. . . . Last year Asian-Americans won the top five scholarship awards in the Westinghouse contest. (Quindlen, 1987, p. 37)

> They make up about 10 percent of Harvard's freshman class and 20 percent of all students at the Julliard School. In California, where Asians are 5.5 percent of the population, they total 23.5 percent of all Berkeley undergraduates. (McBee, 1984, p. 46)

Social scientists are fascinated by this group of minority students and have conducted numerous studies to find out what drives these top achievers to excel. They trace the push to succeed academically to culture, social background, and especially family honor. Unfortunately, while these Asian students continue to work hard, recent reports and statistics have shown that some elite colleges and universities are setting admission quotas to cut down Asian students' admission rates. Some have changed admission policies to make admission harder for them. This quota system worries a lot of Asian students and their parents and makes Asian student associations and communities furious. School officials of these prestigious institutions, however, deny all these charges.   1

Many Asian immigrant families are from cultures "with vestigial Confucian influences, where advancement was entirely based on exam scores" (Biemiller, 1986, p. 35). They understand only grades and academic achievement. "It's hard for them to believe that a female hockey starter has a better   2 chance of getting into college than their son or daughter with 1590 combined SAT scores," says Jayjai Hsia, a senior research scientist at the Educational Testing Service (Biemiller, 1986, p. 35). Mr. Yamashita, an assistant professor at Pomona College, also says that the Confucian tradition, which emphasizes great respect for learning and for teachers, inspires Asian students to excel. Furthermore, students in Asia, for example, in Japan and Taiwan, attend school longer than in America, 240 days versus 180 days a year (McBee, 1984). There is also a different educational form, for example, in Taiwan. "Push, push, push. Much more homework, much more push" (Quindlen, 1987, p. 37). Thus Asian students are used to working a lot and under pressure. Now they are here [in the United States] to get a better education; they work by themselves; they do not need pushes anymore. However, their parents still pressure them.

"The achievements of Asian-American students are rooted in the 3
family," says Emmy Werner, a professor of human development at University of California, Davis. "Our Western idea has always been 'I do well to show I am No. 1.' In many of the Asian families, the idea is to do well to give the family a sense of pride and accomplishment" (Quindlen, 1987, p. 38). There is also a sense of obligation not to embarrass the family; it is called "face" [a Chinese expression] (Williams, 1984, p. 77). Apart from family honor, there is also a difference in attitude and academic standards between Asian parents and American parents. John Whitmore, an Asia expert at the University of Michigan's Institute for Social Research, finds that "if an American student isn't doing well in school, his parents think the teacher or school has failed or the student just doesn't have it. The Asian parents' view is that the student isn't trying hard enough" (McBee, 1984, p. 42). Asian-American parents also have much higher academic expectations than Anglo-American parents (Yao, 1985). For example, in order for the American mother to say she is satisfied, the child has to be just about average. For the Asian mother to say she is very satisfied, the child must be in the highest percentiles. Moreover, unlike non-Asian parents, Asian parents do not encourage their children to participate in extracurricular activities or to play with their friends after school ("Asian-Americans Lead the Way," 1986). Activities for Asian students focus on homework and lessons, for example, music, requiring a lot of practice and concentration.

However, these Asian youngsters are facing an obstacle now—pres- 4
tigious colleges and universities are limiting their admissions. Recently, a lot of Asian students complained that Ivy League schools have set up admission quotas. These complaints have come to the attention of social scientists and researchers. Some have done research with the following findings: The admission rate for Asian-Americans has dropped from 39 percent to 17 percent in the past ten years (Salholz, Doherty, & Tran, 1987). Whenever Asian student admissions reach 10 to 12 percent, a "red light" goes on, and admissions remain the same or are lowered at many famous and influential schools (Perlmutter, 1987, p. 27).

In California, where there is a big Asian community, a task force was   5
assembled by several Asian-American organizations to look at admission
policies there. The report of this task force says that enrollment of Asian
freshman (at UCLA and UC Berkeley) fell 21 percent in 1984; this decline
was attributed to several deliberate policy changes. These changes include
"a decision 'to temporarily employ a minimum SAT verbal score to dis-
qualify applicants,'" as well as a decision to 'redirect' students admitted under
an equal-opportunity program if they were not underrepresented minorities"
(Biemiller, 1986, p. 36). Another report cites that Berkeley changed its
policy in 1983 to give more importance to personal essays and extracurricular
activities, areas in which Asian-Americans are weaker (Salholz, Doherty,
& Tran, 1987). None of these changes or decisions was announced (Biemiller, 1986).

On the East Coast, Brown University limits minority admissions during   6
admission season to achieve a total of 20 percent (Salholz, Doherty, & Tran,
1987). This works out to be the same as a quota. Complaints about Harvard
are even more severe; there is a higher admission standard for Asian-American applicants. In 1982, Asian students who were offered admissions had
combined SAT scores 112 points higher than white students offered admissions (Biemiller, 1986). Furthermore, in 1985, Harvard admitted 15.9
percent of the white students who applied but only 12.5 percent of the
Asians (Biemiller, 1986). At Princeton, the same thing happened. It admitted
17 percent of the white students who applied but only 14 percent of the
Asians (Perlmutter, 1987).

All colleges deny any charges of discrimination—whether it is racial,   7
religious, ethnic, or sexual. In providing proof that they are not discriminatory, many admission officers point out there is a higher percentage of
Asians in their schools than in the national population. They say that if
there are any lower percentages than in the past, "it is only because the
institution has attracted and accepted a wider range of applicants in order
to reflect the population diversity of America" (Perlmutter, 1987, p. 27).
They insist that they need to accept students from a variety of backgrounds
and interests. They prefer the term *enrollment goals* to *quotas* (Salholz, Doherty, & Tran, 1987).

Officials at some schools, Princeton and Harvard, for example, have   8
concluded that "Asian-Americans are admitted at a lower rate only because
they are underrepresented in two important applicant pools—alumni children and athletes" (Salholz, Doherty, & Tran, 1987, p. 60). At Berkeley,
Thomas Travers, assistant vice-chancellor, says that a number of factors
caused the 20 percent decline. Among the factors were "smaller class sizes
. . . and the decision to protect only economically disadvantaged minority-
group students from reassignment to other campuses. He also points out
that Berkeley is under a legislative order "to assure that the composition of
its student population approximates that of graduating high school classes
statewide" (Biemiller, 1986, p. 36).

I cannot accept the thinking of the admission officials. I strongly object   9 to the quota system. America is made up of immigrants from all over the world. People should have equal opportunities to pursue their academic and career goals. Brochures of different colleges throughout the nation spell out that there are equal opportunities for minority and ethnic groups. Why are educators oppressing immigrant students of a hardworking minority group now? After Asian-American students graduate from college, they will be as beneficial to the society as their non-Asian counterparts, both economically and socially. Thus I see no reason for setting up a quota system. It does not solve or prevent any problems (if there are any). On the contrary, it lowers the academic standard of these colleges if non-Asian students do not work harder, and the worst is, it produces discriminatory outcomes. Furthermore, I think that education should be based on fair academic competition. It should not be based on social factors, such as whether the applicant's father is an alumnus or how many athletic awards the applicant won in high school. It is the applicant who is going to school, not his father or his sports awards. When one wants to achieve something, one has to work for it. Hard workers will always be rewarded in the end.

In fact, Asian students are in the same position as the Jews and blacks   10
in the 1920s and 1930s. In 1922, the work of Ralph P. Boas revealed that

> . . . personality, eligibility to social circles, conformity to discipline and acceptable behavior had become the deciding factors, thereby excluding "a large proportion of Jewish students, all negroes, and most members of other immigrant groups." By preferring such qualities over scholastic competition, "the colleges are bound to lose more than they will gain" (Ralph P. Boas, quoted in Perlmutter, 1987, p. 27).

This is really true, only now Asian-American students are the victims!

References

Asian-Americans lead the way in educational attainment. (1986, March). *Phi Delta Kappan*, p. 546.

Biemiller, L. (1986, November 19). Asian students fear top colleges use quota systems. *Chronicle of Higher Education*, pp. 1; 34–36.

McBee, S. (1984, April 2). Are they making the grade? *U.S. News and World Report*, pp. 41–43; 46–47.

Perlmutter, P. (1987, March). Victims of success. *Tab*, p. 27.

Quindlen, A. (1987, February 22). The drive to excel. *New York Times Magazine*, pp. 32; 34–38; 40.

Salholz, E., Doherty, S., & Tran, D. (1987, February 9). Do colleges set Asian quotas? *Newsweek*, p. 60.

Williams, D. A. (1984, April 23). A formula for success. *Newsweek*, pp. 77–78.

Yao, E. L. (1985). A comparison of family characteristics of Asian-American and Anglo-American high achievers. *International Journal of Comparative Sociology*, 26, 198–208.   ●

Write after You Read

1. Make a journal entry on this essay.
2. Write a two- or three-sentence summary of this essay.   ●

Activities for Class Discussion

Working with the whole class, share in the following activities.

1. On the board, write a two- or three-sentence summary of Angela's essay.
2. Discuss your reaction to Angela's essay.
3. Briefly outline the organization of the essay on the board. Distinguish among the introduction, the body, and the conclusion. Discuss whether the writer's ideas flow smoothly in a logical order.
4. Angela presents various opinions about the Asian-American quota controversy. Which sides of the issue does she discuss? Does she include enough discussion of the various sides of the issue?
   a. If the answer is yes, which discussion is most thorough?
   b. If the answer is no, which side of the issue needs more development?
5. Angela makes numerous references to outside sources. Are these references clear enough so that you can understand where the information comes from?
   a. If the answer is yes, which references seem to be the most important or effective? Why?
   b. If the answer is no, where should references be added, clarified, or deleted?
6. Angela wrote this paper for a composition course. Her audience consisted of American and international students and an American instructor. To what extent do you think her knowledge of this audience influenced the way she wrote the paper? Do you think she might have written differently if her audience had been different? To answer the latter question, go through the following list of potential audiences and discuss how Angela might have changed her writing to appeal to each audience:
   - An admission officer at the university
   - A group of non-Asian American students
   - A group of Asians   ●

CHAPTER EIGHT

Guidelines for Finding a Topic and Gathering Material for Essay Assignment 4

W riting an essay based on research is a complex process that requires time and careful planning. You will undoubtedly develop your own way of working, but the strategies listed here suggest approaches you can take to fulfill the assignment. Various stages of research are presented one step at a time, though you will discover as you work that the stages often overlap. To show how the different stages can interact in the development of a research essay, the writing of one student, Angela Gan, is included. Her 1987 essay "Asian-American Students: Why Is Their Success Becoming a Hindrance?" is reprinted on pp. 173–176.

Becoming Familiar with Major Newspapers and Magazines

This assignment asks you to research a controversial topic recently covered in the American press. To prepare for your essay, you should first be familiar with major newspapers and magazines.

ACTIVITY: *Becoming familiar with current newspapers and magazines and selecting potential research topics*

Bring to class a major newspaper such as the *New York Times* or the *Washington Post*, the major newspaper of the state in which your college is located, a major popular newsmagazine such as *Time* or *Newsweek*, or a more specialized magazine such as *Psychology Today*. Then work in small groups.

1. Find the index of a newspaper or the table of contents of a magazine.
2. Look over the headlines or titles of the articles.
3. Look at any accompanying photographs or illustrations.
4. Find the editorial section.
5. Read the opening lines of some of the articles.

From the magazines and newspapers that have been brought to class, select five topics that might be appropriate for a research essay. Share your selections with other groups. Discuss the following questions about each topic with the instructor.

1. Is this topic controversial? In other words, is there a conflict of opinion about this topic?
2. Is this topic researchable? In other words, will there be enough material in the library to draw from? Are there people on campus or in the community who can share their knowledge of this topic through interviews?
3. Is the instructor knowledgeable about this topic? In other words, is this a topic the instructor can evaluate, or is this topic related to a field in which the instructor has little or no expertise?   ●

Finding a Topic That Engages Your Interest

Once you are familiar with several newspapers and magazines and know which kinds of topics might be appropriate, you can begin the process of selecting a topic that is of absorbing interest to you. Since you will be spending a great deal of time researching and writing about it, select a topic that you are curious to learn more about. At first, you may find several topics of interest. With your instructor's and classmates' help, you can narrow down your search to one topic that you can handle during the course.

A STUDENT WRITER AT WORK

Angela's Search for a Topic

Every day for a week, Angela skimmed newspapers and magazines for issues that captured her interest. She brought to class articles on three issues and discussed them with her instructor and classmates. Because of her own Asian background, she decided she was most interested in doing research based on an article in *Newsweek* magazine (February 9, 1987) titled "Do Colleges Set Asian Quotas?" (pp. 180–181). Her topic was approved, and she was given several weeks to complete the project.

ACTIVITY: *Finding a topic*

Skim several newspapers and magazines for several days (you may need more than a week) to search for a research topic. Use your journal to discuss the various possibilities. Remember that you need to select a topic about which there is some controversy, so that you can examine various positions on one issue. On the assigned date, bring articles (or photocopies of articles)

EDUCATION

Do Colleges Set Asian Quotas?

Enrollments are up, but they could be higher still

With a mix of awe and animosity, students in the Boston area joke that MIT stands for Made in Taiwan. Like many of the nation's most competitive schools, the Massachusetts Institute of Technology has experienced huge increases in Asian-American enrollments. Across the Ivy League, Asian-Americans, who make up only 2 percent of the nation's college-age population, account for 11 percent of this year's freshman class. Proud of their high grades and test scores, Asian-Americans say they should be doing even better—and have accused top colleges of imposing ceilings to keep them out. "Asians are being discriminated against," charges Arthur Hu, an MIT alum who has studied Ivy League admissions patterns. "Unwritten quotas are making it more and more difficult to get into selective schools."

Recent admissions patterns do raise troubling questions. The nation's toughest institutions began admitting large numbers of Asian-Americans in the mid-1970s. But as their applica-

tions increased—by as much as 1,000 percent—the acceptance rate dropped; at Yale, the "admit" rate for Asian-Americans fell from 39 percent to 17 percent in the last decade. The timing was no coincidence, charges University of California, Berkeley, Prof. Ling-chi Wang. He claims that when worried schools realized what was happening, they began to curb the numbers.

Colleges deny setting ceilings, but they have taken the charges seriously. A Stanford University subcommittee concluded that "unconscious biases" might be responsible for the discrepancy in admission rates; subcommittee member Daniel Okimoto, a political-science professor, found that Asian-American applicants were often stereotyped as driven and narrowly focused. Princeton and Harvard have concluded that Asian-Americans are admitted at a lower rate only because they are underrepresented in two important applicant pools—alumni children and athletes.

Some critics accuse schools of deliberately adjusting admis-

RICK BROWNE—PICTURE GROUP

Turning affirmative action on its head: *Stanford students*

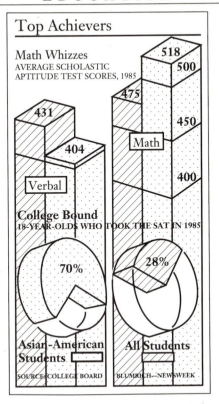

Top Achievers

Math Whizzes
AVERAGE SCHOLASTIC
APTITUDE TEST SCORES, 1985

518
500
475
450
431
404
400
Math
Verbal

College Bound
18-YEAR-OLDS WHO TOOK THE SAT IN 1985

70%
28%

Asian-American
Students

All Students

SOURCE: COLLEGE BOARD   BLUMRICH—NEWSWEEK

sion criteria to keep Asian-American numbers down.

Berkeley revised its procedures in 1983 to give greater weight to essays and extracurricular activities, areas in which Asian-American students traditionally fare less well. The university says Asian-Americans were irrelevant to the decision; they make up 26 percent of the freshman class this year, up from 22 percent in 1978. Brown University, meanwhile, keeps a log of minority admits during admissions season, reportedly to achieve a total of 20 percent. "Asian-Americans should be concerned," says a Brown admissions officer. "We call them enrollment goals, but it works out about the same as a quota."

Assembling a freshman class has always been more than a numbers game at prestigious colleges, based not only on grades but on alumni connections, interviews and a vague sense of who will "fit in." The emphasis on leadership and participation has sometimes hurt Asians, who have the reputation of "being somewhat isolated unto themselves," says Richard Moll, author of "The Public Ivys." Schools also succumb to social and political pressures. "The concept universities love beyond all others is diversity," says Marvin Bressler,

chairman of the Princeton sociology department. "But it's a highly flexible word." Before World War II, for example, "regional diversity" was a way of keeping out Jews, who tended not to live in Montana.

Schools opened the way to previously excluded ethnic groups in the 1960s. Now Asian-Americans have turned affirmative action on its head by outperforming not only other minorities but the majority as well. As a result, educators are asking themselves whether it is legitimate to try to preserve the traditional, largely WASP culture of most prestigious schools. "Stanford could become 40 percent Jewish, 40 percent Asian-American and 10 percent requisite black," says emeritus Harvard sociologist David Riesman. "You'd have a pure meritocracy, and that would create problems for diversity and alumni." Ironically, even their academic competence has sometimes worked against Asians in a milieu that fondly remembers the gentleman's C. Clearly, Asian-Americans have earned a secure place for themselves at America's finest schools, but those institutions are still coming to terms with their changing identity.

ELOISE SALHOLZ *with* SHAWN DOHERTY
in Boston and DE TRAN *in San Francisco*

on three or four topics that you think you might like to research. Present these topics to the class, beginning with the one you would most like to investigate. Your instructor and classmates will help you choose the most appropriate topic for the assignment.   ●

Summarizing a Newspaper or Magazine Article

Once you have selected a topic, you need to clarify the controversial issue for yourself and your instructor. One way to accomplish that goal is to summarize an article that explains the controversy.

News articles report events and usually indicate the significance of those events. In summarizing news articles, you should aim to report both the events and their significance. However, you may find that whereas articles in magazines are usually structured as essays, articles in newspapers are often disorganized and contain short, choppy paragraphs. Both magazine and newspaper writers typically use idiomatic language or slang. Therefore, you need to read carefully to discover the logical order of events and to determine why they are being reported. Ask yourself: What has happened? Why has this newspaper or magazine decided to publish this information? What does the newspaper or magazine want its readers to know or to learn?

A STUDENT WRITER AT WORK

Angela summarized an article on Asian quotas that she found in *Newsweek* magazine (see pp. 180–181).

Angela's Summary

> Summary of "Do Colleges Set Asian Quotas?" by Salholz, Doherty, and Tran, *Newsweek*, February 9, 1987, p. 60:
>
> Recently, there has been an increase in Asian-American students being accepted to colleges throughout the nation. But Ivy League schools have started to set Asian quotas as they did for Jewish people a few years ago. Some don't do it directly; they weight essays and extracurricular activities greater than academic achievements because they know Asian students fare less well on these. Educators are doing this to prevent Asian students from overtaking the American students. Asians are claiming that they are being discriminated against.

ACTIVITY: *Summarizing an article*

Summarize an article connected to your research topic. Show the summary to your instructor.   ●

Writing an Informal Research Proposal

At this stage, you are ready to write an informal research proposal.[†] The purpose of the proposal is to explain to your instructor and to yourself how you want to proceed in your research. In other words, you should state what you want to learn about your topic.

A STUDENT WRITER AT WORK

Angela already had a strong opinion about her research topic, quotas for Asian-American students. Her brief proposal begins with that opinion.

Angela's Informal Research Proposal

> I don't think this quota system is going to do anything good for American students. I want to find out why Asian students work so hard, what are their incentives, goals, and values. I should also find out why Americans are not doing well. I would like to know how there can be fair competition.

ACTIVITY: *Planning your research project*

In one or more paragraphs, write an informal proposal in which you indicate what you want to find out about your research topic. Hand your proposal in to your instructor.   ●

Formulating a Research Question

Research is usually undertaken to find an answer to a question. A research question based on what you want to learn about your topic will guide you in finding sources in the library and elsewhere.

A STUDENT WRITER AT WORK

Angela reread her proposal and narrowed the focus of her research to a question.

Angela's Research Question

> My research question is: "Why are Asian students successful, and are they being discriminated against?"

As you can see, Angela's research question is actually two questions. Her task is to discover (1) why Asian students succeed and (2) if they are

---

[†] This is an *informal* research proposal. A *formal* research proposal would include a list of sources you would draw from to write your essay.

experiencing discrimination because of that success. She will now go to the library to begin to find information to answer those questions.

ACTIVITY: *Formulating a research question*

Reread your proposal and come up with a research question that your research will attempt to answer. Your question should reveal the problem or controversy connected with your topic. (Your question might begin with the word *should*, as in "Should Drug Addicts Be Given Clean Needles to Prevent AIDS?" or "Should Birth Control Clinics Be Allowed in Public Schools?") Show your research question to your instructor.   ●

Finding Needed Information

Once you know what you want to learn about your topic, you need to find information that will help you to answer your research question. At first you cannot know what you will find or what your answer will be. But as you gather information, you will increase your knowledge of the topic. At each stage, you will have a better understanding of what you have already found and a better idea of what you still need to discover.

There are many ways to learn more about a subject. The following guidelines should give you some idea of how to proceed. The order in which you follow the guidelines will be determined by your topic, your working habits, and your instructor's advice.

Becoming Familiar with the College Library

The most valuable source of information is the college library. You may find it intimidating at first; there are many books, and most are written in academic English. But in time, you can find it a comfortable place to do research.

SUGGESTIONS FOR BECOMING FAMILIAR WITH THE LIBRARY

1. Read the library pamphlets to learn where and how to find books, magazines, journals, and other materials.
2. Learn who the reference librarians are. Ask them for help when you need it.

Following Up on Your News Story

If you have chosen a current topic, follow it in newspapers and magazines. In addition to reading news articles, look in the editorial sections to see if there is any commentary on the issue you are researching.

A current major news story will probably be covered for several days or even weeks or months. But many issues have a short life in the American press. So you need to read carefully and ask others—classmates, other friends, family members—to help you find current articles on your topic.

It can be expensive to keep buying current newspapers and magazines. As an alternative, you can read many of them in your college library. The library keeps current newspapers and magazines in a reading room for several weeks or months before they are filed in a different place. You will also want to look at newspapers and magazines that are older. Guidelines for finding those materials will be presented in this chapter.

Determining Possible Subject Headings

Your topic can be described in several ways; in other words, it has different *subject headings*. You need to know how it is listed in the various reference sources in the library so that you can find more information about it. Therefore, you need a list of possible headings before you begin your search for library sources.

A STUDENT WRITER AT WORK

Angela's List of Possible Subject Headings

Asian-Americans

Quotas

College admissions

Discrimination

ACTIVITY: *Listing possible subject headings*

Asking for your instructor's or classmates' help if necessary, make a list of headings that your subject might be listed under. (If you later find that this list is inadequate, check the reference book *Library of Congress: Subject Headings*. The librarian can show you how to use this publication to find appropriate subject headings for your topic.)   ●

Finding Background Information in a Book: Using a Card Catalog or Computer File

Finding out about the background of the issue you have chosen to research will help you to understand it better. One good place to start can be in a book that gives a history or overview of the subject. Begin with a card catalog or computer file that lists all the books the library has. Both usually list books alphabetically in several ways: by author, by title, and by one or more subject headings (see Figure 8-1 on page 186 for a sample card catalog subject card).

Follow these guidelines for using a card catalog or computer file to find book titles related to your topic.

1. Look up the first subject heading on your list. If you do not find books appropriate to your topic, go down your list trying out dif-

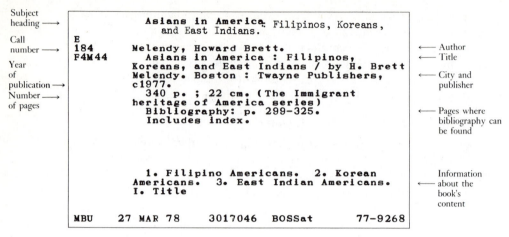

Figure 8-1   Sample Subject Catalog Card

ferent headings. Sometimes you need two headings (or *descriptors*, in computer language)—for example, "Asian-Americans—Education"—to find the books most closely related to your topic.

2. If you find one or more books related to your topic, write the name of the author, the title, and, most important, the *call number*. (If there are many books on your topic, just write down one or two; you will find books on similar topics shelved together). The call number will tell you where the book is shelved in the library. For example, if the number is

E
184
F4M44

the book is shelved, according to the Library of Congress classification system, with books on American history, as indicated by the code letter *E*.

Then follow these guidelines for finding books relevant to your research.

1. Once you find the shelves for the code letter (e.g., *E*), search for the numbers following the code letters (184) and then the final code (F4M44) until you find your book.
2. Skim the book to see if its information is helpful to you. Check the table of contents at the beginning and the index at the end, and read the first few lines of several chapters.
3. If the book is relevant to your topic, check the back of the book to see if there is a bibliography (a list of books and articles used by the author to do the research for the book). You may want to search for one or more of those books or articles.

4. *Important:* Keep a list of the books that you may use in your research. Record author, title, and call number.

A STUDENT WRITER AT WORK
Angela's Search for a Book

In searching for background information on her topic, Angela discovered how frustrating using the library can be. She could not at this early stage in her research find a book that provided an overview of her topic. She did find several books on Asian-Americans, but they focused on the immigration, literature, mental health, and history of Asians rather than on their educational achievements. Following her instructor's advice, she decided to search for information in magazines, journals, and newspapers.

ACTIVITY: *Finding background information in a book*

Following the suggestions for using a card catalog or computer file, search for a book that provides background information on your topic. If you are frustrated in your search, ask for help from your instructor or the reference librarian.   ●

Finding Lists of Magazine Articles: Using a Generalized Index or Computer File

To find magazine articles other than current ones that are kept in the reading room of the library, you need to use *periodical indexes*, which are located in the reference section of the library. These indexes list articles published on a variety of subjects. The most generalized index is the *Readers' Guide to Periodical Literature*, which lists many popular magazines. This and other indexes are organized by year (e.g., articles published in 1987) and are arranged alphabetically. Explanations of the abbreviations the indexes use can be found at the beginning of each volume. Some libraries also have the Magazine Index, Infotrac, or other machines or computers that store lists of recent magazine articles. Some of these machines can generate a computer printout listing magazine articles on a given topic.

A STUDENT WRITER AT WORK

Angela used the *Readers' Guide to Periodical Literature*, searching for articles about her topic under several headings. She had the most luck with the heading "Asian Americans." Angela began with the most recent volume at that time, 1987, and then looked at volumes dated 1986, 1985, and 1984 until she felt she had a useful list of articles.

In a 1984–1985 index, Angela found three articles listed under the heading "Asian Americans" (Figure 8-2, page 188). She eliminated the article on Asian foods and selected the two other articles for her paper.

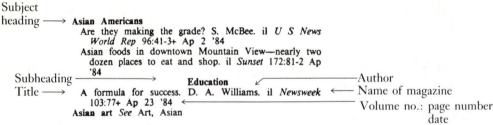

Subject
heading ——→ **Asian Americans**
      Are they making the grade? S. McBee. il *U S News*
        World Rep 96:41-3+ Ap 2 '84
      Asian foods in downtown Mountain View—nearly two
        dozen places to eat and shop. il *Sunset* 172:81-2 Ap
Subheading ———————→ '84
Title ——→   **Education**   ——Author
    A formula for success. D. A. Williams. il *Newsweek* ←— Name of magazine
      103:77+ Ap 23 '84 ←———————————————— Volume no.: page number
    Asian art *See* Art, Asian   date

Figure 8-2   Excerpt from the *Readers' Guide to Periodical Literature*

ACTIVITY: Using the Readers' Guide *or a computer file*

Use the *Readers' Guide to Periodical Literature* or your library's computer
file to look for lists of articles on your topic. Search alphabetically by subject
heading. ●

Finding Lists of Journal Articles: Using a Specialized Index

In college-level research, you need to search not only in generalized
indexes but also in specialized indexes that list (1) journal articles written
in a scholarly way for specialized and academic audiences or (2) articles on
scholarly topics written in a way that is understandable to nonspecialists.
The college library has numerous specialized indexes, for example:

Applied Science and Technology Index   *Humanities Index*
Art Index   *Social Sciences Index*
Education Index

At this stage in your college career, some of the articles you find through
a specialized index may be too difficult to read. But a number of periodicals
in various fields are considered authoritative yet understandable to nonspecialists. The following list may help you; the librarian may provide other
titles in your area of investigation.

EDUCATION

Chronicle of Higher Education
Phi Delta Kappan

**INTERNATIONAL
RELATIONS**

Current History
Far East Economic Review
Foreign Policy
The Nation
World Press Review

POLITICAL SCIENCE

American Political Science Review
Journal of the History of Ideas
Journal of International Affairs
Public Opinion Quarterly
Western Political Quarterly

PSYCHOLOGY

American Psychologist
Psychology Today

SCIENCE
American Scientist
Bioscience
Discover
National Geographic
Science
Science News

Scientific American
Space World

SOCIOLOGY
American Journal of Sociology
International Journal of Compara-
tive Sociology

A STUDENT WRITER AT WORK

Angela used the *Education Index* to find articles about Asian-American quotas in colleges because her topic dealt with an educational subject.

Under the heading "Asian Americans" and the subheading "Education," Angela found a list of four articles in the 1986–1987 index (Figure 8-3). She eliminated two articles—one on Catholic education and one on Asian teachers—because they seemed to be unrelated to her specific topic. She took down the information on the other two articles but later discovered that the library did not carry one of the journals listed. The article Angela did eventually use for her paper is circled.

Heading ⟶ **Asian Americans**
See also
Japanese Americans
Counseling services
See Culturally deprived—Counseling services

Subheading ⟶ **Education**

The Asian American success myth. D. Wei. il *Interracial Books Child Bull* 17 no3-4:16-17 '86
The Asian presence: what Catholic educators should know. P. O. Hwang. *Momentum* 18:45-6 F '87
Asian students fear top colleges use quota systems. L. Biemiller. il *Chron Higher Educ* 33:1+ N 19 '86
Asian teachers: a new dimension. R. A. Rundall and F. Hernandez. *Clearing House* 60:91-2 O '86

Figure 8-3   Excerpt from the *Education Index*

ACTIVITY: Using a specialized index

Use a specialized index to find a list of articles relevant to your topic. If you are not sure which specialized index to use, ask your instructor or the reference librarian for advice.   ●

Finding Lists of Newspaper Articles: Using a Newspaper Index

The college library subscribes to several newspapers, including some from other countries. Some of these newspapers are stored on microfilm after several weeks or months. Microfilm machines give you access to these older newspapers. First, you must find titles and dates of specific articles through a newspaper index. Most libraries have several indexes. Two are the National Newspaper Index (machine) and the *New York Times Index*.

A STUDENT WRITER AT WORK

Angela used the *New York Times Index* because she knew that her college library stored the *New York Times* on microfilm. When she looked under the subject heading "Asian-Americans," she found the list of subheadings shown in Figure 8-4. The subheading relevant to Angela's topic is circled.

Asian-Americans. See also
Assaults, Je 2,3
California, N 10
Colleges and Universities, Ag 3,5
Crime and Criminals, Jl 27, N 30
Education and Schools, Ja 2,5, Ag 3
English Language. N 10
Housing, Ap 18, N 7
Immigration and Emigration, O 26, D 14
Los Angeles (Calif), Jl 6, Ag 24
Medicine and Health, Jl 14

Murders and Attempted Murders, Mr 27, Jl 27, S 13
New York City—Politics and Government, F 13
New York City—Social Conditions and Trends, S 14, O 24
New York City Metropolitan Area, Je 13
Newsdealers and Newsstands, Ja 3
Restaurants, N 24
Science and Technology, Mr 25
United States Economy, N 30
Washington (DC), N 24
  Asian-Americans across country are increasingly targets of racially motivated attacks, and new Coalition Against Anti-Asian Violence has been formed to address problem (M), O 19,I,37:1

Figure 8-4   List of Subject Headings from the *New York Times Index*

Angela looked over this list and decided to look under the heading "Colleges and Universities" to search for the articles on Asian-Americans listed for "Ag 3,5" (August 3 and August 5). The August 3 listing is circled in Figure 8-5.

United States Education Department figures show blacks made up 9.2% of students enrolled in four-year colleges in 1984, down from 9.6% in 1982 and high of 10.4% in 1982; blacks make up 13% of college-age population; drawing (special section, Education Life) (S), Ag 3,XII,12:5
  Remarkable academic success of Asian-Americans is touching off growing debate about whether some colleges are erecting informal quotas to limit their admissions; college administrators deny quotas exist, but Asian-Americans complain that some are being turned down despite having higher scores than other applicants (special section, Education Life) (M), Ag 3,XII,22:1   ← Date, section, page no.: column no.
Student debt is altering financial underpinnings of American higher education, with many colleges reporting that up to one third of their operating funds originate as loans to students and their parents; up to half of nation's 10 million undergraduates are now leaving school with some debts, and debts are shaping their professional and personal decisions; drawing; graph; photo (special section, Education Life) (L), Ag 3,XII,34:2

Figure 8-5   Excerpt from the *New York Times Index*

ACTIVITY: *Using a newspaper index*

Use a newspaper index to find a list of articles relevant to your topic. Be sure to find out which newspapers your library has on microfilm.   ●

Finding Articles in the Library

Once you have a list of articles that you think will help you in your research, you need to find those articles in the library. Follow these guidelines.

1. Check the list of library holdings at the reference desk to see if the library carries the magazines, newspapers, or journals you are interested in and to learn how these materials are stored.
2. Use the card catalog or computer file to find the call number for the volume that contains the magazine or journal (older magazines and journals are bound together in large volumes). Some magazines and journals and most newspapers will be on microfilm or microfiche.
3. If the article you are searching for is in a bound volume, find the volume on the library shelf, and look for the article by date and page number.
4. If the article you are searching for is on microfilm or microfiche, go to the microfilm room and ask the librarian for help in finding the article and using the microfilm or microfiche machine.
5. If you want to make a photocopy of the article, you can do so with a copying machine in the library. Even articles on microfilm and microfiche can be copied. Ask the librarian for help in doing so.

ACTIVITY: *Finding articles in the library*

Using the preceding guidelines, find magazine, journal, and newspaper articles that are relevant to your research.   ●

Reading Strategies

Because you are finding your own reading selections for this assignment, you need effective reading strategies to make wise decisions about which sources to include in your essay. Once you have found material in the library, the following suggestions may be helpful.

Before Reading

Preview an article or book chapter for a few minutes, to gain a general idea of its topic and organization:

1. Read the title and subtitle, if there is one.
2. Read the abstract (summary at the beginning), if there is one.

3. Read the first and last paragraphs.
4. Read the first sentence of every paragraph.
5. Look at any photographs, illustrations, or graphs.

Reading

Initially, you will be reading to discover whether or not the selections are appropriate for your topic. *Skim* the reading: read quickly for the main idea. This will give you an idea of the general content.

Evaluating Sources

Before you spend a lot of time working with a source, try to determine how reliable it is. Even though you are not an expert, you can use several criteria to evaluate each source.

CRITERIA FOR EVALUATING SOURCES

1. Is the information up to date?

Though an older publication may provide background information, it may be outdated, that is, some of the information may no longer be valid. For example, if you are investigating advances in nuclear weapons, a book written in 1958 may not be useful. Check the date of publication.

2. Is the publication fair and trustworthy?

Some popular publications such as *People Weekly* or the *National Enquirer* contain more gossip than information. Others are sponsored by special-interest groups and are therefore biased. If you are not familiar with a particular publication, you can check on the purpose and intended audience of a source by looking it up in a source that evaluates periodicals (a good one is *Magazines for Libraries* by Katz and Katz) or by asking your instructor or a librarian.

3. What is the author's expertise on the subject?

The author may be a news reporter rather than an authority who has done academic research in the subject area. Some reporters, however, have become experts in certain areas (for example, the *Newsweek* magazine bureau chief in the Soviet Union or the *New York Times* health specialist), and their opinions are worthy of reflection. Check on the expertise of the author by reading the description of the author accompanying the article, if there is one, or by consulting an index that discusses authors' achievements and credentials (e.g., the *Biographical Index* or *Current Biography*), or by asking your instructor or a librarian.

4. Is the article well-researched?

To do valid research, you need to find articles that have been carefully researched. Skim the article to find evidence that the author has interviewed authorities on the subject or has done outside reading to deepen the analysis of events. Look at the kind of information used to support major points: statistics, experiences, quotations, theories, and the like.

Rather than limiting your research to popular magazines such as *Time*, try to use more in-depth sources (for example, in the fields of politics and international relations, you could consult *Current History*, *World Press Review*, *Far East Economic Review*, or *Foreign Affairs*). Works that include documentation and a bibliography tend to be most reliable.

Rereading

Scan the reading: look for specific information that you might be able to use in your research essay. Relate what you read with what you already know about the topic.

Making a journal entry

Write in your journal. For example, you can do one or more of the following:

1. Summarize the reading.
2. Write about your reaction to what you have read, discussing how a reading helps (or does not help) you to understand your topic better.
3. Evaluate the supporting material of various arguments (see pp. 122–128).
4. Formulate questions that you want to ask the instructor about your research topic.

ACTIVITY: *Evaluating and recording sources*

Use the criteria for evaluating sources to evaluate the sources you have found in the library. Once you have selected reliable sources, record them in an organized manner.

For each book you use, record these details:

- Call number
- Name(s) of authors or editors
- Title of book, underlined
- City of publication
- Name of publisher
- Date of publication
- Inclusive page numbers, if you have read one article in a collection

For each periodical you use, record these details:

- Name(s) of author(s)
- Title of article, in quotation marks
- Name of magazine, journal, or newspaper, underlined

- Volume number of publication
- Date of publication
- Page number(s)

One efficient way to keep track of sources is to record them on 3- by 5-inch index cards (Figure 8-6).

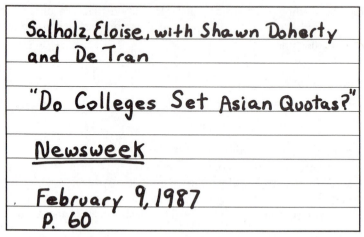

Figure 8-6   Sample Source Card for a Magazine Article

Taking Notes

Once you have found books and articles that you believe are valuable for your research, you can begin to take notes. As with all other aspects of research, the way you take notes is dependent on your material and your working style. The following guidelines suggest a note-taking technique—using 4- by 6-inch ruled index cards—that is popular and efficient. If you use this technique, you can avoid some of the disorganization that often complicates research writing. Notecards can be classified, arranged, and rearranged in a useful order when you start writing your research draft. However, if this technique is not useful for you, take notes in the most efficient and comfortable way possible. For example, you may want to keep notes in a notebook, or you may want to photocopy articles in the library so that you can take notes later on a word processor in your room or at the campus computer center.

SUGGESTIONS FOR TAKING NOTES ON LINED INDEX CARDS

1. In the upper right corner, indicate the source of the notes: for example, the name of the book or author.
2. At the beginning of the note, write the page number of the source.

As soon as the page number in your source changes, write the new number.

3. Try to limit the information you are putting on the card. For example, include only one important idea.

4. At the top, in the left corner, create a heading for the notecard: some word or words that identify the subject of the notecard.

5. Keep separate notecards for your own opinions as they occur to you during your research.

A STUDENT WRITER AT WORK

Angela's Notecards

Two of Angela's notecards appear in Figures 8-7 and 8-8.

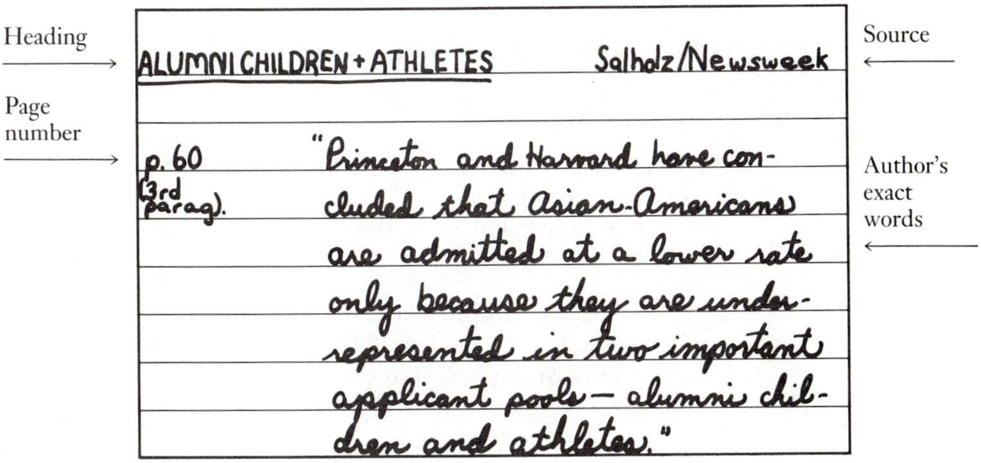

Heading
→

Page number
→

ALUMNI CHILDREN + ATHLETES   Salholz/Newsweek

Source
←

p. 60
(3rd parag).

"Princeton and Harvard have concluded that Asian-Americans are admitted at a lower rate only because they are underrepresented in two important applicant pools — alumni children and athletes."

Author's exact words
←

Figure 8-7   Notecard Containing a Direct Quotation.

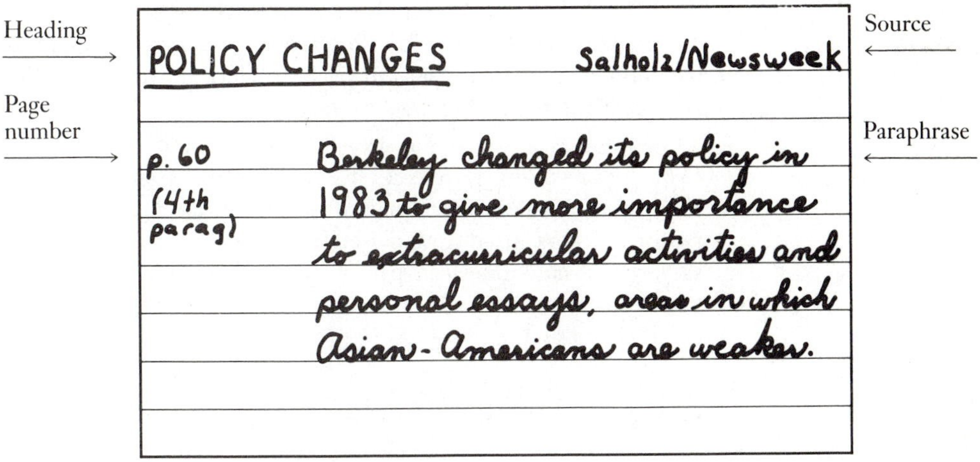

Heading
→

Page number
→

POLICY CHANGES   Salholz/Newsweek

Source
←

p. 60
(4th parag)

Berkeley changed its policy in 1983 to give more importance to extracurricular activities and personal essays, areas in which Asian-Americans are weaker.

Paraphrase
←

Figure 8-8   Notecard Containing a Paraphrase

ACTIVITY: *Taking notes*

Take notes on your library sources, either on notecards or through whatever method is most useful to you. Write down only what you understand. Paraphrase or quote key ideas and information. If you quote, copy exactly what you read, and put quotation marks around what you have written.   ●

Writing a Progress Report

After taking notes from several sources, it is a good idea to stop and assess what you have accomplished. One way to do that is to write a progress report that summarizes what you have done and have learned and indicates what you still need to discover.

A STUDENT WRITER AT WORK

Angela's Progress Report

I haven't changed my mind about this topic. I still think the idea of quotas is wrong.

So far I have found several magazine articles on Asian-Americans:

1. "Do Colleges Set Asian Quotas?" *Newsweek* 2/9/87, p. 60. (This is the first article I found that started my research. It explains that Asian-Americans are complaining that there are quotas limiting their admissions to U.S. colleges.)

2. "A Formula for Success," *Newsweek* 4/23/84, pp. 77–78. (This article is about the positive and negative sides of the achievement of Asian-American students.)

3. "Are They Making the Grade?" *U.S. News and World Report* 4/2/84, pp. 41–43, 46–47. (This article discusses the increasing influence of Asians on American society but also says that Asians still have a long way to go.)

4. "Asian-Americans lead the way in education attainment" *Phi Delta Kappan* 3/86, p. 546. (This article reports on two studies of Asian-Americans. One study says Asian-Americans outperform others in educational attainment. The other study says that Asian-American parents want their kids to study or take lessons after school rather than participate in extracurricular activities.)

I also have a *New York Times Magazine* article someone gave me that I haven't read yet.

I have to go to the microfilm room to find a newspaper article that was listed in the *New York Times Index*.

I'm not sure my information is deep enough. I think I need an article that is a research study. Where should I look for that?

I believe that Asians are being discriminated against in college admissions. I would like to understand why the admission people do this.

Instructor's Response to Angela's Progress Report

You have a good start on your research: you can explain the controversy concerning the quotas and can describe the achievements of the Asian-American students.

To find more in-depth information on Asian-Americans, you can use the *Social Sciences Index*, which lists scholarly articles in journals. You will probably find something on families and educational goals.

I am attaching an article from a local newspaper [*The Tab*] on the quota issue, which you may find useful for your research.

Since you want to understand the rationale behind the admission policy, perhaps you should interview someone in the admission office. You need to find out about the admission process. I think you will discover that the admission committee has some very difficult decisions to make. American universities are looking for a diverse student population.

A STUDENT WRITER AT WORK

Following her instructor's advice, Angela consulted the *Social Science Index*. She searched under the subject heading "Asian Americans." She found the subheading "Asians in the United States" and under that subheading she found the subheading "Education" (Figure 8-9). Under the

Asians in the United States
　　See also
　Chinese in the United States
　Filipinos in the United States
　Japanese in the United States
　Koreans in the United States
　Southeast Asians in the United States
　Vietnamese in the United States
　　　Acculturation
The elusive promise: new immigrants have trouble adjusting to American life [special report] M. Thompson and F. Viviano. *Far East Econ Rev* 134:46-51 O 16 '86
　　　　Education　　　　　　　　←———— Subheading
A comparison of family characteristics of Asian-American and Anglo-American high achievers. E. L. Yao. bibl *Int J Comp Sociol* 26:198-208 S/D '85
The math/reading gap among Asian American students: a function of nativity, mother tongue, and SES. A. Y. So. *Sociol Soc Res* 70:76-8 O '85
The passive-methodical image of Asian American students in the school system. H. Bannai and D. A. Cohen. *Sociol Soc Res* 70:79-81 O '85

Figure 8-9   Excerpt from the *Social Sciences Index*

subheading "Education," there were three articles on Asian-American students. Angela found all three articles in the library. But two of the articles were too difficult for her to understand; they used technical language and statistics that she couldn't follow. She did choose the third article, in the *International Journal of Comparative Sociology*, because the language and methodology were understandable. The article also could supply research findings on the differences between Asian-American and Anglo-American families.

ACTIVITY: *Writing a progress report*

Write an informal progress report—this can be written as a journal entry—in which you summarize your research progress. Include brief summaries (no more than one paragraph each) of at least three articles or book chapters. Use this opportunity to ask for advice or help. Your instructor may want you to write another progress report later in the term or to write weekly progress reports.   ●

Searching beyond the Library: Collecting Data and Interviewing

The library is not the only source of information on controversial topics. You can search beyond the library, on and off campus, collecting pamphlets or other literature on your subject or speaking to people in various departments, organizations, and institutions. Of course, you should be aware that many people may be biased in favor of their side of an issue.

The organizations you choose are dependent on your topic. Here is a partial list of potential places to contact.

1. On campus
   a. Academic departments: Once you have become somewhat informed about your topic, you can consult a faculty member who is knowledgeable in your research area.
   b. Offices: Various offices, such as admissions or a dean's office, can provide you with needed information. Check the college catalog for a list of these offices.
   c. Organizations: Many organizations on campus run by professionals or students specialize in specific areas of interest, for example, Amnesty International. Check with the student activities office for a list of such organizations.
2. Off campus
   a. Institutions and offices: Numerous institutions and offices, many run by the government, provide services to the public. By calling these places, you can be put in contact with specialists who can help to answer some of your research questions; for example:

Consulate or embassy	Mayor's office
Hospital	Museum

Newspaper   Town Hall
State House

b. Organizations and agencies: You can consult a special-interest organization or agency; some are run by the government. Check the yellow pages or government listings in the phone book; for example:

AIDS Action Committee
American Civil Liberties Union
Campaign headquarters
Consumer Affairs Council
Council on Aging
Criminal Justice Department
Department of Education
Drug rehabilitation center
Environmental Protection Agency
Gay rights organization
Handicapped council
Health association
Housing authority
Police Department
Social Services Department
Youth Services Department

GUIDELINES *Guidelines for Conducting an Interview*

1. Choose an interview subject.
2. Contact the person you wish to interview, explain your research project, and make an appointment. Limit the interview to a preset time.
3. Prepare a list of questions about your research topic, based on the reading you have done so far.
4. Be flexible with your questions. One good general opening question may be all you need. Let the interviewee talk. If you are friendly and relaxed, you'll learn a lot more than if you approach someone stiffly, with a set of rigid questions.
5. Use a tape recorder, if you have permission to do so. If you do not use a tape recorder, take brief notes during the interview. But do more listening than note taking.
6. Right after the interview, find a quiet spot to reflect on what you have just learned. Spend some time writing and adding to your notes.

A STUDENT WRITER AT WORK

Angela had not yet interviewed anyone concerning her research project, in spite of her teacher's suggestion to contact someone in the Admissions Office. She felt that she could find enough information in the library; and furthermore, she felt too shy to make the appointment. As you will see, however, she later found it necessary to conduct an interview. That interview is discussed on p. 211.

ACTIVITY: *Searching beyond the library*

To find information other than what can be found in the college library, contact an on- or off-campus department or organization.

1. Ask for any pamphlets or articles that might provide useful facts.
2. Follow the guidelines for conducting an interview. ●

CHAPTER NINE

Guidelines for Planning and Completing Essay Assignment 4

Defining Your Audience

This research essay is an argumentative essay. You will be comparing and contrasting various sides to an issue and explaining your position on that issue. The consideration of audience is a crucial factor in the success of your argument. You need to connect with your readers and move them toward an understanding of your position. You may even want to convince them of the rightness of your point of view. The evidence you provide, the appeals you make, and the language you use will all work together to accomplish the goal of enabling your audience to understand, and perhaps accept, what you believe.

Being aware of your readers as you plan an essay can help you to shape your thoughts. There are two audiences for your research essay: your classmates and your instructor. In orally presenting your research to classmates (see p. 210), you will have the opportunity to teach them about a topic they may be unfamiliar with. Therefore, as you gather material, you can keep that audience in mind.

The primary audience, however, is the instructor, so you should write and organize your essay with the instructor's expectations in mind. Because the research assignment asks you to find your own readings, your instructor's expectations will differ from those for an essay based on course readings. You must determine what those expectations are. The following activity can help you to achieve that goal.

ACTIVITY: *Defining your audience*

As a class, or in conference with your instructor, discuss answers to these questions:

1. What does the reader already know about the topic?
2. What is the reader's attitude toward the controversy?
3. What does the reader want to learn?
4. What kind of appeals might be appropriate?

201

5. What materials must you provide to ensure that the reader learns what needs to be learned and understands what needs to be understood?

Raise any other questions that will help you to define the audience.   ●

Focusing Your Thoughts

Although it takes a lot of time to gather and take notes on material connected with your topic, perhaps the hardest part of research is deciding how to combine all this material into one essay. Many researchers enjoy the process of finding sources and of learning more about their subject but feel enormous anxiety when faced with the task of putting it all together to make sense to others. If you feel that anxiety, you are not alone.

As a first step toward putting the material together, stop, think, and focus your thoughts much as you have done for other essay assignments. You can reread all of your notes and ask, "What do I want to show?" or "What do I want to prove?" By answering these questions and discussing your answers with a classmate, you can create a focal point for your essay, which will guide you as you write a draft.

Creating a Preliminary Outline

Since there is so much material involved in research writing, simply having a focus may not be enough to prepare you to write a first draft. You may need a preliminary outline.

A STUDENT WRITER AT WORK

Angela looked over all her notes and made a list of the headings of her notecards. She saw that much of her information involved the achievements of Asian-American students and the influence of their families. She also had information on the issue of the quotas in many American colleges. She wasn't sure how to combine all this information into the essay or how to make a link between Asian-American achievements and the quota issue. She decided simply to discuss one thing at a time and to see if a logical connection would emerge as she drafted the essay.

Angela's Preliminary Outline

   I. Introduction
  II. Asian students' achievements
 III. Asian parents versus American parents
 IV. Admission quotas for Asian students
  V. Conclusion

ACTIVITY: *Creating a preliminary outline*

Reread your notes. Find the major areas of the subject that you want to present in your paper. Organize those outlines into headings for a preliminary outline. Show the outline to your instructor. This outline is designed to help you focus your thoughts. You may change the order or content of the outline as you continue to work on your paper.   ●

Synthesizing

The term *synthesizing*, as it is used in this textbook, means combining and integrating material from different sources. In writing this research essay, you will be taking material from several sources and putting it together to reveal various sides to an issue. But you must be careful to put the material together carefully, so that each idea is clear and the ideas are logically connected. In other words, you cannot simply copy ideas from the various sources and place them in your paper one after the other. You have to decide which passages to quote directly and which passages to paraphrase. Then you have to think about the relationships between ideas. Furthermore, the paraphrases and quotations have to fit the grammatical structure of your own sentences. This means that you will make thoughtful decisions about what goes into each paragraph of your paper.

There are many ways in which ideas can be related, of course. One of the creative aspects of research writing is discovering relationships for yourself. A first step in writing a paragraph that draws from more than one source is to decide what the paragraph will be about. Then you can look at your notes to see which sources discuss that aspect of the topic.

A STUDENT WRITER AT WORK

When Angela wrote her paper, she discussed the achievements of Asian-American students in the first three paragraphs. Then she began the fourth paragraph by stating that in spite of their achievements, these students are being denied admission to prestigious universities. By reading the beginning of this fourth paragraph, her readers can tell what the paragraph will be about.

Now Angela's job was to produce information to reveal the truth of the statement. If she produced evidence from only one source, her readers might not be convinced. By including information from more than one source, she can persuade her audience more convincingly. Before examining the paragraph, first read passages from the original sources from which she drew her information:

> Recent admissions patterns do raise troubling questions. The nation's toughest institutions began admitting large numbers of Asian-Americans in the mid-1970s. But as their applications in-

creased—by as much as 1,000 percent—the acceptance rate
dropped; at Yale, the "admit" rate for Asian-Americans fell from
39 percent to 17 percent in the last decade.

SALHOLZ, DOHERTY, AND TRAN

In California, where most Asian-Americans live, a researcher recently found that as soon as Asian admissions reached 10 or 12
percent, "a red light went on" and admissions are stabilized or
reduced at a large number of Ivy League schools, including
Berkeley, Stanford, MIT and Yale.

PERLMUTTER

Angela could see the relationship between these two sources: both provide
statistics to show that the Asian-Americans' acceptance rates dropped when
a certain percentage was reached. As she wrote her paper, she began her
paragraph with a main idea, then carefully selected parts of each source to
support that idea. As you read the paragraph she produced, note that she
paraphrased the material and used quotation marks when she used an exact
short phrase from a source and that she gave credit to her sources by
mentioning in parentheses the authors' names, the date, and the page number
for a quotation.

Angela's Fourth Paragraph

However, these Asian youngsters are facing an obstacle now—
prestigious colleges and universities are limiting their admissions.
Recently, a lot of Asian students complained that Ivy League
schools have set up admission quotas. These complaints have
come to the attention of social scientists and researchers. Some
have done research with the following findings: The admission
rate for Asian-Americans has dropped from 39 percent to 17 percent in the past ten years (Salholz, Doherty, & Tran, 1987).
Whenever Asian student admissions reach 10 or 12 percent, a
"red light" goes on, and admissions remain the same or are lowered at many famous and influential schools (Perlmutter, 1987,
p. 27).

ACTIVITY: *Practicing synthesis*

Before you synthesize your own material, you might find it helpful to
practice synthesis on some course reading. Three of the readings in this
book deal with cross-cultural communication: Mead and Metraux's "On
Friendship" (pp. 73–77), Barna's "Intercultural Communication Stumbling
Blocks" (pp. 78–87), and Levine and Wolff's "Social Time: The Heartbeat
of Culture" (pp. 89–96). Working with a partner, find passages in two or
all three of those readings that cover related issues. The authors do not
necessarily have to agree on the issue. Then write a paragraph in

which you make a general statement about cross-cultural communication and support that statement with paraphrased or quoted material from the readings. Make certain that you give credit to your sources. Show your paragraph to the instructor.   ●

Organizing the Essay

To form a whole essay, you must synthesize all of your research material. You need to combine and integrate separate pieces of information and ideas, including your own. The following guidelines will help you to write a logically organized essay that enables your readers to understand all sides of the issue as well as your viewpoint.

1. *Introduction*

The purpose of the introduction is to focus on your topic, to tell your readers what the essay is about. You can open your essay in a variety of ways, for example, relating a case study, quoting a passage, defining a term, or stating an important fact. As you write several drafts of the paper, you can experiment with different openings. But there are certain features that your readers will ultimately need and expect in the introduction to a research essay.

COMMON FEATURES OF THE INTRODUCTION

The introduction of your research essay should achieve two goals:

1. Explain the controversy.
2. Ask or answer your research question.

ACTIVITY: *Evaluating introductions*

The following passages are introductions to student research essays. They are not necessarily good models of introductions. Read the introductions in two ways:

1. Look for the common features of an introduction:
   a. Explanation of the controversy
   b. Research question or answer
2. Examine your response. Discuss your overall impression of each introduction with your classmates. Does it involve you in the topic? (Does reading the introduction make you want to know more about the topic?) Why or why not? Do you like the writing style? Why or why not? If you think the introduction should be revised, what suggestions would you have for the writer? Allow for differences of opinion in the class.

A

Newspapers and magazines are filled with articles concerning the lives and activities of politicians as well as of members of their family and people related to them in one way or another. Many of these articles have a criticizing attitude, and their goal is to twist truth around rather than present it in an unbiased way. Articles that are based on false or nonexisting evidence ruin careers and make families break apart. Politicians, who are in the center of publicity and receive criticism, are most likely to be victims. Other articles, though, reveal facts that are very useful and very enlightening to the public. Especially with presidential candidates, the search for a true image of this candidate always becomes a major issue. However, the things that evolve from this search always leave someone unsatisfied, and we always end up with the question: "What right has the press to interfere in political personalities' personal lives?"

GEORGE

B

Rape, defined by Webster's dictionary as "to have sexual intercourse with a woman without her consent and chiefly by force or deception," is a serious offense to human dignity and probably one of the most devastating experiences a person could ever have. But does the law treat this offense as seriously as it should? Are rape laws fair to the victim? Is the judicial process humane?

These are questions that popped into my mind as I read the article "2 Get Jail in UNH Sex Assault Case." According to the *Boston Globe* article dated September 27, 1987, two college students who raped an intoxicated freshman were formally sentenced to twelve months in jail but the sentence was reduced to three months. The men will serve only two years of probation and be required to attend courses on sexual assault. Furthermore, their criminal record can be expunged three years after they have completed their sentence. And with time off for good behavior, they could be out within sixty days. The victim, who is emotionally traumatized, is now attending a new school.

Even though new laws that favor the victims have been created, in my opinion, the system is still very unfair to the victims. . . .

IDA

C

"Before the 1917 revolution there were 100,000 Orthodox cathedrals, churches and chapels in the country [Russia]. Today there are fewer than 8,000" (Daniloff 68). Indeed, after the establishment of Marxism in the USSR, life became unbearable for believers in God. Marxism, which is based on atheism, has been trying, since then, to drive people away from their religions using every possible way, even violence. Today's Russia under Gorbachev is expected to be different, but is it? "Keston College currently documents 403 Christian prisoners in the USSR (an increase of 223 since 1979). Also under Gorbachev, repressive laws that facilitate resentencing of Christian prisoners without trials have been applied with greater regularity. Radio jamming, house searches, and other repressions and restrictions against believers have not decreased. . . . I've heard that many people in the West think there's more freedom under Gorbachev. In our city, we've been experiencing more repression" (Deyneka 27). Gorbachev himself has declared, in his speeches, a negative attitude toward religion. Are human rights in the USSR being suppressed? Should the USA interfere?

CHRYSTALLA
●

2. Body

In several paragraphs, you will present material that supports the various sides of the controversy. In other words, you will be exploring opposing viewpoints. You do not necessarily have to support one viewpoint over the other; you may find logic in all sides. But you do need to show your readers that you understand the issues well. The body therefore consists of paraphrased and quoted references to your sources. In a research essay, it is necessary to document these sources. (See pp. 247–259 for work on citing and documenting sources. Your instructor will tell you which format to use.)

The challenge in writing this section of the paper is to synthesize the material in such a way that the ideas and information are logically and smoothly connected. There are several ways to do this.

SUGGESTED ORGANIZATIONAL PATTERNS

None of the patterns suggested here is a rigid formula. You may try variations on these structures or devise another structure that is better suited to your topic. You can use the drafting process to experiment with organization; your early efforts can later be revised.

1. *Present one viewpoint at a time.*
   - *First half:* Present one set of arguments first. (If you perceive one set to be weaker, present that set first.) In several paragraphs, explain this viewpoint and include the reasons and evidence used to support it. (You need not evaluate this viewpoint here. Just present the point of view as fairly as possible.)

- *Second half:*   Present the other set of arguments. (If possible, this should be what you perceive to be the stronger set of arguments.) In several paragraphs, explain this viewpoint and include the reasons and evidence used to support it. You can organize this section so that it refutes the weaker set of arguments presented first.

2. *Present and then evaluate opposing viewpoints, one at a time.*
   - *First section:*   Present what you perceive to be the weaker set of arguments. In several paragraphs, explain this viewpoint and include the reasons and evidence used to support it.
   - *Second section:* Evaluate this weaker set of arguments. In one or more paragraphs, explain the strengths and weaknesses of this viewpoint. You can reveal your fairness and credibility as a researcher by treating one or more of the points positively. Keep in mind that there is usually truth in both sides of an argument.
   - *Third section:*   Present what you perceive to be the stronger set of arguments. In several paragraphs, explain this viewpoint and include the reasons and evidence used to support it.
   - *Fourth section:* Evaluate this stronger set of arguments. In one or more paragraphs, explain why you believe this is the stronger viewpoint.

3. *Present both viewpoints together.* In a paragraph, discuss one aspect of the issue. Then show how each side views that aspect. You can do this without evaluating either side. Repeat this procedure for each aspect you want to discuss.

4. *Present and evaluate both viewpoints together.* In a paragraph, discuss one aspect of the issue. Then show how each side views that aspect, and evaluate each viewpoint, showing the strengths and weaknesses of each side. Repeat this procedure for each aspect you want to discuss.

3. Conclusion

The conclusion grows out of the rest of the essay. Up to now, you have given background information on the topic, explained the controversy, raised a research question, and shown that there are opposing sides to the issue. Now you must attempt to answer your research question. But you do not have to "prove" anything. You may have found that all sides have reasonable evidence to support their views. Therefore, in your conclusion, you can either choose a side or explain why you are unable to choose a side. There are several strategies you can use to bring your essay to its end.

SUGGESTIONS FOR A CONCLUDING DISCUSSION

In answering your research question, you can use one or more of these strategies:

1. Briefly review the arguments.
2. Evaluate the sets of arguments, if you have not already done so.
3. Suggest solutions to a problem.
4. Discuss future consequences if no solution is found.
5. Discuss the effect that your research and writing has had on your outlook on your topic.

4. List of Sources

The research essay differs from other essays in that it requires a list of the sources you referred to in the writing of the paper. The list appears at the end of the essay (see sample list on p. 176). By glancing at this page, your readers can see how recent, reliable, and thorough your research is. In addition, they can use the list as a resource if they wish to investigate the same subject.

To learn the correct forms for writing a references list, see pp. 252–259. Your instructor will tell you which format to use.

ACTIVITY: *Organizing the essay*

The organization of your essay is dependent on your subject and on the material you have gathered. If there are two sides to your controversial issue and you want to first present one side and then the other, the first suggested organizational pattern for the body of a paper may work best. If you want to do more than just present the sides one after the other, the second pattern may suit your needs. With this pattern, you can evaluate one side at a time, showing its strengths and weaknesses as you present the evidence. If your issue has many aspects and cannot be broken down neatly into a one-side-versus-other-side discussion, the third or fourth pattern may be most useful for you. You can discuss one aspect of the issue at a time, showing how the various sides view that aspect. Of course, other alternatives exist. If a pattern has not emerged from your material, ask your instructor for advice. You may want to make a detailed outline of your ideas and evidence before you write a draft, to guide you in writing the paper. ●

Writing a Draft to Present for Review

Prepare a draft of your essay to be read and reviewed by your instructor. Before you hand in your paper, use the checklist for content.

Checklist for Content: Self-evaluation

Does my essay provide all of the following details?

1. An explanation of the controversy
2. A research question (or answer)
3. References (through summary, paraphrase, and quotation) to outside sources that represent various sides of the issue
4. Documentation of these outside sources
5. A discussion of my position in relation to the controversy

---

ACTIVITY: *Preparing an outline for oral presentation*

Prepare an outline of your paper to hand out to the class when you do your oral presentation. The outline can be a simple list of the major headings of your topic (see the preliminary outline) or a more detailed outline listing major points made in the paper and some of the evidence provided to support those points. Include the title of your essay.   ●

Preparing an Oral Presentation

Presenting your research report orally to the class can help you to shape your ideas. The best time to do that is between a draft and your final essay. By then you will have done substantial research but can still benefit from comments and questions from your classmates.

ACTIVITY: *Preparing and delivering an oral presentation*

Prepare a five- to ten-minute oral presentation of your research topic by following these guidelines.

1. Photocopy an outline of your draft for each member of the class.
2. Rehearse your presentation before class by following the order of your outline. Plan to tell your listeners three things:
   a. The nature of the controversy
   b. The various sides of the issue
   c. Your position in relation to the controversy
3. On the day of your presentation, hand out copies of your outline to class members, and report on your research in an informal manner. This is a curious but friendly audience.
4. Allow time for answering questions from the class. If you don't have an answer to a question, just tell the class that you will do further research.
5. Take notes on class comments to remember helpful suggestions or further research to be done.   ●

A STUDENT WRITER AT WORK
Description of Angela's Oral Presentation

Angela presented her research orally to the class after she had written a draft to present for peer review. Her classmates were fascinated with her investigation concerning quotas for Asian-American college students. Many of them were surprised to learn about this discrimination, although Angela was careful to point out that according to what she had read, the admission officials denied that it was true. But several students felt that Angela was not treating the issue fairly. Her position against quotas was so strong that she had not explained why American colleges want a diversified group of students. This reaction made Angela realize that she should interview someone knowledgeable about the admission process.

Description of Angela's Interview

Angela still felt too shy to contact someone in the admissions office, so she chose instead to speak to a faculty member she knew who worked closely with international students on campus. During the informal interview, Angela learned that there were some good reasons for an American university's search for a diverse student body. She learned that American universities value extracurricular activities, believing in the adage of "healthy body, healthy mind." She also learned that universities are able to raise much-needed money through athletic events and through alumni gifts.

Description of Angela's Revision

Although Angela did not cite the interview in her final paper, she did make a change in her draft. In an effort to present the opposing side's view fairly, she added material drawn from her reading:

> All colleges deny any charges of discrimination—whether it is racial, religious, ethnic, or sexual. In providing proof that they are not discriminatory, many admission officers point out there is a higher percentage of Asians in their schools than in the national population. They say that if there are any lower percentages than in the past, "it is only because the institution has attracted and accepted a wider range of applicants in order to reflect the population diversity of America" (Perlmutter, 1987, p. 27). They insist that they need to accept students from a variety of backgrounds and interests. They prefer the term *enrollment goals* to *quotas* (Salholz, Doherty, & Tran, 1987).

However, Angela could not accept the idea that limiting the number of Asian students could be justified by the university's economic concerns. She decided not to present that point of view. But she does argue against it in her ninth paragraph (pp. 175–176). You can decide for yourself whether Angela has succeeded in representing all sides of the issue fairly.

Revising

After you have received feedback on your draft from your instructor and on your oral presentation from your classmates, revise your paper. Of course, since every paper and set of responses is different, there can be no rigid rules to follow in revision. The following suggestions may be useful guidelines.

- If there were questions you were unable to answer during the oral presentation, you may need to do some more research. Or you may need to reread some of your articles to find the answers to the questions.
- If you were unable to explain the controversy clearly, you may need to rewrite your introduction.
- If you could not clearly present one or more sides of the issue, you may need to rewrite certain sections of the body of the paper.
- If you did not present one side of an issue fairly, you may need to add material to the body of the paper.
- If you included too many confusing details or statistics, you may need to delete some material.
- If it was hard to follow the logical development of the arguments, you may need to reorganize the paper.
- If your position toward the controversy was not clear, you may need to rewrite the conclusion. If you are not sure of your position, free-write to discover what you think, or discuss the issue with a friend or with your instructor.

Completing the Essay

Once you have revised the essay, read it over to evaluate it as a whole. Make sure that there is a smooth flow from paragraph to paragraph and that every part fits logically. Check to see that the issue raised in the introduction is discussed throughout the body and that the conclusion grows out of the rest of the essay. Proofread and edit the essay, and prepare a neat final manuscript to hand in for evaluation.

Reading and Writing Skills

Part Five consists of guidelines for the skills of summarizing, paraphrasing, quoting, paragraphing, and citing and documenting sources.

The skills of summarizing, paraphrasing, and quoting will be practiced as you are responding to your reading as well as when you are writing and revising your essays.

The skill of paragraphing is also useful to you both as a reader and as a writer. As a reader, you can observe how an author's ideas are linked and organized so that they make sense to you. As a writer, you need to know how to link and organize your own ideas so that they make sense to others. Paragraphing skills can therefore be studied before you write, but they are just as useful when you are making decisions about how to revise your essays.

Finally, the skills of citing and documenting sources will be practiced in essays that include references to your reading.

CHAPTER TEN

Summarizing

Summarizing is a process of condensing, or shortening, a reading selection while preserving its overall meaning. There are many reasons to create summaries. You may write a summary simply to explore your understanding of a reading. You may include a summary in an essay to demonstrate your understanding of the course reading or to establish the ideas that your essay will evaluate or analyze. You may write a summary to inform a reader, as when you summarize a source used for a research paper.

Just as there are different purposes in summarizing, there are different types of summaries. Parts One through Four contain specific guidelines for developing summaries of the various types of reading selections in this book: personal experience essays, research studies, argumentative essays, and news articles. The following general guidelines can help you with all summarizing tasks.

Your primary goal in summarizing is to extract the main ideas, the points that you think are most important. To summarize, then, you need to be able to distinguish between main ideas and secondary details.

Summarizing Passages That Contain Direct Statements of the Main Idea

In short passages and in some complete essays, the main idea may be clearly stated, as in the following paragraph from May Sarton's "Rewards of Living a Solitary Life" (full text on pp. 27–30):

> For me the most interesting thing about a solitary life, and mine has been that for the last twenty years, is that it becomes increasingly rewarding. When I can wake up and watch the sun rise over the ocean, as I do most days, and know that I have an entire day ahead, uninterrupted, in which to write a few pages, take a walk with my dog, lie down in the afternoon for a long think (why does one think better in a horizontal position?), read and listen to music, I am flooded with happiness.

The first sentence of this paragraph contains its main idea. A one-sentence summary of this paragraph could be as follows:

> Living alone is a joyful experience in that it becomes more fulfilling as time passes.

Note that many details of the paragraph have been left out of the summary: the author's 20 years of a solitary life, her watching the sun, writing, walking with her dog, lying down, reading, listening to music, and so on. Most of these details are included in the paragraph to *illustrate* what Sarton means by "rewarding." But they are secondary to the main idea expressed in the one-sentence summary.

Summarizing Passages by Combining Ideas

Though some passages or entire essays contain direct statements of the main idea, more often you must search through the reading, looking at several important ideas. To write a summary, then, you need to combine those ideas in order to establish what the entire passage is about. Sometimes you can be fooled by a first sentence that appears to be the main idea of the passage, but a careful reading will reveal that another idea emerges later on. This can happen, for example, when you read the following paragraph from Kie Ho's "We Should Cherish Our Children's Freedom to Think" (full text on pp. 141–143):

> There's no doubt that American education does not meet high standards in such basic skills as mathematics and language. And we realize that our youngsters are ignorant of Latin, put Mussolini in the same category as Dostoevski, cannot recite the Periodic Table by heart. Would we, however, prefer to stuff the developing little heads of our children with hundreds of geometry problems, the names of rivers in Brazil and 50 lines from *The Canterbury Tales*? Do we really want to retard their impulses, frustrate their opportunities for self-expression?

A first reading of this paragraph might suggest that Ho's main point is that American education does not meet high standards in certain basic skills. Details he includes in the second sentence reveal that this is true. But in the third sentence, he questions the alternatives. And in the final sentence, he suggests that the alternative educational program might prevent opportunities for self-expression. If only the first sentence were used to summarize this passage, the meaning of the passage would be distorted. By combining the idea in the first sentence with the idea in the last sentence, a one-sentence summary that preserves the meaning can be created:

> Though American education does not meet high standards in certain basic skills, it does provide valuable opportunities for self-expression.

This summary, one of many possible, presents two ideas: (1) that Ho acknowledges the weak standards of American education and (2) that Ho approves of the values of American education. The summary is carefully constructed to show the relationship between the ideas. The first clause is a dependent (subordinate) clause (subordinated by the word *though*), showing that this idea is less important to the author. The second clause is an independent (main) clause, showing that this is the main point Ho wishes to make. Note that other details in the paragraph are omitted: ignorance of Latin, names of rivers in Brazil, and so on. These details illustrate what Ho means, but they are secondary to the main idea of the paragraph.

Summarizing Passages That Contain Only Details

Some short passages and occasionally a complete reading selection, such as a narrative, do not contain a direct statement of the main idea. Rather, they are composed primarily of details. It becomes the job of the summarizer to infer a generalization from these details, in other words, to create a main idea sentence.

Such a reading selection is the essay "Zen and the Art of Burglary" by Wu-tsu Fa-yen (p. 3). The essay is composed of details of the story of the son of a thief, who learns the art of theft. The only idea presented by the author is that "Zen is like . . . learning the art of burglary." It is up to the reader to discover what this means. The reader must infer from the details of the story a generalization that reveals the meaning of the story. One possible summary sentence might be this:

The only way to learn something is by experiencing it.

Another possible summary sentence might be this:

Zen is like learning the art of burglary because it can only be accomplished through experience.

Each summary is derived from the details of the story, which show that the son has learned the art of burglary by experiencing it himself.

Since "Zen and the Art of Burglary" is a complete reading selection and not just a paragraph taken from an essay, a longer summary, including the story of the son, can be created, for example:

A son wants to learn his father's trade: burglary. To teach him, the father breaks into a house and locks his son in a chest. The son is horrified; nevertheless, he figures out a way to escape from the chest. When he returns home in anger, his father points out that he has learned the trade. The son has learned that the only way to learn something is by experiencing it.

Identifying Author and Title

In the sample summaries just given, the author and title are not identified. These summaries are restatements of the original passages, directly presenting the information the passages contain. For the writing you do for this course, however, you are more likely to refer to the authors by name, to give them credit for their ideas. If you are summarizing an entire reading selection, you also include the title of the selection.

You can choose from a variety of introductory phrases to identify the author and title, for example:

1. (The author) states in (this article) that . . .
2. (The author), in (this article) shows that . . .
3. In (this article), (the author) writes that . . .
4. As (the author) says in (this article), . . .
5. The main idea of (the author's article) is that . . .

In addition to the above verbs in 1 through 4, many other verbs can be used to introduce an author's ideas, depending on the intention of the author and your emphasis, for example:

maintains	suggests	points out
explains	observes	finds
notes	establishes	reveals
believes	implies	argues
contends	insists	declares
asserts	claims	recommends
asks	advises	proposes

(Check a dictionary of usage, if necessary, to determine which verb to select.)

SAMPLE SUMMARIES IDENTIFYING AUTHOR (AND TITLE):

- May Sarton maintains that living alone is a joyful experience in that it becomes more fulfilling as time passes.
- Kie Ho believes that even though American education does not meet high standards in certain basic skills, it does provide valuable opportunities for self-expression.
- In "Zen and the Art of Burglary," Wu-tsu Fa-yen implies that the only way to learn something is by experiencing it.

When you refer to an author's ideas, use the present tense. In doing this, you acknowledge that the ideas continue to exist even though the author has finished writing about them.

The first time you mention the author's name, include the full name (e.g., Kie Ho). After that, refer to the author by last name only (e.g., Ho).

Guidelines for Writing a Summary of a Reading Selection

1. Reread the reading selection carefully, to understand its purpose and structure. Determine the significance of each idea and example and the way it is linked to other ideas or examples.
2. Decide what you are going to include in your summary and what you are going to leave out.
3. Group the essential information and ideas you have selected in an order that shows the relationships of the ideas and facts. This does not necessarily have to be the order in which the ideas are presented in the article.
4. Write a sentence—or several sentences, as long as the summary is considerably shorter than the original—that reveals what the whole selection is about. You might try to do this orally first, as if you were telling a friend what the author is saying. Then write down your words.
5. Identify author (and title, if you are summarizing an entire essay or article).

EXERCISE: *Writing summaries*

Working alone or with a partner, summarize each of the following passages in one of three ways:

1. Take a direct statement of the main idea from the passage.
2. Combine ideas to create one main idea.
3. Infer a generalization from details and create a main idea sentence.

A

Loneliness is most acutely felt with other people, for with others, even with a lover sometimes, we suffer from our differences of taste, temperament, mood. Human intercourse often demands that we soften the edge of perception, or withdraw at the very instant of personal truth for fear of hurting, or of being inappropriately present, which is to say naked, in a social situation. Alone we can afford to be wholly whatever we are, and to feel whatever we feel absolutely. That is a great luxury!

MAY SARTON, "The Rewards of Living a Solitary Life"

B

Each language has a vocabulary of time that does not always survive translation. When we translated our questionnaires into Portuguese for my Brazilian students, we found that English distinctions of time were not readily articulated in their language. Several of our questions concerned how long the respondent would wait for someone to arrive, as compared with when they hoped for arrival or actually expected the person would come. In Portuguese, the verbs "to wait for," "to hope for," and "to expect" are all translated as "esperar." We had to add further words of explanation to make the distinction clear to the Brazilian students.

> ROBERT LEVINE AND ELLEN WOLFF,
> "Social Time: The Heartbeat of Culture"

C

Few Americans stay put for a lifetime. We move from town to city to suburb, from high school to college in a different state, from a job in one region to a better job elsewhere, from the home where we raise our children to the home where we plan to live in retirement. With each move we are forever making new friends, who become part of our new life at that time.

> MARGARET MEAD AND RHODA METRAUX, "On Friendship"

D

"In the late 1960s," one dean told me, "the typical question that I got from students was 'Why is there so much suffering in the world?' or 'How can I make a contribution?' Today it's 'Do you think it would look better for getting into law school if I did a double major in history and political science, or just majored in one of them?' " Many other deans confirmed this pattern. One said: "They're trying to find an edge—the intangible something that will look better on paper if two students are about equal."

> WILLIAM ZINSSER, "College Pressures"

CHAPTER ELEVEN

Paraphrasing

Paraphrasing is a process of restating a reading passage in your own words while preserving the author's intended meaning and tone. This process is similar to translating; but unlike translating, paraphrasing does not involve changing words from one language to another. Instead, when you paraphrase, you write in the same language, translating someone else's ideas into your own words.

The Purpose of Paraphrasing

Paraphrasing has a number of purposes. For example, you can use paraphrasing to annotate or take notes. As you are reading, you can record certain ideas in a written form that you can clearly understand and re-member. Paraphrasing thus allows you to clarify the meaning of a reading for yourself.

Paraphrasing is also used in essay writing. When you write essays in which you respond to course readings or incorporate outside reading ma-terial, you need to refer to the reading at different points in your essay. Even if your readers have read the same material, they need to know exactly which of the author's ideas you are responding to or have chosen to include. Occasionally, you might want to use the author's exact words (see "Quoting," pp. 228–234), but your readers are primarily interested in seeing how you can make sense of what an author says.

When you paraphrase a passage to include it in your own essay, your goal is to clarify its meaning for yourself and your readers. You take an idea or example from the reading to introduce or support an idea you want to discuss in your paper. Often you incorporate the paraphrased passage into your own sentence. Whether the paraphrase is alone or incorporated, you always need to identify the author on whose words the paraphrase is based (see "Giving Credit to Your Sources" in Chapter 14).

The Process of Paraphrasing

Paraphrasing is not a simple process. You can rarely paraphrase word by word. First of all, some basic words often must remain, for example, indefinite articles, pronouns, and prepositions. Furthermore, even though you need to look up any words you don't know in order to paraphrase, using a thesaurus or dictionary to substitute words can sometimes create sentences that are nonsensical or more difficult to understand than the original:

EXAMPLE

Sentence from paragraph 8 of LaRay Barna's "Intercultural Communications Stumbling Blocks" (p. 82):
Learning the language, which most foreign visitors consider their *only* barrier to understanding, is actually only the beginning.

Word-by-word paraphrase of Barna's sentence:
Acquisition of knowledge of human or written speech, which the majority of alien guests or newcomers think their alone of its kind obstacle to comprehension, is in fact but the commencement.

Obviously, this is not an acceptable paraphrase, since it does not clarify the meaning of the original passage.

Clearer paraphrase of Barna's sentence:
In spite of what most foreigners think, language is not the only factor preventing full communication.

Determining Meaning and Tone

As a paraphraser, you must be flexible if what you produce is to be clear. The best approach is first to think about what the author is really saying. Whenever possible, see how the passage fits into the entire reading selection. How is it linked to the overall message or argument? Once you know that, you can approach the writing of the paraphrase with a better understanding of the author's meaning.

When you paraphrase, you have to think not only about the meaning of the passage but also its tone. For example, if the author is sarcastic or funny or angry or compassionate, your paraphrase should reflect that sarcasm, humor, anger, or compassion. Again, knowing how a passage fits into an entire text can help you determine tone. Look for clues in the title, in the way the author introduces the reading selection, or in the words the author has chosen. Are there any words or phrases that surprise or shock or please you? If so, they are probably reflective of the tone. Capture the tone in your paraphrase.

EXAMPLE

Third sentence of May Sarton's "The Rewards of Living a Solitary Life" (p. 29):
For him it proved to be a shock nearly as great as falling in love to discover that he could enjoy himself so much alone.

Paraphrase:
He was surprised and delighted when he realized that he could find pleasure in solitude.

This paraphrase captures the meaning as well as the tone of Sarton's words. The writer of the paraphrase knows from reading the essay that Sarton believes that being alone is worthwhile. The words *surprised and delighted* reveal the positive connotation of the expression *a shock nearly as great as falling in love.* A paraphrase that does not capture the tone of the passage might look like this:

Paraphrase that does not capture the tone:
He nearly had a stroke when he realized that he liked being by himself.

Here the paraphraser turns the word *shock* into something negative by comparing it to a *stroke.* Furthermore, the expression *nearly had a stroke* is too conversational compared to Sarton's more literary use of the language. This paraphrase does not accurately reflect the author's attitude and writing style.

Incorporating Paraphrases into Your Own Sentences

When you include a paraphrase of a reading passage in your own essay, you need to integrate it smoothly with your own writing. If it stands by itself, your readers will not understand why you have included the paraphrase. Furthermore, without smooth integration, the paraphrase may not match the grammar of your own sentences. Your ideas will therefore be hard to follow. To incorporate paraphrases, you can use one or more of these strategies:

1. Introduce the paraphrase by mentioning the author's name and using a verb that indicates the author's approach to the topic (see list of possible verbs on p. 219).
2. Change an author's first-person or second-person viewpoint to the third person. For example, "I am lonely" can become "the author is lonely"; "you have learned" can become "students have learned."
3. Use words in the sentence to show your own view of the paraphrased material.
4. Check to see that the grammar and punctuation of the sentence help to make sense of what you are saying.

A STUDENT WRITER AT WORK

In writing his paper "Facing a Different Culture" (pp. 98–100), Doxis Doxiadis paraphrased several sentences from LaRay Barna's "Intercultural Communication Stumbling Blocks" (pp. 78–87) and integrated them into his own sentences. In each case, he created paraphrases in which the author's idea is preserved though it is expressed in Doxis's own words. The first paraphrase is analyzed. Working in a small group or with the whole class, you can analyze the others and determine their accuracy.

1. Barna's Sentence

The first [stumbling block] is so obvious it hardly needs mentioning—*language*. (paragraph 7)

Doxis's Paraphrase

The basic problem that an international student faces, as Barna very correctly says, is the language.

Analysis of the paraphrase:
1. The order of the sentence is preserved.
2. The word *basic* is substituted for *first* and allows for the deletion of the phrase *so obvious it hardly needs mentioning*.
3. The word *problem* is substituted for the implied *stumbling blocks*.
4. The paraphrase is then integrated into Doxis's sentence. He is careful to indicate that this idea came from Barna's essay by mentioning her name. By using the expression *very correctly*, he shows that he agrees with Barna.

2. Barna's Sentence

Learning the language, which most foreign visitors consider their *only* barrier to understanding, is actually only the beginning. (8)

Doxis's Paraphrase

However, as Barna points out, language is not the only problem a foreigner will face.

3. Barna's Sentence

The following paragraph written by an international student from Korea illustrates how a clash in values can lead to poor communication and result in misunderstanding and hurt feelings. (16)

Doxis's Paraphrase

One of the most interesting and unfortunately true notions in the Barna article is the fact that lack of communication and comprehension between Americans and foreigners often results in "hurt feelings" and serious misunderstandings.

Note that Barna herself paraphrases other authors whose work she has read. For example, in paragraph 11 she incorporates a paraphrase into her own sentence:

Stereotypes help do what Ernest Becker says the anxiety-prone human race *must* do, and that is to reduce the threat of the unknown by making the world predictable.

GUIDELINES

Guidelines for Paraphrasing

After selecting a passage that you plan to refer to in your own essay, put the passage into your own words. In adjusting the author's words, you can rearrange word order, turn longer sentences into shorter ones, make two sentences out of one, or select only a key idea from a long sentence.

1. Look up the meaning of any unfamiliar words.
2. Think about what the author really means.
3. Use one of these strategies to find your own words to rephrase the passage:
   a. Cover up the passage and write from memory.
   b. Take notes on the passage. Then cover up the passage and write the paraphrase from your notes.
   c. Go word by word, substituting synonyms. Then rewrite the substitute passage so that it makes sense.
4. Reread the original passage to make sure that you have preserved the meaning and tone. Revise your paraphrase if necessary.
5. Integrate the paraphrase into your own sentence.

EXERCISE: *Evaluating paraphrases*

Each of the following sentences is taken from readings in Part One that you have probably already read. Each sentence is followed by a paraphrase. Working in small groups, read each sentence, and then examine each paraphrase. Determine whether the paraphrase preserves the original meaning and tone. (If necessary, reread the entire essay.) Are the key points of the original passage clearly and accurately presented? If not, rewrite the paraphrase.

1. Original sentence:
The tyranny of self-censorship forced me, in my relations with male friends, to seek alternatives to language.

STEVE TESICH, "Focusing on Friends"

Paraphrase:
I did not allow myself to express my feelings with my friends.

2. Original sentence:
What was my little sorrow to the centuries of pain which those stars had watched?

Anzia Yezierska, "College"

Paraphrase:
My unhappiness was unimportant when compared with the suffering that the world has always known.

3. Original sentence:
Solitude is the salt of personhood. It brings out the authentic flavor of every experience.

May Sarton, "The Rewards of Living a Solitary Life"

Paraphrase:
If you sprinkle sodium chloride on yourself, you will really taste what it's like to be alone.   ●

EXERCISE: *Integrating a paraphrase into your own sentence*

Select one of the three paraphrases in the preceding exercise (or your revision of the paraphrase), and integrate it into a sentence of your own. Write with the purpose of including your sentence in an essay about the reading selection. Show the sentence to your instructor.   ●

CHAPTER TWELVE

Quoting

At certain points in an essay, you may want to use the exact words of the author, that is, to *quote* the author. In quoting, as in paraphrasing, you take material from the reading to introduce or support a point you want to discuss. Quoting also enables you to enrich your writing by adding the distinctive flavor of the author's writing style.

However, you need to be careful not to use too many quotations. Too many quotations can break the flow of your discussion. Furthermore, you can become too dependent on the exact language of the reading source. When that happens, you may forget that your readers are primarily interested in learning how you view the material, especially if they are familiar with the original source.

When you do decide to use an author's exact words, you must make it clear that the words are being reprinted from another source (see "Giving Credit to Your Sources" in Chapter 14 and "Quotation Marks" in Chapter 17).

Selecting a Quotation

An important first step in quoting is deciding whether to paraphrase or to quote. The following guidelines can help you to make that decision.

GUIDELINES

Guidelines for Selecting a Quotation

Before you decide to use a quote, ask yourself this question: "Why am I quoting rather than paraphrasing this passage?" If your answer is one of the following statements, include the quotation in your essay.

1. I am quoting this passage because the author's words are so impressive or so clever that to put them in my own words would lessen their impact.
2. I am quoting this passage because the author's words are so precise that to put them in my own words would change their meaning.
3. I am quoting this passage because the author's words are so concise that I would need twice as many words to paraphrase the passage.

EXERCISE: *Selecting a quotation*

Working with a partner, use the guidelines to select a quotable statement from one of the readings in Part Two that you might refer to in an essay.   ●

Incorporating a Quotation into Your Own Text

Once you have decided to use a quotation, you must incorporate it into your essay. And you must do this in such a way that your essay doesn't have a choppy, unnatural rhythm. Otherwise, it may appear to your readers that the quotation has just been dropped into the essay for no reason.

GUIDELINES

Guidelines for **Incorporating Quotations**

When including quotations, you can use one or more of these strategies:

1. Introduce or in some way lead into the quotation so that readers know whose words are being quoted or can understand why the quotation is important.
2. Comment on the quotation after you have included it so that readers understand its connection to other points made in the paper.
3. Insert ellipses (spaced periods: . . .) wherever you delete any words from the original quotation.
4. Use brackets [ ] to add words to or to substitute words for those in the original quotation.

Introducing Quotations

You can choose from a variety of ways to introduce a quotation. You should aim to make the quotation flow with your writing. Whenever possible, the introductory verb or phrase can tell your readers something about your reason for including the quotation.

EXAMPLES

According to (the author), ". . ."
As (the author) says, ". . ."
I agree with (the author's) point that ". . ."
My own experience has shown that ". . ."
(The author) claims that ". . ."
I disagree with (the author's) contention that ". . ."
". . ." admits (the author).

In (the essay), the author concludes that ". . ."
". . . ," remarks (the author), ". . ."
The following quotation reveals (the author's) bias: ". . ."
Unlike most professors, (the author) believes that ". . ."

A STUDENT WRITER AT WORK

In his essay "Facing a Different Culture" (pp. 98–100) Doxis Doxiadis included a quotation from LaRay Barna's article "Intercultural Communication Stumbling Blocks" (pp. 78–87). He integrated the quotation into his own sentence. Note that in introducing the quotation, he is careful to state where the quotation comes from (the Barna article) and who said it (a Vietnamese student), and where in the article it comes from.

Doxis's Sentence Containing a Quotation

> As a Vietnamese student says in the Barna article, "foreigners . . . think that Americans are superficial" (paragraph 2).

Doxis uses quotation marks to indicate that he is quoting, inserts ellipses (3 spaced periods) to show he has deleted a word, and provides the paragraph number for the quotation so that his readers can easily find it in the reading if they want to.

Barna herself quotes from her own outside reading. For example, on page 82:

> As Frankel says, "To enter into a culture is to be able to hear, in Lionel Trilling's phrase, its special 'hum and buzz of implication.' "

(In fact, the single quotation marks reveal that Frankel has quoted Trilling.)

Commenting on Quotations

Obviously, what you say after you have included a quotation depends on your purpose and your subject matter. The important point to remember is that your readers will not understand why a quotation is included unless you tell them. There are many ways to comment, for example:

1. Expand on the quotation: add details, facts, or ideas that reveal its truth.
2. Explain the connection between the quotation and what has already been said.
3. Refer to one important word or phrase in the quotation and explain its significance.
4. Explain your position in relation to the quotation: for example, agree or disagree with the point made in the quotation.

A STUDENT WRITER AT WORK

After introducing the quotation from the Barna article, Doxis comments on the quotation by expanding on it. Note that he picks up the word *foreigner* to show the connection between his comments and the quotation.

Doxis's Comments on a Quotation

As a Vietnamese student says in the Barna article, "foreigners . . . think that Americans are superficial" (paragraph 2). In the eyes of a foreigner, Americans look like happy fools, even though, as I found out, this is certainly not true. However, the first impression of Americans will make most foreigners avoid them, and they won't therefore find their true self.

Barna, too, comments on her quotation, expanding on it and showing its connection to her research.

As Frankel says, "To enter into a culture is to be able to hear, in Lionel Trilling's phrase, its special 'hum and buzz of implication.' " This brings in *nonverbal areas* and the second stumbling block. People from different cultures inhabit different nonverbal sensory words. Each sees, hears, feels, and smells only that which has some meaning or importance for him.

Using Ellipses

Ellipses (spaced periods) can be helpful if you want to delete some words from the middle of a quotation, as long as you don't change the author's intended meaning. Use four periods (. . . .) if the words omitted include a period at the end of a sentence. Otherwise, use three periods (. . .).

There are primarily two reasons to use ellipsis (omission of words):

1. To delete words from a quotation to make the quotation shorter or to select the part of the quotation that comes right to the point.

   EXAMPLE

   Original: "Anonymity, after all, fosters not merely frankness; more ominously (for teachers) it fosters irresponsibility, a trait of character (or a kind of behavior, if we prefer,) that we ought never to encourage in the young." (Paul McBrearty)

   Altered: "Anonymity . . . fosters irresponsibility," according to Paul McBrearty

2. To delete words to make a quotation fit logically into your own sentence.

   EXAMPLE

   Original: "Like historical friends, our crossroads friends are important for *what was*—for the friendship we shared at a crucial, now past, time of life." (Judith Viorst)

Altered: Judith Viorst's definition of crossroads friendship is "the friendship . . . shared at a crucial, now past, time of life."

Using Brackets

If you need to add words to or substitute words in a quotation, put the additional or changed word within brackets. *Note:* Use brackets [ ], not parentheses ( ), for this purpose.

1. Add words to help clarify a potentially confusing quotation.

   EXAMPLE

   Original: "In a foreign land they increase our feeling of security." (LaRay Barna)

   Altered: Barna explains that "in a foreign land they [stereotypes] increase our feeling of security."

2. Substitute words to make a quotation fit smoothly into your own sentence, as long as you don't change the author's intended meaning. You may use brackets, for example, to change verb tenses or to change pronouns to nouns.

   EXAMPLE

   Original: "Man-woman friendships . . . can be just as close and as dear as those that we form with women."

   Altered: Judith Viorst believes that man-woman friendships "can be just as close and as dear as those that [women] form with women."

Combining Paraphrase and Quotation

In your essay writing, you will include a mixture of quotation and paraphrase. If you borrow any uniquely expressed phrases or recognizable expression from the author, even two words, you should put the words within quotation marks. Otherwise, ideas taken from your reading should be paraphrased. In each case, the original author must be identified. For example, Doxis included both paraphrase and quotation in a single sentence.

Doxis's Sentence with Paraphrase and Quotation

One of the most interesting and unfortunately true notions in the Barna article is the fact that lack of communication and comprehension between Americans and foreigners often results in "hurt feelings" and serious misunderstandings (paragraph 15).

(Guidelines for punctuating quotations are on pp. 324–325)

EXERCISE: *Integrating quotations*

To practice integrating quotations into a written text, select a quotation from the source (paragraph 1) and insert it into the paragraph taken from a student essay (paragraph 2). Your goals are, in this order, as follows:

1. To select an appropriate quotation.
2. To incorporate it logically
3. To punctuate it correctly (see pp. 324–325)

Work alone or with partner.

PARAGRAPH 1

The fifth stumbling block is *high anxiety*, separately mentioned for the purpose of emphasis. Unlike the other four (language, illusive nonverbal cues, preconceptions and stereotypes, and the practice of immediate evaluation), the stumbling block of anxiety is not distinct but underlies and compounds the others. The presence of high anxiety/tension is very common in cross-cultural experiences because of the uncertainties present.

LaRay Barna, "Intercultural Communication Stumbling Blocks"

PARAGRAPH 2

Anxiety is the last problem that Barna mentions in her article. Many foreign students get scared because they do not know what to expect. During my first month in America, I did not dare talk to anybody. I often had a stomachache before I went to school. Every time a teacher asked me a question, my legs got so shaky and my voice cracked. I was very afraid that other students might laugh at my English when I mispronounced some words. Everyday I tried to figure out what other people were saying, but it seemed so hopeless. By the end of the day when I got home, I felt so exhausted; I felt like I had been jogging for ten miles or more.

Pat

Follow the same instructions for paragraphs 3 and 4.

PARAGRAPH 3

Crossroads friends forge powerful links, links strong enough to endure with not much more contact than once-a-year letters at Christmas. And out of respect for those crossroad years, for those dramas and dreams we once shared, we will always be friends.

Judith Viorst, "Friends, Good Friends—and Such Good Friends"

PARAGRAPH 4

My best historical friends are the crossroads ones. My best school friends or my playmates will always be in my memory. I would be very happy if I could find out how they are doing and maybe see them again after many years. I will never forget the boy that I shared my desk with at junior school. In the last ten years we have talked a few times on the telephone and met once. We still have a worthy time together.

CHRIS
●

EXERCISE: *Selecting and integrating a quotation*

Using the criteria for selecting a quotation, select a quotation from one of the readings in Part Two or Part Three that you might refer to in an essay. Incorporate the quotation into a sentence of your own.   ●

QUOTING

CHAPTER THIRTEEN

Paragraphing

Determining Paragraph Functions

The paragraphs of an essay are created to serve different functions. In academic essays, opening paragraphs usually serve as introductions; closing paragraphs serve as conclusions. The middle, or body, paragraphs of an essay can have different purposes. They can be created to make a new point, or they can be created simply to expand on a point already made. For example, one paragraph might provide an extended example (or a story, details, or facts) to illustrate or clarify a point made in the preceding paragraph. To gain an understanding of how these paragraphs function, read paragraphs 8 and 9 of LaRay Barna's "Intercultural Communication Stumbling Blocks" (pp. 78–87), reprinted here. The first of the two paragraphs makes a point about the importance of nonverbal cues in communication and then provides evidence to support that point. The second paragraph simply provides an example to illustrate the point made in the previous paragraph.

> Learning the language, which most foreign visitors consider their *only* barrier to understanding, is actually only the beginning. As Frankel says, "To enter into a culture is to be able to hear, in Lionel Trilling's phrase, its special 'hum and buzz of implication.'" This brings in *nonverbal areas* and the second stumbling block. People from different cultures inhabit different nonverbal sensory worlds. Each sees, hears, feels, and smells only that which has some meaning or importance for him. He abstracts whatever fits into his personal world of recognitions and then interprets it through the frame of reference of his own culture.
>
> An Oregon girl in an intercultural communication class asked a young man from Saudi Arabia how he would signal nonverbally that he liked her. His response was to smooth back his hair which, to her, was just a common nervous gesture signifying nothing. She repeated her question three times. He smoothed his hair three times and, finally realizing that she was not recognizing this movement as his reply to her question, automatically ducked his head and stuck out his tongue slightly in embarrassment. This behavior *was* noticed by the girl, and she interpreted it as the way he would express his liking for her.

235

These paragraphs could have been combined into one. It was the author's choice to create two paragraphs. One reason for that choice might have been to break up a paragraph that seemed too long or to allow readers to absorb the generalizations before they read the specifics.

A body paragraph can also act as a transition from one paragraph to another; such a paragraph can be a single sentence. For example, the sixth paragraph of Mead and Metraux's "On Friendship" (pp. 73–77) consists of a question:

> Who, then, is a friend?

This question is the bridge between the authors' general discussion of the different expectations of friendship in different countries and the more specific descriptions of friendship in different nations. By placing the question alone as a paragraph, the authors have given it special emphasis. Readers know that in the rest of the essay, the authors will attempt to answer the question.

In your own writing, the function that your paragraphs serve will be determined by your content and purpose. As you revise your paper, ask yourself why you have created each paragraph. If you yourself understand why your paragraphs exist, you are more likely to create an essay that makes sense to your readers.

(For further work on introductory, body, and concluding paragraphs, see the guidelines for individual writing assignments in Parts One through Four.)

Starting a New Paragraph

The paragraph is an important signaling system. The sight of a newly indented paragraph sends a message to the reader that the writer is introducing a new aspect of the topic or is shifting emphasis. The initial sentence of a new paragraph usually helps readers connect what they have just read with what they are about to read.

EXERCISE: *Analyzing the function of the first sentence of a paragraph*

1. Paragraph 8 and the first two sentences of paragraph 9 of William Zinsser's article "College Pressures" (full text on pp. 132–139) are reprinted here. Discuss how the first sentence of paragraph 9 (underlined) helps readers connect what they have just read (in paragraph 8) with what they are about to read.

"In the late 1960s," one dean told me, "the typical question that I got from students was 'Why is there so much suffering in the world?' or 'How can I make a contribution?' Today it's 'Do you think it would look better for getting into law school if I did a double major in history and political science, or just majored in one of them?' " Many other deans confirmed this pattern. One said: "They're trying to find an edge—the intangible something that will look better on paper if two students are about equal."

Note the emphasis on looking better. The transcript has become a sacred document, the passport to security. . . .

2. Paragraph 1 and the first two sentences of paragraph 2 of Margaret Mead and Rhoda Metraux's "On Friendship" (full text on pp. 73–77) are reprinted here. Discuss how the first sentence of paragraph 2 (underlined) helps readers connect the material in paragraph 1 with the material in paragraph 2.

Few Americans stay put for a lifetime. We move from town to city to suburb, from high school to college in a different state, from a job in one region to a better job elsewhere, from the home where we raise our children to the home where we plan to live in retirement. With each move we are forever making new friends, who become part of our new life at that time.

For many of us the summer is a special time for forming new friendships. Today millions of Americans vacation abroad, and they go not only to see new sights but also—in those places where they do not feel too strange—with the hope of meeting new people. . . .

Providing Connections within and between Sentences to Show the Relationship of One Idea or Example to Another

Connections in writing are made not only between paragraphs but also within paragraphs themselves. These connections occur both between sentences and within sentences, showing how various ideas and examples are related.

Transitional Words and Expressions

One way in which writers show the relationship of ideas and examples is through the use of transitional words and expressions. These connectives enable readers to predict what will follow and to refer to what has just been said. The box titled "Transitions" (p. 238) presents sample transitional words and expressions and their purpose.

TRANSITIONS

Transitional Words and Expressions	Purpose
also, too, in addition, furthermore, moreover, and, besides, in fact	To add an idea or example
for example, for instance, such as, including	To supply an example to support a generalization
first, next, then, last, before, after, earlier, subsequently, later, while, until, initially, at first	To indicate the order in which events occur or ideas are presented
because, since, for, the reason is that	To indicate the cause or reason for something
therefore, so, thus, as a result, so that, consequently, accordingly	To indicate the effect or result of something
but, however, nevertheless, on the contrary, although, unlike, whereas, while, in contrast, despite, yet, on the other hand	To indicate that one thing is different from or contrasts with another thing
similarly, likewise, in the same manner, in the same way, along the same lines, as, like	To indicate that one thing is similar to another thing that was already mentioned
unless, if, even if, or, provided that, as long as	To indicate a condition
still	To indicate that something continues
in other words, that is, that is to say	To indicate that something will be restated for clarity
finally, at last, after all, in conclusion, to conclude, to sum up	To indicate the end of a thought or list

Though you will use some transitional words and expressions in your own writing, you cannot simply memorize the list and then plug the words into your essay for the purpose indicated. The words in each category are not necessarily interchangeable. They have different placements within a sentence, are punctuated differently, and have different grammatical functions. The box titled "Grammatical Functions of Transitions" (p. 239) reorganizes some of the words according to those grammatical functions.

To learn how these transitional words and expressions are used, you need to become aware of them as you read. Notice how the words connect ideas and examples in sentences, paragraphs, and whole essays. Look at the placement of the words within a sentence, and observe the punctuation.

GRAMMATICAL FUNCTIONS OF TRANSITIONS

Transitions	*Grammatical Function*
COORDINATING CONJUNCTIONS:	
and, but, yet, for, or, nor, so	To connect words, phrases, and clauses
SUBORDINATING CONJUNCTIONS (see also additional list on pp. 275–277):	
when, since, where, while, until, before, as, because, although, whereas, unless, if	To transform the independent clauses they introduce into dependent clauses
CONJUNCTIVE ADVERBS (partial list):	
however, nevertheless, similarly, likewise, therefore, moreover, consequently, still, furthermore, otherwise	To join independent clauses; To introduce independent clauses To refer to the preceding clause
ADVERBIAL WORD GROUPS (partial list):	
in addition, as a result, for this reason, in spite of, on the other hand, in conclusion	To join independent clauses; to introduce independent clauses

Through such a process you may eventually internalize the appropriate usage for the terms and come to understand when they may be necessary to indicate the direction of your thoughts.

EXERCISE: *Identifying transitional words and signals*

Most of the transitional expressions and signals have been removed from the following paragraph taken from Rolando Niella's essay "Barriers," in which he compares learning tennis to learning a language (full text on pp. 16–18). Read this paragraph knowing that you will compare it with the paragraph that does contain connectives. Working in a small group or with the whole class, have one student read the paragraph aloud.

Rolando's Paragraph without *Connectives*

A person is aware of my level and tries to go at my pace. I confront some problems. You are a fairly experienced player. You should be familiar with some basic game plans. The way your opponent is sending the balls may lead you to realize which plan he is using to score upon you. In a language you have experience with the cultural patterns of expressing feelings and moods. You distinguish the different connotations of words. You may understand the point he is trying to make to you. I am not very good at predicting what play my opponent is trying to use. I do. It is usually too late. I usually don't react to a joke until it is too late. I have a hard time realizing how annoyed my roommate gets. He selects words to make his point. The connotations of some of them sometimes don't reach me because of my inexperience. I don't know exactly which is worse to him, "mad," "angry," "disturbed," or "pissed off."

Now identify the transitional words and signals in the paragraph Rolando actually wrote. Compare the paragraph with the one without connectives. How does each word or expression serve to reveal the relationship between Rolando's ideas and examples?

Rolando's Paragraph with Connectives

Once a person is aware of my level and tries to go at my pace, I still confront problems. First, in tennis, if you are a fairly experienced player, you should be familiar with some basic game plans. The way your opponent is sending the balls may lead you to realize which plan he is using to score upon you. In the same way, if in a language you have experience with the cultural patterns of expressing feelings and moods, and you distinguish the different connotations of words, you may understand the point he is trying to make to you. In tennis, I am not very good at predicting what play my opponent is trying to use; and when I do, it is usually too late. Likewise, in conversation, I usually don't react to a joke until it is too late. I also have a hard time realizing how annoyed my roommate gets, because he selects words to make his point; but the connotations of some of them sometimes don't reach me because of my inexperience. I don't know exactly which is worse to him, "mad," "angry," "disturbed," or "pissed off." ●

EXERCISE: *Making connections*

Working in pairs or a small group, do the following exercises.

1. The following examples lack subordinating conjunctions. Consider the relationship between the two clauses, and fill in an appropriate conjunction for each example. There may be more than one choice for each one.

   a. _____ she graduates, she will get a teaching job.

   b. _____ she graduates, she can't get a teaching job.

   c. _____ she graduates, she will have to take the exam.

2. The following examples lack subordinate clauses. Consider the subordinating conjunction used, and write an appropriate clause for each example.

   a. Even though ＿＿＿＿＿, he is tired.

   b. Because he ＿＿＿＿＿, he is tired.

   c. He is tired whenever ＿＿＿＿＿.

3. The following examples lack transitional words. Consider the relationship between the two sentences, and fill in an appropriate transition for each example.

   a. You may not succeed. You should keep trying.

   b. You may not succeed. You don't work hard enough.

   c. You may not succeed. You should change your major.

4. Complete the sentence beginning with a transitional expression so that it is logically related to the preceding sentence.

   a. Grades have become so important in the educational system that students work to get good grades rather than to learn the subject.

     As a result, ＿＿＿＿＿＿＿＿＿.

   b. Grades . . . subject. In fact, ＿＿＿＿＿＿＿.

   c. Grades . . . subject. However, ＿＿＿＿＿＿＿.

                                      ●

Transitional words are not the only tactic writers use to connect their ideas and examples. In fact, too many transitional words can be distracting to readers and are often not necessary. If you become aware of how you react to transitions as a reader, you can become more aware of when and when not to use transitions when you write. Use the following exercise to test your reaction.

EXERCISE: *Reacting to transitions*

Compare the following paragraphs. Paragraph A is reproduced exactly as Anzia Yezierska wrote it (full text on pp. 20–25). Paragraph B has been rewritten to include several transitional expressions. Discuss your reaction to A and then to B. Are any or all of the transitional expressions helpful? unnecessary? distracting? Why? Why do you think the author did not include these expressions in the first place?

PARAGRAPHING

A

Darkness and stillness washed over me. Slowly I stumbled to my feet and looked up at the sky. The stars in their infinite peace seemed to pour their healing light into me. I thought of the captives in prison, the sick and the suffering from the beginning of time who had looked to these stars for strength. What was my little sorrow to the centuries of pain which those stars had watched? So near they seemed, so compassionate. My bitter hurt seemed to grow small and drop away. If I must go alone, I should still have the silence and the high stars to walk with me.

B

Darkness and stillness washed over me. Slowly I stumbled to my feet and looked up at the sky. First, the stars in their infinite peace seemed to pour their healing light into me. Then I thought of the captives in prison, and in addition of the sick and the suffering from the beginning of time who had looked to these stars for strength. What was my little sorrow to the centuries of pain which those stars had watched? So near they seemed, so compassionate. My bitter hurt therefore seemed to grow small and drop away. If I must go alone, I should still have the silence and the high stars to walk with me. ●

Other Techniques for Providing Connections

Writers use clues other than transitional words in their paragraphs to show the direction of their thinking. Here are some other techniques you can use.

- Arrange the sentences in a *logical order*, as Yezierska has done in the example in the exercise (she uses a narrative order), so that readers almost expect each sentence that will follow. Of course, this takes careful planning, and usually some transitional words are necessary.
- Repeat *key words* to emphasize a point or example. William Zinsser repeats the word *pressure* in this sentence:

I see four kinds of pressure working on college students today: economic pressure, parental pressure, peer pressure, and self-induced pressure.

Since too much repetition of key words can be tedious for readers, this approach should be used sparingly.

- Use *pronouns* to refer to a word or words previously mentioned. Using pronouns is one way to avoid unnecessary repetition. By using the pronoun *them* in the second sentence, Zinsser can avoid repeating the word *students* and can refer readers to what they have just read:

What I wish for all students is some release from the clammy grip of the future. I wish them a chance to savor each segment of their education as an experience in itself.

- Use *parallel structure*. Writers can repeat similar grammatical structures to tie ideas together (see "Parallel Construction" in Chapter 17). Jacob Neusner repeats the structure "When you (past tense verb) . . . , we (past tense verb)" to link several examples he uses to make a point:

> When you tossed on our desks writing upon which you had not labored, we read it and even responded, as though you earned a response. When you were dull, we pretended you were smart. When you were predictable, unimaginative and routine, we listened as if to new and wonderful things.

Writers link ideas in many other ways as well, and you can discover them through your own reading and through class discussions of the readings.

When you draft your own sentences and paragraphs, you do not need to force connectives onto your writing. If you try to write transitions (or pronouns, repetition, or parallelism) instead of writing ideas, you may block the flow of your thinking. The connections between ideas and examples should emerge as you attempt to transmit your ideas to your readers. If the connections are not clear in a first draft, you can return to individual sentences and paragraphs to revise them for clarity.

EXERCISE: *Combining sentences*

Working in pairs or in a small group, link each pair of sentences in as many different ways as you can, relating ideas in any way you want. Discuss whatever changes in meaning may occur.

1. Learning a new language is difficult. It is a rewarding experience.
2. Women leave college superbly equipped to bring fresh leadership to traditionally male jobs. Society hasn't yet caught up with this fact.
3. American education is tragically inferior. America is the country of innovation.

Creating Paragraph Units

Paragraphs do not stand in isolation, but are linked to form a unit of thought. The following analysis of such a unit of thought should help you to understand better how paragraphing works.

EXAMPLE OF A PARAGRAPH UNIT

First sentence makes a general statement; supporting details follow.

As learners, human. beings display different qualities at different ages. Young children have a spontaneous enthusiasm for learning, but they are easily bored, and their

Signals contrast

Signals addition

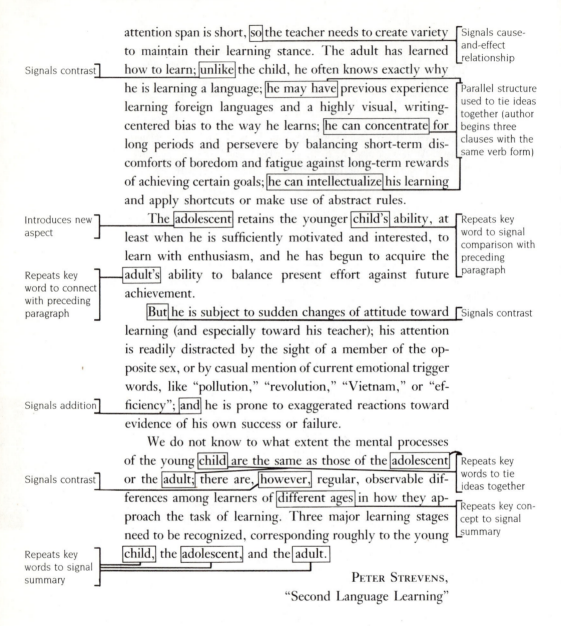

attention span is short, so the teacher needs to create variety — Signals cause-and-effect relationship

to maintain their learning stance. The adult has learned

Signals contrast — how to learn; unlike the child, he often knows exactly why

he is learning a language; he may have previous experience — Parallel structure used to tie ideas together (author begins three clauses with the same verb form)

learning foreign languages and a highly visual, writing-centered bias to the way he learns; he can concentrate for long periods and persevere by balancing short-term discomforts of boredom and fatigue against long-term rewards of achieving certain goals; he can intellectualize his learning and apply shortcuts or make use of abstract rules.

Introduces new aspect — The adolescent retains the younger child's ability, at least when he is sufficiently motivated and interested, to learn with enthusiasm, and he has begun to acquire the — Repeats key word to signal comparison with preceding paragraph

Repeats key word to connect with preceding paragraph — adult's ability to balance present effort against future achievement.

But he is subject to sudden changes of attitude toward — Signals contrast

learning (and especially toward his teacher); his attention is readily distracted by the sight of a member of the opposite sex, or by casual mention of current emotional trigger words, like "pollution," "revolution," "Vietnam," or "ef-

Signals addition — ficiency"; and he is prone to exaggerated reactions toward evidence of his own success or failure.

We do not know to what extent the mental processes of the young child are the same as those of the adolescent — Repeats key words to tie ideas together

Signals contrast — or the adult; there are, however, regular, observable differences among learners of different ages in how they ap- — Repeats key concept to signal summary

proach the task of learning. Three major learning stages need to be recognized, corresponding roughly to the young

Repeats key words to signal summary — child, the adolescent, and the adult.

PETER STREVENS,
"Second Language Learning"

Organizing Body Paragraphs

How you organize the body paragraphs of your essay is dependent on your purpose and content. Some of the possibilities used by the authors in this book are listed here:

- Organize paragraphs *chronologically* (in the order in which things happened), if you are narrating events or describing a process. Examples are Wu-tsu Fa-yen's "Zen and the Art of Burglary" (p. 3) and Anzia Yezierska's "College" (pp. 20–25). Yezierska's narrative is organized according to an expectation-disappointment-discovery pattern.

- Organize paragraphs in *order of importance*, beginning with the least important points and building to the most important (or reversing this order), if you are making a series of points. An example is Paul McBrearty's "We Should Abolish Anonymous Evaluations of Teachers by Their Students" (pp. 145–148).
- Organize paragraphs by *comparison and contrast*, if you are showing the similarities and differences between two or more items throughout the essay. Examples are Rolando Niella's "Barriers" (pp. 16–18) and Margaret Mead and Rhoda Metraux's "On Friendship" (pp. 73–77).
- Organize paragraphs according to a set of *categories*, if you are presenting a series of examples throughout the essay. Examples are Judith Viorst's "Friends, Good Friends—and Such Good Friends" (pp. 68–72), LaRay Barna's "Intercultural Communication Stumbling Blocks" (pp. 78–87), and William Zinsser's "College Pressures" (pp. 132–139).

(For further work on organizing body paragraphs, see the guidelines for individual writing assignments in Parts One through Four.)

EXERCISE: *Analyzing paragraphing*

To understand fully how paragraphing works, you need to look at a complete written text. Working with a small group, or with the whole class, analyze one of the reading selections in this book or a sample student essay. (*Note:* You can use these questions when you revise your own essay.)

1. Determine the function of each paragraph. Does the paragraph introduce the main idea of the essay? Does the paragraph make a new point and provide evidence to support that point? Does the paragraph exist primarily to provide an example to illustrate or clarify a point made in the preceding paragraph?
2. Look at the first sentence of each new paragraph. Does it connect what has just been said with what is about to be said?
3. Determine how the writer links ideas and examples within and between paragraphs. Look for transitional words or expressions; signals such as pronouns, repetition, or parallelism; and other signals.
   a. If you find connectives, do they help you as a reader to follow the logic and sequence of the writer's ideas? Do they reveal the writer's emphasis? Why or why not?
   b. If connections are missing, where would you add connective words or expressions?
   c. If you find any connectives that are distracting (sometimes a

writer can include more connectives than a reader needs), explain where they are and why you would delete them.

4. Look at the essay as a whole. Is the organization of the paragraphs logical? Do the beginning, middle, and ending merge with each other smoothly? If an issue is raised in the introduction, is it discussed in the body of the piece? Does the conclusion relate to the material presented in the introduction and body?   ●

CHAPTER FOURTEEN

Citing and Documenting Sources

Giving Credit to Your Sources

When you incorporate material from other sources into your own text, whether through summary, paraphrase, or quotation, you have an obligation to your readers to cite (mention) the source of that material. You must give credit to another writer for ideas and information by documenting (accurately identifying) your sources. Proper documentation legitimizes your use of the material and allows your reader access to the sources.

To omit this documentation is to commit *plagiarism*, the serious offense of presenting someone else's material as one's own. Discovery of deliberate plagiarism can lead to a student's dismissal from the university.

Documentation is an important convention of American academic writing. In this country, individual opinions are highly valued. Writers want to receive credit for their own unique ideas. Academics are therefore careful to give credit to their sources when they borrow ideas to use in their writing. In some other cultures, the borrowing of ideas is viewed in a different way. Students may learn to write by imitating the work of great writers and be praised for good imitations, even when they include the exact words of the original author without making it clear that the words are being reprinted from another source. These students and other students who do not understand the convention of documenting sources may unintentionally commit plagiarism in an American university.

College professors understand that unintentional plagiarism can occur. However, it is your responsibility to learn the conventions of academic writing to avoid plagiarism in the first place. The guidelines on p. 248 can help you.

In this book, documentation rules are presented in two formats, that of the American Psychological Association (APA) and that of the Modern Language Association (MLA). These rules cover instructions for (1) documenting sources within your text and (2) including a list of sources (a bibliography) at the end of your text. Your instructor will tell you which format to use. In other college courses, you may be expected to use other formats. Your instructors in those courses will provide the appropriate rules.

CITING AND
DOCUMENTING SOURCES

GUIDELINES

Guidelines for Avoiding Plagiarism

Plagiarism is the presenting of someone else's material as your own. Here is how to avoid plagiarism:

- Avoid using the exact words of an author without making it clear that the words are being reprinted from another source. Use quotations marks for short quotations, or set off a long quotation.
- Avoid paraphrasing an author's words without identifying the author.
- Avoid handing in a paper written by someone else and presenting it as your own.
- Avoid having anyone write any part of your paper.
- Use proper formats for citing and documenting sources.

Documenting within Your Text

Deciding What to Document

In your academic writing, you draw on knowledge that you have gained from numerous sources. In writing from course reading or from research sources, you support points that you make by citing facts and opinions from authorities in a given field. By including references to the words of these authorities, you reveal that you are aware of previous writing on your subject and that you are adding to that previous work. Your writing is building on a base of knowledge and thought on your subject.

Once you understand why you document, you need to decide what to document. The following list will help you make that decision.

You should document the following borrowed material:

1. Every quotation
2. Every diagram, chart, or picture
3. Any statistics
4. All ideas, opinions, facts, theories, and information that cannot be considered common knowledge to your audience. The term *common knowledge* means information that your readers already know.

The items in point 4 are the most problematic, for it is difficult to decide what an audience's shared common knowledge is, especially if the audience represents a culture different from your own. Here are several guidelines for determining common knowledge.

- If you yourself were aware of the fact or idea before reading the material, you may assume that this is common knowledge. An exception to this guideline might be that the fact or idea is common knowledge to you because of your cultural background but is not common knowledge to your readers if they have a different cultural background.

- If several of the sources you have consulted mention the same fact or idea without having documented it, you may assume that this fact or idea is part of common knowledge.

(If you are not sure whether something is common knowledge to an American academic audience, check with your instructor.)

Another problem that you might have in documenting sources is that you may have some prior knowledge of your subject—from your own past reading or studying, for example—that you are unable to identify accurately because you no longer remember the exact source. If that is the case, it is wise to include a footnote to your instructor explaining the general source of information. Then your instructor will understand why there is no formal documentation.

Citing Course Material

Much of your college writing involves incorporating material from your course reading. That means, of course, that your readers are familiar with your sources. Nevertheless, you must mention the source if you refer to ideas other than your own. When you cite a course reading, mention the author's name or the title of the reading, or both. This is true whether you summarize, paraphrase, or quote.

EXAMPLES

According to Judith Viorst, friends can be divided into several categories.

In "On Friendship," Margaret Mead and Rhoda Metraux search for a definition of the word *friend* as they contrast friendships in America, France, Germany, and England.

Always include the most precise source location of a quotation (line or paragraph number if these are numbered; page number otherwise) so that your reference can easily be verified. Put this locator within parentheses after the quotation.

EXAMPLE

In "On Friendship," Margaret Mead and Rhoda Metraux define a friend as "someone who chooses and is chosen" (paragraph 15).

Citing Outside Material

When you do research outside the classroom, you may find materials that your readers have never read or have not read as recently or as carefully as you have. Whenever you borrow words, ideas, or evidence from another writer, you need documented references in the text to alert your readers to the borrowed material. Careful documentation makes it possible for readers to find the source of the information you have referred to, if they wish to do so.

Formats for In-Text Documentation

The following guidelines can help you to properly document your sources in your paper. Two formats are demonstrated. Your instructor will tell you which format to follow.

APA Format

The APA format is widely used in social science books and journals. It does not use footnote numbers; the author and date (and the page number, for a quotation) are given in the body of the paper. The author-date citation can be matched with a list of references attached at the end of the paper. A sample student research essay using this format can be found on pp. 173–176.

1. If your in-text reference does not contain the author's name, cite the author's last name and the year of publication of the source within parentheses. Put a comma between the name and the year.

   Students in Asia, for example, in Japan and Taiwan, attend school longer than in America, 240 days versus 180 days a year (McBee, 1984).

2. If your in-text reference includes the author's name, place only the year of publication within parentheses.

   According to McBee (1984), students in Asia, for example, in Japan and Taiwan, attend school longer than in America, 240 days versus 180 days a year.

3. If your source does not have an author, place all or part of the title (inside quotation marks) within parentheses along with the year of publication. Place a comma between title and year.

   Unlike non-Asian parents, Asian parents do not encourage their children to participate in extracurricular activities or to play with their friends after school ("Asian-Americans Lead the Way," 1986).

4. If the same point or statistic appears in more than one source, you can place both sources within the same parentheses, separated by a semicolon.

> . . . (Salholz, Doherty, & Tran, 1987; Biemiller, 1986).

5. If you use a quotation, include the page number(s). Use *p.* for one page, *pp.* for more than one page. Note the punctuation in each of the following examples.

> Many Asian immigrant families are from cultures "with vestigal Confucian influences, where advancement was entirely based on exam scores" (Biemiller, 1986, p. 35).

> Biemiller (1986) points out that many Asian immigrant families are from cultures "with vestigal Confucian influences, where advancement was entirely based on exam scores" (p. 35).

> Biemiller points out that many Asian immigrant families are from cultures "with vestigal Confucian influences, where advancement was entirely based on exam scores" (1986, p. 35).

MLA *Format*

The MLA format is used primarily in the humanities. It is similar to the APA format. One major difference is that in MLA format, the year of publication is not supplied, whereas in APA format it is. Another difference is that in MLA format the page number is supplied for either a paraphrase or a quotation, whereas in APA format the page number is supplied only for quotations.

1. If your in-text reference does not contain the author's name, cite the author's last name and the page number(s) of the source in parentheses. Include no year, no punctuation, and no *p.* for page number.

> Students in Asia, for example, in Japan and Taiwan, attend school longer than in America, 240 days versus 180 days a year (McBee 41).

2. If your in-text reference includes the author's name, place only the page number(s) of the source in parentheses.

> According to McBee, students in Asia, for example, in Japan and Taiwan, attend school longer than in America, 240 days versus 180 days a year (41).

3. If your source does not have an author, place all or part of the title within parentheses along with the page number(s). Include no comma between title and page number.

Unlike non-Asian parents, Asian parents do not encourage their
children to participate in extracurricular activities or to play
with their friends after school ("Asian-Americans Lead the
Way" 546).

4. If the same point or statistic appears in more than one source, you
can place both sources within the same parentheses, separated by a
semicolon.

. . . (Salholz, Doherty, & Tran 60; Biemiller 35).

Preparing the List of Sources (Bibliography)

A list of references, which includes the full bibliographic information
of the sources used in research, must be placed at the end of a research
paper. By glancing at the list, readers can see how recent, reliable, and
thorough the research is. In addition, they can use the list as a resource if
they wish to locate the sources themselves to investigate the same subject.

You are not expected to memorize the rules for citations. Use the
following guidelines as a reference when you are making your own list of
sources. Carefully note the indentation, punctuation, and capitalization, as
well as the order in which the publication information is given.

GUIDELINES

General Guidelines for List of Sources

1. Put the list on a separate sheet at the end of your research
essay.
2. Put the heading References (APA)[†] or Works Cited (MLA) at
the top of the page.
3. Double-space throughout.
4. Start the first line of each entry at the margin; indent the second line five spaces.
5. Put the author's last name first, followed by a comma and
then the first initial (APA) or first name (MLA).
6. Put the list in alphabetical order, according to the last name
of the author. If there is no author, alphabetize according to
the first letter of the title. If the title begins with *A*, *An*, or
The, alphabetize according to the second word in the title.

[†] For a sample page of references in APA format, see p. 176.

Bibliographic Forms for Books

GUIDELINES

APA *General Form*: *Books*

Bibliographic entries for books follow this order:

1. Author(s), last name first, then first initial
2. Year of publication (in parentheses)
3. Title (underlined); capitalize only the first word, the first word after a colon, and proper nouns
4. City of publication (+ state, if city is not well known)
5. Publisher

All of this information can be found at the beginning of the book.

GUIDELINES

MLA *General Form*: *Books*

Bibliographic entries for books follow this order:

1. Author's name, last name first (if there is more than one author, put first name first for all successive authors)
2. Title (underlined); capitalize all words except prepositions, conjunctions, and articles (unless the preposition, conjunction, or article is the first or last word or the first word after a colon)
3. City of publication (+ state, if city is not well known)
4. Publisher
5. Year of publication

All of this information can be found at the beginning of the book.

Forms for Specific Types of Books: *APA and MLA*

The forms for APA and MLA are shown together. Whichever format you use, carefully follow the capitalization and punctuation.

Book by one author:
APA

Frankel, C. (1965). <u>The neglected aspect of foreign affairs</u>. Washington, D.C.: Brookings Institution.

MLA

Frankel, Charles. <u>The Neglected Aspect of Foreign
        Affairs</u>. Washington, DC: Brookings, 1965.

Book by two authors:

APA

Ruesch, J., & Bateson, G. (1968). <u>Communication: The
        social matrix of psychiatry</u>. New York: W. W.
        Norton & Co.

MLA

Ruesch, Jurgen, and Gregory Bateson. <u>Communication:
        The Social Matrix of Psychiatry</u>. New York:
        Norton, 1968.

Book by three authors:

APA

Sherif, C. W., Sherif, M., & Nebergall, R. E.
        (1965). <u>Attitude and attitude change</u>.
        Philadelphia: W. B. Saunders Co.

MLA

Sherif, Carolyn W., Musafer Sherif, and Roger E.
        Nebergall. <u>Attitude and Attitude Change</u>.
        Philadelphia: Saunders, 1965.

Book with an editor:

APA

Hoopes, D. (Ed.). (1972). <u>Readings in intercultural
        communication</u>. (Vols. I–IV). Pittsburgh:
        Regional Council for International Education.

MLA

Hoopes, David, ed. <u>Readings in Intercultural
        Communication</u>. Vols. I–IV. Pittsburgh: Regional
        Council for International Education, 1972.

Book with two or more editors:

APA

Samovar, L. A., & Porter, R. E. (Eds.). (1988).
        <u>Intercultural communication: A reader</u>. (5th
        ed.). Belmont, Calif.: Wadsworth Publishing Co.

MLA

Samovar, Larry A., and Richard E. Porter, eds.
        <u>Intercultural Communication: A Reader</u>. 5th ed.
        Belmont, CA: Wadsworth, 1988.

Book with a corporate (agency, association) author:
APA
Speech Communication Association. (1974).
    <u>International and intercultural communication
    annual</u>. New York.
MLA
Speech Communication Association. <u>International and
    Intercultural Communication Annual</u>. New York,
    1974.

Work in a collection:
APA
Fisher, G. (1988). International negotiation. In
    L. A. Samovar and R. E. Porter (Eds.),
    <u>Intercultural communication: A reader</u>. (5th
    ed.) (pp. 193–300). Belmont, Calif.: Wadsworth
    Publishing Co.
MLA
Fisher, Glen. "International Negotiation."
    <u>Intercultural Communication: A Reader</u>. 5th ed.
    Eds. Larry A. Samovar and Richard E. Porter.
    Belmont, CA: Wadsworth, 1988. 193–200.

Bibliographic Forms for Articles in Periodicals

GUIDELINES   ## APA *General Form*: *Articles in Periodicals*

Bibliographic entries for articles follow this order:

1. Author's name (if there is one), last name first, then first
   initial
2. Date of publication (in parentheses):
   • full date: year, month, and day (for weekly magazines and
     for newspapers)
   • month and year (for monthly magazines)
   • year (for quarterly and monthly journals)
3. Title of the article; capitalize only the first word, the first
   word after a colon, and proper nouns
4. Name of the periodical (underlined)
5. Volume number of a journal (underlined)
6. Inclusive page numbers of the article

GUIDELINES

MLA *General Form*: *Articles in Periodicals*

Bibliographic entries for articles follow this order:

1. Author's name (if there is one), last name first (for successive authors, put first name first)
2. Title of the article (within quotation marks); capitalize all words except prepositions, conjunctions, and articles (unless the preposition, conjunction, or article is the first or last word or the first word after a colon)
3. Name of the periodical (underlined)
4. Date of publication:
   - full date: day, month, and year (for weekly magazines and for newspapers)
   - month and year (for monthly magazines)
   - volume number and year (in parentheses) for quarterly and monthly journals
5. Inclusive page numbers of the article

Forms for Specific Types of Periodicals: APA and MLA

APA and MLA forms for specific types of periodicals are shown together. Whichever form you use, carefully follow the capitalization and punctuation.

SCHOLARLY JOURNALS

Scholarly journals are periodicals that contain articles (especially research reports) written by experts and scholars in a field for other experts and scholars in the field. These journals are available primarily in libraries.

General form:
APA

Yao, E. L. (1985). A comparison of family characteristics of Asian-American and Anglo-American high achievers. <u>International Journal of Comparative Sociology</u>, <u>26</u>, 198–208.

MLA

Yao, Esther Lee. "A Comparison of Family Characteristics of Asian-American and Anglo-American High Achievers." <u>International Journal of Comparative Sociology</u> 26 (1985): 198–208.

MAGAZINES

Most magazines are popular periodicals whose articles are written by reporters or writers for the general public. Other magazines are periodicals whose articles are written by experts and scholars for the general public. These periodicals can be found in libraries and often at newsstands.

Article from a weekly periodical:
APA

Salholz, E., Doherty, S., & Tran, D. (1987, February 9). Do colleges set Asian quotas? Newsweek, p. 60.

MLA

Salholz, Eloise, Shawn Doherty, and De Tran. "Do Colleges Set Asian Quotas?" Newsweek 9 Feb. 1987: 60.

Article from a weekly periodical, with no author given:
APA

AIDS and civil rights. (1985, November 18). Newsweek, p. 86.

MLA

"AIDS and Civil Rights." Newsweek 18 Nov. 1985: 86.

Article from a monthly periodical:
APA

Levine, R., with Wolff, E. (1985, March). Social time: The heartbeat of culture. Psychology Today, pp. 29–30; 32; 34–35.

MLA

Levine, Robert, with Ellen Wolff. "Social Time: The Heartbeat of Culture." Psychology Today Mar. 1985: 29–30; 32; 34–35.

Article from a monthly periodical with no author given:
APA

Asian-Americans lead the way in educational attainment. (1986, March). Phi Delta Kappan, p. 546.

MLA

"Asian-Americans Lead the Way in Educational Attainment." Phi Delta Kappan Mar. 1986: 546.

NEWSPAPERS

Article from a newspaper:
APA

McKibben, G. (1988, August 9). East Europe ponders new Soviet stance. Boston Globe, pp. 1, 6.

MLA

McKibben, Gordon. "East Europe Ponders New Soviet Stance." Boston Globe 9 Aug. 1988: 1, 6.

Article from a newspaper, with no author given:
APA
Tons of drugs from jet seized (1989, April 30). New
    York Times, p. 24.
MLA
"Tons of Drugs from Jet Seized." New York Times 30
    Apr. 1989: 24.

Editorial:
APA
From good news to bad. (1984, July 16). [Editorial].
    Washington Post, p. 10.
MLA
"From Good News to Bad." Editorial. Washington Post
    16 July 1984: 10.

Letter to the editor:
APA
Castillo-Sandoval, R. (1988, August 9). Significance
    of U.S. election to other nations. [Letter to
    the editor]. Boston Globe, p. 14.
MLA
Castillo-Sandoval, Roberto. "Significance of U.S.
    Elections to Other Nations." Letter. Boston
    Globe 9 Aug. 1988: 14.

Bibliographic Forms for Other Types of Sources: APA and MLA

Interview:
APA
Sadow, C. (1987, November 7). [Personal interview].
MLA
Sadow, Catherine. Personal interview. 7 Nov. 1987.

Public address with printed text:
APA
Reagan, R. (1985, November 21). The Geneva summit
    meeting: A measure of progress. U.S. Congress.
    Washington, D.C. Reprinted in Vital Speeches of
    the Day. (1985, December 15). pp. 130–132.
MLA
Reagan, Ronald. "The Geneva Summit Meeting: A
    Measure of Progress." U.S. Congress.
    Washington, DC. 21 Nov. 1985. Rpt. in Vital
    Speeches of the Day. 15 Dec. 1985: 130–32.

Book review:

APA

Slevin, J. F. (1987). [Review of The Nuclear Predicament: A Sourcebook, by D. Gregory.] College Composition and Communication, 38, 241–242.

MLA

Slevin, James F. Rev. of The Nuclear Predicament: A Sourcebook, by Donna Gregory. College Composition and Communication 38 (1987): 241–42.

PART SIX

The Editing Process

Errors are expected and understood as a natural result of the language-learning process, for both native and non-native speakers of English. In fact, most errors have logical causes, and you can learn from your mistakes by examining why you have made them. But since errors can shift a reader's attention away from your meaning, you want to remove from your writing any errors that will prevent someone from understanding what you are saying.

The goal of *editing* is to produce a paper whose meaning is clear. Editing involves both proofreading (reading to look for errors) and the actual correcting of errors. Proofreading and correcting are slow and time-consuming processes, requiring that you closely read and reread your paper and refer to other sources such as a grammar handbook or dictionary. Therefore, it is best to focus on these processes at a later stage in your writing, after you have developed and organized your ideas.

Though proofreading and correcting can be tedious, they are important procedures, for they help you to prepare a clearly expressed and comprehensible paper to hand in for evaluation. A neat presentation that reveals an attempt to edit out mistakes is also a courtesy to your reader. It reflects well on your effort to improve your writing and to do well in the course.

CHAPTER FIFTEEN

Editing and Proofreading

Editing

At the beginning of the term, the instructor or another classmate may mark some of the errors in your paper, probably by underlining the errors or by using symbols to indicate the kinds of errors you have made. Your task is then to make corrections. The following guidelines can help you in that process.

GUIDELINES

Guidelines for Editing

1. When you receive a paper marked for errors, correct every error you can without asking for help.
2. Take time with the instructor or another student to go over any markings you do not understand.
3. Attempt to understand the causes of your errors (see pp. 265–270).
4. Use the Handbook for Correcting Errors (pp. 271–330) or a grammar book to help you correct some errors that you cannot correct on your own.
5. Ask for help if you do not know how to correct an error even after consulting the handbook.
6. Show the instructor or a classmate your corrections.
7. Keep a record of your commonly made errors.

Proofreading

In a composition class, you have the advantage of readers—your instructor and your classmates—who will proofread your paper for you and point out the errors. But because you will not always have this advantage, you need to develop other ways to find your errors. Only then can you feel confident to write papers for other courses.

As the semester progresses, you will take increased responsibility for your own proofreading. There are many ways to proofread. You may want to follow one or more of these suggestions.

GUIDELINES   ## Guidelines for Proofreading

1. *Read for error only.* Read your paper not to develop further the ideas you have written but primarily to find your mistakes. You can devise your own system for this process, but here are two useful techniques:
   a. *Read word by word.* Put your finger or a pencil under each word, and move it slowly across the page. This technique can be especially helpful in finding spelling or typographical errors.
   b. *Look for your typical errors.* Read just to find the errors you know you tend to make, for example, sentence fragments, run-on sentences, or inappropriate verb tenses.

2. *Read your paper aloud.* Read your paper to someone else or to yourself as if someone were listening. If you hesitate as you read your own writing, the reason may be that you have come across an error. Mark the spot on the paper and continue reading. Then go back and make corrections.

3. *Learn the rules.* Before you proofread your paper, review your previously corrected essays and your list of your own errors to remind yourself of the errors you most often make. Then consult a grammar handbook to find the rules to correct two or three of those errors. Then look at your most recent draft, searching for those particular errors, and correct them. You may find it easier to remember the rule once you have applied it to your own writing.

4. *Let someone else proofread your paper.* It can be very difficult to find your own errors. You might find it helpful to have a friend proofread the paper, but only to point out and discuss the reasons for your errors. Only by going through the process of correction yourself will you learn how to correct.

Further Guidelines for Proofreading and Editing

Because several of the assignments in this book ask you to make direct references in your essays to your reading, these are specific areas on which you need to focus. The following suggestions remind you of what needs to be done when references are made to readings.

Guidelines for Proofreading and Editing a Paper That Makes References to Reading

If you have used quotations:

1. Reread the original statements of the author.
2. Check to see that you have copied the passage down *exactly* as it was written originally. This means that your essay should contain the exact words, the exact spelling, and the exact punctuation that you find in the original. Careful quotation reveals your respect for the author.
3. Make sure that the quotation you have selected is logically integrated into your own writing, that credit is given to the author, and that you have included the correct page, paragraph, or line number within parentheses.
4. Consult pp. 324–325 for instructions on punctuating quotations.

If you have summarized, paraphrased, or quoted:

Check to see that all references have been properly documented within the paper. (Consult pp. 247–252 on citing and documenting sources.)

If your paper requires a list of sources (bibliography):

Review the forms (consult pp. 252–259 on preparing the list of sources), and make sure that your sources are listed correctly and alphabetically and are punctuated properly.

CHAPTER SIXTEEN

Causes of Error

Many inexperienced writers, especially when writing in a second language, feel frustrated by their tendency to make language errors. But errors should be considered a natural result of the process of learning to master a language. A variety of reasons explain why they occur in writing.

Some errors are simply mistakes made through carelessness, and they can usually be corrected by careful proofreading. For example, you may know how to spell the word *people*, but in the rush of writing a paper, you write *peeple* instead. By closely rereading the paper before it is handed in to the instructor, you can recognize and then correct this mistake.

Other errors have more complex causes. These errors occur when you face some difficulty expressing and communicating your meaning. Sometimes, in order to avoid error, you may avoid saying something you want to say. But more often, you may use communication strategies that allow you to discuss what you want to discuss, even though these strategies may lead to error. Although you may regret the error, you should not give up. In fact, your instructor will probably encourage you to keep trying. Unless you attempt to communicate ideas, you cannot communicate them. Eventually, your strategies, if you understand them, may lead to successful language learning.

This chapter presents several categories of common causes of errors. By studying these categories, you may come to a clearer understanding of why you make certain errors. You can understand that there is logic behind your errors and that you are not making "dumb" mistakes. If you understand the cause of a frequent error, you will increase your chances of eliminating it in the future.

ACTIVITY: *Examining causes of error*

Read the explanation for each of the following categories, illustrated by student examples. Then, with the class, discuss each error, the student's explanation, and the correction of the error. If you have made similar errors in your own writing, share them with your classmates. Explain, to the best of your ability, why you made the error.　　●　**265**

Interlingual Transfer

Interlingual ("between languages") transfer is characterized by interference from another language. In other words, you apply a rule or sound of a familiar language (another language you speak or have studied) in place of the correct rule or sound in English. Errors may then occur in spelling, word order, verb tense, word endings, use of articles, agreement of adjectives and nouns, and so on.

I. STUDENT EXAMPLE†

In his essay "Barriers" (pp. 16–18), Rolando wrote:

Even so, I am giving it a *tray*.

Rolando's explanation:
"This is a problem of pronunciation. I wrote *tray* instead of *try* because I was trying to get the right English sound [the long vowel sound ī]. To get that sound in Spanish, you need to write *ay*. So when I looked at the word *tray*, a voice inside my head said *try*."

Correction of error:
Even so, I am giving it a *try*.

2. STUDENT EXAMPLE

Rolando wrote:

Is hurting my pride.

Rolando's explanation:
"I forgot to put *It* at the beginning of the sentence. That's because in Spanish, you don't always have to use the [subject] pronoun. You can tell by the verb form what the subject is."

Correction of error:
It is hurting my pride.

Overgeneralization

Overgeneralization is characterized by the inappropriate application of an English-language rule. In other words, you apply a rule you have learned about the English language in place of the correct rule. Errors may then occur in punctuation, spelling, word order, verb tense, articles, and so on.

---

† Format courtesy of Ann Raimes.

1. STUDENT EXAMPLE

In her research essay "Asian-American Students: Why Is Their Success Becoming a Hindrance?" (pp. 173–176), Angela wrote:

It does not *solves* or *prevents* any problems.

Angela's explanation:

"I was thinking that the word *it* is third person singular and so it needed a third person singular verb. I added *-s* to *solve* and *prevent* to make them third person singular. I forgot that *does* already had the *-s* ending."

Correction of error:

It does not *solve* or *prevent* any problems.

2. STUDENT EXAMPLE

In her essay "College: An All-forgiving World?" (pp. 150–151), Ida wrote:

Neusner believes that in college we are trained to think *that*, "*failure* leaves no record."

Ida's explanation:

"I didn't use the correct rule to punctuate the quotation. I used the rule that says that a comma is used to introduce a quotation. When I looked up the rules to discover why the teacher marked the error, I realized that I did not need the comma before the quotation because a comma should never follow the subordinating conjunction *that*."

Correction of error:

Neusner believes that in college we are trained to think *that* "*failure* leaves no record."

Reliance on Incorrect Patterns

A writer can come to rely on word, phrase, or sentence patterns used often without realizing that they are incorrect. Errors can occur in at least two ways: you use a pattern in the wrong context, or you use a word or phrase that doesn't exist.

1. STUDENT EXAMPLE

In an essay about the process of creating a sculpture (not appearing in this book), Efrat wrote:

When I get to a point where I am stuck and don't know how to go on with the work, I use the following strategy: Since I am usually too close, physically and emotionally, to the work, I try to get away from it and to do something else like go for a walk or visit an art show. After a while I know *what is the best way I want to continue.*

Efrat's explanation:

"I used the forms *what is the best way* and *I want to continue* together in my sentence. I didn't know that they couldn't be used in this way. It sounded fine because it is a familiar expression to me. I use it when I speak."

Correction of error:

After a while I know *the best way to continue.*

2. STUDENT EXAMPLE

In an essay about college pressures (not appearing in this book), Al wrote:

Pressure is like a *tumid* in the brain.

Al's explanation:

"I was surprised that the teacher underlined this error. I thought the word *tumid* was correct. But the problem was that I never pronounced the word correctly."

Correction of error:

Pressure is like a *tumor* in the brain.

Appeal to Authority

Appeal to authority occurs when the learner seeks help from an outside source, such as a bilingual dictionary, a thesaurus, or a native speaker of English. In other words, when you do not know a particular form or word, you look it up in a dictionary or ask someone. Errors can occur when the form or word you decide on is not accurate.

I. STUDENT EXAMPLE

In an essay analyzing an argument (not appearing in this book), Som wrote:

I agree with as well as *contradict* some of his ideas.

Som's explanation:

"I didn't want to keep using the same words, *agree* and *disagree*, again and again in my paper. So I looked up the word *disagree* in the thesaurus. I used the synonym *contradict*, but it wasn't the correct substitute. I had to go back and forth in the thesaurus and the dictionary to find the right word."

Correction of error:

I agree with some of his ideas but *reject* others.

2. STUDENT EXAMPLE

In an essay on his high school experience (not appearing in this book), George wrote:

> I was a little bit frightened in the beginning that I would flunk out of the school, but my grades quickly *reassured* my confidence.

George's explanation:
"I wanted to say that my grades made be feel better. But I didn't know how to say it in a sophisticated way. My roommate told me I could say 'my grades were reassuring.' But when I wrote the sentence, I wanted to express the idea that my confidence had changed quickly. I used a form of my roommate's word, but I used it incorrectly."

Correction of error:
I was a little bit frightened in the beginning that I would flunk out of the school, but my grades quickly *bolstered* my confidence.

Risk Taking

Risk taking is a way of getting around English-language rules, forms, or words that have not yet been learned or mastered. In other words, when you want to say something but don't know how to say it, you say whatever you can and hope for the best. For example, you take risks when you make up an expression because you do not know or cannot think of the correct English one. Errors occur when what you choose to say is not correct.

I. STUDENT EXAMPLE

In her research essay on Asian-American Students (pp. 173–176), Angela wrote:

> These complaints have *brought up* the attention of social scientists and researchers.

Angela's explanation:
"I used the expression *brought up* because I just couldn't think of the correct expression in English. I knew the teacher would know what I meant and tell me the correct words."

Correction of error:
These complaints have *come to* the attention of social scientists and researchers.

2. STUDENT EXAMPLE

In an essay analyzing an argument (not appearing in this book), Miltos wrote:

I couldn't believe that the author was right in what he was saying, so I started analyzing his points to find where his reasoning *leaked*.

Miltos's explanation:

"I was thinking that the author's argument had holes in it. I meant that his reasoning leaked out like water leaks out of a pail with holes in it. I wasn't sure if it was the right word, but I decided to try it and see."

Correction of error:

I couldn't believe that the author was right in what he was saying, so I started analyzing his points to find where his reasoning *failed*.

This list of categories does not, of course, cover all possible errors. Other causes exist. For example, errors may result from direct translation of a phrase or sentence from another language into English. Errors can also be the product of misleading, incomplete, or misinterpreted explanations given by textbooks and teachers. You can examine your own writing to find causes of errors not discussed in this book.

Whatever the cause of an error, finding and correcting it yourself is the best way to overcome any difficulty you may have in communicating your ideas.

ACTIVITY: *Finding causes of errors*

You might find it helpful to keep a written record of your errors and their causes in a notebook. You can divide the notebook into different sections, one for each cause. You might need a section for errors that have more than one cause. Follow these guidelines for identifying causes of error in your own writing.

1. Look through your own writing to find errors. These can be errors marked by your instructor or a classmate or errors that you find on your own.
2. When you find an error, underline the sentence that contains the error or rewrite the sentence in your notebook.
3. Explain why you made the error.
4. Correct the error, asking for your instructor's or a classmate's help if necessary. ●

CHAPTER SEVENTEEN

A Handbook for Correcting Errors

This handbook for correcting errors can be used in a number of ways. You can consult it as you are editing your work. You and your classmates may consult it during in-class group editing sessions. You and your instructor may refer to it together during a conference. Or your instructor may use it to teach a point that the whole class is struggling with.

The handbook does not contain all of the rules that govern standard American English grammar and punctuation. Rather, only commonly troublesome areas have been selected for discussion. You may need to refer to a more complete grammar book or handbook for points not covered here and for an explanation of technical terms that you may not know.

Perhaps the most important lesson you can learn from using the handbook is to allow for flexibility in your writing. In many cases, alternatives are provided to show you various ways to correct errors. Emphasis is on the fact that decisions concerning grammar and punctuation are not dependent only on rules. The knowledge shared between the writer and reader as well as the intention of the writer play important roles in determining which forms are used.

SENTENCE BOUNDARIES

The fundamental unit of communication in English is the sentence. It has two main parts: *subject* and *predicate*. The subject is the part of the sentence about which something is stated or asked; the predicate is the part containing what is said or asked about the subject and must always include a verb.

At times, you may not produce a complete sentence even though that was your intention. At other times, you may not punctuate a sentence properly because you don't fully understand how its parts fit together. Since such sentence errors can interfere with your readers' understanding, they must be corrected. To help you remember the acceptable boundaries for written sentences, read the following information on phrases, clauses, fragments, and run-on sentences and comma faults. Most of the examples are taken from the readings in this book.

Phrases and Clauses

EXAMPLES OF PHRASES AND CLAUSES
Phrases a gregarious and charming man to be recaptured slowly have recently experienced *Clauses* INDEPENDENT: I am lonely It takes a while the moment comes DEPENDENT: as I watch the surf that he bored himself when I can converse again with my hidden powers

Phrases

A *phrase* is not a complete sentence. It is a small group of related words that does not contain both subject and predicate. In the following sample sentences, the various types of phrases are italicized.

Noun phrase: a noun and its modifiers (words that describe, qualify, or limit the meaning of other words)

We the faculty take no pride in *our educational achievements* with you.

Prepositional phrase: a preposition and its object and modifiers of the object

Into this empty casing, the teachers are supposed to stuff "education."

Verb phrase: an action or linking verb and its auxiliary verbs

They *had transformed* simple paper lunch bags into, among other things, a waterfall with flying fish.

Verbal phrase: a verbal (word derived from a verb) and all its complements (words used to complete the sense of the verb) and modifiers

- *Infinitive phrase* (verb with *to* before it)

    I spend so much time studying that I don't have a chance *to learn anything.*

- *Gerund phrase* (*-ing* word that acts as a noun)

  But genuine education, as Socrates knew more than two thousand years ago, is not *inserting the stuffings of information* into a person.

- *Participial phrase* (*-ing* or *-ed* word that acts as an adjective)

  Lacking the steadying influence that would be provided by the knowledge that their evaluations, too, are subject to verification, students are under no obligation even to tell the simple truth.

EXERCISE: *Identifying phrases*

In the following paragraph, identify a noun phrase, a prepositional phrase, a verb phrase, an infinitive phrase, and a participial phrase.

> I have painted too drab a portrait of today's students, making them seem a solemn lot. That is only half of their story; if they were so dreary I wouldn't so thoroughly enjoy their company. The other half is that they are easy to like. They are quick to laugh and offer friendship. They are not introverts. They are usually kind and are more considerate of one another than any student generation I have known.
>
> WILLIAM ZINSSER, "College Pressures"

●

Clauses

All clauses have subject and verb combinations.

INDEPENDENT CLAUSES

An *independent (main) clause* is a complete sentence. An independent clause may be part of a larger sentence, but if it is removed from the sentence, it can stand alone as a complete sentence.

Sentence: You have to practice until you master it.

Independent clause: You have to practice

Sentence: When your work came in beyond deadline, we pretended not to care.

Independent clause: we pretended not to care

DEPENDENT CLAUSES

A *dependent (subordinate) clause* is an incomplete sentence that depends on an independent clause to complete its meaning. A dependent clause is introduced by some kind of subordinating word.

Sentence: You have to practice until you master it.

Dependent clause: until you master it (*subordinating word:* until)

Sentence: When your work came in beyond deadline, we pretended not to care.

Dependent clause: When your work came in beyond deadline (*subordinating word:* When)

Punctuation pointer: Put a comma after a subordinate clause that begins a sentence.

A dependent clause can act as adverb, adjective, or noun; for example:

Adverb: It saddens me *because I know them in other corners of their life as cheerful people.* (The adverbial clause modifies the verb *saddens*. *Note:* Adverbial clauses usually modify the whole independent clause.)

Adjective: We have prepared you for a world *that does not exist.* (The adjective clause modifies the noun *world.*)

Noun: We teach them *that ignoring context is a form of falsification.* (The noun clause is a direct object.)

What I wish for all students is some release from the clammy grip of the future. (The noun clause is the subject of the sentence. *Note:* A noun clause used as the subject takes the first person singular form of the verb.)

ADVERBIAL CLAUSES

Many words can transform independent clauses into subordinate clauses. The box on page 275 contains many of the words (called *subordinate conjunctions*) used to form adverbial clauses.

In transforming an independent clause into a dependent adverbial clause, a subordinating word serves to show which clause has more emphasis. For example, observe the transformation of the two sentences in example 1 (two independent clauses) into one sentence (example 2) containing a dependent and independent clause:

1. I was telling the truth. My words sounded like lies.

2. Although I was telling the truth, my words sounded like lies.

In 1, the two clauses are given equal emphasis. In 2, however, the first clause is subordinated to the second clause when it is introduced by the subordinating word *although*. The writer reveals that the emphasis should be placed on the second clause. The writer wants to emphasize the lies

SUBORDINATING WORDS THAT INTRODUCE ADVERBIAL CLAUSES	
Indication	**Subordinating conjunctions**
Time	after once as since as long as so long as as soon as until before when by the time that whenever now that
Condition	as long as on condition that except that only if even if provided that if providing that if only so long as in case (that) unless (=if . . . not) in the event that when(ever) once whether or not
Concession (opposition, unexpected result)	although in spite of (the fact despite that) despite the fact that regardless of (the even if fact that) even though though

Cause or reason	as for
	as a result of inasmuch as
	because (of the fact in that
	     that) in view of (the fact
	due to (the fact that) that)
	     since

Effect or result	because (of this) so that so
Contrast (direct opposition)	whereas while
Purpose	for the purpose of in the hope that in order that so that in order to
Degree or extent	as far as insofar as
Manner	as if as though
Place	where wherever

rather than the truth. If the writer had wanted to emphasize truth rather than lies, the sentence could have read

3. I was telling the truth although my words sounded like lies.

In addition to revealing emphasis, the subordinating word reveals the relationship or connection between the two clauses (see also pp. 237–243 for a discussion of connectives). By using the word *although*, the writer shows that the idea in the subordinate clause is different from what one might expect. In other words, a reader would expect that if someone is telling the truth, lies would not be involved. But that is not the case in this sentence, and the subordinating word shows that.

EXERCISE: *Creating adverbial clauses*

Combine the following sets of sentences with a subordinating word or expression to create a sentence that contains an independent clause and at least one dependent adverbial clause.

1. The library was noisy. I was able to study.
2. The library was noisy. I was unable to study.
3. It is not unusual for students to be in debt. Students work part time at college and full time during the summer.
4. You tossed on our desks writing upon which you had not labored. We read it and even responded. You earned a response. ●

SPECIAL ADVERBIAL CLAUSES

Some pairs or groups of subordinating words are split so that other words come between them. These are used to indicate comparison (or degree) or result.

SUBORDINATING WORDS INDICATING COMPARISON OR DEGREE	
Subordinating words	*Sample sentences*
as . . . as	Students try *as* hard *as* they can.
more . . . than	Jack is *more* intelligent *than* we thought.
less . . . that	She is *less* likely to go *than* he is.
-er . . . than	The biology course is hard*er* this semester *than* it was last semester.

SUBORDINATING WORDS INDICATING RESULT

Note that *so* and *such a* are part of the main clause.

Subordinating words	Sample sentences
so . . . that	I got *so* wild *that* I seized the hurdle and right before their eyes I smashed it to pieces.
	Still, it would be hard for a student not to visualize these officers shuffling *so* many transcripts studded with As *that* they regard a B as positively shameful.
	There is *so* little time *that* I cannot finish my paper.
such a . . . that	She is *such a* friendly person *that* you can feel comfortable meeting her for the first time.

EXERCISE: *Combining sentences to create clauses of comparison, degree, or result*

1. Combine the following sets of sentences with *as . . . as* or *more/less/ -er than* to create a dependent clause.
   a. The cafeteria is usually noisy. The cafeteria isn't noisy today.
   b. Maria had hoped to do well in chemistry. Maria didn't do well in chemistry.
2. Combine the following sets of sentences with *so . . . that*.
   a. He worked hard. He became ill.
   b. He was being stuffed with miscellaneous facts. He had no time to use his own mind to analyze and synthesize the material.
3. Combine the following sets of sentences with *such a . . . that*.
   a. The ice-cream cone was so good. I couldn't stop eating it.
   b. Physics 518 is a difficult course. You have to be highly motivated to take it. ●

ADJECTIVE CLAUSES

A dependent adjective clause provides information about nouns or pronouns in the independent clause that it describes. The noun or pronoun that the dependent clause refers to is called the *antecedent*. The box on page 278 illustrates the use of subordinating words in a number of adjective clauses.

SUBORDINATING WORDS IN ADJECTIVE CLAUSES		
Antecedent	**Subordinating word**	**Sample sentence**
a person	who	I know a girl *who wants to be an artist*.
	whom	I know the girl to *whom you gave the book*.
	whose	I know the girl *whose ring this is*.
	that	She is the student *that called you yesterday*.
a thing	that	To play a sport *that I cannot master* is becoming a pain.
	whose	The poem, *whose author is unknown*, is delightful.
a time	when	Tomorrow is the day *when the exam results will be announced*.
a place	where	She works at the office *where I first worked*.
a reason	why	I don't know any reason *why you can't go*.

Punctuation of restrictive and nonrestrictive adjective clauses

Punctuation can change the meaning of an adjective clause that begins with a relative pronoun (*who, whom, whose, that*, or *which.*) For example, observe the transformation of the two sentences in 1 (two independent clauses) into one sentence (2) containing a dependent and an independent clause:

1. Students are irresponsible. Students often skip their classes.

2. Students who often skip their classes are irresponsible.

In 1, the sentences suggest that *all* students are irresponsible and that *all* students often skip classes. In 2, the sentence suggests that only *some* students are irresponsible. The dependent clause (*who often skip their classes*) *limits* or *restricts* the meaning of the noun (*Students*). The meaning of sentence 2 is this: Not all students are irresponsible; only students who often skip their classes are irresponsible. This clause is called a *restrictive clause*. Note what happens, however, when the punctuation of that sentence is changed:

3. Students, who often skip their classes, are irresponsible.

By using commas to set off the dependent clause from the independent clause, 3 returns to the original intention of 1, the two independent clauses: *all* students are irresponsible and *all* students often skip their classes. The dependent clause *does not limit or restrict* the meaning. This clause is called a *nonrestrictive clause*.

SPECIAL NOTES

1. Relative pronouns replace nouns and pronouns. The noun or pronoun that is replaced should not be repeated. Take these sentences:

   I know a girl. She is an artist.

   The two sentences (two independent clauses) become one sentence when the second clause is combined with the first and the word *She* is replaced by the relative pronoun *who*:

   I know a girl *who* is an artist.

   Not I know a girl *who she* is an artist.

2. When a dependent clause contains a preposition before the relative pronoun, use the relative pronoun *which* (not *that*) immediately after the preposition. Do not repeat the preposition. Take these two sentences:

   I live in a dormitory. The dormitory is too noisy.

   When they are combined into one sentence, the result can look like this:

   The dormitory *in which* I live is too noisy.

   Not The dormitory *in that* I live is too noisy.

   Not The dormitory *in which* I live *in* is too noisy.

3. A noun or pronoun functioning as part of an adjective clause may precede a relative pronoun used in a prepositional phrase.

   • Noun

   They went to a restaurant. I don't remember the name of the restaurant.

   When these two sentences are combined into one sentence, the noun *name* is used in the prepositional phrase:

   They went to a restaurant, *the name of which* I don't remember.

   • Pronoun

   The professor called the students back. Some students had already left the building.

When these two sentences are combined into one sentence, the pronoun *some* is retained in the prepositional phrase:

The students, *some of whom* had already left the building, were called back by the professor.

4. When commas are used to set off a dependent nonrestrictive clause, use the relative pronoun *which* (not *that*) to refer to something:

The teachers' strike lasted ten days. The strike is over.

When these two sentences are combined into one sentence, the result can look like this:

The teachers' strike, *which* lasted ten days, is over.

Not The teachers' strike, *that* lasted ten days, is over.

5. When the relative pronoun is the *object* of the verb in the dependent restrictive clause, it may be omitted, for example:

The woman (*whom*) you met is my professor.

When the relative pronoun is the *subject* of the verb in the dependent restrictive clause, it can never be omitted, for example:

The professor *who* teaches Chemistry 310 is friendly.

6. When the noun in the dependent clause is a *proper noun*, always use commas to set off the dependent clause from the independent clause, for example:

Ronald Reagan, who became the 40th president of the United States, was once an actor in Hollywood.

EXERCISE: *Creating and punctuating restrictive and nonrestrictive clauses*

1. Combine the following pairs of sentences with a relative pronoun, and punctuate the new sentence so that the dependent clause *restricts* the meaning of the noun.
   a. A man was once an actor in Hollywood. The man became the 40th president of the United States.
   b. They seemed to accept the idea. The idea is that someone of status is expected to arrive late.
2. Combine the following pairs of sentences with a relative pronoun, and punctuate the new sentence so that the dependent clause *does not restrict* the meaning of the noun.
   a. To a European, the differences are not clear. A European sees only our surface behavior.
   b. Learning the language is actually only the beginning. Most foreign visitors consider learning the language their only barrier to communication.   ●

NOUN CLAUSES

The following box provides examples of noun clauses.

NOUN CLAUSES		
Subordinating word	*Function of clause*	*Sample sentence*
that	Subject Subject after *It* Object of verb Appositive (restated subject)	*That she is rich* is true. It is true *that she is rich*. I know *that she is rich*. Your assumption *that she is rich* is true.
whether (or not), if	Subject Object of verb Object of preposition	*Whether or not she is rich* doesn't concern you. Do you know *whether or not she is rich?* Do you know *if she is rich?* I was thinking about *whether or not she is rich*.
how, what, when, where, which, who, why, (-ever)	Subject Object of verb Object of preposition	*How she got rich* is her business. I don't know *how she got rich*. I am thinking about *how I can get rich*.

EXERCISE: *Creating noun clauses*

Combine the following sets of sentences to create at least one dependent noun clause.

1. I don't know. They are getting A's or C's. I don't care.
2. They know something. Entrance into the better schools will be an entrance into the better law firms and better medical practices.
3. One appears on paper. One appears in person. One is more important than the other.
4. Your idea is a good one. There should be no grading system.   ●

Sentence Fragments

A *sentence fragment* is only part of a sentence. It is an incomplete group of words punctuated as a complete sentence, beginning with a capital letter and ending with a final punctuation mark (a period, a question mark, or an exclamation point). Most often fragments are phrases or dependent clauses that are disconnected from their independent clauses.

EXAMPLES OF SENTENCE FRAGMENTS

Phrases

Poor students, poor parents.
For example, the guy across the hall.
The result being that you will have to take more courses.

Dependent clauses

When there is no longer a place that is yours in the world.
If you drop out of a class.

Detached predicate

And are used to working under pressure.

Sentence fragments are sometimes used deliberately by experienced writers for emphasis or to express a theme. The following exercise may help you to understand how a writer can use a fragment for a specific purpose.

EXERCISE: *Finding and determining the purpose of sentence fragments*

Working in a small group, have one student read the following passage aloud. Then find the two sentence fragments and discuss what purpose they serve.

> Looking down on those swarming highways I understood more clearly than ever what peace meant. In time of peace the world is self-contained. The villagers come home at dusk from their fields. The grain is stored up in the barns. The folded linen is piled up in the cupboards. In time of peace each thing is in its place, easily found. Each friend is where he belongs, easily reached. All men know where they will sleep when night comes. Ah, but peace dies when the framework is ripped apart. When there is no longer a place that is yours in the world. When you know no longer where your friend is to be found. Peace is present when man can see the face that is composed of things that have meaning and are in their place. Peace is present when things form part of a whole greater than their sum, as the divers minerals on the ground collect to become the tree.
> But this is war.

ANTOINE DE SAINT-EXUPÉRY,
Flight to Arras,
trans. L. Galantière

●

A sentence fragment is an error when you create one unintentionally. Since such a fragment has no purpose, it is distracting to the reader and should be corrected. The box on page 284 shows five ways to correct a sentence fragment.

EXERCISE: *Correcting sentence fragments*

Find and correct the sentence fragments in the following sets of sentences, taken from student papers.

1. Somehow, I drifted into daydreaming. Staring out the window at the high-rise apartment where my best friend lived.
2. After failing to fit my friends into the categories revealed in Viorst's article, I tried to look at friendship from my mother's point of view. Because the women that Viorst has in mind are most likely closer to my mother's age.
3. Talking about the American students' flaws in geography. I think that even though they are taught "creative geography," they should know some practical geography such as which countries exist in the world and where they are situated.
4. Unfamiliar questions came from American students: "How are you?" and "What's up?" I immediately replied, "I'm fine. How about . . ." My sentence left unfinished as the student walked away.   ●

ACTIVITY: *Identifying sentence fragments*

Look through your own writing to see if you have unintentionally created sentence fragments. Check every sentence that begins with a capital letter and ends with a period, a question mark, or an exclamation point. If you find a fragment, turn it into a complete sentence. If you have used a fragment deliberately, explain its purpose.   ●

Run-on Sentences and Comma Faults

Some sentence boundary errors are caused by inappropriate punctuation (see also "Punctuation," pp. 319–328). One common error is the *run-on sentence*. This error occurs when a writer uses no punctuation at all between independent clauses. This is especially confusing to readers, because they are given no clue as to how the words in the sentence should be grouped together.

Another common punctuation error is the *comma fault*, an error that occurs when a writer connects two long independent clauses with only a comma. The comma is not a strong enough punctuation mark to show that there are really two complete sentences.

CORRECTING SENTENCE FRAGMENTS

1. Add a subject or a verb (to complete the predicate), if it is missing.

   Sentence fragment:
   We living in a science and mathematics era.

   Complete sentence:
   We are living in a science and mathematics era.

2. Connect a fragment to the preceding sentence with a comma.

   Sentence fragment:
   Comparable examples are the ladies at the cafeteria telling me about the menu. While speaking at an incredible speed.

   Complete sentence:
   Comparable examples are the ladies at the cafeteria telling me about the menu, while speaking at an incredible speed.

3. Combine a phrase or a detached predicate with the preceding sentence.

   Sentence fragment:
   Thus Asian students are used to working a lot. And are used to working under pressure.

   Complete sentence:
   Thus Asian students are used to working a lot and under pressure.

4. Build the fragment into a complete sentence.

   Sentence fragment:
   For example, the guy across the hall. Yesterday he asked me to turn down my stereo.

   Complete sentence:
   Yesterday, for example, the guy across the hall asked me to turn down my stereo.

5. Change a participle to a verb requiring a subject.

   Sentence fragment:
   Don't drop out of a class. The result being that you will have to take more courses.

   Complete sentence:
   Don't drop out of a class. The result will be that you will have to take more courses.

   Or restructure the sentences.

   Complete sentence:
   If you drop out of a class, next semester you will have to take more courses.

EXAMPLES: RUN-ON SENTENCE AND COMMA FAULT

Run-on sentence

I expected to find a lot of new friends in this country I soon realized that this would not be so easy.

Comma fault

I expected to find a lot of new friends in this country, I soon realized that this would not be so easy.

Fortunately, run-on sentences and comma faults are not difficult to correct. The box shows five ways to correct them.

CORRECTING A RUN-ON SENTENCE OR COMMA FAULT

1. Use a period to create two separate sentences.

   I expected to find a lot of new friends in this country. I soon realized that this would not be so easy.

2. Use a semicolon to connect the two clauses.

   I expected to find a lot of new friends in this country; I soon realized that this would not be so easy.

3. Add a coordinating conjunction (*and, or, but, for, yet, so*) after a comma.

   I expected to find a lot of new friends in this country, *but* I soon realized that this would not be so easy.

4. Use a subordinating conjunction to transform one of the independent clauses into a dependent clause. Put a comma after an introductory dependent clause.

   Although I expected to find a lot of new friends in this country, I soon realized that this would not be so easy.

5. Put a semicolon, then a conjunctive adverb, then a comma between the clauses (conjunctive adverbs are transitional expressions such as *however, thus, therefore, nevertheless, furthermore, consequently,* and *in addition*).

   I expected to find a lot of new friends in this country; *however,* I soon realized that this would not be so easy.

EXERCISE: *Correcting run-on sentences and comma faults*

Correct the punctuation errors in the following sentences, taken from student essays.

1. He would break everything down into pieces and start from scratch he would then build on that slowly so that I would understand.
2. In the past, Americans had a tendency to think that English was the only language worth knowing and that foreigners were forced to learn it so they did not even try to learn another language.
3. However, the fact is that I am not a supernatural being, I could not take the stress.
4. My decision to apply early to college was meant to lighten the burden, unfortunately the three essays and several short questions added to my unbearable load.   ●

ACTIVITY: *Identifying and correcting run-on sentences and comma faults*

Look through your own writing to see if you have any run-on sentences or comma faults. If you find any, correct them, using one of the five options in the box.   ●

AGREEMENT

Subject-Verb Agreement

Verbs in English agree with their subjects in number. That is, if the subject is plural, the verb is plural; if the subject is singular, the verb is singular.

EXAMPLES OF SUBJECT-VERB AGREEMENT

Singular subject, singular verb
Frankness is a virtue.

Plural subject, plural verb
Quitters are no heroes.

Compound subject, plural verb
Peer pressure and self-induced pressure are also intertwined.

Unfortunately, making verbs agree with their subjects is not as easy as it may first appear. The grammatical singular or plural form of the subject is not the only factor. The intention of the writer and current usage may also play a role.

**SUBJECT-VERB AGREEMENT AND THE INTENTION
OF THE WRITER**

The staff *are* leaving separately. (staff = individuals)
The staff *is* leaving. (staff = unit)

Your shouting and screaming *are* annoying. (shouting and screaming = separate items)
Your shouting and screaming *is* annoying. (shouting and screaming = unit)

It is easy to get confused about the proper form of the verb because the real subject of a sentence is not always clear.

RULES FOR CONFUSING CASES OF SUBJECT-VERB AGREEMENT

1. Even when a clause or phrase comes between the subject and verb, the verb should agree in number with the subject.

    A typical *method* used to prevent communication problems *is* to gather information about the customs of the other country.

    What *do* our time *judgments* say about our attitude toward life?

2. When *each*, or *every*, *everybody*, or *everyone* is the subject of a sentence, the verb should be singular.

    Each of his answers *was* correct.
    Everyone is absent.

3. When *who, which*, and *that* are used as subjects, they take singular verbs if the word they refer to is singular and plural verbs if the word they refer to is plural.

    A friend is *someone* who *chooses* and *is chosen*.
    Friends are *people* who *choose* and *are chosen*.

    Current usage provides a choice when the following kind of clause occurs:

    I am one of those people who *prefer* (*prefers*) tea.

    In this case, either *prefer* or *prefers* can be correct.

4. Whether *none* or *enough* is used with a singular or plural form depends on whether the reference is to one item or to more than one.

    Enough *has* been said.
    Enough *are* here to call a vote

Current usage provides a choice in the following kind of sentence:

None of those men *is* (*are*) ready.

In this case, either *is* or *are* can be correct.

5. When compound subjects are joined by (*either*) . . . *or*, *neither* . . . *nor*, or *not only* . . . *but also*, the verb usually agrees with the subject closest to it.

Are the students or the professor to blame?
Is the professor or the students to blame?

6. Whether *there* is used with a singular or plural form of the verb depends on whether the subject of the sentence is singular or plural.

There *is* no *doubt* about his honesty.
There *are doubts* about his honesty.

7. Whether the verb is singular or plural following expressions of quantity with *of* is determined by whether the noun (or pronoun) that follows *of* is singular or plural.

Some of the *money is* mine.
Some of the *dollars are* mine.

8. If an expression of amount or quantity comes before a plural noun referring to time, money, weight, or distance, the noun takes a singular form of the verb.

Six months *is* a long time to be away from home.

9. The expression *the number of* (used as a subject) takes a singular verb. The expression *a number of* (an expression of quantity meaning "several") is followed by a plural noun and a plural verb.

The number of students who take French 210 *is* 12.
A number of students *are* enrolled in Biology 401.

10. Titles of books and articles are considered singular, even if they end in *-s*.

"Intercultural Communication Stumbling Blocks" *is* the title of an article by LaRay Barna.

11. Some nouns that end in *-s* are singular, for example, countries (the Phillipines), stores (Sears), institutions (the United Nations), fields of study that end in *-ics* (economics), and the word *news*.

The United States *is* an enormous country.
The news *is* bad.

EXERCISE: *Creating subject-verb agreement*

Choose the correct answer in parentheses.

1. The extent of my professor's knowledge of the natural sciences (amaze, amazes) me.
2. Two-thirds of the semester (was, were) over before I felt completely adjusted.
3. What percentage of the students at the university (is, are) from other countries?
4. Everybody (is, are) required to take a year of science.　　　●

ACTIVITY: *Identifying and correcting errors of subject-verb agreement*

Look through your own paper to search for errors of subject-verb agreement. If you find any errors, correct them, asking for help if necessary.　　　●

Pronoun Agreement

Pronouns are substitutes for nouns or noun phrases. They agree in number (singular or plural) and gender (masculine, feminine, or neuter) with the words they refer to or replace.

EXAMPLES OF PRONOUN USE

A *pronoun agrees in number and gender with the word(s) it refers to*

An American girl in the same class gives *her* view . . .

How *a country* paces *its* social life is a mystery . . .

Today *millions of Americans* vacation abroad, and *they* go not only to see new sights . . .

Peer pressure and self-induced pressure are also intertwined, and *they* begin almost at the beginning of freshman year.

Selecting the correct pronoun is sometimes dependent on the writer's intended meaning. The table on page 290 illustrates, for example, how different pronouns might be used with certain collective nouns and indefinite pronouns to convey different meanings.

PRONOUN AGREEMENT

With Collective Nouns

The *staff* congratulated *itself* on the victory. (collective noun refers to a unit)

The *staff* had smiles on *their* faces. (collective noun refers to the individuals)

With Indefinite Pronouns

Each expressed ideas. (neutral)

Each (man) expressed *his* ideas.

Each (woman) expressed *her* ideas.

Problems with pronoun use can create confusion or misunderstanding in the mind of the reader. To present your ideas as clearly as possible, follow these guidelines.

SOLVING PRONOUN AGREEMENT PROBLEMS

1. Be consistent in your use of first, second, and third person pronouns.

   Inconsistent:
   At college, *people* must learn to budget *their* time (and money!) and to be tolerant (otherwise *you* wouldn't survive in a crowded triple!). *We* meet people from different parts of the world . . .

   Correct:
   At college, *we* must learn to budget *our* time (and money!) and to be tolerant (otherwise *we* wouldn't survive in a crowded triple!). *We* meet people from different parts of the world . . .

2. Avoid exclusive use of the masculine pronoun (*he, him, himself, his*) in referring to human beings in general. This use of the masculine pronoun was common practice before the 1980s. You may notice it in materials published before 1980. However, the use of the masculine pronoun to refer to all human beings is now considered sexist (unnecessarily specific with respect to gender) by most readers and editors. One way to avoid a sexist pronoun is to use the alternatives *he or she, him or her, his or hers,* if your instructor accepts them. Other options include the following:

   a. Change the reference to a plural form.

      Previous practice:
      The *American's* characteristic openness to different styles of relationship makes it possible for *him* to find new friends abroad.

Current practice:
Americans' characteristic openness to different styles of relationship makes it possible for *them* to find new friends abroad.

b. Rewrite the sentence to avoid pronouns with gender.

Previous practice:
Each sees, hears, feels, and smells only that which has some meaning or importance for *him*.

Current practice
Each sees, hears, feels, and smells only that which has some *personal* meaning or importance.

Note: Usage is changing in regard to the indefinite pronouns *each*, *everybody*, and *everyone*. For example, informal usage allows for a plural pronoun to refer to everybody or everyone, even though the verb is singular:

Everyone has *their* own luggage now.

However, such usage may not meet with universal approval or acceptance. Discuss usage of indefinite pronouns with your instructor.

3. Refer to these rules regarding an *antecedent* (the word a pronoun refers to).

   a. Use a plural pronoun to refer to an antecedent that consists of two or more nouns joined by *and*.

      If *Neusner and McBrearty* want to understand college life from a student's point of view, *they* should read my essay.

   b. Use a singular pronoun to refer to an antecedent that consists of two or more singular nouns or pronouns joined by *or* or *nor*.

      If *Neusner or McBrearty* wants to understand college life from a student's point of view, *he* should read my essay.

EXERCISE: *Completing sentences with pronouns*

Complete the following sentences with pronouns. In some of the blanks, there is more than one possibility. In some cases, there is a choice of verbs.

1. The American educational system allows students to think for themselves, but it does not provide everyone with the best education _____ can pursue.

2. From that experience, I have learned that fear is not the answer to any problem; instead, _____ should always try things that

have even a little chance of success. Unless _____ (try,

tries), _____ will never know what will happen. (Choose

from these pronouns: *I, one, we, they, you.*)

3. Each of her women friends (has, have) _____ own career.

4. Neither the professor nor the students expressed _____

appreciation.   ●

ACTIVITY: *Identifying errors of pronoun agreement*

Look through your own writing to search for errors of pronoun agreement. If you find any, correct them, based on the guidelines. Ask for help
if necessary.   ●

VERBS

Verb Tenses

Tense relates the verb form to the meaning of the sentence. Selecting
the appropriate verb tense when writing in English is not always easy
because, grammatically, tense is not the same as clock time. It is possible,
for example, to use the present tense to express future time ("She is going
to college next year"). Factors involved in selecting verb tense include not
only the time of an activity but also the habitual nature of an activity, the
meaning of the verb, the intention of the writer, and the conventions of
writing. Some of the tenses you are likely to use in your writing are
discussed.

Simple Present Tense

COMMON USES OF THE SIMPLE PRESENT TENSE
1. Expressing situations (feelings, perceptions, conditions) that exist at the moment of writing: I think he *is* wrong.
2. Describing habits or routines: I *study* every day.
3. Expressing long-term beliefs or perceptions: I *believe* in helping the homeless.

The simple present tense has other uses as well.

SPECIAL USES OF THE SIMPLE PRESENT TENSE

1. Expressing a universal truth or permanent situation:

    The earth *revolves* around the sun.

2. Indicating the near future, in cases of scheduled activity (with words such as *open, close, begin, end, start, finish, arrive, leave, come, return*):

    My class *starts* in an hour.

3. Discussing the ideas of an author:

    In "The Commencement Speech You'll Never Hear," Jacob Neusner *argues* that college is not a good preparatory school for life.

    [This acknowledges that the ideas continue to exist even though the author has finished writing about them.]

Present Progressive Tense

This tense, formed by *be,* (*am, is, are*) + *-ing,* refers to actions that are in progress at the time of writing and will probably continue for a while. The progressive is often used for activities that are temporary.

COMMON USE OF THE PRESENT PROGRESSIVE TENSE

Expressing situations that are in progress at the moment of writing:

    I *am waiting* for inspiration.

The present progressive tense has other uses as well.

OTHER USES OF THE PRESENT PROGRESSIVE TENSE

1. Describing an activity occurring over a specific period of time:

    I *am studying* composition this semester.

2. Indicating an activity that will occur in the near future:

    I *am studying* literature next semester.

3. Expressing an emotion (such as annoyance or anger) about some habitual action, with *always:*

    She *is always complaining.*

Several verbs describe states (rather than actions) that usually cannot be used in progressive tenses. These include verbs of perception, verbs of emotion, verbs of relationship, and verbs of measurement. Examples of such verbs appear in the following box.

VERBS THAT ARE NOT USUALLY USED IN THE PROGRESSIVE TENSES

Verbs of perception

believe	imagine	prefer	seem
doubt	know	remember	suppose
forget	mean	resemble	understand

Verbs of emotion

appreciate	envy	love	trust
care	fear	mind	want
desire	hate	need	
dislike	like		

Verbs of relationship

belong	contain	include	possess
consist of	entail	owe	

Verbs of measurement

cost	equal

EXERCISE: *Using present tenses*

Use either the *simple present* or the *present progressive* form of the verb in parentheses.

1. Maria has gone to work in France. At first, her French wasn't very good, but now it _____ (improve).

2. The library _____ (open) at 8:00 A.M and _____ (close) at 1 A.M. every day.   ●

Simple Past Tense

This tense refers to activities or situations that began and ended at a particular time in the past. The box on the top of page 295 shows uses of the simple past tense.

USES OF THE SIMPLE PAST TENSE

1. Specifying a definite time in the past:

    She *dropped* the course (last Thursday).

2. Describing activities that existed or occurred over a period of time in the past:

    She *stayed* in the course for two months.

3. Describing activities that existed or occurred at intervals in the past:

    She *skipped* a class almost every week.

Past Progressive Tense

This tense, formed by *be* (*was, were*) + *-ing*, refers to temporary actions in progress at a particular time in the past.

USES OF THE PAST PROGRESSIVE TENSE

1. Describing a temporary activity that was in progress at the time of another activity in the past:

    I *was studying* when the fire alarm sounded.

2. Describing a temporary activity that was in progress at a point in time in the past:

    They *were studying* in the library last Thursday night.

EXERCISE: Using past tenses

Use the *simple past* or the *past progressive* in the following sentences.

1. I _____ (understand) what he was saying.

2. I _____ (take) the exam when I noticed that it _____

    _____ (snow) outside. ●

Simple Future Tense

This tense, formed by *will* or *be going to* + the simple form of the verb, expresses activities that will exist or occur in the future. (See also "Auxiliary Verbs," pp. 298–304, for a discussion of *will, be going to*, and future time.)

USES OF THE SIMPLE FUTURE TENSE

1. Expressing an action that will take place at some definite future time:

    He *will take* the bus to school tomorrow.

2. Expressing a future habitual action:

    He *will take* the bus to school next year.

3. Expressing a future state:

    Don't worry; everything *will be* fine.

Future Progressive Tense

This tense, formed by *will be* + *-ing* or *be going to be* + *-ing*, expresses temporary activities that will be in progress at a particular point in time or will extend over a limited period of time.

USES OF THE FUTURE PROGRESSIVE TENSE

1. Indicating an action that will be in progress at a specific time in the near future:

    They *will be driving* to work at 8 A.M. tomorrow.

2. Indicating the duration of some specific future action:

    She *will be reading* that book for the next three hours.

EXERCISE: *Using future tenses*

Use either the *simple future* or the *future progressive* form of the verb in the following blanks.

1. I _____ (lie) on the beach in Puerto Rico by this time

    next week.

2. Angela _____ (be) here next week.   ●

Present Perfect Tense

This tense, formed by *have* + past participle, refers to activities that began sometime in the past but extend to or have relevance to the present. Several expressions of time are commonly used to indicate a past-to-present event:

1. Prepositions: *since* (gives the beginning point of the event), *for* (gives the entire span of the event)
2. Adverbial expressions: *so far, up to now, until now, up to the present*

USES OF THE PRESENT PERFECT TENSE

1. Describing an activity that began in the past and has continued up to, and may extend beyond, the immediate present (the actual time of writing):

    I *have been* at this university for one month.

2. Describing an activity that has existed or occurred (or did not exist or occur) in an unknown or unspecified time in the past:

    I *have been* there.
    I *have* never *studied* Russian history.

3. Describing an activity that has been completed a short time before the immediate present:

    I *have* just *finished* my paper.

4. Describing an activity repeated in the past (that will possibly be repeated in the future):

    I *have written* my introduction three times so far.

Past Perfect Tense

This tense, formed by *had* + past participle, refers to a past action that occurred before another past action.

USES OF THE PAST PERFECT TENSE

1. Describing an activity that ended before another activity in the past:

    The plane *had* already *left* by the time she reached the airport.

2. Describing an activity or situation that existed or occurred before a specific point of time:

    I *had* never *seen* a horror film before tonight.

Future Perfect Tense

This tense, formed by *will have* + past participle, refers to actions that will be completed before another time or event in the future.

USE OF THE FUTURE PERFECT TENSE

Indicating a future action that will be completed prior to a specific future time:

    I *will have written* five pages by six o'clock tonight.

EXERCISE: *Using perfect tenses*

Use the *present perfect*, the *past perfect*, or the *future perfect* in the following sentences.

1. I _____ (lived) here since 1988.

2. You'll miss her if you don't arrive until 10:00. She _____
   (go) home by then.

3. I was too late. The professor _____ (give, already) the
   quiz when I got to class.   ●

Perfect Progressive Tenses

These tenses, formed by adding *-ing* to the perfect tense verb forms, indicate the duration of events in progress immediately before, up to, or until another time or event.

EXAMPLES OF THE PERFECT PROGRESSIVE TENSES

Present perfect progressive:

   I *have been writing* for three hours now.

Past perfect progressive:

   I *had been writing* for three hours before you arrived.

Future perfect progressive:

   I *will have been writing* for three hours by the time you arrive.

Figure 17-1 on page 299 shows the relationship of several tenses on a time line. You may find this helpful in determining which verb tenses to use in your writing. You can design a time line for your own essay.

ACTIVITY: *Identifying and correcting errors in the use of verb tenses*

Look through your own writing to search for errors in the use of verb tenses. Look closely at the various actions or situations you have described in relation to the time at which you are writing. Decide whether the verb tense used accurately reflects what you want to say. Ask for help if necessary.   ●

Auxiliary Verbs

Auxiliary verbs in English are known as *helping verbs* because they help bring structure or meaning to the verbs they are used with. There are three

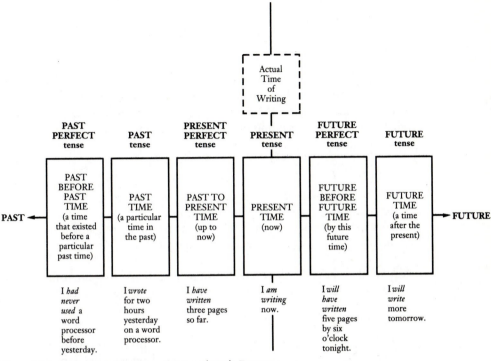

Figure 17-1   Time Relationship of Several Verb Tenses

types of auxiliary words: tense auxiliaries, *do*, and modal auxiliaries. Each type has a different purpose, although most can be followed by *not* in negatives and can be reversed with the subject in questions.

Tense Auxiliaries: be, have, will†

The tense auxiliaries add structure. *Be* occurs in progressive tenses (e.g., "I *am* waiting for inspiration") and in passive forms ("The door *was* locked last night"). *Have* is used for the perfect tenses ("I *have* gained 3 pounds since September"). *Will* is used for future tenses ("I *will* write tomorrow").

Do

Do is used with the simple form of the verb (the infinitive without *to*) primarily to create questions or statements of emphasis. This auxiliary is used only in the simple present tense ("*Do* you like your psychology course?" "He *does* study, but his grades are poor") or the simple past tense ("The package I was expecting never *did* arrive").

Modal Auxiliaries

These auxiliaries, used with the simple form of the verb, add meaning to the verb. There are three groups of verbs that act as modals.

---

† *Will* is also a modal auxiliary.

GROUP 1

can	may	must	should	will
could	might	ought to	would	

The first group of modal auxiliaries is characterized by a lack of tense and a lack of subject-verb agreement (note especially that there is no -*s* ending for third person singular). The meaning of the verb that the auxiliary is added to changes, depending on the writer's intention and attitude and on the verb used.

GROUP 2

be able to (ability)	have got to (necessity)[†]
be going to	have to (necessity)
be supposed to	used to[‡] (repeated past action; situation that
be to	existed in the past)

Most of the verbs in the second group have tense, require subject-verb agreement, and are followed by *to*. Some carry particular meaning.

GROUP 3

had better (advice; threat)	would prefer to (preference)
would like to (desire)	would rather (preference)

The words in the third group lack tense and subject-verb agreement and carry a particular meaning.

Note: Modals are also illustrated in the box on pp. 301–303 and in sections on sequence of tenses (pp. 304–306) and conditional clauses (pp. 308–310).

[†] *Used to* has no subject-verb agreement; in questions or negative statements, the form is *use to.*

[‡]*Have got to* is used in present tense only.

MODAL AUXILIARIES

Meaning Added to the Verb	Present or Future Time	Past Time
ABILITY		
can	I can see.	
be able to	I am able to see.	
	I will be able to see.	
could		I could see.
ADVISABILITY		**UNFULFILLED OBLIGATION**
(in order of increasing urgency)		
should	You should go.	He should have gone (but he didn't).
ought to	You ought to go.	You ought to have gone.
had better	You had better go.	
have to	You have to go.	
must	You must go.	
CERTAINTY		
will	She will be here.	
be going to	She is going to be here.	
DESIRE		**UNFULFILLED DESIRE**
would like	I would like to go.	I would have liked to go *or* I would have liked to have gone.
EXPECTATION		**UNFULFILLED EXPECTATION**
be supposed to	It is supposed to start at 5:00.	It was supposed to start at 5:00.
be to	It is to start at 5:00.	It was to start at 5:00.
should	It should start at 5:00.	It should have started at 5:00.
ought to	It ought to start at 5:00.	It ought to have started at 5:00.
IMPOSSIBILITY		
cannot	She cannot go.	
could not		She could not go.
LACK OF NECESSITY		
do not + have to	You don't have to go.	You didn't have to go.
NECESSITY		
have to	He has to go.	He had to go.
have got to	He has got to go.	
must	He must go.	He had to go.

Continued on p. 302

MODAL AUXILIARIES (continued)

Meaning Added to the Verb	Present or Future Time	Past Time
PAST REPEATED ACTION		
used to		I used to dream of being a pilot.
would		When I was eight, I would dream of being a pilot.
PERMISSION		
may	Yes, you may go.	
can	Yes, you can go.	
PLAN		**UNFULFILLED PLAN**
be going to	I am going to go to France. (decision made earlier)	I was going to go to France.
will	I will go to France. (decision made at time of speaking or writing)	I would have gone to France.
POLITE REQUEST		
may	May I go?	
can	Can I go?	
could	Could I go?	
will	Will you help?	
would	Would you please help me?	
POSSIBILITY		
can	It can rain.	It could have rained.
may	She may go.	She may have gone.
might	She might go.	She might have gone.
could	It could rain.	
PREDICTION		
will	He said it will rain tomorrow.	
be going to	He said it is going to rain tomorrow.	
PREFERENCE		
would rather	I would rather go than stay.	I would rather have gone.
would prefer to	I would prefer to go.	I would have preferred to go *or* I would have preferred to have gone.

302

Continued on p. 303.

MODAL AUXILIARIES (continued)		
Meaning Added to the Verb	**Present or Future Time**	**Past Time**
PROBABILITY (in order of increasing probability) could might may should must	He { could might may should must } be home by now.	He { could might may should must } have arrived by now.
will	He will leave by then.	He will have left by then.
PROHIBITION OR STRONG RECOMMENDATION AGAINST must not	You must not go.	
SITUATION THAT EXISTED IN THE PAST used to		I used to live in Italy.
SUGGESTION could	If you don't understand, you could ask him to explain.	If you didn't understand, you could have asked him to explain.
WILLINGNESS will	I will do that for you.	I would have done that for you.

EXERCISE: *Using modal auxiliaries*

Put a modal auxiliary in the blanks. Explain the meaning you want to convey.

1. I want to see that movie tonight. It _____ be interesting.

2. We _____ hurry. The train _____ leave in an hour.

3. The plane _____ landed by now. It took off three hours ago.

4. She _____ walk along the Seine every day when she lived in Paris.   ●

ACTIVITY: *Identifying and correcting errors in the use of auxiliaries*

Look through your own writing to search for errors in the use of auxiliaries. If you have used *be, have,* or *do,* make sure that the subject-verb agreement is correct and that the verb tense reflects your meaning. If you have used any modal auxiliaries, make sure that you have not added an *-s* ending to third person singular with *can, could, may, might, must, will,* or *would* and that you have used the simple form of the verb after the auxiliary. Check to see that the modals used fulfill your intentions.   ●

Sequences of Tenses

Sequence of tenses refers to the relationship between the verb in the independent (main) clause of a sentence and the verb in the dependent (subordinate) clause(s) of the same sentence.

The sequence of tenses must be logical. But determining which tense to use to describe the activity or situation in each clause is not always easy. The tense chosen to indicate the time of an activity or situation is dependent on its relationship to the actual time of writing. A key factor is what the writer perceives and what the writer intends to convey.

Fortunately, there are some rules for sequences of tenses, summarized in the box. These rules govern sequences that include dependent clauses that function as adverbs "*Although I was telling the truth,* my words sounded like lies") or dependent clauses that function as nouns ("I know *that she is rich*"). In these sequences, the tense of the verb in the main clause ordinarily controls the tense of the verb in the dependent clauses.

SOME RULES FOR SEQUENCE OF TENSES

The terms *present, past,* and *future* refer to several tenses: simple, progressive, perfect, perfect progressive.

Tense of Main Clause	Relationship of Action in Dependent Clause to Action in Main Clause	Tense in Dependent Clause(s)	Examples
Present	Simultaneous	Present	He *knows* that you *are* late.
Present	Earlier	Past	He *knows* that you *were* late.
Present	Later	Future	He *knows* that you *will be* late.

Continued on p. 305.

	SOME RULES FOR SEQUENCE OF TENSES (continued)		
Tense of Main Clause	**Relationship of Action in Dependent Clause to Action in Main Clause**	**Tense in Dependent Clause(s)**	**Examples**
Past	Simultaneous	Past	He *knew* that you *were* late.
Past	Earlier	Past perfect	He *knew* that you *had been* late.
Past	Later	*would* + infinitive	He *knew* that you *would be* late.
Future	Simultaneous	Present	He *will know* if you *are* late.
Future	Earlier	Past or present perfect	He *will know* if you *were* late. He *will know* if you *have been* late.
Future	Later	Present or future	He *will know* if you *are* late. He *will know* if you *will be* late.

EXERCISE: *Producing correct verb sequences*

Fill in the blanks with the appropriate form of the verb in parentheses.

1. His professor was pleased when she _____ (discover) that Michael _____ (pass) the exam.

2. His professor will be very pleased when she _____ (discover) that Michael _____ (pass) the exam.

3. Caroline will learn that she _____ (fail) her biology course when she _____ (check) the grade list posted on the professor's office door.

4. While Stephanie _____ (have) a conference with the professor yesterday, John _____ (wait) in the hallway.   ●

ACTIVITY: *Identifying and correcting errors in sequences of verbs*

Look through your own writing to search for errors in sequences of verbs. Check every dependent clause that functions as an adverb or as a noun. To find and correct errors in sequences, use the box titled "Rules for Sequence of Tenses." Ask for help if necessary. ●

Verb Forms in Clauses Involving Wishes, Requests/ Demands/Recommendations, or Conditions

Certain verb forms in English require separate discussion because they do not conform to the rules that govern the sequences of the various tenses.

Wishes

The verb *wish* is often used to express that something is impossible or improbable. The writer wants reality to be different, to be something other than it is.

After the verb *wish*, a *that* noun clause is used ("I *wish that* I could go"). The introductory *that* is often omitted, especially in informal usage ("I *wish* I could go").

PRESENT OR FUTURE TIME

When a wish is made for something in present or future time, use either of the following:

1. The simple past or past progressive form of the verb (for the verb *be*, use *were* for all persons)
2. *could (would)* + simple verb form

NOUN CLAUSES AFTER *WISH (THAT)* REFERRING TO PRESENT OR FUTURE TIME

1. A situation does not exist, but you wish that it did:

    I am not an A student, but I wish (that) I *were.*

2. A situation exists, but you wish that it did not or that it were different:

    I wish (that) the professor *weren't speaking* (or *didn't speak*) so rapidly.

3. A situation is in progress or is continuous, but you wish that it would change:

    I wish (that) he *would end* the class on time.

4. A situation cannot exist, but you still wish it could:

    I wish (that) I *could fly* home tomorrow, but I know that's out of the question.

Continued on p. 307.

**NOUN CLAUSES AFTER *WISH* (*THAT*) REFERRING TO
PRESENT OR FUTURE TIME** (continued)

---

5. A situation does not yet exist, but you wish for it:

  I wish (that) he *would give* me an A.

PAST TIME

Wishes referring to past time are not fulfilled. Past perfect forms are used in such wish clauses.

**NOUN CLAUSES AFTER *WISH* (*THAT*) REFERRING
TO PAST TIME**

---

1. A situation did not exist, but you wish that it had:

  I wish (that) I *had taken* Chemistry I.

2. A situation existed, but you wish that it had not or that it had been different:

  I wish (that) I *hadn't taken* Chemistry II.

Request, Demands, and Recommendations

After expressions of urgency that request, demand, or recommend, a *that* clause is usually used, followed by the simple form of the verb. This simple verb form is used regardless of the tense of the main verb or the number of the noun or pronoun that follows the expression ("I demanded that he *go* home." "It is important that she *stay*").

**EXAMPLES OF EXPRESSIONS THAT REQUEST, DEMAND,
OR RECOMMEND**

The following words take a *that* clause. Verbs marked[†] can be followed by a *that* clause or by a noun or pronoun + infinitive ("He advised her to drop the course").

Verbs		Adjectives with **It is**	
advise[†]	order[†]	advisable	imperative
ask[†]	propose	crucial	important
beg[†]	recommend	desirable	mandatory
command[†]	request	essential	necessary
demand	require[†]	good (better,	urgent
desire[†]	suggest	best)	vital
forbid[†]	urge[†]		
insist			

Conditions

Clauses of condition (usually *if* clauses) indicate the circumstances under which the situation expressed in the main clause may exist or occur.

Some clauses of condition state real or factual circumstances in present or future time. The *if* clause presents the possible condition; the verb form in the *if* clause is the simple present tense. The main clause expresses results.

REAL OR FACTUAL CIRCUMSTANCES IN PRESENT OR FUTURE TIME

1. When a condition in the *if* clause is possible, the future tense form or an equivalent form is used in the main clause:

   If I have time, I *will* (or *may*) *finish* my book today.

2. When a condition in the *if* clause is habitual or true in general, the simple present tense or an equivalent is ordinarily used in the main clause:

   If I *have* enough time to study, I usually *do* well on my exams.

3. When a condition in the *if* clause expresses an established, predictable fact, either the simple present or the future tense form is used in the main clause:

   Water *freezes* (*will freeze*) if the temperature *goes* below 32° F (0° C)

4. When a request or suggestion is expressed, a verb form used in making polite requests is used in the main clause:

   If you *go* to the library, *would* you please *return* my book?

Other clauses of condition state unreal, contrary-to-fact, or hypothetical circumstances under which the situation in the main clause might be or might have been realized. When the circumstances occur in the present or future time, the simple past tense is usually used in the *if* clause. (Use *were* for the verb *be*.) An auxiliary + simple form or the past progressive form of a verb can also be used in the *if* clause. The verb in the main clause is *would* (*could*, *might*) + simple form (+ progressive form in progressive situations).

**UNREAL, CONTRARY-TO-FACT, OR HYPOTHETICAL
CIRCUMSTANCES IN PRESENT OR FUTURE TIME**

Simple past tense in *if* clause:

> If I *were* the professor, I *would explain* the material more clearly.

Auxiliary + simple form in *if* clause:

> If I *could switch* classes, I certainly *would do* so.

Past progressive verb form in *if* clause:

> If I *were living* at home, I *would not be* so tired.
> If I were living at home, I *would be studying* more.

PAST TIME: UNREAL CIRCUMSTANCES

Other clauses of condition state circumstances that are unreal, contrary-to-fact, or hypothetical in past time. The past perfect tense is usually used in the *if* clause. An auxiliary + *have* + past participle or the past perfect progressive form of a verb can also be used in the *if* clause. The verb in the main clause is *would* (*could*, *might*) + *have* + past participle (+ progressive form in progressive situations).

**UNREAL, CONTRARY-TO-FACT, OR HYPOTHETICAL
CIRCUMSTANCES IN PAST TIME**

Past perfect tense in *if* clause:

> If I *had known* the answer to the last question, I *would have gotten* an A on the exam.

Auxiliary + *have* + past participle in *if* clause:

> If I *could have had* a choice, I *would have taken* Professor Brown's course.

Past perfect progressive verb form in *if* clause:

> If it *had not been snowing*, I *would have gone* for a walk.
> If it had not been raining, I *would have been skiing*.

Besides the *if* clause, there are other ways to state conditions.

EXAMPLES OF VARIOUS WAYS TO STATE CONDITIONS

If our professor *becomes* ill, our class *might be cancelled.*

Should our professor *become* ill, our class *might be cancelled.*

Continued on p. 310.

> ### EXAMPLES OF VARIOUS WAYS TO STATE CONDITIONS
> (continued)
>
> Were our professor *to become* ill, our class *might be cancelled.*
>
> *In the event that* our professor *should become* ill, our class *might be cancelled.*
>
> *Even if* our professor *is* ill, our class *might not be cancelled.*
>
> Our class *might be cancelled whether or not* our professor *is* ill.
>
> Our class *will be cancelled only if* our professor *is* ill.
>
> *Only if* our professor *is* ill *will* our class *be cancelled.*

EXERCISE: *Completing clauses containing wishes, requests, demands, recommendations, or conditions*

Complete these sentences with an appropriate verb form.

1. I _____ (visit) my brother more often if he didn't live so far away.

2. The striking teachers are demanding that their salaries _____ (be) increased.

3. She didn't tell them about the fire. I wish she _____ (tell) them about it.

4. It is essential that he _____ (study) the material.   ●

ACTIVITY: *Identifying and correcting errors in verb forms in clauses involving wishes, requests, demands, recommendations, and conditions*

Look through your own writing to search for errors in the verb forms just discussed. Check any clauses containing *if*, *wish* (*that*), or expressions of request, demand, or recommendation. If you find an error, correct it, using the guidelines. Ask for help if necessary.   ●

Verbs Followed by Gerunds or Infinitives

A *gerund* (the *-ing* form of a verb) functions as a noun. A gerund phrase can be used as a subject ("*Learning a new language* is challenging"), as an object of a preposition ("I'm interested in *going*"), or as an object of a verb ("I enjoy *learning Russian*").

An *infinitive* (*to* + the simple form of a verb) may function as a noun.[†]

[†] An infinitive may also function as an adjective or adverb, but that is not relevant to this discussion.

As a noun, an infinitive phrase can be used as a subject (*"To err* is human") or as an object of a verb ("I attempted *to register*").

One of the hardest decisions to make about the use of gerunds and infinitives concerns which one to use after a verb that requires an object. Principles govern some of the choices. For example, an infinitive usually follows verbs that relate future, unfulfilled events (*hope, want*). A gerund usually follows verbs that represent real, fulfilled events (*enjoy, finish*). However, since no one principle explains all gerund and infinitive uses, you must learn them through your own listening and reading. You may also refer to the following charts of common verbs as you write and revise your papers.

VERBS FOLLOWED BY A GERUND

Verbs Followed by a Gerund

Example He *dislikes* waiting.

admit	deny	justify	practice	resist
anticipate	detest	keep	quit	risk
appreciate	discuss	mention	recall	stop[†]
avoid	dislike	mind	recollect	suggest
can't help	enjoy	miss	recommend	tolerate
consider	finish	necessitate	resent	understand
delay	imagine	postpone		

Verbs with the Preposition to followed by a Gerund

Example I *object to* your going.

accustom oneself to	limit oneself to	reconcile oneself to
allude to	look forward to	resign oneself to
confess to	object to	resort to
confine oneself to	plead guilty to	revert to
dedicate oneself to		

[†] The verb *stop* can also be followed by an infinitive of purpose ("I *stopped* to ask for directions").

VERBS FOLLOWED BY AN INFINITIVE

Verbs Followed by an Infinitive

Example She cannot *afford* to buy a computer.

afford	ask	consent	expect	intend
agree	beg	decide	fail	learn
appear	care	demand	hesitate	manage
arrange	claim	deserve	hope	mean

Continued on p. 312.

VERBS FOLLOWED BY AN INFINITIVE (continued)

need	pretend	seem	threaten	want
offer	promise	struggle	volunteer	wish
plan	refuse	swear	wait	would like
prepare				

Verbs Followed by Noun or Pronoun + Infinitive

Example   I *urge* you to wait.

ask†	dare	instruct	persuade	tempt
beg†	enable	invite	remind	urge
cause	expect†	need	require	want†
challenge	forbid	obligate	teach	warn
command	force	order	tell	wish
convince	hire			

† These verbs may be used with or without noun or pronoun objects.

VERBS FOLLOWED BY EITHER A GERUND OR AN INFINITIVE

Examples   I *regret* informing him. I *regret* to inform you that you failed the exam.

advise†	continue	like	prefer	remember
attempt	encourage†	love	propose	start
allow†	forget	permit†	regret	try
begin	hate			

† These verbs require a noun or pronoun with an infinitive.

EXERCISE: *Selecting gerunds and infinitives*

Fill in the blank with the appropriate gerund or infinitive.

1. I look forward to _____ (see) you again.

2. The head of the department agreed _____ (let) me take History 911.

3. We can leave as soon as it stops _____ (rain).

4. My professor advised me _____ (take) English 201.   ●

ACTIVITY: *Identifying and correcting errors in the use of verbs followed by gerunds or infinitives*

Look through your own writing to search for errors in the use of the verb forms just discussed. Check to see if you have used any of the verbs that are followed by gerunds or infinitives. If you find an error, correct it. Ask for help if necessary.   ●

ARTICLES

Each time a writer writes a noun in English, a decision must be made concerning the use of articles. The writer can choose the indefinite article, *a* (or its alternate form *an*, used before words beginning with vowel sounds); the definite article, *the*; or no article at all, ∅.

EXAMPLES OF THE USE OF ARTICLES

1. *A* book was lost.   (One specified book was lost.)
2. *The* books were lost.   (All of the books were lost.)
3. *The* book was lost.   (One particular book was lost.)
4. ∅ Books were lost.   (Some of the books were lost.)
5. ∅ Book was lost.   (ungrammatical)

Several factors determine the use of articles, among them these:

1. Whether the noun is countable or noncountable, singular or plural
2. Whether the writer believes the noun referred to is familiar or unfamiliar to the reader
3. Whether the statement that contains the noun is general or specific
4. Whether the noun is modified

Because there are so many factors, it is impossible to memorize all the rules for using articles. Much of what you learn will be derived from your reading and listening in English. But in the following box are a few guidelines that may help you to determine when to use or not to use an article.

NOUNS AND ARTICLES

1. English nouns are *common* (person, car, country) or
                         proper (Maria, Volvo, Japan).
2. Common nouns are *countable* (car, cars; chair, chairs) or
                    noncountable (courage, furniture, work).

Continued on p. 314.

NOUNS AND ARTICLES (continued)

3. Singular countable nouns require an article:
   - *a car* (unspecified, any car, or one car)
   - *the car* (specific, familiar, or previously referred to) even if an adjective precedes the noun:
   - *a shiny new car*
     unless there is a determiner[†] other than the article:
   - *another car*
4. Plural countable nouns do not require an article:
   - *Cars are dangerous.*
     unless they refer to something specific or familiar:
   - *The cars he owns are nice.*
     but they are never used with *a* or *an.*
5. Noncountable nouns require no article:
   - *Life is hard.*
     but some can take *the* if a modifier follows the noun:
   - *The life we lead is hard.*
     or *a* or *an* if they are used as countable nouns:
   - *We want a life of ease.*

[†] *Determiners* are articles, possessives (my, Maria's), demonstratives (this, those), and words of indefinite quantity (some, more).

One area of difficulty is the use of articles with names of places. Some names need to be memorized because they are exceptions to the rules (The Hague, the Sudan). But you can refer to the following lists to learn when to use *the* and when to omit it.

USE OF ARTICLES WITH NAMES OF PLACES

1. Geographic subdivisions on land typically *don't* take *the:* continents (Europe), countries (Nicaragua), cities (Boston), individual islands (Long Island), individual mountains (Mount Fuji)

   EXCEPTIONS:

a. Deserts and forests	(*the* Sahara Desert)
b. Regions	(*the* Middle East)
c. Points on the globe	(*the* South Pole)
d. Mountain ranges	(*the* Rocky Mountains)
e. Groups of islands	(*the* West Indies)

2. Public structures typically take *the* (*the* Guggenheim Museum, *the* Washington Monument, *the* Golden Gate Bridge, *the* Ritz Carlton Hotel, *the* Globe Theater).

Continued on p. 315.

USE OF ARTICLES WITH NAMES OF PLACES (continued)

EXCEPTIONS:
a. Universities   (Stanford University)
b. Streets   (Pennsylvania Avenue)
c. Parks   (Central Park)

3. Bodies of water typically take *the:* rivers (*the* Mississippi River, oceans (*the* Atlantic Ocean), gulfs (*the* Gulf of Mexico), seas (*the* Red Sea), canals (*the* Suez Canal), groups of lakes (*the* Great Lakes)

EXCEPTIONS:
a. (Individual) lakes   (Lake Ontario)
b. Bays   (San Francisco Bay)
c. Harbors   (Sydney Harbor)
d. Sounds   (Puget Sound)
e. Creeks   (Rock Creek)

4. Names composed of common and proper nouns with *of* phrases take *the* (*the* University of Wisconsin, *the* United States of America).
5. Multiple-word names of countries ending in common nouns take *the* (*the* United Arab Emirates, *the* German Federal Republic, *the* United Kingdom).
6. Plural names of countries take *the* (*the* Netherlands).

Certain grammatical constructions require the use of *the*.

THE IN SPECIAL GRAMMATICAL CONSTRUCTIONS

1. With adjectives used as nouns:

   She teaches *the* underprivileged.

2. With gerunds or abstract nouns followed by *of* phrases:

   The taking of prisoners is inevitable.
   The courage of soldiers is admirable.

The following is a list of other uses of *the*.

OTHER USES OF *THE*

1. Points of time   (*the* beginning)
2. Physical positions   (*the* top)
3. Names of historical periods   (*the* Ming Dynasty)

Continued on p. 316.

OTHER USES OF *THE* (continued)

4. Names of historical events	(*the* Civil War)
5. Names of legislative acts	(*the* Bill of Rights)
6. Names of law enforcement bodies	(*the* police)
7. Names of institutions, foundations, and organizations	(*the* United Nations)
8. Names of branches of the government	(*the* executive branch)
9. Names of political parties	(*the* Labor Party)
10. Plural of family names	(*the* Joneses)
11. Names of newspapers	(*the New York Times*)

The following is a brief list of special uses of *a*.

SPECIAL USES OF *A*

1. To classify a noun:

   Alice is *a* teacher.
   Joe is *a* bright student.

2. After *such* or *what* used with a singular countable noun:

   He is *such a* nice man.
   What a nice man he is.

3. After certain adverbs or adjectives—*not a, many a, quite a, rather a:*

   There was *not a* dry eye in the room.

EXERCISE: *Determining use of articles*

Working with a group of classmates, fill in an appropriate article in the blanks in the following passage. Choose either *a, an, the,* or Ø (no article). Remember to consider the writer and reader's familiarity with each noun, as well as the degree of specificity of each noun. Be prepared to explain your choices. After you have completed the exercise, compare your choices with the original text. You may discover that more than one choice is possible.

What I wish for all ＿＿＿＿＿ students is some release

from ＿＿＿＿＿ clammy grip of ＿＿＿＿＿ future. I wish

them ＿＿＿＿＿ chance to savor each segment of their education

as ＿＿＿＿＿ experience in itself and not as ＿＿＿＿＿ grim

preparation for _____ next step. I wish them _____
right to experiment, to trip and fall, to learn that defeat is as instructive
as victory and is not _____ end of _____ world.

WILLIAM ZINSSER, "College Pressures" (paragraph 5)

●

EXERCISE: *Correcting errors in the use of articles*

Correct all errors in the use of articles in the following sentences, taken
from student essays.

1. The report said that large percentage of American high school students do not know where Moscow is or who Deng Xiaoping is.
2. On May 19, 1986, I received diploma from the Museum School of
   Fine Arts after four years of the rigorous studio work.
3. Many times students do not learn the material at all but just try to
   memorize it for a good grade. Therefore, grading system should be
   eliminated.
4. Listening to older friends makes me think more and look at things
   from different angle.   ●

ACTIVITY: *Identifying errors in the use of articles*

Look through your own writing to search for errors in the use of articles.
Check each noun. If you find an error, correct it. Ask for help if
necessary.   ●

PARALLEL CONSTRUCTION

Parallel construction, the balancing of grammatical structures in a pair
or a series, allows readers to see the relationship between ideas. Parallel
structures can also serve to dramatize or emphasize a point.

Parallel construction is achieved by joining words, phrases, or clauses
that are similar grammatically and logically connected in meaning. This
can be accomplished in a number of ways:

- Use of the coordinate conjunctions *and, or,* or *but*

  She wants to take chemistry, physics, *or* biology.

- Use of words like *not* or *than* that give the meaning of "and not"

  His employer was impressed by his ability, *not* his charm.
  She was more embarrassed *than* angry at what he had said.

- Use of paired coordination conjunctions: *both . . . and, either . . . or, neither . . . nor, not only . . . but also*

  She is *either* at the library *or* in the cafeteria.

- Careful placement of commas between similar items

  They came, they saw, they conquered.

EXAMPLES OF PARALLEL STRUCTURES

Balancing of nouns:

Darkness and *stillness* washed over me.

Balancing of adjectives:

Mr. Martin was a *fat, easy-going, good-natured* man.

Balancing of verbs:

We view friendship more tentatively, subject to changes in intensity as people *move, change* their jobs, *marry,* or *discover* new interests.

Balancing of words ending in *-ing:*

I had stayed up night after night, *washing* and *ironing, patching* and *darning* my things.

Balancing of prepositions:

We move *from* town *to* city *to* suburb, *from* high school *to* college in a different state, *from* a job in one region *to* a better job elsewhere, *from* the home where we raise our children *to* the home where we plan to live in retirement.

Faulty parallelism occurs when grammatical structures are not balanced. For example, a student writer wrote:

Annie saw her classmates picking up their pencils and started writing as fast as they could.

In this sentence, the structure appears to be balanced, but in fact it is not. There are two past tense verbs (*saw* and *started*), but the rest of the sentence is off balance. It doesn't make sense for the writer to say "*Annie* saw . . . and started writing as fast as *they* could"; the noun (*Annie*) and the pronoun (*they*) do not agree. Depending on the writer's intention, the sentence could be rewritten in at least two ways. If the classmates are the ones writing fast,

Annie saw her classmates picking up their pencils and starting to write as fast as they could.

In this sentence, the balanced structures are the *-ing* words *picking up* and *starting*. If Annie is the one writing fast,

> Annie saw her classmates picking up their pencils and started writing as fast as she could.

In this sentence, the balanced structures are the simple past tense verbs, *saw* and *started*; the pronoun *she* agrees with the noun *Annie*.

EXERCISE: *Balancing grammatical structures*

Make the items in parentheses grammatically parallel to the items that precede *and*, *but*, or *not*.

1. Wanting to achieve something and _____ (if you actually achieve it) may not be the same thing.

2. Slowly but _____ (in a forceful manner), she argued her point.

3. She always says what she wants to say, not _____ (the thing she should say).

4. We were surprised not only about his idea but _____ (that he decided to express it).   ●

ACTIVITY: *Balancing grammatical structures*

Look through your own writing to search for grammatical structures in a pair or series of items. If you find any that lack parallel construction, create a balance.   ●

PUNCTUATION

Punctuation is a tool writers use to help their readers understand how to read their sentences. Though there are many principles which govern punctuation, how a sentence is punctuated is often dependent on a writer's style or intended meaning. For example, read this sentence and then explain what it means:

> A woman without her man is lost.

Now discuss how the meaning of the sentence is changed when the punctuation is changed:

> A woman: without her, man is lost.

Punctuation can be changed further to reflect the writer's style or emphasis. Discuss the effect of the following changes:

1. A woman without her man is lost.

   A woman, without her man, is lost.

   A woman without her man is lost!

   A woman without her man is lost?

2. A woman: without her, man is lost.

   A woman: Without her, man is lost!

   A woman—without her, man is lost.

   A woman. Without her, man is lost.

Many of the following guidelines for punctuation exist to help readers avoid misreading of sentences. Your guiding principle in determining which mark of punctuation to choose should be to find a way to transmit your ideas as clearly as possible to your readers.

Period (.)

Periods are used in these situations:

1. At the end of statements and commands or requests:

   I pressed my face against the earth.

2. After indirect questions:

   I don't know what time it is.

3. After deliberate sentence fragments:

   A fiasco.

4. After abbreviations:

   Dr. Jones is on vacation.

Question Mark (?)

Question marks are used in these situations:

1. After direct questions:

   What do our time judgments say about our attitude toward life?

2. At the end of doubtful statements:

> A woman without her man is lost?

Exclamation Point (!)

Exclamation points are used after emphatic or emotional statements, phrases, words, or expressions:

> What a beautiful day it was!

> Good news!

Comma (,)

A comma is used to indicate a natural division or slight pause in a sentence. Commas are usually used in the following situations:

1. To separate three or more items (words, phrases, or clauses) in a series:

   > We owe our students rather more than lectures on Keynesian theory, computer language, and topic sentences.

2. Between two independent clauses connected by coordinating conjunctions (*and, but, or, nor, so, yet,* or *for*):

   > The country needs them, and they will find satisfying jobs.

3. Following introductory elements:
   a. Dependent clause:

   > When you were dull, we pretended you were smart.

   b. Phrase:

   > Back home in California, I never need to look at a clock to know when the class hour is ending.

   c. Transitional or adverbial word or expression:

   > Inevitably, the two are deeply intertwined.

4. To set off interrupting elements:

   > My wish, of course, is naive.

   > It was, as I said, not to be liked.

5. To set off appositive phrases:

   > The transcript has become a sacred document, the passport to security.

(See also "Punctuation of Restrictive and Nonrestrictive Adjective Clauses," pp. 278–280.)

Semicolon (;)

A semicolon indicates a major division in a sentence, marking a stronger pause than is indicated by a comma. Semicolons are usually placed as follows:

1. Between two independent clauses when they are not joined by co-ordinating conjunctions:

   The parents mean well; they are trying to steer their sons

   and daughters toward a secure future.

2. Between two independent clauses joined by a conjunctive adverb such as *furthermore, nevertheless, moreover,* or *consequently:*

   I know how to hold the racket and basically how to hit the

   ball; however, I still can't say that I actually play tennis.

3. Between independent clauses if there are commas within the clauses, even if they are joined by a coordinating conjunction:

   Vocabulary, syntax, idioms, slang, dialects, and so on, all

   cause difficulty; but the person struggling with a different

   language is at least aware when he's in this kind of trouble.

4. Between items in a series if the items contain internal commas:

   We will discuss the essays of several writers this term: Ye-

   zierska, Sarton, and Tesich; Viorst, Barna, and Levine; and

   Neusner, Zinsser, and Ho.

Colon (:)

A colon marks a major break in a sentence and directs attention to what follows it. Colons can be used in three situations:

1. To separate two main clauses when the second clause explains or expands on the first:

   College should be open-ended: at the end it should open

   many, many roads.

2. To set off a listing or series of items:

> In another newspaper I wrapped up my food for the journey:
> a loaf of bread, a herring, and a pickle.

3. To introduce a full-sentence quotation:

> I see the tension in their eyes when exams are approaching
> and papers are due: "Will I get everything done?"

Apostrophe (')

An apostrophe indicates either possession or the omission of one or more letters in a word.

1. To indicate possession

   a. Add *'s* to form the possessive of these words

     • Singular nouns and pronouns

      the girl's hair

      the class's opinion

      nobody's business

     • Plural nouns that do not end in *-s*

      the children's books

   b. Add *'* to form the possessive of plural nouns ending in *-s* or *-es*:

      the girls' hair

   c. Add *'s* to last word in a compound noun or pronoun:

      his brother-in-law's house

      someone else's notebook

   d. Add *'s* only to the last item to indicate joint possession:

      Levine and Wolff's article

   e. Add *'s* to each item to indicate individual possession (separate items):

      Neusner's and Zinsser's articles

2. To indicate omission of a letter:

      it's (contraction of *it is*)

Quotation Marks (" ")

Quotation marks are used to indicate the beginning and end of a quotation.

1. Use double quotation marks at the beginning and end of a direct quotation.

   According to Mead and Metraux, "Between friends there is inevitably a kind of equality of give and take."

2. Use single quotation marks to enclose a quotation within a quotation.

   Robert Levine tells of his experience in Brazil when he rushed to be on time to teach a class, only to hear "gentle calls of 'Hola, professor' and 'Tudo bem, professor?' from unhurried students."

3. Use quotation marks to enclose titles of articles, poems, songs, stories, chapters, and names of TV shows.

   As Judith Viorst depicts in her article, "Friends, Good Friends—and Such Good Friends," friends can be grouped into different categories.

4. Place all periods (.) and commas (,) that come at the end of a quotation *before* the end quotation marks.

   "Once you have twenty or thirty percent of the student population deliberately overexerting," one dean points out, "it's bad for everybody."

5. Place all semicolons (;) and colons (:) and dashes (—) that come at the end of the quotation *after* the end quotation marks.

   William Zinsser writes that students should "break the circles in which they are trapped"; that is hard to do.

6. Place question marks (?) and exclamation points (!) *before* the end quotation marks if the quotation itself is a question or an exclamation.

   Kie Ho asks, "If American education is so tragically inferior, why is it that this is still the country of innovation?"

7. Place question marks and exclamation points *after* the end quotation marks if your own sentence is a question or exclamation.

Can we believe Zinsser when he says that "there will be plenty of time to change jobs, change careers, change whole attitudes and approaches"?

8. Use a comma to separate an opening quotation from the part of the sentence that follows:

   "The pressure on students is severe," admits Zinsser.

   Do not use a comma if the quotation ends with a question mark or exclamation point or dash:

   "Why can't the professor just cut back and not accept longer papers?" asks Zinsser.

9. When a quotation is interrupted by explanatory words, set off the explanatory words with commas, and add an extra set of quotation marks.

   "For four years," says Jacob Neusner, "we created an altogether forgiving world."

10. Use a comma to introduce a quotation.

    Neusner says, "Failure leaves no record."

    Do not use a comma if the quoted statement follows the subordinating conjunction *that*.

    Neusner argues that "failure leaves no record."

11. Set off a lengthy quotation (more than about 40 words) with a colon, without adding quotation marks, by indenting five spaces from the left margin.

    The language of Paul McBrearty's argument is extremely biased. This is especially true when he says:

    > When we assure students that we will not under any circumstances reveal their identities, we in effect tell the weak, the confused, the vindictive, the morally obtuse, and the less courageous among them that they may say what they please without having to stand behind their words.

    Words like *vindictive* and *morally obtuse* are hurtful terms, and they weaken his argument.

Parentheses ( )

Parentheses may be used for these purposes:

1. To enclose comments or explanations that interrupt the main thought:

    There appears to be a very strong relationship (see chart) be-
    tween the accuracy of clock time, walking speed and postal effi-
    ciency across the countries we studied.

2. To expand on an idea:

    But according to Hall, in many Mediterranean Arab cultures
    there are only three sets of time: no time at all, now (which is
    of varying duration) and forever (too long).

3. To indicate documentation of sources:

    They prefer the term *enrollment goals* instead of *quotas*
    (Salholz, Doherty, & Tran, 1987).

Brackets [ ]

Brackets are used to indicate that you have added words to quoted material:

    Barna explains that "In a foreign land they [stereotypes] increase our
    feeling of security."

Ellipses (. . .)

Ellipses or ellipsis points are a series of three spaced dots used to indicate that words have been omitted from a quotation. If the words omitted include a period at the end of a sentence, four dots are used.

    As a Vietnamese student says in the Barna article, "Foreigners . . .
    think that Americans are superficial."

Hyphen (-)

A hyphen is used for these purposes:

1. To divide words between two lines when handwriting or typing (divisions are made only between syllables of words of more than one syllable):

The hyphen's major uses are to divide words between lines and to join compound words.

2. To join compound words:

thirty-three

a well-known candidate

Dash (—)

A dash marks an emphatic or abrupt break. It can replace a colon, semicolon, comma, or parenthesis in some of their uses, for example:

1. To expand on an idea or add details:

   The intellectual faculties developed by studying subjects like history and classics—an ability to synthesize and relate, to weigh cause and effect, to see events in perspective—are just the faculties that make creative leaders in business or almost any general field.

2. To indicate an interruption in the expression of an idea:

   She is a free spirit in a campus of tense students—no small achievement in itself—and she deserves to follow her muse.

3. To set off a final item, for emphasis:

   But the sons and daughters want to major in history or classics or philosophy—subjects with no "practical" value.

Note: A dash typed on a regular typing keyboard consists of two consecutive hyphens.

Underlining

Underline titles of newspapers, magazines, books, and films. (One way to remember whether to underline or to use quotation marks is this rule of thumb: Underline long works; use quotation marks with short works.)

The essay "Focusing on Friends" was originally published in the New York Times.

"College Pressures" first appeared in Blair and Ketchum's Country Journal.

"Solitary Confinement" is a chapter in Nien Cheng's book <u>Life and Death in Shanghai</u>.

"Don't Worry, Be Happy" is a song on the album titled <u>Simple Pleasures</u>.

Note: Underlining corresponds to italics in most publications.

PROGRESSIVE REST SYMBOLS

Many punctuation marks are actually pause or stop symbols, telling the reader when to rest. These rest symbols represent progressively longer pauses:

,	--	;	:	.
comma	dash	semicolon	colon	period

EXERCISE: *Punctuating sentences*

Working in a small group of two or three students, punctuate the following sentences. First, punctuate each sentence twice so that two different meanings emerge. Then use various forms of punctuation on each sentence to reflect a different writing style or emphasis. Refer to a dictionary to look up vocabulary words, if necessary.

1. A woman without her man is lost
2. See the elephant eat Maria
3. Give the bird to my cousin Sylvia
4. She said hold it softly
5. I can can can but I cant cant can you
6. That that is is that that is not is not ●

ACTIVITY: *Identifying and correcting punctuation errors*

Look through your own writing to search for punctuation errors. Begin by focusing on the punctuation marks that give you the most trouble, for example, semicolons or commas. Using the guidelines for punctuation, check to see if you have punctuated your sentences correctly. Correct any errors, asking for help if necessary. ●

MANUSCRIPT FORM FOR FINAL COPY

After you have revised and edited your paper, you are ready to write or type the final copy for presentation to the instructor. The way your paper looks can have a positive or negative psychological effect on the reader. It is therefore important to make your paper as neat as possible, and to follow certain guidelines for writing or typing the paper.

Whether a paper is handwritten or typewritten, it will usually mention these features:

- Your name
- The course name and number
- Your instructor's name
- The due date
- The title

The pages will be numbered and stapled together.

The boxes on pages 329–330 provide guidelines for handwritten, type-written, and computer-generated papers.

GUIDELINES

Guidelines for a Handwritten Paper

1. Use a pen.
2. Write on white, lined paper measuring 8½ by 11 inches.
3. Write neatly and legibly.
4. Write on every other line.
5. Leave margins on both sides.
6. Write on only one side of the paper.
7. Indent each paragraph.

GUIDELINES

Guidelines for a Typewritten Paper

1. Use 8½ by 11-inch unruled paper of good quality. (Avoid onionskin paper and erasable bond.)
2. Use a good ribbon.
3. Double-space.
4. Leave at least 1-inch margins all around.
5. Indent each new paragraph five spaces.
6. After you have typed, check for typographical errors.
7. If you find any errors after your paper is finished, use white correction fluid to cover the errors and then handwrite or type in the correction.

Guidelines for a Computer-generated Paper

1. Use white paper.
2. Use a ribbon that produces clear copy.
3. Set the printer to double-space.
4. Set the top and side margins at 1 inch; set the bottom margin at 1¼ inches.
5. Set unjustified margins.
6. Set the page length setting at 66 lines.
7. Set the default tab stop at five spaces in from the left margin, to indent your paragraphs.
8. Instruct the printer to number the pages.
9. Select the print mode that produces the best copy.
10. Use a style or spell checker program, if you have one.
11. Proofread carefully to check for errors that may have occurred as a result of deleting or moving text.

INDEX

Instructor's Manual
to accompany

GUIDELINES
A Cross-Cultural
Reading/Writing Text

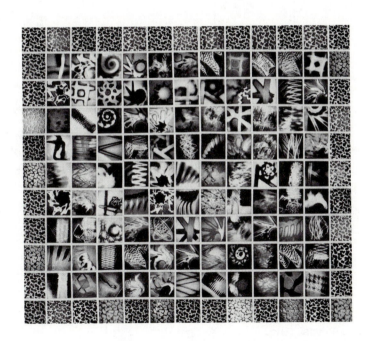

RUTH SPACK

Prepared by Ruth Spack

For information, write:
St. Martin's Press, Inc.
175 Fifth Avenue
New York, NY 10010

ISBN: 0-312-25903-4

CONTENTS

I. OVERVIEW

Through naturally sequenced, culturally relevant reading selections and writing assignments, **GUIDELINES: A CROSS-CULTURAL READING/WRITING TEXT** builds on language resources students already have while providing the structured support students need as they undertake new and increasingly complex tasks. The guidelines within the text show students how to integrate new procedures and information with previous knowledge and experience. Students can gradually internalize these guidelines and use the strategies effectively in other contexts.

GUIDELINES contains four essay assignments that are presented in a logical progression so that students can build on what they learn from one assignment to the next. All assignments are supported by reading and writing tasks that allow students to write from their own perspective as they examine the perspectives of others. Students begin with writing from experience and move to writing from course readings, using their experience and background knowledge to evaluate and analyze what they read. Then they write from outside sources, using the academic skills practiced in previous assignments and synthesizing new material, in order to examine a controversial issue.

The INTRODUCTION introduces students to reading and writing strategies that will be used for many tasks throughout the semester.

PARTS ONE through FOUR contain the four essay assignments, with several related reading selections and with demonstrations of student writers at work as they fulfill each of the assignments. PART ONE describes in detail various processes including finding and developing a topic, focusing, organizing, drafting, peer reviewing, revising, and completing an essay. These processes reappear in PARTS TWO through FOUR, with variations appropriate to the particular assignments. Special attention is paid to determining effective organizational patterns for the different types of essays.

PART FIVE provides guidelines for utilizing several skills required to fulfill the essay assignments: summarizing, paraphrasing, quoting, paragraphing, and citing and documenting sources.

PART SIX provides guidelines for proofreading and editing as well as a handbook for correcting errors.

Reading Strategies

PARTS ONE through FOUR include suggested reading strategies for the different types of selections: personal

essays, research studies, argumentative essays, and news
articles. You can discuss these strategies in class.

Before Reading. Preceding most of the reading selections is
a Write before You Read activity that directs students to
write about something connected to the selection they are
about to read. I ask students to do this at the end of a
class period on the meeting before the reading assignment is
due. They are given ten to fifteen minutes to write and
time to discuss what they have written, either in small
groups or with the whole class. This activity stimulates
their interest in and often facilitates their understanding
of the reading. Of course, it is not always possible to
find class time for each Write before You Read entry. Some
entries can be written outside class or skipped.
    Biographical information can facilitate comprehension by
helping students to understand who the author is and why the
piece was written.

Reading, Rereading, and Making a Journal Entry. Students
are given specific suggestions for reading and for writing
about the reading in their journals.

Summarizing. The instructions for summarizing the readings
follow the suggestions for making a journal entry. Writing
summaries is not easy. Journal writing loosens students up.
They understand what they have read better after they have
written about it informally.
    Initially, the summaries will be used just for class
discussions. Eventually, summaries will be incorporated
into student essays (Essay Assignments 2, 3, and 4).

Discussing and Taking Notes. The discussion activities take
place primarily in small groups to provide a cooperative
classroom atmosphere. The intimate nature of small groups
allows for more opportunity for individual students to
speak, a more equal relationship among students, a higher
level of student motivation, and the development of greater
respect and tolerance of students toward one another.
Nevertheless, I sometimes turn small group activities into
whole class activities if I feel they will be more
productive in a particular class.
    Some students feel comfortable taking notes in class;
others do not find it necessary.

Activities for Class Discussion

    I divide the class into discussion groups of 3 or 4
students, initially assigning the groups, later in the
semester allowing students to form their own groups. (Some
groups may stay together the whole semester; more commonly

they make frequent switches.) Their journals and summaries
act as the springboard for class discussions.

Since their summaries are likely to differ, students are
invited to discuss the reasons for the different
interpretations and to negotiate the meaning of the text.

Each group is responsible for the vocabulary in the
reading. A list of potentially difficult words is included,
and students are asked to guess their meaning from the
context. Some groups spend a lot of time on this task;
others go through it quickly. Each group controls the pace
of the discussion.

The rest of the discussion activities -- some oral, some
written -- involve the students in the text, asking them to
select memorable passages, compare experiences, evaluate,
analyze, interpret, argue with, paraphrase, examine the
organization of, and expand on the reading. All of these
activities are designed to lead students toward developing
ideas for their own essays.

Guidelines for Fulfilling the Essay Assignments

The guidelines are just that -- guidelines. They are
not rigid instructions that students must follow. Students
are encouraged to use strategies such as invention, journal
writing, note taking, interviewing, researching, drafting,
organizing, peer reviewing, and revising to develop their
essays. But the guidelines are presented with the
understanding that different assignments require different
strategies and processes. Some strategies may carry over
from one assignment to the next, but new strategies are
always needed for new contexts. If students have
internalized procedures, instructional support for
previously-practiced strategies may no longer be needed.
Class time can be spent instead on providing the framework
for newly-needed skills and approaches. For example, class
time can be spent on teaching the invention strategies of
list making, freewriting, looping, and cubing while students
are developing Essay Assignment 1. But when students are
finding and developing a topic for Essay Assignment 2, class
time can shift to an emphasis on taking notes on,
paraphrasing, and quoting from the readings.

Understanding the Assignment. Sometimes students do not
write well simply because they do not understand an
assignment. Analyzing the directions can help them to
understand what is expected.

Note: Discussions of the specific guidelines for fulfilling
each of the four essay assignments can be found in **CHAPTER
COMMENTS AND SUGGESTIONS.**

II. SUGGESTED COURSE PLAN

The following plan shows how the material in **GUIDELINES** can be covered in a 14- to 15-week semester.

Weeks 1,2   INTRODUCTION: Reading, Writing, and Keeping a Journal. Begin work on Summarizing (PART FIVE) and on PART ONE.

Weeks 2,3,4   PART ONE/ Writing from Experience: Expressing a Personal Viewpoint. While students are reading assigned selections, begin following the guidelines for fulfilling Essay Assignment 1. Work concurrently with PART FIVE (summarizing). After peer reviewing and while students are revising and editing Essay 1, begin work on PART TWO.

Weeks 4,5,6   PART TWO/ Writing from Course Readings: Relating Reading to Experience. While students are reading and discussing assigned selections, work concurrently with PART FIVE (paraphrasing, quoting, paragraphing, citing course material). After students discuss the readings, begin work on finding and developing a topic for Essay 2.

Weeks 6,7   While students are drafting and reviewing Essay Assignment 2, work on PART FOUR/ Writing from Outside Sources: Researching a Controversy. Guide students toward finding a research topic and writing an informal research proposal. While students are revising and editing Essay 2, begin discussions of readings in PART THREE.

Weeks 7,8,9   PART THREE/ Writing from Course Readings: Analyzing an Argumentative Essay. As students complete discussions of the readings, begin work on finding and developing a topic for Essay 3.

Weeks 10-15   After students have drafted and reviewed Essay 3 and while they are revising Essay 3, continue classroom work on PART FOUR. Work concurrently with PART FIVE (Citing and Documenting Sources).

Note: See **Appendix** for a more detailed course plan.

III. CHAPTER COMMENTS AND SUGGESTIONS

INTRODUCTION: READING, WRITING, AND KEEPING A JOURNAL

The **INTRODUCTION** provides several reading and writing strategies that are useful for many tasks.

What Is a Reading/Writing Journal?

The reading/writing journal project entails keeping an an informal record of responses to the course reading and writing assignments. Students may have difficulty understanding exactly what "journal" means if they have never kept a journal before or if they have written a more personal version than what is asked for in this course. This section provides an explanation of the reading/writing journal by answering several questions students may have.

Some of the answers are purposely vague to allow you to determine how you want to incorporate journal writing into your own course. Over the years, I have experimented with several approaches, all successful: (1) students write entries both in and out of class; (2) students write entries only out of class; (3) students hand in one journal for each class meeting (2-3x a week); (4) students hand in journals (at least one entry) only 1x a week; (5) students write entries throughout the semester; (6) students write entries for 3/4 of the semester (until there are no more assigned course readings), with occasional research progress reports during the last 1/4 of the semester.

Whatever approach I have used, my pattern has been to collect journal entries at the beginning of class and to hand back at that time each student's previous entry, on which I have briefly commented. In each case, I respond positively to the content of the entry, answering questions, expanding on a point, providing suggestions, or asking clarifying questions or questions intended to challenge the student further. My responses range in length from two words to a paragraph, depending on my time allotment and on my reaction to what I have read. I neither correct nor grade the entries, though I do keep a record of them; and I expect students to hand in the assigned number of entries.

You may choose to respond to only a few of each student's entries or even to none; and you may want some sort of grading system, such as check/check plus. You may even want to make selected corrections. My practice has been to respond to each entry not only because students appreciate the feedback but because positive responses can encourage students to engage in a close, thoughtful, and honest reading of a text and in a valuable exploration of their own writing. I believe that individual grades (such as A, B, C...) are counterproductive, implying

inappropriately that there are right and wrong responses.
And I believe that correction of errors on journal entries
sends the wrong message: that error should be the central
focus of writing. Instead, students can learn early in the
course that exploratory writing is valued, that taking risks
to develop ideas is a worthy process. By responding to what
the students say rather than to the particulars of how they
say it, I can convey interest in the students' viewpoints.
Since that interest carries over to the more formal essay
assignments, students are motivated to compose essays not
just to elicit a good grade but to communicate ideas.

Reading and Writing about What You Read

Depending on the group of students and the level of
chaos vis-a-vis course registration, I try to spend at least
part of the first class getting started on the journal
project. A "training session" during the first week of
classes helps students to understand what is expected. I
take students through a process of reading and responding to
a short reading selection and have them observe the process
one student went through to produce a journal entry on that
reading.
     Since textbooks are rarely brought to class on the first
day, I bring in mimeographed copies of the reading ("Zen and
the Art of Burglary") and of Chrystalla's annotations.
During the first class, students may be able to do a first
reading of "Zen," annotate the piece by writing double-entry
notes, examine Chrystalla's annotations, and write a journal
entry on the reading.
     First previewing a selection and then reading without
using a dictionary encourages fluent reading. Annotating a
selection encourages a careful, engaged reading of a text.
Writing double-entry notes to separate the author's ideas
from their own reactions leads students to understand as
well as to take a critical stance toward what they read.
Shortening summaries gives them practice in expressing an
author's ideas succinctly.
     By the end of the first week of classes, students may be
able to complete the work outlined in the INTRODUCTION.
After reading and discussing Chrystalla's and their own
annotations and journal entry, students can apply these
reading/writing strategies to the essay, "What True
Education Should Do." [I sometimes skip this activity and
go right to PART ONE, if time is of the essence. This essay
by Harris will be used again in PART THREE when students
practice analyzing an argumentative essay.] The essay can
be read aloud or silently, and students should have adequate
time to annotate and write a journal entry on the essay.
(The time will vary from class to class; you should probably
plan for at least 30 minutes.) During this time, you can

move around the room, stopping to answer questions and make suggestions (some students may persist in writing over-long summaries and need help). If any students seem to have writer's block when it comes to the journal entry, you can briefly discuss with them their reactions to the reading and encourage them to record those reactions without focusing on the mechanics of writing. Assure students that there is no "right" response.

If there is time, divide the students into small groups (simply group 2 or 3 students who are sitting next to one another) to discuss what they have written. This will serve as a model for the small group discussions that will take place as students work through PARTS ONE through FOUR. Move from group to group to provide assistance when needed.

You may be able to begin work on PART ONE or on Summarizing (PART FIVE) during the first week of classes. A first lesson in summarizing can be to combine marginal paragraph summaries (from double-entry notes) into one or two sentences.

Sample Student Writing: Reading/Writing Journals

The sample journal entries show that no two journal entries are alike. Some students may write one paragraph, others several pages. These journals cover issues connected to student writing or to ideas discussed in class. Sample journals about the readings are included in PARTS TWO and THREE.

Keeping a Teacher Journal

You might want to consider keeping your own journal in response to the course work and mimeographing your entries to share with the class. By including excerpts from student journals, you can extend and enrich the student-teacher interaction and lead to a more dynamic group awareness and exchange of ideas. Through your journal, students can view the writing instructor not only as critic but also as participant in the writing process. Of course, the length and number of journal entries you write is dependent on the amount of time and energy you can devote to the project. For further reading on student and teacher journals, see Spack, Ruth, and Catherine Sadow. "Student-Teacher Working Journals in ESL Composition." TESOL Quarterly 17 (1983): 575-593.

CHAPTER ONE: Responding to Reading

The selections in PART ONE are expressive essays on subjects close to students' experiences. Students may use these (or other personal essays you assign) as stimuli or models for their own personal essays. Essay Assignment 1 asks them to write an essay in which they express a belief or share an insight drawn from their own experience.

Rolando Niella, "Barriers" (student essay)

Rolando compares the experience of learning to master a second language with the experience of learning how to play tennis. He reveals the frustration and discouragement that occur when he cannot sustain a conversation or keep a ball in play. Yet he concludes that practice will result in mastery and that the effort is worthwhile.

This essay receives mostly positive responses from students, who find that the often humorous tennis comparison allows readers to truly understand the communication barrier. One student wrote in his journal, "I have to admit that when I realized that the author was really just a student like me I was dissapointed. I thought that it would be a boiring and meaningless text that would make me more sleepy than I allready am. But fortunately I was wrong. It may not be a masterpiece but it is very direct and touches a problem that I also have." Another student: "The strongest reason why I liked it was because it made people ask themselves the question 'What if I was him?!'"

Rolando's essay does sometimes come under criticism for going off the subject or dragging out the analogy.

Anzia Yezierska, "College"

In this excerpt from an autobiographical novel, Yezierska reveals the disappointment of a poverty-stricken immigrant who finds that college life is not what she had hoped for. Impressed by the beauty of the campus and of the students, she wants to become an integral part of this scene but instead is overworked, rejected, and humiliated by her isolation. She ultimately finds strength in the realization that her suffering pales in comparison to the pain that others have experienced.

Although this selection is lengthy compared to the other personal essays in **GUIDELINES**, it is quite easy to read. Students can examine the organizational pattern of the entire piece: expectation-disappointment-discovery. This can be an effective pattern for students to follow in writing about similar experiences.

This selection usually receives wildly different responses. Some journals contain statements such as "I love this essay"; others contain negative comments such as "I found 'College' to be one of the worst story I've ever read." Some students find her too self-pitying: "I understand that she was poor and wanted her life to change but nothing can change over night, and she's got to learned to live with that." Yet others admire the vivid description and are touched by the tender conclusion: "the sense of loss of the author was digging into the reader's heart."

May Sarton, "The Rewards of Living a Solitary Life"

Sarton believes that being alone allows us to be truly ourselves and to perceive things with originality. Although she temporarily feels lonely after being with other people, she finds that her solitary life brings with it the reward of time to explore her thoughts and experiences.

One student was so moved by this essay that she made copies for all of her friends. The more typical response is for students to find Sarton's philosophy interesting but inadequate: "From my point of view, being alone is sometimes rewarding, but searching for knowledge throught others is more rewarding than everything else." Other students find Sarton too defensive: "It make me sad because I feel the writer wrote it from an apologic approach. I think she feels she has to explane the fact that she leeves alon to the majority of people do have spouses. Its' not that I don't believe what she is saying, I do, and she probably believes it but it is sad that she has to justified it to society and to her self." The most humorous response I have received: "p.s. Does 'salt brings out the authentic flavor of food'? or does it cover it?"

Steve Tesich, "Focusing on Friends"

In his essay comparing his male and female friendships, Tesich reveals that he finds it easy to tell women he loves them but is unable to verbally express his feelings to his male friends. After describing the richness of his relationships with males, relationships in which he shows rather than tells his love, he decides that it is time to change the nature of his relationships with women.

Often, students misunderstand Tesich's discovery. They assume that since it is preferable in this culture to express feelings, Tesich's male friendships are the ones that need changing. Many are confused because Tesich discusses friendships in cinematic terms ("I didn't quite understand the ending. I don't know what he would

accomplish by freeing the women from those close-ups").
Therefore, the group discussions are extremely useful in
helping students come to an understanding of the author's
message. Once that is understood, students can share their
opinions on same-sex and different-sex friendships.

CHAPTER TWO: Guidelines for Fulfilling Essay Assignment 1

In this chapter, students are able to see the process
Rolando Niella went through to produce his personal essay,
"Barriers." This is an eye-opener for most of them. Their
earlier journals, written just after they had read the
completed essay, reveal students' insecurity about writing:
"I wish my pepers will be as good as the 'Barriers' but I
don't think they will be. I can't think of a topic orginal
enough and within my knowledge." As they watched the
unfolding of his essay, their reactions changed: "I was
very impressed by the way his essay improved. I could tell
that he put a lot of time and effort to the essay. Now I
understand that I can do it too."

Practicing Invention Strategies

Several strategies for getting started on and developing
ideas for an essay are described and demonstrated in this
chapter. Teaching these techniques can be fun, but they
don't work for everyone or for every assignment. As long as
these are presented as strategies and not as rules that must
be followed, they can enhance classroom teaching. You might
want to write along with your students. Your participation
may validate the procedures.

I space these techniques out as students do the readings
in PART ONE. For example, on the day they read "Barriers,"
I might ask them to make a list and then to freewrite on one
item. On the day they read "College," they may loop. On
the day they read "The Rewards of Living a Solitary Life,"
they may cube. They work on their own essays as they read.

Making a List. Students can work in groups to expand on the
lists already given. Some of the topics they come up with
may sound outrageous, but they usually have fun with this
exercise, and taking risks should be encouraged. This
activity can be completed in 5 to 10 minutes.

Freewriting. This is done individually. I usually give
students 5 to 8 minutes to write, with instructions to keep
the pen moving. If they get stuck, I tell them to write "I
have nothing to say" or to repeat the last word they have
written over and over until an idea emerges. Most students
find this to be a liberating experience, but some may be

intimidated at first; so be prepared to offer aid and comfort to anyone who seems paralyzed by the task.

Looping. This is an extension of the freewriting exercise. Looping also asks students to reflect on what they have written. I often stop after each loop and ask students to read aloud what they have written or to read just the summary sentence. I sometimes volunteer to read my own "loop" first to get things going. Sometimes this activity goes quickly; sometimes it takes 30 to 45 minutes. If you run out of time, they can finish looping outside class.

   Note: Almost all of the student writing in **GUIDELINES** has been corrected. This is mentioned several times in the text, but students still may believe that Rolando's looping and other writing was error-free. In fact, quite the opposite is true. Here are the last two sentences of Rolando's first loop (which were originally a handwritten mess!), which you can show to your students.

   Are they bodered by my language problem, can't they carrie on coversation with me because they always talk about local or national subject of which I 'not inform. This is really hard and some time make me feel like an estranger in a group were everybody is lauphin and talking and they sopposly were my friends.

Cubing. The secret of successful cubing is to spend only two to three minutes on each perspective. The fast pace stimulates the imagination. I often stop after one or two perspectives to see what students have written, to get their reactions, and to encourage them. This activity can also take 30 to 45 minutes and can be completed out of class.

   You might want to have students cube with a tootsie roll lollipop or other object brought to class to see how far the imagination can stretch to generate ideas. The lollipop tends to tap childhood memories, which can lead some students to a topic for the first essay.

Focusing Your Thoughts

   The focal point is not necessarily the thesis or message of the essay. If you read several expressive essays, including the ones in **GUIDELINES**, you will discover that the thesis is rarely stated outright at the beginning. Instead, writers of personal essays typically indicate in the opening paragraphs what they will focus on in the essay. This focal point is all I ask of students at this stage. If they are not ready to do this, they are encouraged to use the drafting process to discover a focus. If the draft handed in for review is not well focused, I ask them in conference to explain their focus to me and to write it down and then to revise the paper to match their intention.

11

Writing a Trial Draft

For the first essay assignment, I usually have students write a trial draft in class or bring one to class (and later another draft to be presented for review). The purpose of this trial draft is simply to get them started. Some students write a whole essay, others half an essay, others one paragraph, others one line crossed out. I accept everything. Once they have started, they have an idea of what they need to do; and they have practical questions. Working in small groups, they can share reactions and get ideas for proceeding. They can spend time expanding on an idea by discussing or writing out a specific example.

Organizing

The structure of personal essays is determined largely by the writer's subject matter and intentions. Still, students should create an essay whose organization has an internal logic: beginning, middle, and ending.

For some students, the organizational pattern is clear from the outset; they may make mental or written outlines. For others, the pattern does not emerge until after they have written one or more drafts. Much of my advice on the drafts I receive is to revise for a more logical organization, and I give students suggestions for doing so.

Writing a Draft to Present for Review

As noted earlier, students may write poorly-organized drafts even though they have been given instructions about creating a logical framework. This is understandable, given the pressures and constraints of a writing course. Some students have not had the time to devote to the essay; others cannot see the problem. Given the opportunity to bring the draft to class for review, students are made aware that composing is an evolving process. Of course, this system may have its drawbacks. Some students may not put much effort into a first draft, and what we get to read may not be worth the time we have to put into it. But that is more the exception than the rule.

The class can practice reviewing Rolando's draft. This is a nonthreatening way to prepare them to review each other's drafts. I model approaches to work in progress, helping students to focus initially on communicating ideas rather than prematurely on correcting errors. You may want to use a draft of one of your students.

Before they bring their own papers to class, students should be encouraged to use the Checklist for Content to do a self-evaluation. This puts them into a position of some control when their own papers are being reviewed.

12

Peer Reviewing

Establishing successful peer review sessions can be a difficult goal to achieve. My own experience differs from year to year, from class to class, from assignment to assignment. Some classes settle comfortably into groups of 2 or 3 or 4, and the class hums along as students read and comment on each other's papers. But other classes are uneven, with one group finishing 20 minutes before another or with an entire group unable to make progress. Sometimes one recalcitrant student can throw the whole session off balance. The instruction to show their work to classmates can be met with horror by competitive students who have always jealously guarded their written ideas. Shy students or those who lack faith in their own writing may want to skip class on the day of peer review. Most believe that only an experienced English teacher is capable of making good judgments about writing.

Nevertheless, I believe in the value of peer review; it trains students to internalize criteria for evaluating written work. Students who do not see problems in their own papers usually can see them in others', and this helps them to understand how a reader might react to what they have written. But before I ask students to share in this very sensitive task of giving and receiving criticism, I devote class time to preparing them for it. My own approach has been (1) to model the peer review process by using a draft from a student in a previous class, and (2) to open up discussion about peer review so that students can air their concerns. Students have always responded well to the excerpt from Koberg and Bagnall's book on problem solving, which is reprinted in **GUIDELINES**: "How to Criticize Painlessly/ How to Accept Criticism." These authors recommend that negative criticism be placed within the context of positive reinforcements. I find that to be productive advice, and it is given in good humor (although I recommend stronger negative criticism than Koberg and Bagnall do). Equally important is the advice to resist being defensive and instead to accept any negative comments for further evaluation. Students can choose to ignore suggestions that they don't find valuable or workable.

I mimeograph copies of the blank peer review form, have students fill out and discuss them, and collect them when I collect the drafts. I have students write down their reactions to other students' papers because this helps reviewers organize their thoughts and gives writers something concrete to deal with. The written student comments can be helpful in my own evaluation of the draft. I indicate on the form my agreement or disagreement with the peer reviewer's comments.

The note students write indicating how they might revise their drafts helps me to shape my comments and is often the springboard for discussion in an individual conference.

If, in spite of all precautions, some peer review groups are less than successful, I intervene. If I think a peer review group can benefit from my help, I join the group. If one student is having a problem, I work individually with that student. As with all teaching practices, I find that flexibility is a valuable asset.

Responding to Reviewer's Comments

Sample reviewer responses and Rolando's subsequent revisions are included to show how a reviewer's specific suggestions can help a writer. The emphasis in discussing these comments is on their specificity. Reviewer responses can help only if the reviewer identifies the problem area and (though this is not always possible) suggests a solution. Note that even while giving criticism, the reviewer finds something positive to say about the writing.

Revising and Teacher Conferences

Revising is often the heart of writing, and I do much of my teaching at this stage. When I get a draft, I first read it, to see what it says. Then I read critically and write comments in the margins related to content and organization about sections I particularly like and about specific areas of concern. When I hand back these drafts, I leave class time for students to ask questions about my comments. Later I discuss the drafts in brief (10-15 minute) conferences outside class with all students or with those who request or need a conference. In conference, I ask questions, let students do most of the talking, and have them take notes on what they are saying about the changes they want to make. Some students make revisions and return for another brief conference to show me what they have done in an interim draft before a final draft is completed. I don't expect every student to follow the exact same procedure.

I usually give students at least a week to revise their papers. While they are revising, I begin work on the next essay assignment. Students are usually working on more than one project at once.

Completing the Essay

Students are directed at this stage to make sure that the essay hangs together, to proofread and edit, and to prepare a neat final copy. Proofreading and editing are important processes discussed at length in PART SIX.

PART TWO
WRITING FROM COURSE READINGS: RELATING READING TO EXPERIENCE

CHAPTER THREE: Responding to Reading

PART TWO builds on what students have practiced in PART ONE. In writing from experience, students have employed invention strategies and found ways to support generalizations with examples. They will now learn how to integrate material from their experience with material from the course reading. Their experience will become the support or refutation of generalizations made by other writers.

The selections are essays and reports based on the authors' research on the subjects of friendship and cross-cultural communication. In presenting contrasting values and behavior in several different countries, these selections may challenge or reinforce student readers' assumptions about their own and others' cultures. Students will use at least one of these course readings as source material for their essays. (Students may write about a selection in PART ONE or another selection you have assigned.) Essay Assignment 2 asks students to examine the relationship between what they have read and what they know from experience; its purpose is to illuminate, evaluate, or test the validity of the ideas contained in the reading. It will be necessary to work concurrently with PART FIVE on paraphrasing, quoting, and citing course material.

Judith Viorst, "Friends, Good Friends -- and Such Good Friends

In searching for an understanding of what it means to be the best of friends, Viorst categorizes her friendships by their function and intensity. Her categories include convenience, special-interest, historical, crossroads, cross-generational, part-of-a-couple, and man-woman friendships. She concludes that being best of friends involves love, support, trust, truthfulness, and, perhaps most important, tolerance of differences.

Students generally like this piece very much, because they can identify with it, but most dislike the numbered list format Viorst uses. I've had varied reactions from male students. Negative: "She's using the female gender as her basis of categorizing -- this makes me lost somewhere between the lines when she mentions about eyeshadows and hemlines." Positive: "I thought it was going to be just another women's lib thing, but I found myself fitting my friends into the categories. It really works."

The style of the essay is extremely informal, sometimes irritatingly so. You can speculate with students as to why Viorst uses so many sentence fragments. This might be a good time to do the exercise on sentence fragments in PART SIX ("Finding and determining the purpose of sentence fragments"). Despite the informality of the Viorst piece, it can work well for the assignment. Nevertheless, first drafts often sound choppy, and I need to work with students to help them establish a stance toward Viorst's ideas and to make smooth transitions from one category to another.

Margaret Mead and Rhoda Metraux, "On Friendship"

To define the word **friend**, Mead and Metraux compare friendships in four countries: The United States, France, Germany, and England. Though they have discovered that different expectations about what constitutes friendship exist in different cultures, they conclude that in all cultures friends choose one another, make each other feel special, and allow for a balance of give-and-take. The authors advise Americans who travel abroad to be open to different styles of friendship.

The concept of different expectations of friendship in different cultures comes as a new idea to some students. Students from different cultures immediately make comparisons: "The difference between latin friendships and American friendships is that we the latins demonstrate our affection by more physical contact." Some of these students find the information personally useful: "This article helped me through my way in finding out where my difficulty in making real friends with Americans lied upon." Others object to the generalizations about different cultures, feeling that they are a form of stereotyping.

In first drafts, students may have a tendency to repeat rather than to explain Mead and Metraux. Some may write too many generalizations and need more specific examples.

LaRay M. Barna, "Intercultural Communication Stumbling Blocks"

Barna examines five barriers to successful cross-cultural communication: language, nonverbal signs, preconceptions and stereotypes, the tendency to evaluate, and high anxiety. She believes that awareness of these stumbling blocks, knowledge of the values and attitudes of other cultures, and a nonjudgmental attitude can help to facilitate communication.

This is the most difficult reading selection in **GUIDELINES** because of its professional jargon. Though most students have to struggle to understand it, they like the student quotations and find the article accessible because of their inclusion.

By following the stages Doxis Doxiadis went through to write his essay on Barna's article (Chapter 4), even the weakest students can get a good grasp of its meaning. This is a popular choice for fulfilling Essay Assignment 2. Some students need to revise drafts to explain what Barna means rather than just to quote what she says.

Robert Levine with Ellen Wolff, "Social Time: The Heartbeat of Culture"

The research Levine and Wolff report reveals that ideas of time, punctuality, and pace of life are closely bound to culture and differ from place to place. These differences, when not understood, lead to confusion when people from different cultures interact. Though speed is often equated with progress in industrialized countries, the authors warn that a fast pace of life may compromise health and may therefore be undesirable.

Because Levine begins the essay by humorously describing his own experience as an American professor in Brazil, this research report is accessible and amusing to most students. With this article (and, in fact, with any of the articles), students may write about their own experiences and forget to refer to the reading, in spite of all instruction to the contrary. Revision takes care of that problem.

Doxis Doxiadis, "Facing a Different Culture" (student essay)

Doxis agrees with Barna that language and nonverbal signs are serious and sometimes painful communication barriers for foreigners, but he feels that she underemphasizes both the role Americans play in isolating foreign students and the stress that the different pace of life places on a student.

Having a sample student essay can help students to get an idea of what their own essays might look like, and so students like to see it. On rare occasions a student has told me that when it came time to write her essay, she had to choose another article to write about since "Doxis said everything I wanted to say." Most students, however, want to share their own experiences; and Doxis has actually covered very few of Barna's ideas.

CHAPTER FOUR: Guidelines for Fulfilling Essay Assignment 2

In this chapter, students are able to see the process Doxis Doxiadis went through to produce his essay, "Facing a Different Culture." By comparing this process with that of

Rolando Niella as he was composing "Barriers" (Chapter 2), they can observe and discuss how writing from course readings can build on but differ from writing from experience.

Defining Your Audience

When they write from experience alone, students know more about the source material than their readers do. But when they write from course readings, students are aware that their reader knows this source material. They therefore need to make adjustments to accomodate the reader's prior knowledge. Students often question the need for summary, paraphrase, and quotation since the instructor is already familiar with the reading. Many do not realize the importance of specifying enough of the supporting evidence within the source to allow the reader to follow their line of thinking. I explain that summary, paraphrase, and quotation not only help me to see whether they understand what they have read but also to know exactly what in the reading they are referring to. Some students may have been trained not to quote or not to paraphrase or have been allowed to quote or paraphrase without crediting sources. These students need to understand the rationale behind these conventions of academic writing. This is a good time to turn to PART FIVE to discuss citing sources.

Essay Assignment 2 asks students to integrate their background knowledge into the course material and to reinterpret their experience or the experiences depicted in the sources in a new way. From this unique perspective, they can bring original insights to the instructor even though the instructor is already familiar with the source.

Finding and Developing a Topic

This section explains how students might choose a reading to write about, take notes, develop experiences, gather information related to the reading, and organize their essay. Again, students can see how the sample student essay evolved. Students can be assigned to read this section on their own, but it is preferable to use some class time for students to go through one or more of these steps.

Focusing Your Thoughts

For Essay Assignment 2, the focus should be on the relationship between what the student has read and what the student has experienced. There is no need to formalize this procedure beyond reminding students that readers will expect and need a focal point. Again, the focal point is not necessarily a thesis statement. In fact, a thesis statement

18

spelling out exactly what the essay will do would diminish a reader's interest. Instead, students should aim to arouse the reader's interest by allowing the reader to make inferences about the direction of the paper and its development.

Organizing the Essay

Although there is flexibility and room for creative approaches, this type of academic essay must fulfill audience expectations for an introduction, body, and conclusion. Some students are able to use these guidelines for organizing before they write a draft. Others find them more useful during revision.

Introduction. The introduction is an important feature of academic writing. Students need to learn to focus clearly on the issue at hand. The activity "Evaluating introductions" is designed to help students to see for themselves when introductions fulfill expectations and when they do not.

Body. What each student chooses to write about will determine which organizational pattern works best. A variety of patterns are presented to show both the importance of structuring thought and the flexibility of the genre.

Conclusion. To compose a conclusion, students need to go back over what they have written and to draw from that to give their readers something to think about. This is an area that often needs revision. Students can usually give helpful suggestions to one another during peer review sessions.

Note: From here, PART TWO follows the cycle of PART ONE: writing a draft to present for review, peer reviewing, revising, and completing the essay.

PART THREE
WRITING FROM COURSE READINGS: ANALYZING AN ARGUMENTATIVE ESSAY

CHAPTER FIVE: Responding to Reading

Reading Critically

In PART THREE, students again practice the skills of summarizing, paraphrasing, quoting, and citing sources. To those skills and to other strategies employed in PARTS ONE and TWO, students add the strategy of critical reading, which is necessary in the analysis of an argumentative essay. Critical reading is discussed in the "Reading Strategies" section.

To demonstrate critical reading, I have included a sample analysis of an argumentative essay, Sydney J. Harris's "What True Education Should Do" (reprinted in the INTRODUCTION to **GUIDELINES**). Note that in the section on evaluating the supporting material, students are to judge the effectiveness of the argument. For example, they are told, "If your answer is yes, you may conclude that the argument is strong. If your answer is no, you may conclude that the argument is weak." This allows students to give their own opinions about Harris's essay as they are addressing the various questions. They can truly practice analysis rather than just have it "stuffed" into them. This analytical approach will be brought to bear on the readings in this chapter; the questions in this section are repeated in the "Activities for Class Discussion."

The Readings and Essay Assignment 3

The selections in PART THREE are argumentative essays on the subject of teaching and learning. The authors present strong opinions on education in Western and non-Western cultures, opinions that are likely to cause student readers to question what they are reading and to reexamine their own views. Students will use at least one of these course readings (or Harris's essay or another argumentative essay you have assigned) as source material for their own essays. Essay Assignment 3 asks students to analyze an argumentative essay and establish and support a position toward some key ideas or issues raised in the reading.

Jacob Neusner, "The Commencement Speech You'll Never Hear"

Neusner claims that professors inadequately prepare students for the real world because they reward mediocre work and tolerate rude behavior, and he recommends that students unlearn the lessons of college in order to avoid failure in the outside world.

The reactions to this essay are strong, wide-ranging, and often hilarious: "He told the honest truth." "I could never be a teacher as I do not have the patience and tolerance like Jacob Neusner." "It surprises me that some of the professors only be nice to students to get rid of them. Somehow, I think some students are deserved to be rid." "All I can tell him is just wait and see your misjudgment. We are going to get somewhere wheather you believe it or not." "I really think this man fits into the case of social rejection." Students often prefer to discuss this and other argumentative essays with the whole class rather than in small groups.

The Brown University **Daily Herald** received over 200 letters within five days of the publication of Neusner's essay. Many students accused Neusner of insanity and incompetence and demanded that he be fired (he almost was). You can read his self-defense in his book **How to Grade Your Professors** (Boston: Beacon Press, 1984).

This has been a popular choice for fulfilling Essay Assignment 3. Each student essay is unique, attacking or defending Neusner on a variety of points. Some students may attack Neusner (or any of the authors in this chapter) without explaining the author's position; they need to revise to include his point of view.

William Zinsser, "College Pressures"

Although he recognizes that today's college students are pressured into treating their education primarily as a step toward career and financial security, Zinsser believes that college should be a place for students to take risks, develop intellectual faculties, and gain the power to shape their future.

Needless to say, most students identify strongly with the piece. They appreciate his compassion (especially after having read Neusner!). Many find that it helps them to understand their own college experience. But some students think Zinsser overgeneralizes about students or that he underestimates the value of fierce competition. Others disagree with his notion that pressure is a negative force.

This can be a hard essay to analyze if students completely agree with Zinsser; it's easier to argue when you disagree. Some students have written successful essays by comparing Neusner and Zinsser. For example, they use examples from Zinsser to refute Neusner's points.

Kie Ho, "We Should Cherish Our Children's Freedom to Think"

Kie Ho argues that although American education does not meet high standards in certain basic skills, it is a superior system because it allows for free experimentation with ideas.

Although some students agree with Ho, most find his argument flawed; and they enjoy analyzing it. One discovery is that although the author has a weak case, his words and tone are persuasive (this is true of other authors in PART THREE).

Paul McBrearty, "We Should Abolish Anonymous Evaluations of Teachers by Their Students"

Believing that anonymity allows for student evaluations of teachers that are irresponsible, inaccurate, unreliable, and unfair, McBrearty argues that either students should sign their names or these evaluations should be eliminated altogether.

A few students in the class may never have written an evaluation of a teacher, and so this is the time when they learn about the process. For others, it's a good time to reflect on a process that they may not fully understand or that they take for granted. Feeling under attack, they work hard to analyze the flaws of this argument.

Ida Timothee, "College: An All-forgiving World?" (student essay)

Ida argues against Neusner's notion that a college education is not preparation for real life by showing that college life is full of pressures, challenges, and experiences that strengthen students' characters and broaden their world view.

CHAPTER SIX: Guidelines for Fulfilling Essay Assignment 3

Defining Your Audience

If you prefer a more formal style of argumentative writing than Ida has produced, explain your evaluative criteria to your students.

Note: From here, PART THREE follows the cycles of PARTS ONE and TWO: finding and developing a topic, focusing, organizing, drafting, peer reviewing, revising, and completing the essay.

PART FOUR
WRITING FROM OUTSIDE SOURCES: RESEARCHING A CONTROVERSY

CHAPTER SEVEN: Preparing for Research

This chapter contains the fourth essay assignment: a research essay on a recent controversy. Students choose their own topics, through investigation of various publications, and find their own reading materials.

Because gathering and synthesizing sources takes time, this project should begin early (you may even want to begin the first or second week) and continue throughout the semester. Students work on the research essay as they are writing and revising other essays for the course. The research should be based on at least six sources; the essay will be between 5 and 10 pages typewritten, double-spaced.

All of the skills practiced in previous assignments come into play in fulfilling the research assignment. In addition, by observing a student writer at work, students learn how to use the college library, conduct an interview, examine various sides of an issue, make an oral presentation, and synthesize material from several sources.

The reading strategies used in PARTS TWO and THREE will be brought to bear, as students read research studies and argumentative essays (e.g., editorials) to complete this assignment. Additional strategies for reading and summarizing news articles and for evaluating sources are included in Chapter Eight.

Angela Gan, "Asian-American Students: Why Is Their Success Becoming a Hindrance?" (student essay)

Angela's research shows that Asian-Americans are admitted to elite colleges at a lower rate than their high academic achievement would suggest. Although admissions officers deny it, evidence exists to suggest that these colleges have set admissions quotas for Asian-American students or have established admission policies that discriminate against these students. Angela believes that education should be based on fair academic competition, and she maintains that the colleges are the losers.

Students are interested in debating this issue. This is, I think, a welcome change from discussions of sample student research papers that focus only on organization and documentation. Students become enthusiastic about the research project when they realize that they can select a topic that will be of interest to their readers.

CHAPTER EIGHT: Guidelines for Finding a Topic and Gathering Material for Essay Assignment 4

Becoming Familiar with Major Newspapers and Magazines

This activity can build confidence because students use class time to determine which kinds of topics might fulfill the assignment. They then feel more prepared to find topics on their own. I discourage topics that repeat generalized, well-worn, emotional discussions of abortion, euthanasia, capital punishment, and so on. I prefer topics that allow students to be original researchers on a recent or current controversy. Students have researched issues such as whether or not gay couples should be foster parents, whether or not businesses should provide day care, whether or not maternity and paternity leave are a right, whether or not athletes should be tested and punished for steroid use, whether or not the U.S. should support Pinochet, whether or not the Seabrook (N.H.) nuclear plant should be closed, whether or not we should invest in exploration of Mars, whether or not American students are culturally illiterate.

I emphasize that this is a research **essay**, not a research paper. I am not requiring that students follow the conventions of writing of other disciplines, as I am not a qualified evaluator of papers in other disciplines. I am interested in students' opinions on issues of significance; research is the way they educate themselves.

Finding a Topic That Engages Your Interest

Some students find a topic immediately; others labor over their decision; some panic. I usually step in to help struggling students. One potentially useful library source is **Facts on File**, a weekly world news digest. **Editorials on File**, a twice-monthly newspaper editorial survey, is useful both for finding and following up on topics. Students can skim accessible specialized journals, such as those listed under "Using a specialized index."

On the day(s) that students present their topic choices in class, many students change their minds when they hear other topics. I give students until the next class meeting or two to make a final decision.

Summarizing a Newspaper or Magazine Article

Writing an Informal Research Proposal

Formulating a Research Question

These activities can be done in or outside class, on the same day or on different days. The research proposal and

question can be done together. I collect these, make a
brief comment (such as a suggestion for how to proceed with
the research), and return them.

Finding Needed Information

I like to bring students into the library and give them
hands-on activities so that they use the library's resources
to find materials. For example, to show them how the
microfilm machine works, I ask them to find a newspaper
published on the day they were born to see what news made
the front page. Students use indexes and computer files to
find books, magazines, and journals. They walk through the
reading room and peruse the current periodicals. They walk
through the reference section and peruse those sources. I
introduce them to the reference librarians.

Library research can be extraordinarily frustrating and
time-consuming for students. I try to make several visits
to the library with the class so that they can use class
time and take advantage of my help to find materials. If
students have already found materials, they use the library
time to evaluate sources, take notes, or discuss their
topics with me.

Taking Notes

Students can benefit from the notecard method of
notetaking, but it is not wise to force this method. Many
have success with other ways of taking notes. However, it
is a good idea to periodically check students' notes,
especially to see that they are matching notes with sources
and keeping track of page numbers. Some students do not
understand how specific the documentation must be.

Writing a Progress Report

To write a progress report, students stop what they are
doing and assess what they have done. I can intervene to
provide support and give useful suggestions for proceeding.
The progress reports do not have to look like Angela's.
Most students write them as journal entries; each is
different. You may want to assign weekly progress reports.

Searching beyond the Library: Collecting Data and Interviewing

Students can collect data from sources other than the
library early in the research project. I recommend that
they wait for interviews until they have become reasonably
knowledgeable about the subject. Then they know what
questions to ask. Some topics lend themselves well to

interviews; others do not. I do not force this aspect of
the assignment.

To model the interviewing process for your students, you
can invite an expert to your class. One possibility might
be to invite an admission officer to answer questions about
quotas for Asian-American students. Before the officer
comes to class, students can prepare a list of questions.
In class, the students can take brief notes; after class,
they can reflect upon what they have heard and perhaps
speculate on how this new information could be incorporated
into Angela's essay.

CHAPTER NINE: Guidelines for Planning and Completing Essay Assignment 4

Defining Your Audience

When they write from course readings, students draw from
sources familiar to their readers. When they write from
outside sources, they need to fulfill needs and expectations
of an audience unfamiliar with the source material. You can
discuss with students the need to establish a context for
the reader and to relate new information to something the
reader already knows. Since students are arguing a
controversial issue, they might want to consider opening
their essays with an aspect of the issue that might be
universally agreed upon and then presenting increasingly
controversial material.

Since each student has a different topic, you may want
to discuss your role as audience with individual students.
But the questions in this activity can be discussed with the
whole class. It's another welcome opportunity for students
to learn about each other's research projects.

Focusing Your Thoughts

Creating a Preliminary Outline

I usually take some class time for students to write
preliminary outlines. To model the process, I take one
student's topic and make an outline on the board as the
student explains it.

Synthesizing

It takes time for students to synthesize material
effectively because many skills are involved. The writing
activity recommends that students practice using three
readings on cross-cultural communication in **GUIDELINES**. You

can instead have students practice on their own research materials by having them bring books or xeroxed copies of articles to class.

Organizing the Essay

Since there is so much material to organize, these guidelines are usually helpful before students begin the drafting process. As part of that process, students should be keeping track of sources so that they include a list of sources (bibliography) at the end of the paper.

Writing a Draft to Present for Review

This draft is written for the instructor. Students spend class time doing oral presentations rather than reviewing each other's written drafts. Of course, if you wish to have peer review for the research essay, you can add it to your course plan.

Preparing an Oral Presentation

Students photocopy outlines of their drafts for each class member; otherwise they present their drafts orally. I leave two or three class meetings for the presentations. One student at a time speaks while the rest of us listen. (If you have a large class, you can divide students into groups.) These are usually remarkable sessions. Since students are reporting on recent or current newsworthy events, there is high interest. Many ask questions, offer opinions, challenge the presenter. Since this presentation occurs between the draft and the completed essay, students are given a valuable opportunity to shape their thoughts.

Note: From here, students follow the cycle of doing more research or reading, revising, and completing their essays.

PART FIVE
READING AND WRITING SKILLS

Summarizing, paraphrasing, quoting, paragraphing, and citing sources are practiced as students are engaging in the reading discussion activities in PARTS ONE through FOUR. PART FIVE provides detailed explanations and demonstrations of these skills and can be used concurrently with the other parts of **GUIDELINES**. The exercises can help students to practice these skills before they apply them to their own writing. Students can also use PART FIVE as a reference while they are writing and revising their essays.

CHAPTER TEN: Summarizing

This chapter provides general guidelines for summarizing tasks. (Guidelines for writing summaries of specific types of texts are included in PARTS ONE through FOUR.) It is not necessary for students to write each of the four summaries in the exercise at the end of the chapter. Students practice and improve this skill as they write summaries throughout the semester. My students hand in a summary of each course reading along with a journal entry on the reading. Summaries of readings are incorporated into Essay Assignments 2, 3, and 4.

CHAPTER ELEVEN: Paraphrasing

Refer to this chapter when you get to PART TWO. Students need to practice paraphrasing to prepare for Essay Assignment 2, and they need a lot of practice. Essay Assignments 2 and 3 give them the opportunity to become relatively proficient paraphrasers before they are faced with research writing in Assignment 4. You can go through this chapter in class and then have students do the exercises at the end, either in groups or with the whole class. In addition, they should practice paraphrasing as part of the discussion activities for several of the readings. If you sit in on one of the small group efforts to paraphrase, you will discover why this is such a difficult skill to master.

Some students need extra help with this task. In conference, I read aloud a passage, have them tell me in their own words what it says, then have them write down what they have just said (if it was accurate), and then say, "That's a paraphrase!"

Remind students that paraphrasing without giving credit to the source is a form of plagiarism.

CHAPTER TWELVE: Quoting

Some students do not like to use quotations; others use too many. It takes time to learn how to achieve an effective balance of paraphrase and quotation when referring to a source. Students can practice selecting and writing about quotations during discussion activities connected to PARTS ONE through THREE. Incorporating quotations into their own text becomes necessary for Essay Assignments 2, 3, and 4. They can refer to this chapter for instructions on smooth integration. The exercise on integrating quotations from the readings into student paragraphs should be useful practice.

Remind students that quoting without quotation marks or without making it clear that the material is being reprinted from another source is a form of plagiarism.

CHAPTER THIRTEEN: Paragraphing

Paragraphing skills are, of course, necessary for all of the essay assignments. Student awareness of paragraphing can grow out of discussions of course readings. In addition, PARTS ONE through FOUR provide guidelines for organizing paragraphs for specific types of essays. This chapter reveals several general ways to develop and organize paragraphs and to link ideas and examples within and between sentences and paragraphs. Students can refer to this chapter for their own writing. As a reference it is probably more useful for revising than for drafting. Overemphasis on transitional words and expressions before students begin composing can block the rhythm of their thinking and writing.

Exercise: Analyzing the function of the first sentence of a paragraph

1. The underlined sentence, <u>Note the emphasis on looking better</u>, refers readers back to the last line of the previous paragraph and reveals what this new paragraph will discuss.

2. The underlined sentence, <u>For many of us the summer is a special time for forming new friendships</u>, reveals that the focal point of the previous paragraph is on making new friends and that this new paragraph will further develop that idea.

Exercise: Identifying transitional words and signals

Although some students may find that Rolando used too many transitional expressions, most will discover that without them it's hard to follow his line of thinking.

Exercise: Making connections

Several of the many possible answers are suggested.

1. Students can turn to the section on adverbial clauses in PART SIX to consult the box containing subordinate conjunctions. Note the change in meaning when different subordinate conjunctions are used.

   a. When/ If/ By the time that/ As soon as/ After/ Once
   b. Unless/ Until/ Even if
   c. Before/ If/ When/ Whenever/ After

2. a. Even though he slept for ten hours, he is tired.
   b. Because he woke up at four a.m., he is tired.
   c. He is tired whenever he works the second shift.

3. a. Even though you may not succeed, you should keep trying.
   b. If you don't work hard enough, you may not succeed.
   c. Since you may not succeed, you should change your major.

4. a. As a result, the quality of education has declined.
   b. In fact, the pressure to achieve high grades has led to an increase in cheating on campus.
   c. However, this phenomenon is preferable to a situation in which students do not make enough effort.

Exercise: Reacting to transitions

Students may not have identical responses. Their different reactions can show them that there are no hard and fast rules for using transitional words. Writers make choices based on their own intentions and their awareness of audience needs and expectations.

Exercise: Combining sentences

There are many possible answers. Several are suggested here. This is a good exercise to make students aware of the flexibility of sentence structuring. They should practice variations on their own sentences. Note that some differences in emphasis and meaning may occur.

1. - Although learning a new language is difficult, it is a rewarding experience.
   -- Learning a new language is a difficult but rewarding experience.
   - Because learning a new language is difficult, it is a rewarding experience.

2. - Women leave college superbly equipped to bring fresh leadership to traditionally male jobs, but society hasn't yet caught up with this fact.
   - Society hasn't yet caught up with the fact that women leave college superbly equipped to bring fresh leadership to traditionally male jobs.
   - Although women leave college superbly equipped to bring fresh leadership to traditionally male jobs, society hasn't yet caught up with this fact. (Zinsser, para 13)

3. - In spite of the fact that American education is tragically inferior, America is the country of innovation.
   - Whereas America is the country of innovation, American education is tragically inferior.
   - If American education is so tragically inferior, why is it that this is still the country of innovation? (Ho, para 2).

Exercise: Analyzing paragraphing

An exercise similiar to this one is included in the discussion activities following many of the readings. Students can be directed to this exercise when they are revising their own essays.

CHAPTER FOURTEEN: Citing and Documenting Sources

The first few pages of this chapter need to be covered in class so that students understand the importance of the convention of citing and documenting sources. This section contains a discussion of when to document and how to avoid plagiarism. It can be supplemented by any materials your own university may publish.

This chapter is largely a reference section for students to look up documentation formats. For a fuller description of these formats, see the **Publication Manual of the American Psychological Association** or the **MLA Handbook for Writers of Research Papers, Theses, and Dissertations.**

PART SIX
THE EDITING PROCESS

CHAPTER FIFTEEN: Editing and Proofreading

Students are advised to focus on the processes of editing and proofreading only after they have developed and organized their essays. This initially directs their attention to meaning, structure, and style rather than to grammar rules and correctness. An early focus on rules and correctness can do more harm than good if students spend too much time worrying about making errors and too little time thinking about how to develop an idea. When students attend to error at a later stage in writing, grammar can be presented not as a way of memorizing rules but as a way of solving problems as they arise out of real writing situations.

It is impossible to evaluate every single error every student makes. I have to set limits on what I and my students can accomplish; there simply is not enough time for students to absorb what they need to know. I focus on errors that interfere with comprehension and errors that are frequently made.

There are many ways to call attention to error, for example, symbols and abbreviations, references to rules, checklists, underlinings, and peer correction. But each is effective only insofar as it provides clues for self-correction. I don't make it a practice to simply supply the correct answer. Students need to undergo a complex cognitive operation to correct error if they are to remember how to use correct forms. The ultimate goal is for students to identify their own errors and to become responsible for their own editing.

I mark errors (primarily by underlining) only on a second draft or during a second reading of a first draft. I then work with students to solve the individual technical problems that have emerged. When I hand papers back, I ask students to correct the underlined parts in class. If they do not know how to make a correction, I discuss the grammar on the spot, make a conference appointment, or direct the student to the appropriate section in the Handbook for Correcting Errors (Chapter 17) or in a grammar book. Students who make similar errors can work together. Students have time to edit before they turn their papers in for a grade.

CHAPTER SIXTEEN: Causes of Error

Students can apply to their own writing the categories which linguists use to identify sources of error. While this process does not necessarily result in immediate elimination of that error, it does heighten students' awareness and allows for a positive rather than a negative evaluation of what they have done. This has helped to ease the stress that writing for academic courses incurs. I reassure my students that making errors is not a sign of failure.

There are many causes of error other than those described in this chapter. Many errors occur because students are making an effort to follow previous writing instruction that may have been incomplete or misunderstood. Showing our understanding of this phenomenon can help our students to build confidence and take risks.

It is not necessary to insist that students keep a record of the causes of their errors. The suggestion to do so will be taken up by students who find it useful.

CHAPTER SEVENTEEN: A Handbook for Correcting Error

Only a few of the possible answers are demonstrated.

Exercise: Identifying phrases

noun phrase: a portrait
prepositional phrase: of today's students
verb phrase: have painted
infinitive phrase: to laugh and offer friendship
participial phrase: making them seem a solemn lot

Exercise: Creating adverbial clauses

1. Although the library was noisy, I was able to study.
2. Because the library was noisy, I was unable to study.
3. It is not unusual for students to be in debt, even if they work part time at college and full time during the summer.
4. When you tossed on our desks writing upon which you had not labored, we read it and even responded, as though you earned a response. (Neusner, para 4)

Exercise: Combining sentences to create clauses of comparison, degree, or result

1. a. The cafeteria isn't as noisy today as it usually is.
   The cafeteria is less noisy today than it usually is.
   b. Maria didn't do as well in chemistry as she had hoped.

2. a. He worked so hard that he became ill.
   b. He was being so stuffed with miscellaneous facts that
      he had no time to use his own mind to analyze and
      synthesize the material.

3. a. That was such a good ice cream cone that I couldn't
      stop eating it.
   b. Physics 518 is such a difficult course that you have
      to be highly motivated to take it.

Exercise: Creating and punctuating restrictive and nonrestrictive clauses

1. a. The man who became the 40th president of the United
      States was once an actor in Hollywood.
   b. They seemed to accept the idea that someone of status
      is expected to arrive late. (Levine & Wolff, para 13)

2. a. To a European, who sees only our surface behavior, the
      differences are not clear. (Mead & Metraux, para 4)
   b. Learning the language, which most foreign visitors
      consider their only barrier to communication, is
      actually only the beginning. (Barna, para 8)

Exercise: Creating noun clauses

1. I don't know if they are getting **As** or **Cs**, and I don't
   care. (Zinsser, para 11)
2. They know that entrance into the better schools will be
   an entrance into the better law firms and better medical
   practices. (Zinsser, para 9)
3. How one appears on paper is more important than how one
   appears in person. (Zinsser, para 9)
4. Your idea that there should be no grading system is a
   good one.

Exercise: Finding and determining the purpose of sentence fragments

This passage is taken from Saint-Exupery's **Flight from
Arras**, a book about his experience as a pilot during WWII.

Sentence fragments:
When there is no longer a place that is yours in the world.
When you know no longer where your friend is to be found.

In sentences 3, 4, and 5, the structure begins with a
simple subject-verb pattern: "The villagers come home...,"
"The grain is stored...," "The folded linen is piled...."
As sentence 6 tells us, "... each thing is in its place."
The author's sentence structure reflects his theme. As the

34

short simple declarative sentences show, in time of peace everything is in a simple order.

Sentence 9 acts as a transition to break that peace and order, beginning "Ah, but..." and telling us that "peace dies when the framework is ripped apart." Note that this sentence contains an independent and a dependent clause.

In sentences 10 and 11, the dependent clauses have been ripped away from their main clauses and stand alone as fragments. Again, the author's sentence structure reflects his theme. In time of war, life is fragmented.

Sentences become whole again (12 and 13) when peace is defined as the bringing together of parts to form a whole.

Exercise: Correcting sentence fragments

1. Staring out the window at the high-rise apartment where my best friend lived, I somehow drifted into daydreaming.
2. After failing to fit my friends into the categories revealed in Viorst's article, I tried to look at friendship from my mother's point of view because the women that Viorst has in mind are most likely closer to my mother's age.
3. In addition to being taught "creative geography," American students should know some practical geography such as which countries exist in the world and where they are situated.
4. Unfamiliar questions came from American students: "How are you?" and "What's up?" I immediately replied, "I'm fine. How about...." My sentence was left unfinished as the student walked away.

Exercise: Correcting run-on sentences and comma faults

1. He would break everything down into pieces and start from scratch. He would then build on that slowly so that I would understand.
2. In the past, Americans had a tendency to think that English was the only language worth knowing and that foreigners were forced to learn it; so they did not even try to learn another language.
3. However, the fact is that I am not a supernatural being. I could not take the stress.
4. My decision to apply early to college was meant to lighten the burden; unfortunately, the three essays and several short questions added to my unbearable load.

Exercise: Creating subject-verb agreement

1. The extent of my professor's knowledge of the natural sciences amazes me.

2. Two-thirds of the semester was over before I felt completely adjusted.
3. What percentage of the students in the university are from other countries?
4. Everybody is required to take a year of science.

Exercise: Completing sentences with pronouns

1. The American educational system allows students to think for themselves, but it does not provide everyone with the best education they can pursue. (**Note:** If you do not accept this usage, have students rewrite the sentence to avoid the problem.)
2. From that experience, I have learned that fear is not the answer to any problem; instead, we should always try things that have even a little chance of success. Unless we try, we will never know what will happen.
3. Each of her women friends has her own career.
4. Neither the professor nor the students expressed their appreciation. (**Rule:** When the antecedent is a compound of singular and plural nouns joined by or, nor, either...or, or not only...but also, make the pronoun agree with the part of the compound that is closer to it.)

Exercise: Using present tenses

1. Maria has gone to work in France. At first, her French wasn't very good, but now it is improving.
2. The library opens at 8:00 A.M. and closes at 1 A.M. everyday.

Exercise: Using past tenses

1. I understood what he was saying.
2. I was taking the exam when I noticed that it was snowing outside.

Exercise: Using future tenses

1. I will be lying on the beach in Puerto Rico by this time next week.
2. Angela will be here next week.

Exercise: Using perfect tenses

1. I have lived here since 1988.
2. You'll miss her if you don't arrive until 10:00. She will have gone home by then.
3. I was too late. The professor had already given the quiz when I got to class.

Exercise: Using modal auxiliaries

1. I want to see that movie tonight. It should be interesting.
2. We must hurry. The train is going to leave in an hour.
3. The plane should have landed by now. It took off three hours ago.
4. She used to walk along the Seine every day when she lived in Paris.

Exercise: Producing correct verb sequences

1. His professor was pleased when she discovered that Michael had passed the exam.
2. His professor will be very pleased when she discovers that Michael passed the exam.
3. Caroline will learn that she failed her biology course when she checks the grade list posted on the professor's office door.
4. While Stephanie was having a conference with the professor yesterday, John was waiting (or: waited) in the hallway.

Exercise: Completing clauses containing wishes, requests, demands, recommendations, or conditions

1. I would visit my brother more often if he didn't live so far away.
2. The striking teachers are demanding that their salaries be increased.
3. She didn't tell them about the fire. I wish she had told them about it.
4. It is essential that he study the material.

Exercise: Selecting gerunds and infinitives

1. I look forward to seeing you again.
2. The head of the department agreed to let me take History 911.
3. We can leave as soon as it stops raining.
4. My professor advised me to take English 201.

Exercise: Determining use of articles

If students discover that more than one choice is possible (for example, Zinsser could have said "the chance" instead of "a chance" or eliminated "a" from "a grim preparation"), they will learn that several factors determine the use of articles.

Exercise: Correcting errors in the use of articles

1. The report said that a large percentage of American high school students do not know where Moscow is or who Deng Xiaoping is.
2. On May 19, 1986, I received a diploma from the Museum School of Fine Arts after four years of rigorous studio work.
3. Many times students do not learn the material at all but just try to memorize it for a good grade. Therefore, the grading system should be eliminated.
4. Listening to older friends makes me think more and look at things from a different angle.

Exercise: Balancing grammatical structures

1. Wanting to achieve something and actually achieving it may not be the same thing.
2. Slowly but forcefully, she argued her point.
3. She always says what she wants to say, not what she should say.
4. We were surprised not only about his idea but about his decision to express it.

Exercise: Punctuating sentences

1. A woman without her man is lost.
   A woman: Without her, man is lost.

2. See the elephant eat Maria!
   See the elephant. Eat, Maria.

3. Give the bird to my cousin Sylvia.
   Give the bird to my cousin, Sylvia.

4. She said, "Hold it softly."
   She said, "Hold it" (softly).

5. I can can-can, but I can't cant, can you?
   I can. Can can. But I can't cant. Can you?

6. That that is, is. That that is not, is not.
   That "that is" is that. That is not "is not."

IV. Appendix: DETAILED COURSE PLAN

The following plan shows how I usually use the material in **GUIDELINES** in a course that meets twice a week for 14 to 15 weeks. In addition to the four essay assignments, this plan includes an in-class essay for which I assign outside reading. The reading may be different articles related to one issue (such as civil rights), different reviews of a movie students have seen, or an autobiography such as Maya Angelou's **I Know Why the Caged Bird Sings** or Richard Wright's **Black Boy**. Students read the material outside of class and later write an essay in class in response to the reading. They may evaluate or argue with what they have read, using the skills they have practiced throughout the semester.

To accomodate your own teaching schedule and preferences, you might want to eliminate an essay assignment or some of the activities. Or you might choose to substitute or add readings, activities, exercises, and assignments that will enrich the material in **GUIDELINES**.

Tu 9/5   Introduction to the course: syllabus, course
              guidelines, Reading and Writing about What You
              Read (in INTRODUCTION), Write before You Read

Th 9/7
  READING: Keeping a Reading/Writing Journal
              Expressing a Personal Viewpoint/ Reading
              Strategies
              "Barriers" by Rolando Niella
  WRITING: Journal #1 due
              Summary of "Barriers"
  IN CLASS: Activities for class discussion (Niella)
              Discussion of ESSAY ASSIGNMENT 1 (draft due 9/21)
              Making a List; Freewriting
              Write before You Read

Tu 9/12
  READING: "College" by Anzia Yezierska
              Summarizing (Chapter 10 in PART FIVE)
  WRITING: Journal #2 due
              Summary of "College"
  IN CLASS: Activities for class discussion (Yezierska)
              Looping
              Write before You Read

Th 9/14
  READING: "The Rewards of Living a Solitary Life" by May
              Sarton
  WRITING: Journal #3 due
              Summary of "The Rewards of Living a Solitary
              Life"

IN CLASS: Activities for class discussion (Sarton)
          Cubing
          Focusing Your Thoughts
          Writing a Trial Draft
          Write before You Read

Tu 9/19
  READING: "Focusing on Friends" by Steve Tesich
            Organizing the Essay
  WRITING: Journal #4 due
            Summary of "Focusing on Friends"
            Bring TRIAL DRAFT of Essay Assignment 1 to class
  IN CLASS: Activities for class discussion (Tesich)
            Writing a Draft to Present for Review

Th 9/21 **DRAFT OF ESSAY ASSIGNMENT 1 DUE:** Expressing a
            Personal Viewpoint. Before you bring your paper
            to class, consult the Checklist for Content.
  READING: Peer Reviewing
  IN CLASS: Peer reviewing
            Write before You Read

Tu 9/26
  READING: Relating Reading to Experience/ Reading
            Strategies
            "Friends, Good Friends -- and Such Good Friends"
            by Judith Viorst
            "On Friendship" by Margaret Mead and Rhoda
            Metraux
  WRITING: Journal #5 due
            Summaries of "Friends, Good Friends -- and Such
            Good Friends" and "On Friendship"
  IN CLASS: Activities for class discussion (Viorst)
            Activities for class discussion (Mead & Metraux)
            Discussion of ESSAY ASSIGNMENT 2 (draft due
            10/12)
            Write before You Read
  Draft of Essay Assignment 1 will be returned, with
  suggestions for revision. Revising (in Chapter 2) and
  Paragraphing (Chapter 13)

Th 9/28
  READING: "Intercultural Communication Stumbling Blocks" by
            LaRay Barna
            Paraphrasing (Chapter 11)
  WRITING: Journal #6 due
            Summary of "Intercultural Communication..."
  IN CLASS: Activities for class discussion (Barna)
            Evaluating paraphrases (exercise in Chapter 11)
            Editing of Essay Assignment 1 (Bring draft to
            class)
            READING: Editing and Proofreading (Chapter 15)
                     Causes of Error (Chapter 16)
            Write before You Read

Tu 10/3	**REVISION OF ESSAY ASSIGNMENT 1 DUE**, stapled together with previously-corrected draft. See Completing the Essay.
READING:	"Social Time: The Heartbeat of Culture" by Robert Levine with Ellen Wolff "Facing a Different Culture" by Doxis Doxiadis Quoting (Chapter 12 in PART FIVE)
WRITING:	Journal #7 due Summaries of "Social Time..." and "Facing..."
IN CLASS:	Activities for class discussion (Levine & Wolff) Activities for class discussion (Doxiadis) Selecting a quotation (exercise in Chapter 12) Integrating quotations (exercise in Chapter 12) Defining Your Audience Reading: Giving Credit to Your Sources (in Chapter 14)

Th 10/5	
READING:	Finding and Developing a Topic (for Essay Assignment 2)
IN CLASS:	Finding and developing a topic Reading: Citing course material (in Chapter 14)

Tu 10/10	BRING TO CLASS A MAJOR NEWSPAPER SUCH AS THE NEW YORK TIMES, OR A MAJOR NEWS MAGAZINE SUCH AS TIME OR THE ECONOMIST, OR A MORE SPECIALIZED MAGAZINE SUCH AS PSYCHOLOGY TODAY.
READING:	"Asian-American Students: Why Is Their Success Becoming a Hindrance?" by Angela Gan
WRITING:	Journal #8 due Summary of "Asian-American Students..."
IN CLASS:	Activities for class discussion (Gan) Discussion of Writing from Outside Sources: Researching a Controversy (ESSAY ASSIGNMENT 4; draft due 11/21), Chapter 7 Becoming Familiar with Major Newspapers and Magazines

| Th 10/12 | **DRAFT OF ESSAY ASSIGNMENT 2 DUE**: Relating Reading to Experience. Consult the Checklist for Content. |
| IN CLASS: | Peer reviewing
Finding a Topic (for the research essay) |

| Tu 10/17 | BRING TO CLASS: ARTICLES (OR XEROXED COPIES OF ARTICLES) COVERING 3 or 4 DIFFERENT TOPICS THAT YOU THINK YOU MIGHT LIKE TO RESEARCH. |
| WRITING: | Journal #9 due (you can discuss potential research topics) |

IN CLASS: Discussion of research topics
          Summarizing a News Article
          Write before You Read
 Draft of Essay Assignment 2 will be returned, with
 suggestions for revision. Analyze paragraphing.
Th 10/19   RESEARCH PROPOSAL AND QUESTION DUE
 READING: Analyzing an Argumentative Essay/ Reading
           Strategies
           "What True Education Should Do" by Sydney J.
           Harris (in INTRODUCTION)
           "The Commencement Speech You'll Never Hear" by
           Jacob Neusner
 WRITING: Journal #10 due
           Summary of "The Commencement Speech..."
 IN CLASS: Reading Critically
           Activities for class discussion (Neusner)
           Discussion of ESSAY ASSIGNMENT 3 (draft due 11/2)
           Write before You Read
Tu 10/24   REVISION OF ESSAY ASSIGNMENT 2 DUE, stapled
             together with previously-corrected draft.
 READING: "College Pressures" by William Zinsser
 WRITING: Journal #11 due
           Summary of "College Pressures"
 IN CLASS: Activities for class discussion (Zinsser)
           Defining Your Audience
           Write before You Read
 Research proposal/question will be returned. Discussion
 of finding, evaluating, and taking notes on library
 sources.
Th 10/26
 READING: "We Should Cherish Our Children's Freedom to
           Think" by Kie Ho
           "We Should Abolish Anonymous Evaluations of
           Teachers by Their Students" by Paul McBrearty
 WRITING: Journal #12 due
           Summaries of "We Should Cherish..." and "We
           Should Abolish..."
 IN CLASS: Activities for class discussion (Ho)
           Activities for class discussion (McBrearty)
Tu 10/31
 READING: "College: An All Forgiving World?" by Ida
           Timothee
           Finding and Developing a Topic (for Essay
           Assignment 3)
 WRITING: Journal #13 due
           Summary of "College: An All Forgiving World?"
 IN CLASS: Activities for class discussion (Timothee)
           Finding and developing a topic

42

Th 11/2   **DRAFT OF ESSAY ASSIGNMENT 3 DUE**: Analyzing an Argumentative Essay. Consult the Checklist for Content.
 IN CLASS: Peer reviewing
Tu 11/7   CLASS WILL GO TO THE LIBRARY. Meet in the classroom first.
  Draft of Essay Assignment 3 will be returned, with
  suggestions for revision.
Th 11/9   **RESEARCH PROGRESS REPORT DUE**
 READING: Searching beyond the Library: Collecting Data and Interviewing
 IN CLASS: Defining Your Audience
            Creating a Preliminary Outline
            Synthesizing
Tu 11/14   **REVISION OF ESSAY ASSIGNMENT 3 DUE**, stapled together with previously-corrected copy.
 IN CLASS: Organizing the (Research) Essay
            Preparation for in-class essay (to be written in class 11/28)

Th 11/16   CLASS MEETS IN LIBRARY

Tu 11/21   **DRAFT OF ESSAY ASSIGNMENT 4 DUE**: Researching a Controversy. Consult the Checklist for Content. Review formats for in-text documentation and list of sources (in Chapter 14).
 IN CLASS: Preparing an Outline for Oral Presentation
            Preparing an Oral Presentation
            Preparation for in-class essay (to be written 11/28).

Th 11/23   NO CLASS - Thanksgiving recess

Tu 11/28   **IN-CLASS ESSAY**
  Draft of Essay Assignment 4 will be returned, with
  suggestions for revision

Th 11/30   Oral presentations of research

Tu 12/5   Oral presentations of research

Th 12/7   Oral presentations of research
                (last day of class)

Tu 12/12   **REVISION OF ESSAY ASSIGNMENT 4 DUE**, stapled together with previously-corrected draft

St. Martin's